In 1996, David McMillan was held in Thailand's infamous Bangkok Hilton prison. As his near-certain death sentence approached, he escaped from the maximum-security jail and disappeared into the hinterlands of Baluchistan, Pakistan. Despite Interpol alerts, McMillan continued his smuggling trade, although at a low level. Even so, he was caught and imprisoned several times. Eventually settling to a modest life in London – far removed from the high life and wealth of his twenties – he wrote and published *Escape: The True Story of the Only Westerner Ever to Break Out of Thailand's Bangkok Hilton*. The book was successful, and did not go unnoticed in Thailand. A slow but relentless process began to return McMillan to chains in Bangkok.

Escape, McMillan says, "made no apologies for drug smuggling; I told the story through those who suffered in Klong Prem prison, with no real explanation of my choices or history. I didn't expect sympathy from readers, nor do I now. Although I accepted that those forty years of contraband trading needed a full interpretation. That is not easy when churned in the smuggling whirlpool."

With *Unforgiving Destiny – The Relentless Pursuit of a Black Marketeer*, David McMillan brings together the threads of his successes and misadventures. He details his large courier operations, his links in Colombia and to the mafia in New York City, and the mini empire he had built. Then, the downfall, as his couriers turned state witnesses, resulting in a long prison term. After his Thailand escape, McMillan became Western advisor to a tribal lord on the Afghanistan border before creating a new life and identity in London. Long haunted by the death of his first wife a decade earlier, McMillan courts and wins the English girl who cannot know his past. Yet a call to Afghanistan during Taliban rule, destroys, again, all he has built. Freed from the torture cells in Karachi, McMillan begins once more. The reader may condemn his ethics, yet admire his resilience.

"The only linking cord over those years," writes McMillan, "was DEA man Bill Shenkmann — he appeared before me for all the major arrests." That twine of the US agent's obsession binds this 37-year chronicle together, as McMillan survives alone, culminating with the final attempt in 2016 to extradite him through the London courts.

Unforgiving Destiny is an extraordinary work as biography: a rare underground life exposed beyond the usual true-crime standards, told with compassion and honesty.

davidmcmillan.net

UNFORGIVING DESTINY

The Relentless Pursuit

of a

Black-Marketeer

David McMillan

Copyright © 2017 David McMillan

All rights reserved.

ISBN: 1544253052
ISBN-13: 978-1544253053

WELCOME

In the course of any criminal enterprise there is usually someone who makes a complete pest of himself. If that person is on the side of the team, the solution is simple. He goes. Unfortunately, if he's an agent of the US Drug Enforcement Agency, he is then an almost intractable problem. He has at least 6,000 colleagues to take his place should he fall. One of them, against whom I held no special grudge, made it his business to end my life. Bill Shenkmann appeared before me at the times of major arrests for over thirty years, even though not one of the cases had a US connection. That's devotion.

Unforgiving Destiny follows the threads that link those unwelcome visits and the background fire of the smuggling trade that drew him close. It is also a story of survival. I'm too old to apologise for my life, and have made too many apologies to the dead to care how evil readers believe I am. Set that aside and look to the payoff: would a good guy tell you what you really want to know?

CONTENTS

	Notes on disclosure	i
1978	A Peaceful Crossing	1
Part 1	Airports & Americas; Couriers & High Life	17
Part 2	Destruction & False Dawn; Thailand & Death	103
Part 3	The Lord of Baluchistan; A London Gentleman in Love	200
Part 4	The Ghosts of Afghanistan; Scandinavian Summer	322
	TERMINATION; Old Thais & Headstones	400
	Index of Names	404
	(*All those who appear in the text*)	
	Pakistan prison phrases	410
	Dedication	410
	ABOUT THE AUTHOR	411

NOTEWORTHY

When making notes for this book some time ago, I took some care submitting Freedom of Information Act requests to find out just what officials from agencies recorded. I was seeking some motive beyond the routine task of capturing scoundrels. Of the documents, I received little more than sheets of thick black lines where the text had been hidden. Concealed, explained the cover letters, as revelation might, *'jeopardize ongoing operations or reveal investigative methods.'* The standard justification for secrecy. Fortunately, retired police in several countries were more talkative. Some matters concealed in earlier writings I am now free to print; the players involved have considerately died.

All of the people in *Unforgiving Destiny* are real; no composites have been created. That would be fiction – a different deal altogether. Only in five cases have I changed the names. A necessary protection of the guilty. Best they keep their lonely identities. Anyway, who'd want to hear from a utter snitch: they never know when to shut up.

▽

Rest easy as you follow in my steps: many people appear and disappear throughout *Unforgiving Destiny*. After all, this was real life. Yet, there is no need for the reader to keep track of them as named identities, just how they played out their moment. While the names are not important and most do not return, some key players re-appear. For those without the luxury of reading a book in one week without distractions, I have included an index from p.404 that outlines their place in these years of my life.

▲

*The lands where I found maps
grew more from distant imagination,
and where the real ground blurs all lines...*

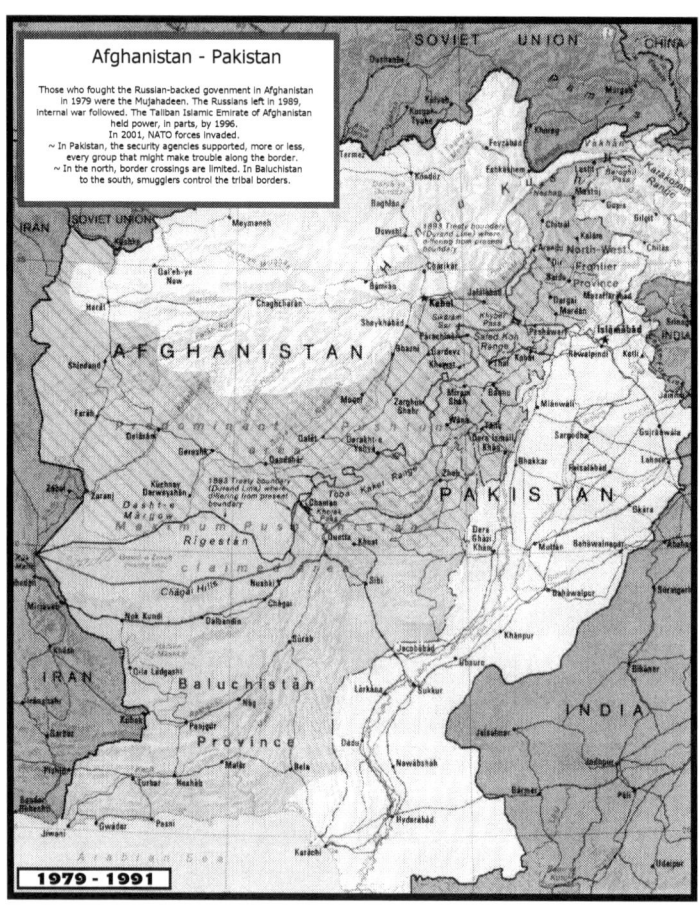

A Peaceful Crossing

A moment when nothing happened has stayed in mind for decades. It was 1978. The check-point at the border crossing between Afghanistan and the Pakistan province of Baluchistan was little more than a battered office – a room of plywood and tin – next to an iron boom gate counterbalanced by an old oil drum filled with concrete. The crumbling barrier and three officials in worn uniforms suggested that this crossing on a minor road was barely used. Yet the deep and wide wheel ruts in the stony ground spoke of frequent heavy vehicles. To my eyes that day, the fact that everyone was armed to the teeth told another truth: anything worth carrying long distances through hard and dangerous country is often worth more than other travellers' lives. I hoped it would not be mine for I was twenty-three and too inquisitive to die soon.

Of the four groups of the interested parties at that moment on the border, I was the only person without a gun. Knowing that, I relaxed. If it came to shooting, I wouldn't be the first to be shot - one of many lessons that taught me that only the brave and foolish bear arms. The parties included our group in two old cars with my Thailand business partner and our guides; then, a feared and respected provincial leader from Baluchistan returning home in shiny four-wheel drives; and on the Pakistan side of the boom gate, the worried saps, the border officers hoping to survive and make a few rupees. Next in line, four Pakistan army rangers looking smarter, more professional yet taking their cues from a darkly evil spook type from some PK intelligence service dressed head to foot in white robes.

After twenty minutes stalled at the crossing with lots of fake friendly greetings and patting of the heart, we were cleared to go. A uniformed officer parked his fat gut on the oil drum to raise the barrier. Then the spook raised a soft hand and whispered to the ranking solider.

The ranger spoke.

"Wait."

Funny I remember this command in English. It wasn't, of course. Languages amongst us included Baluchi, Pashtu, Sindhi, the universal market language Urdu and taxi-driver English but 'wait' at a border crossing needs no translator. Besides, my attention was drawn immediately to the tightening of hands on gun stocks and straps.

The tension was broken by the friend I'd made just forty-eight hours earlier, the Baluchi chief. Also dressed-to-kill in white, he moved effortlessly to the spook and within seconds they were brothers. Clearly, the tribal chief had a reputation. With the wrong look, the wrong move, it could have been different. Half of us, maybe all, dead. But then there would be nowhere to go. You need a survivor to tell the story.

Two days earlier, when we were still far from the border, Lee, my Thailand-based contact, was grumbling about our water supplies. Our drivers were unhappy about leaving our two cars lightly protected, and our guides worried about everything. Our little caravan had left Kandahar that morning but when I'd seen the cliff-top ruins of some old fortress nearby, I decided I wanted to enjoy a night communing with the spirits of the ancients.

"Lee, there couldn't have been any monasteries in Afghanistan?" I asked.

Following a triple translation (Pashtun – Urdu – English), Lee answered.

"The Persians built it. One thousand years."

"Persians? I thought they used mud brick, mostly?" I gave up the search for accurate history. Whoever built the fortress, they were surely long dead. It would have been ages since anyone dropped in for good old commune.

Lee was my fixer for all Asian mischief at the time. In the '70s this was heroin and local marijuana with the potent buds threaded on thin bamboo sticks. The heroin was cooked up from village-grown opium, packed and branded, not by the refinery, but with the stamp of whichever of four warlords guaranteed the safety of transport from field to lab and, importantly, to the Thai wholesalers of the north around Chiang Mai. Lee would deal with the northern people. I stayed in Bangkok apart from a little tour of the Golden Triangle – the touching borders of Burma, Thailand and Laos – so I could see for myself how it all worked.

As expected, all my early ideas about the opium and heroin trade were wrong. I do so understand how the English enjoy being told everything they have understood to be true throughout their lives is completely wrong. I'd formed the idea of the narcotics trade in the Golden Triangle from the movies where a secret encampment has armed men protecting a massive laboratory where the workers are forced to toil over a boiling pot while the big cheese sits in luxury, holding court for evil-eyed foreigners coming to buy the illicit goods.

In fact, there are no such places. When a city wholesaler expects an order for, say, 10 kilos of dope, he first sees a village headman from an opium-poppy growing area and puts a deposit on the 100 kilos of opium paste needed to refine enough morphine to make the 10 kilos. When that thick, black morphine base is ready, the wholesale trader arranges transport to one of hundreds of independent farmhouse laboratories where the morphine will be cooked upon with acids into heroin, then filtered through charcoal and dried in a huge, slowly turning glass globe. This last trick leaves the white powder in coffee-granule sized balls that if squeezed, lose five times their size. That extra effort is to prevent easy mixing of the 88% pure heroin with any adulterants. Even in the cities of Thailand, you can find drinking straws a half-inch long sealed with hot scissors with just this high-quality dope, since any self-respecting junkie can recognise the unique appearance before parting with his 50 cents for a single blast. Back in the labs, the heroin is sealed in bags weighing over 1100 grams (30 Chinese *tael*) – bags bearing the seal and logo of the warlords. Those private armies (not all in uniform – some as mercenaries only sent in if needed) were rarely around during any of this. The seal of General Lei or 'warlord' Khun Sa was simply a guarantee of safe passage: a sign that the quality of the drugs was assured. Safety guaranteed, too, for the mule teams transporting chemicals, drugs, and as importantly, the supplies needed to maintain hillside forces. The big names are not directly involved in the trade, it's the businessmen and middlemen who run it. As almost everywhere, those who stamp their names and gaudily flourish their violence are quickly replaced, while business trades on.

Lee, my Thai friend (no relation to General Lei, a Chinese nationalist leader in exile turned warlord-trafficker) had saved me from ruin and I him from the shanty towns behind Bangkok's main streets. He'd learned his many languages driving taxis on three continents and had great-grandparents ranging from Bangladesh to the borders of Iran. This journey – to establish a source for several tonnes of hashish – allowed Lee to introduce himself to relatives lost across the frontier when Pakistan's birth changed the map of old India. It gave me a chance to play explorer into the unknown. Of course, the great unknown is well-known to those who live there.

We'd flown from Bangkok to Karachi, a very quiet town in 1979, being under the control of General Zia al-Haq who had a way with rope if not with words. He'd hanged the prime minister and would stay in power for years. Lee had brought a young apprentice and we arranged for drivers and guides before heading west. Eventually, we found the village where lived Lee's elders. Along the way, I'd been so absorbed by the unfamiliar and utterly new, I had yet to go beyond the surface. That changed when I stood among the crowd of well-wishers who'd gathered on our arrival.

A very old man, clearly respected, came forward. Lee introduced himself, explaining our journey. They embraced and I saw the old man's tears. He wiped them away with a corner of his dusty robe. He wiped them gently. He'd had a young niece who'd gone away in childhood. The word, so often wrong, was that the entire branch of the family had been killed in the waves of violent and effectively forced migrations after India's independence from Britain. Lee was that niece's grandson and there were many family survivors unknown to this western branch. I felt honoured to be welcomed to the moment when that spring of kinship, barren for so long, flowed once more. Gifts were given, builders and well-drillers paid, and a traders' meeting held, at which we promised to return for a modest 500 kilos of local hash. Lee and I considered flying back east from Kandahar but concluded troublesome airport officials might be difficult to settle with me around. There were few western visitors then. Anyway, I was enjoying the roads.

It was a few days later when just three of us spent the one night sleeping at the top of the ancient fortress. Our porters and protectors were spread about in what I understood as strategic guard posts. I was enjoying the moment.

"You know what this place is?" I said to Lee in the strong moonlight. "It's probably some Buddhist's temple. I heard there's some huge statues farther north."

Lee waved a finger as I searched for my flashlight.

"David, you know there's a war. The guys worry everyone thinks we are Russians."

"I thought the government was already communist?" I stowed the flashlight thinking I could look for inscriptions in the morning.

Lee spoke to the stars. "In Afghanistan, the village we came from is government." He propped on an elbow, circling the air with a hand. "Here, is government."

We both knew that for smugglers, there's always an advantage when officials become rebels and then back again. Instability allowed people to take what they could. For us, the fees might be higher but the delays less.

Our departure the next morning was delayed by the men's insistence at pulling down and coiling up all the rope my cliff-top sleepover had unrolled. Leave no traces. As we were about to depart, a four-wheel drive appeared, followed by new BMW and Mercedes sedans easing aside the lines of passing sheep and shepherds on the road. Our guides and guards adjusted their rifles casually, making them more visible, and brushed their jackets to check the readiness of handguns. They looked at me – wishing, I supposed, that I wasn't around – so I stepped forward toward the little convoy, all smiles and child-like curiosity.

The new vehicles had pristine plastic over seat covers although the amount of dust coating these German cars looked as though it'd been applied by hand. Perhaps so, to look like local traffic. The accompanying Land Rover was packed with fuel cans and the original tyres of the Merc. Good, I thought, these guys were fellow smugglers.

During the elaborate greetings, one of them stood above the others. With a generous, rounded and open face, the traditionally (Baluchi) dressed man was deferred to at every moment. We all looked each other over and decided that for now, at least, there was no need for immediate slaughter. Intentionally yet cautiously, we misled each other as to our ultimate destination. Even I, a relative greenhorn knew never to tell strangers where you've been or where you're going. Lebanon had taught me that.

After I safely established myself as an exploring Englishman, we all shared breakfast. Their leader introduced himself as Mir Noor Jehan Magsi from the coast below the Makran desert in Baluchistan.

"He's a tribal leader," Lee told me, "very good man." Lee explained this clan chief would have many useful contacts but added quietly, "And big danger. Not civilized. There are some like these." Apologising, needlessly.

Yet I would have much to do with this provincial noble over the next twenty years and Noor Jehan would twice save my life; twice I knew of, anyway.

As we all moved toward his lordship's homeland, Russia was invading Afghanistan, and the Americans were to arm the local Mujahedeen fighters with stinger missiles, and the soon-to-become Taliban boys were still kids and turning red with embarrassment under the smart glance of the high-school girls in Kabul (*"Oh, how those girls will pay one day!"* and, *"God, when my beard only grows..."*). Our two happy bands of smugglers edged toward the border at Pakistan wondering, each, if we'd made a mistake joining forces. We came to a halt at a roadhouse before the checkpoint, parking the cars at a distance but failing to deceive anyone.

Noor Jehan swigged on a Coke, looked to the checkpoint, then assigned his - well, scribe, I suppose you'd call him - to translate between his fragments of English. I was expecting a dozen reasons why only he could get us through the crossing and why it would cost a fortune. We were sitting at a metal table outside the roadhouse. Instead of some pitch, Noor Jehan looked back to the northeast, from where we'd come. I give his words in English.

"That fortress you slept in the other night," he began - although I'd not yet spoken of it - "it is very old. A city built by your people. It was called Alexander and there are many more north and south. Your Alexander took his army through there before going to India through the mountains. You made your bed on the stones of the temple. His people made it for their woman god. Those people had sons but you won't find their children. Just in the light of their eyes."

"Thank you," I said, genuinely. "There's much I don't know here," and I gestured toward the checkpoint, now holding army rangers. "But let me help if I can."

And that's where you came in as I began writing this. I was happy to pay the crossing charges and bribes for all of us. Also, to play the part of the stupid foreigner in whose river of money the true sons of the soil could wash. Yet throughout, I was pleased to see Noor Jehan give me secret signs that it was just us against them. Maybe that was simply part of his charm but history would prove otherwise.

By that time, I had money. Somehow dying an unreasonable and violent death while poor seems so much more unjust than dying rich. Being rich was not always so. I look back to an even earlier time when I had been ever so much younger than twenty-three.

I was nineteen and driving in the late afternoon traffic circling the city of Melbourne, Australia. Sitting alone in a '61 Ford (this was 1975) coated in pale blue house paint with rust and matching faded number plates. A car bought three months before for $100 and just car enough to keep me moving until I could leave the country and begin again the job I'd failed on a first try, the path of the smuggler.

I was overdressed for the heat, the best of my clothes under a long-rider's leather coat. As a stranger by then from home, I kept everything that mattered close. Though my passport was kept at a distance, concealed between dusty planks of a disused factory crumbling between old warehouses of the inner city, a bolt hole where my sleeping bag and a second pair of boots were out of sight under broken work benches.

I rolled to a stop at the lights next to a police cruiser I'd half-expected would run the amber rather than stop. Yet they were in no hurry. I could see the driver's mouth move as he spoke. His partner casually scanned the surrounding cars. He paused at the sight of my old Ford Anglia, then looked to me trying, in that automated policeman's way, to marry the car to its driver. The lights dropped to green. The cruiser inched forward, forcing me to move ahead so he could read my number plate. A glance to my mirror gave a picture of the two cops looking ahead and now with one holding his radio mic.

The fuzzy number plate would only lead to the phoney name I'd used when buying the Ford. Unfortunately, I'd burned my licence doing 120mph along a beach road months ago, but the real trouble lay next to me in a trembling paper bag. Inside was $7,000 stake money for the first India run just days away. That money and

I had to stay free, yet as the police car moved forward alongside, I knew I'd lost the edge.

I pushed the Ford's side-shift lever into second gear and took a right turn. Even when simply curious, cops don't worry about blocking traffic and so stopped to look sideways. As soon as I'd taken the next left, I gunned the old slant-six engine. I'll have to take my hat off to that old rust bucket – it took me to the next crossroad within 20 seconds. Unfortunately, at 19 seconds, the patrol cruiser was just able to see me speeding into the next turn, cutting left again, back on myself. That was enough evasiveness for the police, and the chase was on.

I cursed myself and began stuffing the bank notes down my shirt front. I'd need to ditch the Ford fast *and* in a good place to leg it. Heading toward the city centre (never go country starting a car chase), I knew by then the cops' radio check would have replied 'all clear' and they'd conclude that whatever I wanted to hide would be with me. Dumping the car was essential; you can't tear away from officers in a car without breaking at least five laws. On foot, you're just Joe Citizen until found otherwise.

Even with my Ford flat out it would take a full minute to reach the city centre. I knew Melbourne's inner city streets as well as a London cabbie knows his. Even so, from my mirror I saw the cops had tapped their siren lights and bullied their way through the main crossroad. I had perhaps thirty-five seconds to side-line my car and lost twenty of them trying to think ahead. If I'd turned to the freeway I'd never leave it without handcuffs. Better to stay near buildings I knew and accept a plan no matter how rough.

My eye caught a block of flats whose layout appeared standard. Turning in, I raced to the nearest residents' parking-bay cover, killed the engine and jumped out with the keys. I was wrong about the layout so had to run around a brick partition to reach the back fence. I didn't need to look back: the pitch of the police siren told me I was losing ground. Still, a misleading U-turn around a hedge path gave me invisibility for the price of a few seconds. In any chase the value of being out of sight while on the move is massive, and so is the value of luck as two close fences gave the chance of getting back on course toward the city centre.

I could hear the sounds of more police. New voices. Another carload had joined the pursuit. At the end of a lane the road ran alongside a large, and mostly empty, market car park. If there is ever a benefit from running when chased – oddly, that's almost never – do your running out of view. My watch told me I had eight minutes to get to the big department store I needed before it closed. Crossing the road at a walk, I'd been seen by one of the original cops. Unlucky.

He called, "Hey, you!" and, "Stop running!"

(As though anyone would actually stop.)

His voice was about fifty feet away. I took off.

I moved papers, keys and wallet from inside pockets to secure side pockets and then took off across the open car park to the city shopping arcades, keeping high on the balls of my feet, allowing a slight curve in my path to suggest I was heading for a random isolated car at the far side so not to acquaint myself with two men at another car beginning to take an interest, good citizens as they might have been. By chance, I was in decent shape at nineteen. It's hard not to be at that age unless you've gone out of your way.

I made it to the sidewalks and slowed to a fast walk, saying to some confused women, "some crazy old guy with an axe!" and nodding. "The police think he's around here." Doubly confused, the women moved away and I cut into an arcade to remove my coat. The last policeman I saw was still in the car park but talking into a big hand-held radio.

Sticking to plan, even though the cops might have then lost interest, I walked quickly to the big department store. As I turned into the store as they readied to close, I saw two uniformed policemen and two patrol cars circling.

In the store, I took the stairs to the first floor, then a lift to the seventh, which had access to a rooftop terrace – used only for staff smoke and lunch breaks – and climbed the low partition to the smaller department store next door where they also had an open terrace, never used at that hour when most were heading home. Ducking inside, I had time, just, to buy a cream woollen pullover and that gave me a useful store bag, into which I packed my (reversed) leather coat. I was safe, and I'd kept to places I knew well.

Back on the street, the police were in little bunches, chattering and joking. The chase had been simply because they had nothing better on and happened to be nearby. And now over. I was simply the rabbit.

This tired and homeless rabbit then walked uptown to the theatre district to sit in a café and wonder at the exhausting nature of being a forager.

Some indistinct but worrying sounds later woke me deep into the night. I had been sleeping nights in the empty small-industry factory for those last few weeks as I'd need every penny for the India job. The skinny tin shed had been gutted except for the skeleton of an iron press. Too heavy, perhaps, to drag across the dirt floor. No electricity but blessed with running water and a toilet. The human sounds grew closer. My dark home had no windows beyond the front and just one door I kept locked. I'd been given the key by a busy agent believing I'd been looking for a place to store company accounts.

"I'm not sure it'll suit you," he'd said. "It might leak. The Anglican Church wants to sell its old city properties."

After checking the place out, I'd returned the original key after keeping a copy.

"You're right," I'd told him. "Water stains down two walls."

I looked at my watch as I interpreted the sounds that had woken me. They were low and gritty sounds from a private security patrol car's radio. Lights glowing on the frosted glass of my factory told of a stationary car. I lifted myself from my sleeping bag and eased on shoes over bare feet. The dirt floor, forty years of machine dust dislodged from the ceiling and walls by city vibrations, muffled most sound. From a crack in the old glass I could see two uniformed men sniffing about the gates of the newer warehouses. I held back a few feet so they couldn't catch even a glimpse of my face, and rolled my head to provide a limited panorama of the real world. When remaining invisible, every moment has its own rules. In four days, I would be airborne once more. I'd been rich once before for five months and planned, this time, to be more careful.

The security men returned to their car and were soon gone. I had made no noise but had they sensed human life amid the still machines? I moved close to the crack. All quiet at five to three. A few cars sifting along the main streets, one pitching laughter from side windows. A star blinked.

No, not that, and here now is why I remember that otherwise unexceptional night. A remodelled office block of around twelve storeys offered this unusual sight: a man, I could just make out, walked through the night sky, floating effortlessly with his hands in the trouser pockets of a pale-yellow suit. He halted and looked down upon the town, maybe smiling; he was too far away to tell. The body language of this sky-walker was utterly sure, as if some powerful god might smile down upon a hungry mortal. The man then turned as though responding to a friendly call and returned across the sky to the gargoyle-cornered slate rooftop of the building. Then, the clearing moon revealed the illusion.

A balcony of thick glass and matt-black tubing had been built as a projecting walkway from the modern penthouse atop the old structure so that it was almost invisible at night. Anyone standing on the platform could feel the thrill of the suspended flight. To me, the manner of the man's movements suggested he was a visitor, someone with complete confidence in his world and its obedience in his hands. He, I was sure, would be one of the few with the edge: an athlete's balance, an artist's control and the vision to be blind to the distractions of weakness.

A few people grow naturally with that edge, that advantage. I had no such natural talent, only the realization that I would need to attend constantly to hone such sharpness and hope to keep it safe within my grip.

A few days later as I wiped away the signs of my existence from that tin shed, I thought, 'Well, at least I have the gift of nothing.' That no one knew of me or cared what I might do. My first business partner had disappeared, the marijuana grocery store had been closed, the newspaper folded, old friends scattered, I would be nothing in the ashes.

I was wrong but many years would pass before my earliest and most implacable enemies would be revealed.

I'll take a couple of pages before we return to Afghanistan to outline why, previously, I'd always written of my own smuggling adventures as no less than a relentless pursuit of money. If only my objectives then had had such heartless purity. True devotees of money stay with money – stock contracts, securities, hedge funds, futures and bonds; actual cash would be too visible. For lovers of money, open crime, especially drugs, usually goes beyond acceptable risk. Amongst my friends back then, our motivation flowed from that troublesome occasion in most teenagers' lives: believing things to be true.

In the last of my school years, I'd taken an interest in chemistry while raising pocket money trading hash at New-Age grocery stores and hallucinogens in burger joints around Melbourne's hippie district. This was the early 1970s when some major dealers of quality would direct some profits into counter-culture doings. Burt Deling's dramatic comedy of dopers' lives, *Pure Shit*, is almost the only Australian movie of that era that today can be viewed without cringing, perhaps helped by cast members being dopers themselves. Others published drug-law reform newspapers, as did my friends. Few western papers now can boast that each edition would be banned outright, as was *The Australasian Weed*.

Those born after, say, 1980 would struggle to get a feel for just how low was the regard held in the '70s for governments and public institutions and how naively high the hope for their transformation. As for the law, even an older generation at that time believed moral crimes laws would soon become dust. Few then would have believed the quantity each year of new laws enacted in Britain, Europe and America prohibiting immoral private behaviours and improper speech in public. Many of us in the '70s insisted that our hired administrators – the governments – had no authority to make laws restricting sexual activity, public expression or private risk-taking. We saw all moral law-making as merely politicians assuming the robes of ancient priestly castes, and that the only laws that are changed are the laws that are broken. But enough of all that – it's pointless to speak of a time long gone and a lie to understate the pleasures of black-market cash.

Yet for today's age of smirking obedience that masks unspoken fears (that broken spirit perhaps from the online stream, when everything's already pictured and done better than you ever could), it is perhaps comforting to know that it wasn't so very long ago that to be young permitted the illusion that we might make a new world.

Adapting song lyrics as some step-by-step instruction manual for even a peaceful revolution was as lame then as now. Yet the first step for our presumptuous little group was to ignore the existence of separate countries and violate border rules. Hypocrisy, of course, as the next move relied on the economic differences those borders enforce. Never mind, on to Step 2 which was: smuggle drugs and turn everyone on (at a competitive price). Step 3: buy an island and start a country (Orange Island off Guinea-Bissau was considered) with the profits, where we'd all live free. Step 4 – well, not much point listing the rest of the plan. We never got past Step 2 before The Man, (as government agencies were then called) was on to us. Besides, step 2 seemed so much fun. And, never surrender, did I mention that? We might allow ourselves to be organised but never became part of organised crime since we saw The Mob as just another style of government but without a media division. Few of us saw the danger in this, for being truly independent might mean being truly alone. That's the last I'll say of what we thought about society. It might have been a deceptive belief but a belief is a fine thing to have. Anyway, within a year most of us were broken up by toxic combinations: greed and generosity, lovelessness and love; thinking stubbornness is being wisely determined, and worse, personal ambition and unbridled intoxication. The smartest among us took his dog into the Blue Mountains and single-handedly grew a huge crop (only visiting the town shop fifteen miles away every month to buy dog food), then harvested and bulk-sold. He bought a yacht and sailed the world happily ever after. Well, maybe not *ever*.

I had a job in advertising but it didn't take. Fooled by my new profession, in my after-hours, I set up a too-ambitious scheme to fly $3m-worth of Thai-stick marijuana by Lear jet, island-hooping after Chiang Rai, across the Isthmus of Kra, Malaysia, even a risky refuel at the Cocos Islands before dropping into the western deserts of Australia.

Working with grown-ups for the first time, I foolishly set aside all the cautions I'd apply if any had been school friends. The players included a banker, the Lear jet salesman (or, so he said), a slick American investor in futures (a con artist and part-time spook – which means being an informer was always his fall-back position) and the only good guy in the show disappeared just before the money. Too sad to detail. Worse, too, was my family lawyer calling me in from the cold only to warn me I was treading on the toes of some 'Americans'.

"Is that bad?" I said to Ralph Renard, the lawyer, affecting the voice of a spoiled child.

In fact, it was. I returned to my cute and much-loved city apartment to find it stripped to the floorboards with even wallpaper half torn away. What I did not know was that this was the first time my name became known to the US Drug Enforcement Administration – then only a few years old. Or rather, my face. They had only a false passport photo, and it reached the desk of Bill Shenkmann, then a young intelligence analyst in Washington. The US was still running air-force bases in Thailand as part of the Vietnamese war, and the drug connection was surfacing. Shenkmann took an interest in the private Lear jet's movements and that led to a name at the old Bangkok Sheraton, which led to me. The DEA, as far as I know, had nothing to do with my downfall, but I was then a face to be found.

Penniless, I kept on, leaving for Lebanon a few months later to arrive just as the 15-year civil war broke out. I think I could have been successful in Lebanon. Except I'd be dead. Again, I tried fresh ground to seek my fortune. This time, India. I worked from the gutter up – but stayed there – well, I guess I did advance, worked my way up to the footpath. Eventually, I began to run out of mistakes to make and in Thailand finally got it right, if I can put it that way. Made my first million. I returned to Europe after waiting in a Bangkok hotel room for three weeks with a slight case of raging heroin addiction but with enough dope around, I didn't notice at first. That passed with the help of whisky and Xanax, and later I met an Italian girl and life was fine. But still dangerous. Even in barren Afghanistan.

Six weeks later, our little band drove through the same checkpoint from Afghanistan back to the Baluchi heartland. The checkpoint appeared abandoned: the office-shack was a ruin of corrugated metal; a burned husk of a pick-up truck lay blacked at the side and the twisted pole of the boom gate was caked with dried blood. Nothing else.

At least they bury their dead.

Our cargo that day was no more than Lee's personal hash stash – a kilo built into a carved box. Personal consumption, in that part of the world. Besides, such times beyond the west were holidays compared with working under the roar of jet engines and the glare of our modern inspectors, which is where we'll go next, as soon as some passengers are collected.

Part 1

1

One overcast dawn in the 1990s I sat aboard a long speedboat as it edged away from a beach near Singkawang City. On shore, Indonesian police aimed machine guns at the Malay smugglers who ducked for cover between the large bales they'd just unloaded before returning fire. Within minutes four policemen and half a dozen Malays were dead, the crimson-dashed cargo falling to the sand. That cargo was garlic. Fourteen tonnes of it. Those flavoursome bulbs turned into food to die for by the Indonesian government's decision to impose a 400% duty on imports. That year, for six months, cloves of garlic gave illicit traders a greater return than moonlighting the famed Thai marijuana sticks. Garlic, gold or drugs – anything can be contraband at the right time and place.

The foundation of smuggling is ordinary trade; the price one person is prepared to pay another person for goods acquired within risks the buyer might reward but not suffer himself. On the numbers, most smuggled goods are not absolute contraband in themselves, merely unlicensed and so, untaxed. Another level of premium is added by danger.

Most smugglers worth attention survive early collisions until a final crash and burn. My own career seemed a landscape of winding bridges. But I never looked down to the deep cavities below. Before we crawl together from the first dark crater, let's return to days before the fall. As these events cover decades, you'll hear many names. Most will appear to make good or do bad as I go along, but it is not worth keeping track of the names before they disappear. (I've listed them anyway in a descriptive index.) Only to note their help or hindrance. Yet Michael remained a lifelong friend.

I'd met Michael Sullivan by chance in the 1969 when I was fourteen. He was lounging around the swimming pool of a Melbourne doctor. I was visiting with family. Michael was the weed dealer to a group of respected gynaecologists who were quietly paying off local cops so they could continue providing the only safe abortions available under the law. I thought him odd, interesting perhaps, then forgot him. Those doctors soon challenged the payoffs, brought the matter to law, and ultimately helped change the restrictive laws. The glare of police sent Michael underground. Again, by chance, five years later, at an all-night hot-dog stand – the only place in town then to eat after 3:00am – we exchanged a five-minute conversation. Michael was at the height of his earning capacity; the link-man between Italian farmers growing marijuana and city folk. He didn't give his number. Too cautious, which struck me as pointless, considering he was dressed in a snakeskin musician's suit and a cowboy hat and drove a 19-foot Lincoln town car. I'd heard he'd had trouble in the following years.

So, when Clelia suggested one night that we drive across town to meet a couple she had found in her travels, I didn't make the connection. Clelia's travels were often through the local dope scene, something she did almost as a hobby during my frequent trips to Asia and Europe. I had met Clelia Viganò eighteen months earlier while eating at her father's restaurant. She was the youngest daughter of a line of successful Italian restaurateurs and troubled her parents with her choice of friends. She was beautiful yet liked to act the tough girl, which was a cover for a natural shyness she hoped to overcome. A year earlier we had bought a house together. We were happy.

"And, who is this Michael?" I asked as we drove through the outer Melbourne suburbs, heavy weeping trees making the street lights dark. "Another dealer?"

"He doesn't deal much. Just a couple of customers," Clelia swung the Porsche into a curved street to park. "He was some kind of pole-vaulting champion, and his wife is a South American girl. Pretty. I thought maybe he could do some work for you. He needs the money and looks good." By work, Clelia meant working as a courier. In those days, I paid $20,000 for each run. Not only paying for quality, but with $350,000 for each kilo imported (that's $1.5 million today), I could afford to pay four times the usual rate.

As we left the car and approached the dim lights of the house, I remembered that the Michael Sullivan I'd met years earlier had been a top athlete until one knee failed him. I was about to say that to Clelia when we stopped at the front door. At was an inch open and splinters of the door frame looked freshly exposed. I peered through the side-window curtains. I caught sight of a tall figure in a ski mask striding about the living room. The indoor skier had an old double-barrel shotgun held with one hand at the barrels. Two pair of knees sitting at a sofa. I looked to Clelia.

"Seems as though they have company," she whispered.

Using hand signals, I gestured for Clelia to wait in the near shadows of the front garden. I backtracked to the car and took a handgun from its stash in a false panel. By the time I returned, Clel had little to report.

"A lot of talk. Not much with the shotgun."

I slid my handgun into the belt at my back. Awkward as it had a fat 6-inch silencer connected to its 9mm barrel. Gently moving the door open, I stepped in first, pausing just inside to listen. The masked man was talking.

"I don't like to do this stuff," he was explaining. "I mean, we could be friends. But you have to share, you know."

Clelia was behind me. She tapped my shoulder and pointed. There was a second visitor in the room, sitting on a stool by a small living-room bar. His mask was no more than a knitted winter cap with a jagged hole around the eyes – cut with scissors for the occasion, I guessed. These guys didn't have a professional tailor. The one with a gun was still talking.

"Now, if that's all you've got – and I want to believe you – we can come back next week..." I'd heard enough from this considerate robber.

I stepped in to the living room just as I saw the gunman walk alongside a heavy coffee table, mid-room. This meant his barrel would catch the table if he tried to swing it up quickly. Before that happened, I was a few feet into the room, my gun aimed at his face.

"Long time, no see," I said, for I had recognised the voice and manner of Lou Speechly, a jailbird loser and fringe player. I'd met him once with a customer. He was big on show, terrified in action. I nodded at the shotgun. "I hope you didn't put shells in that thing." I then looked to Lou's friend on the barstool. "You can take the sock off your face, too."

While I took the shotgun from Lou, Clelia introduced me to Michael and his wife Marie. It looked as though they'd been trying to make the best of a bad situation. Lou and his sidekick had crashed in around thirty minutes earlier. Robbing dealers was common enough but selective. Those who did so were too fearful to steal from those who might shoot back. Looking at Michael, at over six feet, though slim, I imagined him a match for the rangy Lou. Maybe he was being protective of his wife. Such invasions were not a problem I had. Not because of any dangerous reputation, but because the people I supplied wouldn't tolerate any interference in their business. Lou knew this.

After fifteen minutes Lou and his stooge left, having given Michael back the $1700 he took from the cookie jar. I then assured him Lou wouldn't be back. The only reason I had a gun in the car was that it was one of a bagful I'd acquired after friends robbed a firearms warehouse. The crew's engineer had made well-machined silencers for the automatics, and I knew the opportunity wouldn't occur again. Yet, even then, I knew the limitations of guns. A couple of months earlier, I'd been at a restaurant with friends when a disagreement needed settling by fetching a document from my car. I left the table, crossed the street, and as I approached my car, I saw five young men mercilessly kicking another young man in the gutter. After collecting my papers, I returned with a gun in my hand. It was an impressive weapon: a VP70M silenced pistol that held 18 rounds and fired in bursts of three once modified. After waving it at those doing the kicking, they looked at me blankly. The only reaction came from the kid in the gutter, who immediately jumped up and told me to mind my own business. I shrugged and returned to my dinner companions. So much for weaponry.

"It's just as well you arrived when you did," Michael said, still a little unsure.

I shrugged. "Any idea who set this up?" There'd be no point asking Lou. He'd say anything. Michael didn't know.

Clelia and I spent a couple of hours more in the house. It was well furnished, clean. Some damage to a large stereo speaker that Lou had kicked. We were given drinks and snacks as Michael took out a photo album to show me pictures of the small yacht he once owned. A couple of cars he had. A bigger house. All gone. He'd been betrayed by a business partner. His large stake money taken. Michael was now dealing in a very small way. Just enough to get by and pay for his heroin habit. Most addicts take heroin because they must or become sick. Michael did it because he loved it. One of the minority of users who don't feel quite right without it. Still, he kept it clean. He used three times a day at the same hours. Never more than 140mgs per dose. Wife Marie had a habit, too, to keep him company.

"Marie has tiny veins," Michael reported. "We have to get Duncan over to give her a hit." Duncan was Michael's one real customer. Took a couple of ounces each week on credit and served it up in bits. Being drop-in nurse to Marie was taken as a sign of loyalty.

Driving home, Clelia asked me what I thought of Michael. I had a question first.

"Does every visitor get the photo album?"

"Well, I did." Clel thought for a moment as she drove. "I don't think they have many visitors."

"They'll get more if this Duncan has his way." I was almost certain loyal Duncan had set up Lou for the raid. "Michael's a little pompous in his way. Spends a lot of time trying to impress with a past that doesn't matter. But there's something there I like."

Even though Michael made some people turn on him, I sensed a good man. He was capable of being dedicated – the athletic training – and not afraid of work. He once been an art teacher, and there were signs of his touch around the house. As well, I had heard a fine story from when Michael had been arrested by the fledgling Narcotics Bureau. He'd sat in a chair for eight hours without saying a word to police. Not because he was a hardened criminal but because he simply hated authority. You can't buy that. Of course, police took the view that he held them in contempt – and he would pay for that attitude during his life. Michael had been impressed at the sight of me waving a gun around his living room at his lame and temporary enemies. He should not have been. I didn't tell him what Lou knew well: that the cash incomes of several major villains around town depended on my safety. A young man can afford to be brave when unseen shadows demand his continued existence.

Michael became one in a team of couriers who travelled the world blind. That is, they never saw the dope, never met anyone other than me – and every element of their journey from tickets to hotel rooms was arranged. I didn't want them thinking about what they were doing – the less they had to do, the more they would daydream in a fantasy of safety. Yet they were safe. I didn't want couriers at first. I didn't want people who might need to make decisions. Decisions and choices that would always be wrong. However, the more smuggling I did on my own, the greater the risks I'd take, simply to understand what was possible. I found myself taking chances I'd never allow any courier. With the couriers, I could usefully obsess over their routes, the best arrival and departure times for each airport, and how they would spend their few days in Bangkok, Cali or Islamabad.

The fantasizing by couriers was no small side effect. It was important. As long as they were in a make-believe world where everything seems perfect, they would not be looking at imagined dangers. The real danger was that they would draw attention to themselves by changing the plan. Head for the wrong exit or tear off their luggage tags to hide their origin airport. This meant that I followed their route to watch and intervene if possible.

One time in Vancouver I passed immigration into the customs hall to watch Michael and Peter Dale make a bag switch. Peter Dale was a fine courier. He had the shining confidence of a pathological liar. In his thirties with a perennial near-tan, Peter often dressed in white to set off his blond hair. In business, he'd single-handedly ruined some boutique plant shops and needed the money ferrying suitcases across borders.

Here, in the airport, he was free of his concerns and had assumed the manner of a record producer. He looked like one. Not simply the suit and white shirt but the walk and gestures of a man for whom time is money. Michael had flown in from Bogota with the case containing the dope. He waited for Peter – who had flown from London - to pick up his bag. The bags were matching but had a small sticker on each to distinguish them. I was holding back searching my papers but quietly looking at the arriving passengers.

The hall is a strange arena. Everyone wants to get out. No matter how innocent a passenger may be, each has a secret fear they could be stopped. A nuisance for most, dangerous for some. The fact that it is confined space surrounded by officials with unlimited powers of search and intrusion affects everyone. My scan of the room passed the retired couples returning from vacations, and focussed on those likely to be checked. Young men travelling alone, women too pretty to resist a counter check, and those dressed to attract attention. Soon enough, I began to see that there were just too many damn hippies in the hall to count as an ordinary day. Well, not just hippies: sure, there were three couples with long hair and beads fussing over backpacks, but there were three separate guys that looked down-and-out yet brushing their hands over their clothes and running fingers through messy hair. They were all part of the same outfit. A smuggling group had developed a practice of landing a dozen couriers at the airport at the same time. Ten were from US flights but went out of their way to look dishevelled and suspicious enough to attract the Canadian search teams. This way, the organizers hoped, their two couriers would sail through unmolested while the hippies were turned upside down. This expensive trick worked well at the time.

Taking advantage of the confusion, I signalled Peter Dale to move. He picked up Michael's bag as planned and walked through. We all met in the carpark. Of course, I said nothing to either about the hippie group. I didn't want them thinking too much about other passengers. The job was successful. Peter was paid his $20,000 and spent it mismanaging his plant shops. Michael buried his under his rear garden steps, while I traded to my wholesale customers, retired bank robbers, who shared my certainty that police would like most to catch us all. The couriers knew nothing of that world of informers and surveillance. As our taxi drove us into town where we could collect our own cars, Michael remarked, "That was easy – I should have been doing this years ago." By which he meant, *I can do this myself*. Since I'd said nothing of the complex arrangements, his was a natural – if wrong – thought.

2

In the early '80s in Australia, the economics of the dope trade allowed something that has never been repeated. A kilo of heroin would wholesale for over a million dollars in today's money - twenty times its current value. Not in one transaction for anyone but perhaps five, and still a momentary glitter as might a diamond twinkle when turning under a light that has not shone since.

For me this allowed fast operations by air with elaborate safety measures while paying everyone more than they had hoped and never to question any decision I made. If this seems a monumental arrogance, it is truly a sheer wonder that the laws of the world could bring about such a foolhardy prohibition. The high returns permitted the expense of complex relays where those who crossed borders at international airports would always appear to have come from a safe western country. With up to four couriers plotted across the globe some operations would demand great care.

One such operation will serve as an example for many. The couriers often changed names as they travelled. Anyone on board would have at least two passports and never in their own name.

I'll describe the operation in detail, something rarely done truthfully in print. The operational moves are the easy part. More demanding is the management of the half-focussed personalities as they shade themselves from a risk made greater by their blindness.

A word about passports and identities. In my late teens, an old-fashioned policeman took me aside.

"Don't use all these different names," he warned in a tone that suggested to do so would not be playing the game fairly. "We won't know it's you."

Puzzled, I ignored the advice. Having grown up in a household full of women, I viewed men of authority mostly as hopeless nuisances.

In the smuggling world, you learn quickly that, for customs inspectors, there is no time to check every item in a passenger's luggage. It is the intelligence on a traveller that makes the difference. And with a fresh identity, there is no intelligence beyond the manner of each traveller.

Another thing: false documents are best obtained from the ground up. Beginning with a real birth certificate and creating all the on-line data so that the new person appears to have a past. A lazy imbecile criminal (and I've met a few) once lamented, *"But Dave, surely you'd have to get guys in the passport office to put the fix in?"* Not good. The higher your man in the government office, the more damage follows if one among you is somewhere identified using false papers. The feds would look at every passport that left his desk, unmasking the entire crew. Besides, if he's selling his documents to you, he's probably selling to others: more notorious villains who are bound to be spotted. Tedious and time-consuming as it is, do the work yourself. I learned that the hard way, as you'll later see.

In my twenties, I hadn't the maturity to slow down, or the experience to know I'd enjoy adventures more with a stroll of appreciation rather than the gallop of recklessness.

The three-week operation below involved two kilos of China White heroin going to Colombia where it would be exchanged for four kilos of double-hydrated cocaine. Pearly, smooth, layered and almost mellow in its super-charged way. Need I say, worth having. The coke was wanted in Sweden.

The first of the four couriers to drift from the plan was George.

George the Greek was in his fifties and a small-time fence who believed he had expertise in gemstones. If you're thinking his qualifications were poor for a courier, you're right. He was passed to me by a shabby group of Australian crooks. He'd run up gambling debts and those debts passed to the crooks for collection.

They collected little but for a $5,000 fee, offered George as a courier. George liked the idea; he would think himself his own man and seize every opportunity he saw. In my defence of the poor decision, I can say only that at the time I had yet to nail down my own *Villain's Book of Rules*. The first rule is to select a team based only on suitability and talent.

Remember the old *Mission: Impossible* TV show? No? Well each episode began with Jim Phelps, the leader, sifting through files of those he would need. Rejecting those without experience and selecting for skills. Mr Phelps was not governed by sentimentality or wanting to be loved for providing work to the needy. Think of how different your own life would be if you approached your life choices of accomplices with such cool.

George was sent to London where his brief was to wait out ten days before returning to Australia with two kilos of heroin another courier would bring from Asia. I had a couple of kilos stashed in the UK in case the first courier fell. George's ten-day stay was to give plausibility to his travel itinerary, that of visiting British relatives – not that he had any. When returning to Sydney his passport would have no entries other than a short trip to a country from which no one is likely to export drugs. See the sights, I told him. Visit the waxworks museum, I thought, he might learn a few things about expression from the dummies.

I'd given George a message-service number to call in case he had a dire problem. I received a call eighteen hours after he'd checked into his hotel. Good of him to keep it bottled for a night.

When I phoned his hotel from a payphone in Miami, George told me he'd lost his expense money. Fortunately, his ticketing was already paid (and by a third party so he couldn't exchange his Business Class for Economy and pocket the difference) but he said he'd need another £1,000 for expenses.

"Don't tell me how it happened," I began to say as he coughed out some story about a light-fingered call girl in his hotel room.

Later, I would learn the truth. George had spent a night in a casino. Keep in mind George was a man who thought life had cheated him. To George, there was only one explanation for his years of hard luck. Fate must have a big win due to him. Not for the first time, he'd spent a night in the casino plotting strategy only to be cleaned out by the double zero by which the house takes all bets. Not only was George a fact-free optimist, he was an *impatient* dreamer. The casino had been in Sydney. He'd blown his expense money before stepping foot on the plane.

I called a friend in London, made arrangements to pre-pay nine days at another hotel, and added, "Put £4,000 in an envelope so it's waiting for him. Don't leave a number or a name."

I knew there'd be trouble with George and his villain owners in Australia. Even so, the job was safe.

To most, the idea of anyone viewing heroin with anything but horror might seem strange. The picture is less black-and-white if examined in its parts. However scary the word is, ask anyone who has suffered great pain and been given morphine you'll hear good things. Those who take it for their imagined pain are not depriving the genuinely pain-racked, they are being indulgent with a very useful drug.

A sympathetic friend of learning and high standards once said to me, *"But really, David. Heroin! I mean, really* not *heroin!"*

How to explain. Okay, one view. I'm rotten to the core. But that's no explanation. Did it matter that my stuff was always kitchen-clean at lower prices? No, that doesn't mean much if you're not involved. Does it matter that that the high price is set by governments, not the dealers? This is so. By the simple act of the law's prohibition, a black market is instantly created with long sentences pushing up risk and consequently prices. That, too, doesn't matter. If we all set our scruples upon government behaviour, we'd be pretty ruthless.

Let's look closer at the trail. I've used heroin (it's very moreish) and worked the street, so I know all about it. When I've had large, sealed bags of top grade smack or snow on my desk I've looked at them hard. A smuggler sees the hands of those skilled hill chemists in hidden laboratories and the extraordinary path those smooth blocks have taken to make it so far into my care. I rarely wanted to let the white bricks leave my hands, knowing that once the seal is broken, some creeps will stomp all over it with crappy additives. Once, in my late teens, I encased a block of Chinese 999 heroin in acrylic glass, framed it and mounted it above my bed. A million-dollar artwork. The combination of threat, purity and understated opulence held me spellbound. By my time, the Burmese chemists had adapted the old French recipe purifying with farm charcoal before a second clean with hydrochloric acid to make the powder water soluble. Then, the fifty *tolas* (580 grams, about one Chinese pound) would be dried in a giant, turning wok over a blue flame. The drying with constant rotation resulted in those tiny, light balls (like bean-bag Styrofoam) I spoke of with that important characteristic. Almost any touch would see them collapse to a white dust. They could not be messed with. This allowed my buyer in Chiang Rai to see at a glance that he had the right stuff. The twice-sealed bags had the Double-Lion brand logo as well, the stamp being the symbol of the protective militia who taxed both laboratory and hill trader. I'd known western junkies take the trouble to travel to that part of the world to free themselves of heroin habits. Using pure dope not only makes it easier to regulate doses but to slowly reduce over weeks to avoid excruciating withdrawal effects. East or west, a strong determination is needed, but at least if you know what you are using, you have a chance.

I could argue about drug law, make feeble comparisons with legal drugs, mumble something about worse things. I could bore everyone silly by dusting off the survey of heroin use I published with the Economics School at Adelaide University (1989). In brief, the survey, conducted from street to car park to a hundred mid-level dealers suggested two thirds of users were not addicted but recreational. They couldn't afford otherwise and were not prepared to wreck their lives.

Yet nothing of the above weighs in as a solid justification. But do ask yourself, along that path, who did you begin to despise?

If 'Do No Harm' is good enough for physicians, it's certainly good enough to apply to the likes of me. No matter how you play the dope game, you're still part of it. More to the point, if a person can do something to make the world better, then he should do it. By that simple standard, I have betrayed my world. Yet, I've spent a lifetime arguing for complete legalization. Drug supermarkets. Come in, sign a waiver, knock yourself out. It will happen.

I got out of the trade for two reasons. Firstly, because I found I'd been on all the rides in the park, and secondly, because I was tired of being imprisoned. As you'll see, getting out was easy enough but being imprisoned is another matter. That depends on whom you've annoyed.

That's the last I'll say on all that. Anyway, if I'd given up at twenty this book might be about fly-fishing in the Sahara, and as at this recalled moment I've got four couriers and twenty-two dependents scattered across the world, we'd best get on the move.

Three days in Cali were enough to make the arrangements for the cocaine. The town had not been as I'd expected. By 1980, its reputation beyond South America was that of some Colombian Wild West. Yet I'd found a sprawling modern city with pleasant shopping arcades at its centre, relaxed and civilized on the surface.

However, one incident should give a glimpse beneath the easy urban life. My driver, a local, was delayed by having to borrow a car. His own had been stolen by some city villains. In the Cali style, Diego had been contacted and given the price for the return of the old jalopy, at least two-thirds of its actual value.

"This is a tough town," I suggested to Diego. "Why can't our friends take care of it in their way?"

"Not worth it," said Diego, "too much money."

The cost of getting his car back from the thieves was $1,500. If I went to my coke friends for help, they'd of course refuse money, or even gun-fare, to sort the problem. For them to get that car back it would mean a serious fight – even street thieves stand their ground in Colombia. A serious fight would mean rewarding those who did the fighting. It would be cheaper to pay the $1,500 as my drug friends would never fight for Diego without expecting to effectively own him later. If involved, my people would probably manage $500 for the car but – once I was out of town – tell Diego it cost $1,000 to settle. He'd have to pay that or, worse, be in debt for small errands of major risk. So, thanks to my bravery by proxy, Diego would've had his rust bucket, be in debt for $1,000 and have made sworn enemies of a gang of street toughs.

As Diego drove me to the airport, I was grateful to have had this explained to me. I gave him $500 above his tip, a fine imposed on myself for speaking without thinking.

My private viewing of the four kilos of cocaine had been on a glass coffee table in one of the new apartments built among the many hills of Cali. I'd kept such things away from my hotel room as hotels are full of informants, the amateurs more dangerous that the professionals. It's worth saying, that for a smuggler the best hotels are those that, while not cheap, are not five-star, where the elite stay. When you think of the elite in colourful countries, imagine how they became that way. The elite have public security against their political rivals and private security against their friends. Why should a smuggler add professionals to the hotel employees' amateur sleuthing? A four-star hotel of no less than fifty rooms is perfect. The apartment I'd borrowed to do my dope packing was one I'd later rent.

Each of the four compressed blocks of coke was cling-film wrapped, then sealed in black rubber. A standard form of travel wear for your cocaine brick as it might never know when it had to jump ship. Not always standard was the impressed seal on the surface of the coke, and here as in the East, the marks were of the protectors, not the manufacturers, humble technicians all. Peeling back a flap of the black rubber I felt a ridged shield and noted the winged bird that advertised its Ecuadoran origin.

"You want us to keep it safe for you until you come back?" My supplier had asked, fishing.

"I'll take it with me to the hotel tonight," I said, "if Diego can get me there without getting car-jacked." My vendor shrugged as I cut out about an ounce (or two) as a treat for my travels.

"My girl will be leaving the airport Friday," I lied. A white lie. It wasn't a woman who left, it was a man, and Diego later took me (and the stuff) to a shopping complex from where I jumped into a taxi to a another friend's house where the dope – by then part-packed – would spend the next week. It was always essential to have everything ready to go before flight bookings took hold.

The Colombians were expecting two kilos of heroin as payment for their coke and I'd already given them $5,000 'expenses' money, which in reality would have been close to the cost – to them – of the four kilos of coke. They could afford to trust me. I honoured agreements and made it a point not to do business with anyone who doesn't trust me. Movie dope transactions that take place in empty warehouses among armed men are as unreal as they look. In the real world, if you're invited to a trade at a warehouse (or hotel, or car park), expect to meet police or worse – you've been set up. Besides, four kilos as a sale was small trade to them yet I thought I wanted to meet these big traders. But was there any point?

I'd been offered tonnes of grass and hundreds of kilos of coke on credit. But there was an obvious catch: such people want to be partners. And they make it their business to know the wholesale prices of every country where people come equipped with a nose. Like most partners, they'd want half, at least.

That month's business, as I'd planned it, was worth a million to me at a cost of $100,000, including the threefold bonus of $10,000 to the Colombians (based on their purchase price) once my safe landing was assured with the cargo in Europe. Sure, this Colombian adventure was not as profitable as my usual Thai-Australian runs but otherwise, it would've been a quiet month. I'd found I couldn't sell an ounce more in Melbourne.

The reason for this became clear through a chance meeting at a notorious pub in North Melbourne. A couple of months earlier I'd called in at the Cumberland Arms to meet a friend only to find six of the biggest dealers in Australia. Danny Porcini from Sydney, Joe F from Perth, a dressed-down biker from Queensland, the son of a NSW casino owner and two others who were big movers in the trade. We got to talking shop and discovered that what each of us sold affected the sales of the others. Sounds obvious. Yet we had no customers in common or even customers of customers, as far as we could guess. What astonished us was that while countrywide we might have bumped up against the limit, the entire market – even allowing for a probable third who we didn't know, with customers who knew none of the people who might know *our* customers. The six degrees of separation is about two in the dope world. You mostly get to hear about everyone else. Because of that meeting, I began the informal drug-use survey I spoke of earlier. Even in the '80s, there were limits to expansion.

I'd flown to Miami by a multi-stop route. This was, in part, due to the four ounces of powder in my pocket (my underwear pocket, that is). I'd taken a short domestic flight to Cartagena on the coast, then across the Caribbean Sea to Nassau in the Bahamas. Nassau is one of the dullest towns among many of the pretty-beach island groups yet with the virtue of a seaplane connection to Miami. After checking in your bags at Nassau airport, passengers walk through a doorway in one wall to find a large sign saying, 'WELCOME TO THE UNITED STATES'. Those bags don't go far. In fact, you are in the USA, under a special consular annex deal with the Bahamian government. Rather than overload Miami International, immigration and customs checks are made offshore.

The seaplane with its eight passengers skimmed into Miami Port where I stepped lightly ashore without an official in sight. Although I'd wanted to check this route was still intact for some future mission, those few ounces upon my person were not to be dismissed as a minor risk. A bust was a bust and if I'd been grabbed much would fall with me. I suppose I could have held off indulging until the cargo reached Europe but what would have been the point of those elaborate schemes if I could not think of a formula to equal cake + eating?

Risky arithmetic aside, the introduction of couriers to my little world followed an understanding with Clelia that I should step back from the front line. Even so, I was rarely at ease having couriers – except for Peter Dale, super confident and so super courier – no matter how thoughtfully the cargo might be concealed.

I would routinely remain close to my powder porters at airports as they departed. I'd fret as might a teacher when a troubled student sits an exam.

By 1980, Clelia and I had been together for only three years but we were stuck fast. I suppose the glue held so well because we'd been good friends for a year before. With an unvoiced determination, we'd decided to blend.

As friends, we'd share secrets like school pals and marvel and laugh at the same things – mostly at each other. As well, we shared some similarities despite our separate pasts. Clelia's grandparents had been rich Italian immigrant restaurant owners. When the old business folded – brought down by too many idle aunties and uncles on the payroll – Clel's dad had to start again. Through hard work and a cash loan from a tough trucking company owner he'd turned an unpromising hotel into a fine twin-restaurant, bar and reception complex along Melbourne's beachside. The background match ends halfway as my side of the family didn't prosper after botched divorces. The point is, Clelia had almost as many changes in location and new faces as had I. When we met, the Viganò clan had three hotels and new houses along the bay.

All the restaurants and the private family houses were fixed with hundreds of locks and different keys as you'd expect. One Sunday evening at the start of our union, when every customer had gone and family and friends were abed upstairs, Clelia and I sat on the carpeted stairs between floors. Clel lifted with her finger a shoelace tied around her neck. Looped through was a single key.

"This key," she smiled, coyly, "it's the master key and it opens every lock in the family business and every house, every door."

"That's impressive," I mumbled.

Clelia then pressed something sharp into my hand while still tugging at the string around her neck.

"Here's one for you. In case," she said without explaining before adding, "I *can't* lose it."

We'd had a scare in '78 when I was arrested and jailed for six months when stopped with a few grams of hash at London's Heathrow airport. The day of that arrest led to a long night and only Clelia's wit in pretending she hardly knew me deflected customs investigators from knowing where the main stash lay – within millimetres from their fingertips at one stage. [1]

So, I agreed with Clelia that on any smuggling run, the crucial walk past customs would be done by couriers. I'm sure I took more care of them than ever I did with my own arrangements. Only once has a courier under my control been stopped and arrested. My own arrests have been for trivial amounts for all of which I've been sentenced to the maximum penalty. I'm not complaining, simply noting that the courts take any opportunity when compensating for failed investigations. From another angle, perhaps those couriers were valuable beyond their excess baggage. I'd sweat over their documents and schedules knowing that they were gamblers all; against the house and that in each case the house must never win.

In Miami, I found a hotel – far from my own – with a quiet payphone offside from the lobby to call all the players in that month's show. 1980 was before the common use of mobile phones and the absence of reliable tracking devices was a clear advantage. Because of land-lines, crooks had to think before deciding to make a call. A heavy and visible wire focuses the mind on the kind of talk that follows.

Nestled in the phone nook of the Omni Plaza hotel's conference centre, I took out two phone cards. Both were prepaid international calling cards linked to UK call-routing networks. I would use the first card to connect to its UK network, and once online, dial the second card's access number. I could call them anywhere in the world without giving away my location. It sounds complicated but it is just a method to lose the hidden caller ID that is signalled with any call. The technique still works today

---

[1] I've written of that night in *Escape: The Past* (2011)

providing the cards come from different companies. That day I was phoning hotels in London, Amsterdam and Bangkok.

The first call was to Peter Dale, the fabulist. In his case that means he would mentally live in the fables of his own creation, and as a courier he would radiate that false reality so well the aura of innocence would carry him through a wall of the most suspicious customs inspectors. He was in Bangkok where he was waiting to take four kilos of heroin that I had bought but not yet finished packing. Peter was fine and chirpy even if a little tired from telling whoppers to everyone from bar companions to uncomprehending taxi drivers. His job was to fly to London – indirectly – before going on to Colombia – empty – to then take half the cocaine (two kilos) back to Europe. This would keep him away from Australia for a few weeks where he was mismanaging his chichi plant shops. This was good for me, too, as I was the primary investor at his giant-palm and twitchy Venus fly-trap emporiums. While Peter was away, the shops might inadvertently turn a profit.

Such grumbles were petty of me. Peter was born to be a dark-side courier. While some couriers might gulp nervously on first seeing the false passports I'd given them, Peter would take one look at the details page and hum softly, nodding and smiling. I'm sure at these moments he would be summoning from his symphony of personalities a fresh identity that chimed with the sound of the new name.

I'd seriously considered retiring the other couriers and assigning the run segments to Peter alone, giving him perhaps four identities to slide amongst. After all, he absorbed readily a world that was laid before him. But who would remain as backup if Peter fell? I never worried about Peter's chameleon abilities as a danger if he ever turned to working as an undercover spy. He would be lost without a script in that alien world.

I next phoned George the Greek in London – where the time was 10pm. Not in – according to reception. I checked with my London eye who reported that George was still at the hotel. George's segment was London-to-Sydney where he'd be landing with two of the four kilos flown in by Peter Dale.

A throaty voice sounded on the line after I connected with Sue Noel in Amsterdam. It was 11pm. Secretary Sue had been asleep. Wise. Sue's task would be going to Colombia to take the other half of the four kilos of coke back to Europe. I allowed time for Sue's sleepy murmurings to make sense, and then spoke.

"Guess what, Sue?" I said, unplanned. "You've been promoted."

"I have?" Sue said, still unfocussed.

"You're now an architect."

"That's nice," she said.

Sue had looked the part of a secretary – today's PA – but calmer, less needy. Tall, pleasant face, around thirty. Single, unhappily. Unchivalrously, I knew such characteristics would help prevent her being stopped by either male or female customs officers. Though I felt, more than most in her life I suspected, a real duty to protect her from harm. She'd done a little work for me in the past, posing as an assistant in a law firm whilst applying for birth certificates, collecting new passports. She'd then sniffed out that I was a coastal trader and put herself forward as a courier.

I paid $50,000 (in today's money) for each segment. The task of presenting her as an architect would take an afternoon's schooling and some new clothes. The smart suit would make her more confident, although of doubtful benefit on *the Walk*. That one-minute walk through the line of customs officers. A female architect in 1980. Good for South America, not good for Australia where the resentment of flash sisters had yet to subside. I gave her an edge for Colombia in the device used, the form of concealment of the two kilos: an architect's portable drawing board. The coke was already pressed flat between 0.8mm sheets of plywood. I'd seal the slab within an acrylic plastic. I'd bought a drawing-board from an artist's supplies shop in London and added a new base. Using ever-useful Lego blocks, I extended its thickness by 2cm to form a mould. After mixing white polymer resin and added catalyst, I fitted the sealed coke slab in place before pouring the liquid resin onto the upturned base. After overnight hardening, I removed it from the Lego mould and sanded the small line indentations. The board, complete with its spring-guided L-square ruler, was given a final touch. A thin layer of cork glued to its underside. If the board was tapped with a suspicious finger, the cork would muffle any ring of hollowness – an effect faintly present even with tightly pressed powder. Then a garnish with some working-life scuffs and, of course, sketches of modest houses.

A further element of protection for Sue was in her route. To get to Colombia, Sue would take a KLM flight to Bonaire, an external Netherlands territory and tourist island just north of Venezuela. By noon the following day, she'd board a propjet for the 90-minute flight into Colombia's Cartagena, considered – in Colombia at least – a beach resort. Cali, the chosen destination, is an hour south by jet. The advantages of island-hopping are on two fronts: direct flights to Colombia from Europe are all to the capital, Bogota. I've seen passengers at London's Heathrow in the boarding lounge bound for Bogota stopped at the gate and questioned by plain-clothes customs police. Secondly, Sue could leave Colombia from the same city as her arrival, Cartagena, a town and airport where American agents rarely spend time needling the local law into bothering passengers. A courier, having finished the task she's prepared for, is prone to giving careless answers to officials. I wouldn't want the Americans – then very much the world's police – sending their doubts to European and Australian counterparts.

I didn't explain any of that to Sue during my call from Miami. Only that I'd squeeze in a day to fly over to Amsterdam from London before her journey to Cali. She sounded lonely.

Michael Sullivan was staying with his Marie at my flat in Charles Street, London. I could have had Michael check on George the Greek but it's a rule never to allow couriers to mingle while the work is in train.

Part of Michael's job that month was to meet me in Colombia to make an introduction to people who could supply me with emeralds. His girl Marie was born in Cartagena and schooled in Miami, elements when combined with her good looks made her, for Michael, the embodiment of perfection.

Michael was also being paid for the task of running half of the coke back to Europe. So, the expense of flying him and Marie Business Class around the world via London might seem a high cost for an introduction. Generous of me, yes? No. Michael had worked for me twice before as a courier. In an operation of this complexity, should one of the others fall ill – in any sense – Michael could stand in. Again, I never spoke of this thought. I had phoned him on a second set of calling cards to isolate my London home from the hotels. We chatted briefly.

"What's Marie think of London?" I asked.

"She doesn't think much of the weather."

"No one does. Been to the galleries? The V&A is your sort of cave."

"Not yet." Michael had the tiniest wobble behind his voice.

"Busy with the paperwork, I suppose," I said, knowing somehow Michael hadn't yet taken advantage of his new and phony Australian passport to open bank accounts and get a driver's license.

"I've made enquiries."

Michael was defensive. The flat was big, lush and comfortable and I doubted they'd been farther than the food shops. I told him all was well and I'd see him in a week.

I had just enough credit on the calling cards to try another call to George. He was in.

"I tried you twenty minutes ago," I was keeping it short.

"Yeah, sorry I was in the shower," he lied.

"Well, all's fine. Nine days to go. Thereabouts."

"Listen, Dave – I need an advance on my payment. There's a top deal here in London – you know I know all about precious stones. I've met—"

The card had run out. I didn't call back.

So, everyone was in place. I cabbed to Miami's domestic airport and spent the remaining hour in the first-class lounge reading local papers in detail before my flight to New York City. Never miss a chance to read local papers. City news and the small ads. Forget the opinion pages and editorials. Those and a dollar fifty will get you a cup of coffee. Free in my lounge, of course.

Clelia was out when I got in. We'd taken a suite at *The Pierre* hotel for five days. A note from Clel as I got in told me she was in Central Park. Riding a horse. It shouldn't have surprised me that one can hire a nag in NYC for an afternoon. The hotel's rooms seemed dated in style even for the '70s but its best feature was a tiny desk by Reception at which a friendly woman kept a selection of good tickets to Broadway shows. After a first night playing around the suite we went to a fine revival of *West Side Story*. This five-day mini vacation before business resumed included a casual assessment comparing London with New York City as alternatives to life in Australia. New York was winning. Less stressful and not as coded as London. In either city, I'd conduct no trade nor provoke any mischief with the reasoning that one should not think through crimes large or small in the place of their commission. This is different from that old nonsense about not pooing where you eat. If you ever find yourself noshing pizza on the throne, you're beyond help.

Even so, curiosity dignified by the word 'research' can be entertaining anywhere, and many questions about New York drug business were answered by chance as Clelia and I were wandering back from Broadway to *The Pierre* having underestimated the size of the city's blocks.

A couple of those blocks astray and looking for a cab, we passed McHale's bar on 8th Avenue. A familiar face was visible through the window. It belonged to Francesco Turchurello, a young man of style I'd met in '78 when, independently, we'd found trouble struggling through London's Heathrow Airport. We both said we'd keep in touch but nothing came of it.

Clelia read my expression as I said, "Hey, I know that guy."

"David, it's late."

"I'll just say hello," I said, as I squinted through McHale's glass to see what sort of company Francesco might have. "Anyway, you know the rule, never walk away from a chance meeting," a rule Clelia would not likely have known since I'd just made it up. She moved in front of me.

"So you'll remember that next time we run into one of my friends?"

That said lightly enough as Clelia accepted passage through the door I'd opened.

Francesco was with Bobby C, a fellow (yet second-generation) Milanese but all New Yorker. An hour had passed and Bobby had made a show of strength by keeping his space his own – although it wasn't crowded. We introduced ourselves and sat. I nudged the talk toward the dope trade. Looks were passed between the two Italians. We were okay, apparently. Or Clelia was. We talked through our credentials. Mine were anonymous but enthusiastic solutions for solving technical dope-smuggling problems. Bobby was now prepared to show more than I was prepared to tell. We were soon off, in his car. His driver was respectful, silent.

"You should know from the get go this is not my thing," Bobby stressed. "I get a couple of guys to check things are running okay, make sure things don't get out of hand."

He would, it seemed, often make a statement and then provide a contradiction. Bobby clarified that the mafia and his boroughs were not part of the heroin trade.

"But somebody has to keep a strong hand on it. You know what these people are like."

I should. Clelia stared at the streets with a distant expression, which was her way of avoiding these wordless conversations between lovers that disturb outsiders. She was thinking perhaps we should leave for the hotel now – but as curious as I was.

Parking at an all-night garage in the Lower East Side, we walked through the back entrance of some tenements before meeting another two Italians and a couple of black guys. Francesco was explaining the set-up as Bobby C tried to hold back, failing mostly.

"The heroin," Francesco said, "is packed in ten and twenty-dollar little plastic. Then they use the house to work." His accent had remained strong.

"Must be the same where you come from?" Bobby asked, but didn't wait for an answer. "They don't know me here," he added proudly as the black guys nodded us through, making Bobby's statement meaningless.

As we moved along the corridor that would be the path to dope headquarters for these hours – the fourth location since sundown – the apartment's residents glumly walked out to let trading begin. An old man and a fat girl holding a blanket. They took the stairs going up. Perhaps settling at a neighbour's place.

Inside the apartment, in the kitchen, a pale young man was unpacking wads of what were then called 'dime bags', despite their varied amounts and prices. Bobby's underlings held the front door open while a freestanding, steel, door-sized barrier was clamped in its place. At eye level, a two-inch hole could be opened by a pivoting disc. One of the black guys signalled from the window to the street. The customers started coming.

A tap or scrape on the temporary steel door and the porthole was opened: money in, packets out, and little conversation. Clelia made some excuse about coffee to talk to the bagman in the kitchen.

The transactions went on. All quite efficient and grim. At first.

Through a slit above the porthole, I looked at the customers as Bobby and Francesco, seated at a table, talked nonsense. The customers were a mix of black and mostly white, some scruffy, some neat. They said little to each other until they'd bought their bits. Yet once holding (though not yet fortified) they'd pocket their fixes and strike up a conversation in the corridor. One of Bobby's lesser wranglers, left in the passageway, would try to shoo them on their way. The conversation would then move to the stairs, like an overflowing party.

Moving to the kitchen, I suggested to the bagman that the changing locations every few hours was not to avoid police but to avoid a block party.

"Oh, the police," he said, "they give us two hours at each place." Not interested in the social scene.

Clelia and I then made our excuses and Francesco led us down to the apartment below which was under the eye of more friends. Francesco and I exchanged contact names as he concluded, "the police take money, of course."

After yet another driver dropped us uptown, we wearily returned to our suite and ordered room service, sitting propped up in bed watching late shows.

I snuggled against Clelia and thought aloud.

"I can't picture Bobby clambering down that fire escape," and then, "what's the gear like?"

"Rubbish," said Clelia. "Five percent. Maybe." Clelia had scored a $20 bag from the kitchen man. Clelia toyed with the television remote. "Do you think anyone was watching from outside?"

"I don't think there was anyone who *wasn't* watching."

One last thing about that time in NYC, less to do with chance.

Looking for a good bug detector, I was directed to CCS, what was then (and for years after) a big counter-surveillance store with five branches across the country. The retail outlet had a big showroom, heavy on telephone-monitoring equipment. Many customers were from the Arabian Gulf states which liked to listen to their citizens. The prices of CCS's electronic boxes were wildly inflated. Even so, I bought a wide-band detector worth $100 for $4,000 so I'd be invited into the back room to talk to the boss. The manager said they were all ex-CIA people who'd turned private after post-Watergate changes in the law cut back the tech staff.

Would I care to take some discounted items for trade sale in the UK?

You might think my night with Bobby C and then walking into the obvious Trojan Horse set-up at CCS was inviting trouble. I knew I'd be photographed from a distance on the Lower East Side – and snapped up close in the showroom along with the Arabs. But in those days, we consciously put ourselves out there. It is not easy from the perspective of the Puritan early years of this century to imagine those of us who believed we were on the right side who were convinced we would eventually win. Over-weening arrogance? Maybe. A folly of youth? Certainly, not.

Anyway, surely, I was not an enemy of the United States of America.

Clelia accompanied me to Los Angeles even though I was to continue alone westward across the Pacific to Bangkok while Clelia would fly east to London. One night in LA. Clel wasn't keen on so much flight-time.

"This'll cost you," she'd said, mock-grumpy as we queued along Hollywood Boulevard to see *The Shining*, which had just been released.

"That's okay," I said, regretting the long line ahead. "Name it."

"Concorde. JFK to London."

"Fine. But the seats aren't any bigger than the ones we're about to take," I said, as I realised we were in line for a much later screening. The similarly long queue for the current session was full of people who'd already bought tickets. I had to convince another couple to part with their tickets. The boy jumped at the offer – $200 – against his grouchy girlfriend who surely would make *him* pay.

A day later, I was on board a Philippines Airlines flight changing at Manila for Bangkok. I wanted time undisturbed to think to the days ahead. The airline had the upper deck of a few of its 747s fitted with 6 small bedrooms.

My luggage contained a stereo amplifier, the wood casing of which contained $US120,000; the 100-dollar bills recently given at Kahani & Co off Rodeo Drive in Los Angeles for bundles of Australian 50-dollar notes. In those days, large wads of cash were not the signs of horrible terrorists, merely honoured tax dodgers. In Bangkok, the same stereo would be packed with four kilos of heroin in time for Peter Dale to take it to London. The dope was already paid for and the cash was for preparation of the next run, rewards to the faithful for the last job. Also, money for a stop I'd make in Antwerp, Belgium, to buy diamonds to clean the cash I'd made on earlier runs.

After the jet cruised into clear air, I ate lightly and prepared my bed. I thought of the players in the month's run. Peter was by then the most professional. I resolved to work with him more. Keep him moving and try to persuade him to take on a manager for the plant shops. A manager who'd not – like Peter – simply hire his mates and undertake never-ending glitzy renovations.

Secretary Sue – even as Executive Architect Sue – would have to work in other ways. At the completion of this job her earnings through me would have topped $60,000. Yet I didn't think she'd be content to sit around hotel rooms, as rewarding as it might be. At the end of each run, she declined the next until she somehow (a boyfriend?) ran low on money and requested more work. Something about her sadness – a sadness that would always lift after a few hours' pleasant company – made me think her decisions might not remain rational. After three years of working with people whose thoughts I had to consider carefully, I'd begun to believe people so often simply reacted; decisions were what they later told themselves they'd made.

I'd not again employ George the Greek. So far, he'd yet to carry so much as an aspirin and twice called for help. He was trouble and I was sure he'd cause more.

Michael Sullivan, despite his ambitions to run his own show, (that is, to imitate mine), was family by then. Colombia, I thought, would reveal the complexion and depths of those ambitions. More important than any of that, Michael was by nature honest and loyal. He would never bring harm to our door other than by carelessness. His wife, Marie, was Colombian. Colombia is a land of few rich and many poor, and in such a place the value of loyalty is made plain to the young.

Drawing the shades of my room aboard the jet as it flew toward the sun, I pressed on my Walkman to listen to a tape compiled by a fellow whose job within our little company was to record good music for me. Some Marc Jordan selections, Garfunkel's *Breakaway* and Steely Dan's *Aja*, I remember. As *Black Cow* began, I removed a tiny plastic tube from a special pocket in my underwear. I tapped out a line of heroin to snort. Relaxed then, I imagined I'd enjoy being someone's music finder. I drifted into sleep trying to find flaws in the technicalities of my smuggling devices. Not only the hiding containers but identity, documents, communication trails and the chosen routes. It was my belief then that if the plans were airtight, then the people should take care of themselves.

I'd met my business partner, Lee, by chance when he was living in near poverty behind the old Metro Hotel in Bangkok. I'd not long been smuggling out of Thailand, and soon dumped the pimps and loose-mouthed halfwits I'd dragged out of the red-light district.

Working at night from the bedroom of Lee's new house in Bangkok's outer suburbs, I first removed the wooden casing of the stereo amp before carefully peeling away the lightly-glued veneer. Small blocks held the cash tight, which I removed and set aside. Then, the dope had to be packed. I took the large bags of fluffy white heroin from Lee's travelling bag. (He'd bussed from Chiang Mai in the north two weeks earlier.) The elaborate red stamps of quality on the plastic bags indicated the dope was made and transported from the Burma border under the shield of Khun Sa, still one of the Big Three. It would be foolish to get romantic – or hostile – as to the role of Khun Sa's outcast army in protecting the trade. His was more than a tax and very close to extortion. The real protection of drug movements followed from the feudal nature of life in the Golden Triangle and invisibility under the rugged terrain.

After playing with the closed bags for a few minutes, I scooped out the powder and pressed it deep and tight into the hollowed side panels of the stereo. The sealing was first with silicone gel, then thin rubber foam, more wood and finally veneer strips glued with contact adhesive, smoothed flat with pressure from the edge of a steel ruler. A touch of alcohol to wipe away even the glue line; a brief, fine sanding then finished with stain and a polish buff. Even a close inspection would keep the illusion of a case made from solid wood.

I wasn't finished 'til dawn but didn't begrudge the work. Just such precautions had allowed, a year earlier, one of the stereo amps to survive a bomb alert on a halted KLM flight. It was not so much that I took immodest pride in the long packing task as much as I thought less of those in the trade who would ask, *"Who do you get to do the packing?"* as though unwilling even to spend time in the same room with the material that provides their bread.

After lots of blessings from Lee's wife, a nervous Lee drove me back to town.

"Don't worry, Lee," I said. "A friend is taking this out and he's a good man."

Lee pulled up behind the Nana Plaza where I took the large satchel with the stereo from the back seat of his old Dodge. Lee had a new car but he'd had the 1971 Sedan when I'd first met him, his last thing of value. He would always dust it off at the end of my visits for the final drive as he would see me leave.

"I'll phone as soon as it's back in Europe," I said.

"Never mind the stuff," Lee said. "Call me when you're safe in home."

After I saw Peter Dale safely checked into his Scandinavian Airlines flight to Copenhagen, I boarded Air France to Paris. Peter didn't need nurse-maiding, and if anyone might be subject to surveillance it would be I. He'd merely spent his time at the

Montien Hotel telling fibs to those he met in the bar, despite not being much of a drinker. By contrast, I was the one spending time with drug connections. Yet the chance of being detected was remote. Lee had done well but lived modestly. His dope links were limited to mid-level wholesalers in Chiang Mai. Best of all, Peter was safe; I hadn't needed to give him a story to tell if he were nabbed – and if he was, at least I'd see it at check-in so I could cancel my flight and get to work freeing him.

Peter would transit in Copenhagen, avoiding the long-haul Asian arrivals by taking a smaller jet to Brussels. It would be for those Bangkok arrivals that troublesome customs inspectors would wait. Peter would collect his luggage around 11am in Belgium when the morning shift had finished nosing around. The next sector, Brussels to London, was safe, too, as he'd be joining the lunch-home business commute. Although those added hops were tiring, they were essential. British customs keep on station until noon, particularly aware of transit links.

After landing at Paris, I took a train to Antwerp, arriving after lunch and for a meeting with an old diamond seller. I deposited the remaining US currency with an order for the usual parcel. One-carat, VVS-2 quality, F-colour stones are the easiest to sell and reliably hold their value. I planned to collect the stones in time for my return to Australia. The diamond trade is a closed shop and I would certainly take a small loss if I sold them in Melbourne. But the transactions would serve their purpose: leaving a faint but traceable record of David, the diamond smuggler.

My detour made me late to meet up with Peter in London but I'd given him some business to do. I insisted he lodge his suitcase at the land-side left-luggage depot at Heathrow. That would take him an hour.

One last matter on Peter's journey, and although a standard measure, I'll mention it once just to stress that details make the difference.

I'd arranged for Peter to have two passports, in new names, in addition to his own. And since he'd used his own name three times on jobs over the past two months, the Peter Dale identity was set aside on operations, tucked away in his office in the plant shops. As with agriculture, passports should 'lie fallow' lest customs people become curious about apparently regular journeys.

So, Peter travelled to Asia as Mr X, keeping Mr Y in a panel of his carry-on bag. After landing at Brussels, he would clear customs, then check-in as Mr Y, using the new passport with no immigration stamps – Mr Y not having travelled through iffy countries.

The risk of Peter being thoroughly searched in Europe was low - especially as Mr Y – but I didn't want him carrying Mr X's passport. A two-minute discovery would inevitably lead to disaster. Peter's one job in Belgium was to go to the airport post office and mail Mr X to London. I'd prepared a typewritten envelope for him (already with stamps in case the post office was closed) and a mail drop address in London to receive it.

At Heathrow, I waited in a taxi as Peter collected his suitcase.

Finally, Peter and I were in the taxi, heading to his hotel.

"You'll like it," I said.

"What's the name?" Peter asked.

I tapped off the intercom button of the black cab.

"Peter, it's the one around the corner from the one I told the driver." Often, surveillance watchers take a cab's number rather than tailing if they're acting on a hunch.

I left Peter at The Brompton in South Kensington. Not a grand hotel but one that is discreet by default. Only one person on reception and often a student worker after 6pm.

Before leaving Peter's room, I couldn't resist opening his suitcase to look at the stereo amp. I tapped the casing and patted it as though congratulating the machine itself.

After a night's sleep at the Charles Street flat, Clelia and I had late breakfast with Michael and Marie. I'd already had something of a report from Clel.

"They never go out," she'd told me. "I had to drag them to a restaurant."

"I won't ask who paid," I said.

"Worse than that. Michael let me pay half."

While one must admire a fellow who's successfully spent a lifetime dining out at others' expense, one must condemn a check-dodger who settles for half portions. I supposed Michael-Marie had decided all things were chargeable to the company.

I lightly questioned Michael about the thing I'd asked him to do: if you have a temporary identity, open a bank account and buy a yearly rail ticket or any document with the look of stability and permanence.

"I hear you've been wearing Clelia out bouncing her around town," I said with casual sarcasm.

Michael missed the point for a moment.

After a pause, Michael said, "I went to two banks. No luck. They wanted all sorts of info. Who I work for, if I owned property…" and then he stopped.

The sun from the rear garden swept across the table, lighting the blue-and-white striped crockery. I was reminded of my childhood. I thought of the sixpenny account opened for me on bank visiting-day at school. I looked to Michael.

"Today, I'll drop you off at an Australian bank in the Strand. Australian passport, Australian bank. Say you were working in Paris last year – private secretary to a clothes designer." I gave Marie a look as though saying, 'You can help.' And to Michael, "Go to ANZ bank, here. Your own bank should be some other Aussie bank, you tell them. Open the account with £200 and say you'll wire-transfer a lump next month."

"Won't they ask—?" Michael began.

"No," I said, trying to convince myself all this paperwork would be useful. "Banks work from home office rules. Here, banks make their money from the sizeable overdrafts. Even opening a current account is like asking for a loan."

I had one other question. I was wondering if Michael had stuck to the warning not to use the flat's phone. I made my next question casual.

"Say, did Marie get through to her folks? They must be looking forward to seeing her."

"The line was bad. She only talked for a few minutes." Michael then cottoned on. "It was just a family call. No business by phone, of course."

"What business?" I said, not really asking.

As Michael and I were friends, this lecturing and cross-examination might seem harsh, if not forensic. The assumptions that often ride with friendship can be dangerous in a merciless joust with the law. I'd known people jailed for a decade for mistimed courtesies.

I gave Michael a card for a call shop and then explained I'd be leaving for Sydney the next day but would meet them all in the Dutch Antilles off the Colombian coast. Marie wanted to know why they couldn't fly direct – London to Bogota and then on to her home town on the coast.

"I mean," Michael spoke for her, "I'll only be running a risk flying out from Colombia."

"Michael, you'll be alone leaving Cartagena," I said, repeating gently for Marie, "yes, alone. And I want you to be in a familiar airport, even if the layout for arrival is different from departure."

Michael's job was in two parts. First, to fly two kilos of heroin Peter Dale had just brought on to Amsterdam. There it would go to Architect Sue who'd fly it on to Colombia. The second task was to take two of the four kilos of the Colombian coke back to Europe. There were some things he would later need to know but after dealing with a few Amsterdam matters, I took Clelia's breakfast upstairs. I made a mental note to include Marie in any business conversations with Michael. This would surely save misunderstandings.

The next day at Peter's hotel, I removed the casing from the stereo so I could separate half the stash for George the Greek to run over to Australia. The wood casing, once separated, had the shape of an oversized hollow brick, like a breezeblock. Using needle-nosed pliers, I eased out six wood pins from the inner side. That freed the upper panel, which I then replaced with a solid rectangle that I'd made to fit in my workroom at Charles Street. The rectangular panel I'd removed had – on the inside - a covering of fake wood veneer, which I then peeled away. This revealed a chessboard with neat contrasting squares of light and dark wooden inlays, and discs at each side on which to sit chess pieces. The entire device had been made with the intention of dividing the load.

An hour later, George the Greek admired the chessboard.

"What's inside?" he asked.

"Plutonium," I said.

"I mean, well, what's it worth in Australia?"

We were walking by the weatherworn shops near Paddington station. The gambler in George was tugging at new possibilities, all beyond his reach. He couldn't help himself.

"But the stuff must be worth millions."

"Not to me," I answered before turning the conversation to describe the shop from which came the receipt I'd given him for the chessboard. A board I'd bought and dumped just for the receipt.

"Now, don't carry this in your wallet. If you get into a conversation with customs people about the board, hunt around for it in your suitcase like you can't find it."

"I'll put it in my toilet bag…"

I sighed. When it comes to smuggling, it seemed that even with the most trivial choice, the greedy scammer would always choose the wrong one, since he believes his ideas are best.

Up early the next day, Clelia and I put on Gerry Rafferty's *City to City* to wake Michael and Marie.

"Should I pester Michael about the bank?" Clelia asked. "He said postcodes aren't important in Australia."

"They are here," I said. In the UK, you can forget your name but not your postcode. "No, sweetheart. That's dead. If Michael needs so much pushing when we're here, he'll never manage the paper world on his own."

Clelia was only accompanying me as far as the airport. I tried to talk her out of the dull taxi ride back but she said no, so in hopeful compensation I'd ordered a plush car for the day. There was just time for a stop at a camera-maker's shop in Soho where a small team were modifying a Linhof Aero Technica camera into a monster handheld machine. I had no devious plans for this camera. It was costly (£30,000) but unique, and important because it would allow things that had never been done before.

It might seem an irrelevant detour to talk about the camera but it is worth knowing about because of what happens to things of quality in the next chapter.

You've probably noticed those super-sharp pictures on magazine covers with their lush colour. Even today (well, until yesterday), those pictures are taken with large-format cameras using sheets of film up to ten inches wide. The images are better than most electronic camera available. But such cameras are usually confined to photo studios and are slow to use.

The camera I was putting together used the 4x5-inch format, not using boxed sheets but 33 feet of film, wound into fat rolls. The film would be carried in a motor-driven pack normally used in aerial photography but here mounted behind the large camera and fitted with a battery-powered vacuum pump. The vacuum would suck the film flat, so not even the tiniest ripple in the film might blur the image. The film itself had to be custom-coated by Kodak and rated at only 6 ASA to provide sharpness over 1,000 lines per millimetre. Test images allowed landscapes that could be printed over an entire wall of a gallery providing a vista beyond the range of human eyesight. The lens-makers were quite excited at the challenge. Such a camera had never been constructed before or since. I planned a three-month trek through India. Although the machine was like holding three house bricks, I would try to use it like a photojournalist's camera and capture ways of life fast disappearing in such sharpness as to make memories real. It was one of the few worthy enterprises I undertook with my drug money.

"Kodak will want Ministry of Defence clearance on the film," Tommy the Tech advised as we stood in his workshop. "I told them you weren't planning aerial shots over parliament but they still want your details."

"Don't worry about the film, Tom," I said, as I held a heavy lens with the care as if it were some religious relic. "I'll order it in Australia. They don't worry about Ruskies photographing the desert."

Back in the taxi, Clelia had a suggestion.

"I could wait for you if you're only going to be a few days in Australia." We were airport-bound.

"Three days plus another two before I catch up with you," I said.

"Stop playing with that and look at me!" Clelia was only half-joking. I was marvelling at the 13mm Nikkor lens I'd picked up.

"Look at this, Clel. No curvature at all. And an f/2.8 – not easy to get." I gave her the Nikon. "Sit in the yes-mans' seat and take a photo." In those days London black cabs had two drop-down rear-facing seats,

"You know nothing will be ready, don't you?" Clelia said, trying to get arty lying on the floor pointing the super-wide lens. She meant we'd be delayed by Marie's family fussing around getting a deal on the emeralds. Emeralds supposedly waiting for us. Another money-cleaning purchase.

"A hundred and ten degrees wide," I said, ignoring the problem.

"Shut up and look sad like you'll miss me."
Click.

The Australian segment of the job went fine. I picked up George the Greek from Melbourne even though I'd been lurking about when he arrived in Sydney. He'd been nervy with a chance of showers when he left London.

Now that he was in the clear and had flown south domestic without incident, he was all puffed up.

"David, I'm willing to do another job for you," he said with pride. "But I'll have to ask for twice the money. I know this stuff is worth it."

"The waiting in hotel rooms didn't put you off?"

"I mean the risk. I could go to jail."

"I could go to jail selling it," I said. "I'll let you know if I need you."

George was next to me in Clelia's sports car yet I caught the look in his eyes. He was thinking of me not being around. He cleared his throat.

"Dave, I'm worth more. Not everyone is honest like me. Some people, they could just fly off with it."

I smiled a shrug.

George sat silently chewing himself up as we took the freeway into the city. No doubt he felt he should have taken the chance he'd been twisting over every minute since he stopped shitting his pants at Sydney airport: to keep the stash and run. All that confirmed my suspicions of the hold George's owners – the gangsters – had on him. Since George was plainly a hopeless gambler, they'd probably bought (with talk) his debt from one of the small clubs he'd use to lose money. That's why they'd insisted I not pay George his fee but that they'd settle with him. I bet they would, in their own way.

I pulled up near a taxi stand in town. I'd already separated the stereo from George's smelly luggage. I gave him a $50 note for his cab fare.

"So, when do I get paid?" asked George trying to sound manly.

"George, I don't like a lot of talk so I'll keep it brief. We all agreed you and the people you owe money to – for a fee of 25,000. That's over the odds but let's call the 5,000 they'll get a spotter's fee. You know, like the spotter's fee tow-truck people pay someone who phones in an accident.

"Now, our muscle-headed acquaintances no doubt took on some gambling debt of yours. One of them – don't interrupt please – with a promise they'll never keep, to pay off your debts with the casino. They asked me not to pay you a cent. To pay them. But I won't."

George looked confused, so I continued.

"At your feet is a shopping bag. In it, $15,000. The remaining ten I'll give to your friends. They won't be happy that I've not allowed them to leave you with nothing but I don't much care."

"They're big guys," George seemed to have lost his bluster.

"If they had the stomach for gunplay they'd be out robbing banks, not cheating the weak. If this casino debt thing is all in my imagination, you'll get the rest of your money from them. I'll be in touch in a month to see how it went."

I unlocked the car doors. George was now as I'd met him.

"Is that when the next job is on?"

"I don't plan so far ahead," I said starting the engine and thinking George must owe all his fee. He'd had a good day.

Two islands north-east of Colombia form part of the Netherlands Antilles, sixty kilometres apart: Curaçao and Bonaire. Postcard-perfect, peaceful and an exact vantage point of safety for anyone contemplating the playing fields of Colombia. Both with good air connections to coastal Barranquilla and Cartagena cities, while the return journeys are met as casual and official-lite.

By travelling east from Australia to Mexico City I could investigate – alone and with concentration – potential exits from the world's cocaine capitals.

If, today, people imagine Colombia as some coke-fuelled Wild West in the 1980s, then at worst, the country held a controlled civil war. The big boys of Medellin and Cali (less a cartel, more like a mistrustful gamblers' club) thought of their turf with the same limited vision of their beginnings: mostly street traders; one boss cut his teeth and competitors' throats selling black-market cigarettes before rising to hero-outlaw status by showering silver upon the poor while giving the police the choice of gold or lead, to translate a local expression. Cigarettes or cocaine, it was still only boxes of stuff, even when bundled from jungle labs in the same busted trucks that had hauled stolen goods and wrinkled ciggies.

Beyond the cities lived people just as ruthless. In Colombia, a self-styled Marxist guerrilla army called FARC. Over the border in Peru a mad rebel group called 'The Shining Path'. The coke cooked and blocked within both groups was cheap at source: a little over $US1,000 per kilo. The city men shopped for their blocks of dope in the countryside but city and country distrusted each other, the city seeing the uniformed guerrillas as foolish outcasts, the country people saw the city boys as lazy and corrupt. Both made money and both saw the United States as a surreal cash machine that simply gave away money for their local magic.

As I sat by the window in my modest hotel room at Willemstad, I stared at an unfolded world map and asked what I wanted here and beyond. Even allowing the comparatively radical world view of the 1970s, the toughness of the Colombians was something to behold.

A US funded anti-narcotics force had been set up in downtown Bogota. Full of men with a mission, its people cruising around town in masks and SWAT-team rigging. Not long after the unit was operational, a truck bomb levelled the building, killing hundreds. Even more impressive, in 1985, was a peculiar understanding with *Movimiento 19 de Abril* (M-19). After an agreement was made allowing the extradition of cocaine bosses to the United States, a legal challenge reached the Supreme Court of Colombia. When lawyers and money failed, M-19 arrived to make a final submission. They took over the entire Supreme Court building resulting in the death of half the high-court judges, throwing some from the eleventh floor. Did I want to buy into that world? As I left Curaçao, I decided to let risk-benefit economics decide my options.

Cartagena. More hotels. Michael and Marie were staying at a huge, busy, tourist hotel by the beach rather than with Marie's family.

I'd suggested, "Just check-in for a couple of days. You'll be able to shake off jetlag before the family onslaught." Marie had a large family.

In truth, although the coke would be packed by the time it was in Michael's hands, I didn't want it in the Marie family home where, regardless, it would be discussed. As it was, the hotel was paid for a week: Michael and Marie didn't move.

With Clelia, I made a quick trip to Cali to greet Sue who'd arrived with the two kilos of heroin for the Colombians. I lost half the day finding the right hotels: three-star, off-the-main-drag inns with few English speakers. I'd left the dope in the chessboard. Smuggling in chessboards must be a hundred-year-old tradition by now, and even then, not good enough to run coke *out* of South America. I'd use a different method.

When I gave the chessboard to the Cali people, mid-level dealers, they opened it in front of me. We were in a high-rise apartment overlooking the city. At first, I thought they didn't trust me. But it wasn't that.

The smarter of the two young men peeled away some of the veneer, removed the wooden blocks and knifed out a small pile onto a plastic bag. He approached the little white hill cautiously, breathed in a proto-sniff and then, well, sort of played with it using the letter opener. He'd never seen it before and couldn't wait another minute to see this China White everyone had spoken of.

"It's good," he said, for want of something to say.

I smiled to myself. This stuff wasn't going into business. The 1980s Colombian entry into white heroin was just an experiment. At the time, nearby Mexican heroin was low-grade, acidic tar. Not for them. I guess the Colombians had standards – or white expectations, anyway.

The dope I'd brought, I was sure, would be passed around, divided, used as a talking point and finally be absorbed by friends of friends. Then celebrated or rejected, when, as first-time users often say, *"Never again!"* and mean it. Maybe I was getting a better deal with the swap than I thought. I was pleased, too, as always when I know where it's going. I never like to let it go to strangers.

I took an extra day stashing the coke into the devices that would be used by Peter and Michael to carry the cocaine to Europe.

You won't need a degree in chemistry to understand a couple of things about cocaine important to a smuggler. First, it dissolves completely in alcohol, and secondly, when that alcohol is evaporated, it recrystallizes with virtually no loss. Cocaine has been smuggled in rum bottles, half-dissolved to a cream to look like shampoo, and sometimes variations of the method I used here. Working from a small holiday flat, I dissolved the cocaine in ten litres of pure alcohol (at least 98%) and stirred in five cups of almost microscopic black nitrocellulose fibres. You know you've put enough in when light is slightly blocked through the glass container. I then heated the mix on an electric stove until it evaporated as a thick paste. By the way, no smoking near the stove! Two Samsonite hard-shelled suitcases would be enough to take the load, using the lid and base of each. I removed the lining of each case, trowelled in the paste, smoothing it up the curves of the corners. A firm patting down the lining and sealing the rims with silicone and let it dry. My sample piece had dried overnight, now appearing as a solid, grey plastic.

I packed the cases with towels to allow more drying, and paid a last call on Secretary Sue. Then, with nothing more to do, she flew across to Bogota enroute to her home in Melbourne, Australia.

"So, what did you think of Cartagena airport?" I asked Michael.

"Seems okay," Michael answered, without adding detail. He was still sulking about travelling inward from Europe in Business Class while the girls had First Class seating. I'd wanted them separated with the hope Michael would take in more of the airport and its procedures.

We were on the balcony of his hotel suite. I was using the light to examine $50,000 worth of emeralds one of Marie's sisters had purchased for me.

Michael thought this a good moment to return to his pitch to take on a dope run of his own.

As I've said, Michael had been quite a player in the marijuana trade in Australia in the 1970s. With a lucky connection to the Italian growers along the Murray River, he'd rapidly found himself with property, boats, big cars and a fine pair of snakeskin boots whose heels took him to six foot four. He'd also taken on partners he couldn't trust. Like me, for our counter-culture pretentions, he'd thrown bits of money at drug-law reform outfits and '70s art, including that movie, *Pure Shit* (the name referring to the quality of heroin) featuring the lives of a handful of happy urban junkies.

Michael's partners had turned on him in 1970, and by the time we'd met he was ready to resume the life narcotic. He had to, he'd been cleaned out by his friends. Michael made friends easily but lost them in quick time. He didn't care. He had Marie.

"They're good stones, no?" Michael asked, as I folded the emeralds into a cotton-wool pouch.

"Good enough," I said, turning the magnifier in the sun. "But I'll only know for sure when I sell them. Some cracks and inclusions, though small." I was learning that emeralds have more flaws than diamonds.

Michael nodded. "I think we can make some money here." He didn't mean with gemstones. He meant from Marie's connections, one of whom we'd met the night before as we tried to chew our way through local meat innards. Our soft European tastes had not hardened for bulls' foreskins and other South American specialities. The men we'd met through Marie's line had offered cocaine in bulk, delivered anywhere along the Central American coast but no farther. And hundreds of tonnes of local marijuana shipped within 120 miles of any coast, worldwide. Michael thought this worth grabbing.

"We could sell the puff easily enough," he said, stretching his arms over the balcony.

The guy we'd met was Alphonse and spoke good English, having had a Miami high-school education. I had a thought.

"How far do you think Alphonse is removed from the people who count?" I thought him no more than a man who knew a man who has a friend. "He'll want to be a partner and the real people will want to be partners, too. His English was business-like, at least."

"Yeah," Michael said brightly. "You'd think I'd have learned some Spanish by now."

Michael had missed my point. The people who counted here had no reason to live beyond Colombia, or Spain, maybe. No reason to bother with English. And Alphonse would want to keep himself (and his share) in between us, even though the biggies would want to meet us, *Los Gringos*.

The problem is part of a general one when dealing in black markets. I've met people in Pakistan who I've paid to buy dope for me. 'If the kilo costs $2,000, I'll pay you $4,000. $2,000 before you go shopping, the same again before I leave, so you don't even have to use your own money while being paid twice the rate.'

You'd think locals would be happy with this deal but they rarely are. They'd say, 'I hear you get $50,000 in your country for one kilo. Let you and me be partners,' - with an expectation of half the profit. 'Sure,' I'd say. 'Your half of the stuff will be waiting for you in London – *you sell it!*' So, instead of that set-up, I'd pay a further 2,000 if the deal works out over time. The wedge doesn't end there. After a couple of loads, one supplier said, 'I'll give your couriers an extra kilo, can you sell it for me?'

Rejecting such hopes must be done thoughtfully. There are times, when smugglers are foolish enough to let source-country suppliers know when a courier is leaving, they find a courier arrested at the airport. Often, the supplier is working with customs people and the confiscated dope kept and split between them. There are even double-cheats in such arrangements where the crooked customs people claim the dope had to be written up as a bust because the big chief was on duty.

Another scam might be where the local tells the smuggler, 'I can fix everything at the airport so your man will be safe.' There's a fee, of course. The size of the fee will give you an idea of your supplier's ambitions. Often, you'll hear that dope with a value of, say, $2,000 will have a 'clearance fee' of $10,000 per kilo. In response, I asked, 'How would the customs people know how many kilos are packed?' The following pause told me the truth: there would be no fix, just a premium going to the supplier. If a smuggler were to be gullible enough to fall for the scam, he'd be later told, (a) go at a particular time, or (b) their official will be watching, both vague enough to make easy excuses in the event of failure. It's the rainmaking con. If the courier boards (or clears) okay, the supplier takes credit. If the courier falls, it will be due to some behaviour by the traveller or the unexpected arrival of some special anti-narcotics outfit. In fact, the range of excuses is limited only by the versatility of the spoken word.

I've never been inclined to pay off policemen, prison guards or customs officers whose job usually involves a lot of standing around watching, doing nothing. He who pays a man to do nothing in a job that requires mindful inactivity often invites a burst of mindless frenzy. Soon enough, the officials' uncharacteristic efficiency being on-point arouses suspicion, and when they collapse, they fall talking.

It was just these formulae I was trying to avoid. If I hooked up with the big Colombian outfits, sure, they could provide hundreds of kilos and maybe even deliver to some Spanish port but there would be this catch: the Colombians know to the penny the wholesale and retail price of drugs in destination countries. Out of a kilo of coke landed in Europe they'd want - today - £30,000 and their middleman £7,000 more. In effect, I'd end up working for them. I didn't think Michael saw this – or understood the business – and what he said next proved it.

"David, after this job I'll be ready to do my own run from Thailand."

"That's great, Michael," I said. "By my count, I would have paid you a hundred thousand or more. So, what you have got in mind?"

"Pretty much the same way I did it for you," he said. "Only I'll be putting in all the money. You think I'd be safe with two kilos?"

Michael had been hinting at this for some time and it was a conversation I wanted to have with Marie present.

"Let's save it for Curaçao," I said. "We're in the middle of a job."

"What about the big load of puff?" Michael asked of the shiploads of marijuana. "Or should I ask Marie to tell them we're not interested?"

"Never say that, Michael. Let's meet the highest man we can. Tell them we are still building up the bank but will be back. We want to get out of here without accidents, no?"

Of course, I kept Peter Dale's presence in Colombia a secret from everyone other than Clelia. It was good to have someone in my life in whom I could confide. And whatever you may hear, women are better than men at keeping secrets. I suppose the cold truth might be that considering what men do to women, they should learn to keep secrets.

It would be prideful of me to list all the chores necessary to ensure the safe exits of Michael, the girls and Peter Dale from Colombia. Peter Dale was the least trouble, even though he was leaving from nearby Barranquilla, a rougher town than Cartagena.

All of us had one night in Curaçao before the long-withheld announcement of our next destination, an island among the Caribbean's Windward Islands.

"Where?" asked Marie.

"Saint Martin," I said.

"French?" suggested Michael.

"Yes and no," I said.

"I suppose we should know where we are going," Marie said, looking at Clelia unhappily.

Michael added, "That's true."

By contrast, at his hotel, Peter Dale had said, "Okay, when do I leave?" Peter then read the ticket saying, "Five hours. Anything I should know?"

Saint Martin is a most civilized island, then of some 20,000 people and called Sint Maarten by the Dutch, who own half. Each half is treated as an external territory of France and The Netherlands respectively. There are no customs officers, as such, on arrival or departure yet the island has links to France and the US and none directly to troublesome Britain. All good, no bad.

I'd rented a villa for three days on the Dutch side of the island. Wide doors at the rear opened to white sands, and the beach was rarely crowded since the airport was close by with planes landing and taking off every twenty minutes until nightfall.

"Couldn't you find one not so close?" Clelia asked, even though we'd grown accustomed to the sound within hours.

"Just want to get Michael to zone out to the sounds at the airports," I said. I also wanted him to take another two kilos of heroin from London to Australia. This was two kilos I'd had in reserve in the UK in case something had happened to Peter leaving Thailand. Without the certainty of that dope mid-point in London all the arrangements for the month would collapse, along with extra funding to lift Peter out of trouble. I'd seen too many elaborate deals collapse due to everything riding on a single wheel.

Clelia understood. "You'd better get Michael used to the French since he'll be landing at Paris. How about we eat in France tonight?"

A few minutes later we were in a taxi for a ten-minute ride to the French side of the island.

"Marie," I began, while playing with the table candle, "Michael tells me he wants to go out on his own. Let's all hear about it."

I add this to the list of things a smuggler must know as, at some point, usually too early, those coasting atop the surf of your complex arrangements will come up with plans of their own. If, indeed, plans of their *own*.

Michael hesitated as people do when telling you something they fear you already know.

"Well, the same sort of thing as I did for you. Thailand. Get it back to Australia."

"I'm always here for advice," I said, looking at Clelia as though to say, *'I'm being reasonable, am I not?'* And then, to the heart of it, "How do you plan getting it back?"

"In one of those stereos, I suppose," Michael said with doubt, adding, "Peter Howard could knock one up for me."

I frowned. "You really want Peter H knowing you're planning a run?"

I didn't like Peter Howard. He was the kind of phoney mock hippie who would steal your teeth while you were chewing your food. He had no men friends. That was just the sign my mother had warned me about as a rule against sleaziness.

"Unless I could use one of your stereos you're finished with?"

Michael almost made it sound like he'd just thought this up.

Clel jumped in. "I think David's finished with them when they fall apart."

"It's a small matter, Michael," I smoothed. "Would I be wrong in thinking you'd want to do your buying from Lee?"

"David's friend, Lee?" Clelia pointedly asked. I tapped her foot with mine under the table. There's more to come.

"That's fine with me, probably with him," I said. "When are you planning to go?"

Marie couldn't hold on even though she was playing the subdued Latin wife.

"David, don't you want Michael to be free to get his own things?"

Michael calmed her down. "That's okay, Marie. So, ah, David. Well, next time you're going over anyway. I could do my thing then."

"Passport?" I asked.

Michael looked upward as though he'd never thought about it. He'd be wanting to use one of the work passports I'd given him.

"One thing, I suppose, Michael," I put on a look of slow uptake. "Two kilos. You've got customers – well, one – for about two ounces a week. Two kilos. Who'd put that out for you? Not Peter Howard, is it?" I said as though that was incomprehensible. Peter would certainly take it from Michael. He'd never pay and give some feeble story.

"Maybe you could take it yourself," Michael moved from light-bulb moment to beaming saint. "I'd give it to you, you know, at a good price."

I let a silence stand. Only the sound of other diners, some boats sloshing at anchor in Marigot Bay. If that was Michael's clincher, it wasn't well thought out. I guess he thought I'd prefer to take on his dope rather than allow Peter H to know more of our business. It stank. Clelia was preparing for a fit.

"Michael. Marie. Let me lay this out," I said. "You want to use my method, my devices, my contacts and have me travel with you to make sure everything goes well and then I'm to be honoured with selling your heroin paying twenty times the price I could get it myself? Have I missed anything?"

"Passport," Clelia muttered.

"That's true. If you come unstuck using one of my passports it will burn the entire series." I meant all those gained by the same phoney lawyers. My face would appear on many of them.

I began to see why Michael's friends turned on him in the weed trade.

And yet, I liked Michael. I didn't like the implied threat of him risking himself – and indirectly me – in doing business with Peter Howard but I knew Michael would do anything I asked. Complete loyalty must be rewarded by the same; the same, yet never sacrificial. The fact Michael would pay for his little expedition meant nothing.

"Funny thing about the economics of the trade in Colombia," I said to Michael. "They don't care about the price of the dope. They know it might be the heart of the business but it's the long-range customers they want."

True enough, the business is weighted on the man who has the customers. Anyone who has plans on becoming a smuggler need not first concern himself with devices and routes. If he has customers he's almost there except for things he can learn while travelling. You can scrape a fair supplier from the floor of any third-world bar; a customer who's reliable is a rare thing.

"Okay, Michael," I concluded. "We'll make some kind of deal. You can buy from Lee providing you pay him what I pay him. For the rest, make me an offer on services. Ideas are free." I didn't want to go further until the month's tasks were done. There's nothing quite so sure as planning the future for cursing the present.

Later in bed, Clelia passed on a message from Marie. An apology of sorts. Clel railed a little.

"Michael should be grateful. Has he forgotten about the days people used to come visiting with guns?"

"Relax, sweetheart. Michael was being pushed. You know that. And one thing is certain. No matter what happens, Michael will never talk."

"How can you be so sure?"

"He's a snob. He thinks he's better than the cops. They'll hate him for it but he'll never lower himself – as he sees it – to talk to them."

Clelia flopped on me and punched off the television with the remote.

"So how come you're worried?"

"I'll have to keep track of Michael's friends. He'll never see them coming."

Clelia leant on an elbow. "And how about you, David, will you see them coming?"

That sounded like something important. If only I knew who *they* were.

There's a trick to getting safely through Paris having come from the Caribbean. The long-haul flights arrive at Charles de Gaulle airport and the cops loiter around the luggage carousel. Any advantage for the smuggler comes from knowing airport configurations. Sure, your suitcases are checked through as transit bags to a final European destination but you can be pounced upon if you walk from Terminal F to the short-haul departure gates. First, take the stairs to Terminal G and wait 30 minutes. Then, move. Always put a three-hour wait in transit before the last sector. That allows you to go to the Business Class lounge near the shopping arcades. Whatever is going on within Europe is not of much interest to French customs. The same applies to passengers taking connections long-haul to, say, China or the US. The Americans do their own sniffing about but that's on the land-side, mostly.

As I'd bought the girls' tickets separately, I let Michael and Marie sit together (arranged only at check-in as though they'd just met) while Clelia and I went First.

"It means I'll be off before you," I said to Michael. "If there's something bad ahead I'll cause a distraction." That got a laugh.

It was at my boot maker's when I decided that London would make a better base than New York. (Coincidentally, the boots I picked up that day lasted another 13 years until falling apart on the streets of Bangkok.) And certainly, it was not as though a good life couldn't be had in the Big Apple, but Europe is essential along the smuggler's route and only an hour from base. A rail link to Paris was planned (it would not open until 2003) and there was talk of open borders within Europe. Living in London would mean I shouldn't do any domestic trade in the UK but prices were low then, less than a tenth of Australian returns. As well, in those days, UK passports were issued without much fuss.

I had a cool weekend with Clelia in Stockholm, meeting Peter Dale who'd arrived with half the coke from Saint Martin. I gave my Swedish connection two months to play with it. He could take the balance from London if he did well. Peter switched to his second – clean – passport for the return trip from London to Australia. Just because he was landing in Sydney without cargo, that was no reason to allow curiosity from Australian customs. People most often become a *person of interest* on one trip only to be targeted on the next. I didn't want him to become a face familiar to those roaming CCTV cameras at Sydney.

Clelia and I detoured to Belgium after a return to London. There, at Antwerp, I met an old contact, a South-African-Iranian carpet dealer. We met near the staggeringly rich but wonderfully subdued diamond exchange. Since the 1978 revolution in Iran, a squeeze had held on the export of large silk Qum carpets so he was happy to trade in diamonds.

On my side, the '80s were years when governments were enacting laws to confiscate drug money. The new powers unearthed tax dodgers, and few drug lords. Perhaps that was the intent, especially directed at American citizens since they must pay tax on income no matter where they live. I needed to craft an explanation for my own odd travels. If the day came when I found myself accounting for all the destinations and false passports, then diamond smuggling might seem credible if I could claim I bought cheaper than the real price. No one makes money from diamonds who is not part of the circle. That month I'd bought $180,000 in diamonds, and it would cost nearly $16,000 for the pleasure of playing with them for a couple of months. Well, maybe more. Clelia liked to play, too.

With the detail I've given in these last pages for the month's work, it might seem very complex. It is less so on the ground: Peter Dale leaves Bangkok for London with four kilos of heroin. Then, George the Greek takes two, back travelling to Australia while Secretary Sue takes the other two to Colombia where I swap them for twice their weight in cocaine. That load is split in two: Peter and Michael separately take two kilos of coke each to Europe where

Michael does double duty running the reserve two kilos of heroin to Australia as it is no longer needed as a fall-back supply. What was it worth? Difficult to say as no transaction ever stood still and money mumbles when it talks. Less than a million, anyway.

Clelia and I were so tired arriving at Melbourne I took no precautions for our landing. Our passports showed two trips to Bangkok so we were directed to a customs counter for inspection.

Australian customs inspectors at airports have an effective routine. Given that there's not time to probe into every item a passenger has in his luggage, they use an observational trick. Working in pairs, one officer opens each suitcase. He then drops the suitcase lid to his left hand to judge the weight. You get quite good after much practice, and even a kilo drops distinctively. Next, he or she will pick up each item – hairdryer, Teddy Bear; it doesn't matter – and give it a cursory glance. It's quick, and he hasn't got x-ray eyes so it's up to the second officer to call the hit. Let's say the swag is hidden inside Teddy, and so the bear is picked up and set aside (they place checked items on the lid side), which, for the passenger, would signal, 'Yes, no problem with Teddy' while officer #2 is watching the passenger closely. Well, it takes a very well-controlled smuggler not to give the game away by suddenly relaxing, or lifting his style of speech, suddenly blabbing tourist stories. I've seen just that happen with the observing officer gently touching the searcher who then returns to Teddy. Anyone capable of holding his nerve under such close observation is quite slick and deserves a seat at a high-stakes poker match.

So, it was with expectation of a long delay that Clelia and I found ourselves at a customs counter with our bags open in front of two officers. Yet they didn't begin their routine. The lead man, looking at my passport, spoke simply.

"Why did you go back to Bangkok?"

Visibly exhausted, I replied, "Because we like the place."

"Fair enough," said the border-protection officer in perfect Australian. "That'll do. Welcome home," and then closed our bags.

Of course, it helped that we had nothing to declare.

Although I took care to keep vigilant for anyone who might thwart or interfere with my travels that month, my cares were mostly for the frailties of the couriers and the state of the airports through which we moved. If a plainclothes policeman or customs officer looked on with interest, I kept mental notes. Yet I failed to read the consequences of the minor field notes that officials pass on. Trivial mentions occurred: I was seen by an observer in Cali in a car; my meeting in NYC with Francesco was photographed by an undercover cop on a separate mission; another mention in Cartagena, and a peevish report by a French detective. Each mention fell into a paper dump, with no action taken. Yet most found their way to the US Drug Enforcement Agency's mountain of foreign field reports where they would have rotted with time. Yet, by chance – and such mischances increase with the size of the agency concerned – these mentions came to the fixed stare of Bill Shenkmann, who saw the poor-quality surveillance pictures and remembered the look of a young fellow at the edges of the failed Lear-jet operation out of Thailand in the '70s.

Perhaps Bill was bored or just as likely, simply didn't like the look of me. Whatever the reason, he kept me in mind. And if there's any mind you don't want to be in, it is that of an agency man.

3

The story I'm telling is not especially a history of smuggling runs, although there is much smuggling. It's a story of pursuit by agencies we blindly termed, the Forces of Darkness. By world standards I was a minor player in the greater game. Compared with the tonnes shipped daily through the worlds ports, the kilos I moved around could never justify the money spent on pursuing me. I was an independent in that greater game. A game certainly for the police and special agencies. And a chase that remains a game only for smugglers who remain under the radar, or those big enough so an actual arrest becomes unlikely when players include governments themselves. From the police standpoint, independents are the ideal targets. They can be crushed without any fear of backlash.

It is difficult to imagine, say, murder being legalized, even though the penalty is the same in many jurisdictions. Stealing made lawful? No. Arson, sex crimes – none of these offences against people will ever be legal. Yet, eventually, all criminal sanctions over drugs will be dropped. As I write, marijuana is produced commercially in four American states, with five more to follow. So, it is not an aversion to the stuff that drives police. It is the chase. If peanuts were freakishly outlawed, police agencies would not hesitate to hunt down nut-fiends.[2]

---

[2] During World War II, Britain formed GHQ Auxiliary Units, teams whose task was to act as resistance fighters should Germany invade England and form a military government-of-occupation. Drawn from local men, prime minister Churchill instructed the teams to first kill the village police chief as a priority. Churchill believed police would not only cooperate with

From the other side, I have fallen into the trap of the game. Smuggling drugs rapidly becomes as much about defeating the opposition as it is black-market money. Sure, I put money into legalizing drugs but I put more into becoming my own force of darkness.

Such philosophical thoughts were not in mind after returning to Australia. Thoughts were few, too, concerning the selling of the dope or fussing over accounts, providing I was paid.

Drug selling is the dullest trade-work, although I was fortunate. Early on, I'd made good connections with former safe-crackers who'd kept themselves a cash income with narcotics. At a higher level this doesn't demand much time while the risks keep you sharp. More importantly for me, these were old-school guys who'd proved their worth by sticking to their few words and could take a police interrogation.

Until the next operation, I had a couple of weeks to enjoy the summer and play with my toys. I kept a few houses and apartments around Melbourne and in one I'd soundproofed to prevent eavesdropping while I worked on stash containers for smuggling. The large room had quickly become a listening and thinking room with recordings using the now forgotten CD-4 quadraphonic audio system. Huge speakers thundered the bee swarm from *Tubular Bells* as I'd sit in the middle of the room daydreaming.

Every so often in most lives a little reality seeps in. After three years in contraband, it seemed to me I'd become nothing more than a businessman without scruples. Gone were the days where I'd openly take a stand on anything. Beyond conservative dress sense and skill ordering from foreign menus I'd few rules of

---

the invaders but were in the best position to supply the names of likely rebels and sympathisers. A deeply cynical view of lawmen, yet historically reliable. Under occupation, Danish police rounded up Jews, as did police in other European countries. Those in resistance units regarded themselves as patriots; to the police, they were simply lawbreakers.

behaviour. *The Australian Weed*[3] had folded and my views were too extreme for NORML. The National Organization for Marijuana Legalization was a one-drug cause whereas my belief was for every drug to be sold by pharmacies without restriction, merely consent. A NORML-party mantra proclaimed, *'No law changes without it first being broken'*, and while I was pleased enough to do the law-breaking, I felt the issue trivial. I foolishly hoped for tougher nuts to crack. If someone had told me then that thirty-five years later the laws would tighten in many countries, I could only have imagined some mad religion, a new puritanism, had taken control. I suppose the reluctance to allow change is just one of those political stalemates. With three-percent voting swings deciding victory between barely different parties, no sensible politician would buy into the no-win issue of drug law. More immediately, I had to keep an eye on my own rules.

Driving toward the city, I had to be gentle on the accelerator. I employed a mechanic for our little company and he'd not long replaced the engine of the Ford Cortina XLE with a 327 ci Chevrolet. Twin mufflers made the engine's growl almost silent with extra air pumped into the carburettor through concealed vents. There were few outward signs of the transformation but even a light touch with a foot would tear up the road. A heavy water tank in the rear kept the wheels gripping and its contents could be dumped in five seconds. Tests had found water as good as oil for losing any chasing cars.

I called in at the flat where I kept my dope. I'd rented it myself while disguised and using documents unconnected with anyone in my world. This is not easy to do, especially if one needs to give references. Yet, because the flat would hold quite a few kilos, it was worth the extra effort creating the identity from nothing. Borrowed or stolen documents would not do.

---

[3] A pro-legalization monthly newspaper I had a hand in distributing. Banned afresh with every issue, it had to change its name to *Australasian Seed*, then *Australasian Greed* and finally, *Australasian Need*.

Posing as a grad-student I followed up shared accommodation ads until I found the right set up: a single man with a girlfriend who did not live in. I'd become the ideal flat-share tenant, paying full rates while staying (in fact, visiting) only four out of seven nights, explaining I lived with country parents for the other three. The trick was to move him out and take over the lease. I'd been using the address as nothing more than a mail drop and packaging bolthole for five months before encouraging my novice landlord to move out.

"This'll be great," he said. "My girl wants to move from uni halls – she can move right in, if I can find a place." I found him a place.

We'd shared a lottery ticket one long weekend when he was going away with his girl. And guess what? We won. His share of the $15,000 prize capped the money he needed for the deposit on a house he (and she) had been sniffing at. I'd bought the ticket from a gambling club for $17,000 – in some circles, the true owners of mid-level lottery wins never cash their tickets. Not when there were people like me who'd pay an extra ten percent to clean up a little cash. You might think people – such as my flatmate – would become suspicious at so much good fortune walking into his life. They don't. Most of us stumble through life without ever getting a break. When one arrives, only the most extreme pessimist thinks it's anything other than that long overdue shred of good luck.

For me, the combined hours on this identity amounted to less than a week, and provided a completely untracked, credible and proven character. His doctor became mine; his accountant gave me investment advice; I think his girlfriend had a date lined up with her BFF if my mysterious girl went her own way. And, should the need arise some dark day, I had a credible and ready-to-wear life into which I could step within minutes. Yes, creepy, too.

Now, the place was empty and as I approached the apartment block I turned on my car radio. It had been tweaked to tune into 87mhz so I could listen through the bug I'd installed in the flat. The advantage of bugging oneself is to avoid any unpleasant surprises upon entering. Everything was quiet.[4]

Inside, I made tea, rotated the refrigerator contents, ran the dishwasher and checked the tape counter. I'd concealed a small voice-activated Dictaphone within a door panel. The counter had moved. I listened to the recording. Only a phone ringing. After a bit of unpacking and packing, I left, taking my disposable gloves with me. Using gloves for such brief visits spared a full clean.

I drove to the centre of Melbourne where I kept a high-rise apartment. Useful if Clelia and I had spent a late night taking in a show. The one-bedroom apartment was attached to a major hotel and office-space high-rise. This provided room service as well as five alternate ways out once in the main corridor.

That afternoon, there was a note on the back of a business card belonging to the estate agency that kept offices along the hallway. "Call me," didn't say much but I remembered Vincent Price wanted to use the flat during a two-week run and I saw no reason why he should not. I kept $20,000 in $10 postage stamps in the place but nothing that needed explaining. Stamps are portable (here, only twenty sheets) and rise with a value that exceeds most basic savings accounts.

Outside the living room was a rooftop garden – part of the lease – complete with furniture. One item I'd added was a low, heavy wooden table, hidden in plain view. By turning a small key (an Allen key concealed by a knot hole), the underside would drop down, revealing a fine stash box.

Walking through the place, I did my usual housekeeping and opened the sliding glass doors that lead to the patio-garden. This time of day the sun glints over the city office blocks showering light across the paving. Turning back, I looked to the table. Its underside panel was down. About $60,000 in bundled notes had rolled onto the stone tile. I didn't freeze, I moved fast, thinking the

---

[4] I'd chosen 87mhz because, at the time, police bugs were around 110mhz, just below the aviation band, another quiet spot of the radio spectrum. If you want to bug your own house today use the intercom function of an unconnected multiphone handset. They use spread-spectrum technology and can't be overhead.

cops were waiting for me two floors below in the lobby. Speeding into the bedroom, I grabbed a pillow, flinging the inner padding across the room. I quickly went outside and stuffed the cash and half-a-dozen passports into the pillow case. Then I froze. Surely, they knew the layout and the exits – even the corridor wasn't safe. I ran to the building's edge and then over to the fire escape, down two flights, sliding down another until there were no more. A door, leading those fleeing any fire back toward the lobby. Instead, I dropped down to the roof of a Chinese restaurant and then to an alley. As a general precaution, I kept a car tucked away for emergencies in one of the big, multi-level car parks in town. Then, in the street, I froze again but this time in thought.

Passports? Still with the money? The feds would have taken them – or at least opened the plastic bags in which they were sealed. So, the false-table-top discovery was not by the cops.

It had been an unusual accident, one confirmed when I rang the out-of-hours number of the letting agent. In fact, I'd lucked out despite my carelessness. The woman I'd dealt with at the office was streetwise from years of renting space to call girls – there were a half dozen around the building complex. She'd learned the value of discretion.

"I'm really sorry, Lucas," she said to me. "We were having our carpets cleaned on the rooftop and spread them over your table to dry. Well, it dropped, and— that's quite a clever place you've got there. Of course, I told them to leave everything as soon as I saw…"

So, it was a nothing. Or perhaps someone playing a very long game.

As my sweat dried under my car air-conditioning, I decided it was the Fates giving me a warning. Or, if you want to be technical, I'd used up a bit of good luck and so must reduce any subsequent dependence on chance. I even turned on the portable scanner on my way home, something that should've been routine.

Clear of any disturbing reports, I made a stop at another house, one I kept just for those moments when all other places have come under a shadow. I left the cash there. Money likes to travel, I thought.

Driving on to the beach road, I called in on a soap maker to smell what was new. As I returned to the car, the handheld radio was making scratchy, indistinct noises. It was tuned to the channel used by undercover police but I didn't have time that night to go chasing shadows. When the Bearcat scanners first allowed monitoring of police, we'd sit around all night listening to undercover operations. Sometimes Rocky (my old partner) and I would try to warn the poor slobs that they were being watched and tailed. Usually, they just freaked out, fearing the messenger as much as the message. Maybe I wouldn't need to go hunting – the signal was getting stronger as I neared my house.

"Clelia, I've brought you some fine new soaps," I said, as I kissed her hello. I was late as usual. "Shaped like jellyfish."

"You bought them for yourself, you buttyboy." Clelia was always pleased to see me.

"And some jerk is under observation, as police politely call it," I said, moving to the little radio room in the house. "Must be close by. Clear as a bell."

It wasn't until I'd recharged the portable and driven out for the evening paper that I realized the truth.

"He's backing out of the drive now," a voice said as I did just that.

In the shop, I added milk and eggs to the newspaper but the voices were still suspicious.

"Why you s'pose he didn't stop on the way home?" one asked. I heard six distinct voices but could only count four cars, most very plain. A 1960s VW; a white-van workman's transport – even a station wagon with a kayak on its roof and a bent coat-hanger for an antenna. They were good.

I overreacted. Clelia and I grabbed emergency passports, some cash, and drove to her dad's seaside restaurant to have a meal. We sat where we could be watched. After ordering dessert, we separately walked through to the kitchen and then to the staff garage where Clelia's sister was waiting. The entrance to the staff garage couldn't be seen from the street. Crouched down, we hid as Teresa drove us away. Clelia's Porsche remained visible in the customer car park.

I won't tire you with the intermediate steps, but ten days later I was in the Caribbean again. Nassau. Or, near Nassau. As Clelia relaxed on a boat, I was sitting alone on the beach of an uninhabited island, just having a think. Fuck it, I thought. Go back and fight. There's no sense to such a thought. At twenty-three, go back and fight always seems right.

Clelia and I were the only people in the cinema. I'd arranged a special screening, and although I'd planned to invite twenty or so; in the end, I didn't. The movie was *Head*. Quickly, I saw it for what it was, a self-indulgent Monkees' vehicle. Still I was enjoying the music but drifting silently to an odd moment of the day.

I'd left my office around four. The office was the shop front of a converted bijou terrace house, all renovated to suffocating cuteness. What did I do there? Ask Clelia.

"David? He just wanders around the shops all day," she'd told a girlfriend who'd asked about my work.

Not true. Her remark only reflects the assumptions any observer of our conversations might have. I'd try to interest her in my leisure pursuits while she'd speak of hers. Most recently, of Sascha, our German Shepherd. Clelia dismissed mine. She was terrific.

In the darkness of the cinema:

"I bought two tonnes of Huon pine today," I whispered.

"Sascha did well at doggie school," Clelia said. "And why are you whispering?"

"You rich girls are only interested in animals, you know that?"

"I found a home for the last puppy but we'll keep one."

"I've found a craftsman," I said. "An artist. He's making us a gearbox."

"A what? Think of a name for the dog," Clelia said.

"Rodney," I'd only just stopped whispering. After all, only two of the 550 seats of the old theatre were occupied. "He thinks he can make a working, six-speed gearbox with no metal parts. A huge, skeletal —"

"If you don't want to watch the movie, we'll go home. It's almost midnight."

I paused. "George the Greek is giving trouble. I won't pay him off. The gangsters cheated him."

"See, I told you. You didn't need him," Clelia had grown out of her interest in gangsters.

Playing with my toys allowed calm time to think. I'd decided – even though the surveillance cops had suddenly disappeared – that a major Colombian operation would mean talk that would leak down. I'd allowed Michael his one operation, giving him just enough responsibility to put him off future runs alone. He had money now – not that much, a few hundred thousand – but that could mean others might return to prey on him. He still insisted on selling ounces for extra money to Duncan – the guy I felt sure had steered night raiders upon Michael before we'd met. As for me, I'd keep my operations tight and close.

That afternoon, before the movie, I'd left the office with a plan to do a Bangkok run in complete blackness. As I drove into town calling past houses and flats I owned, I realized I'd need to sell off assets that were probably known to the police, even if that news got back to them. Already, Clelia and I had leased our Brighton (the Melbourne suburb) house and moved to a rental house with guest rooms and a pool.

"The puppies will like that," Clelia had sniffed, unhappy when I began reducing our expanded world.

As I drove in an s-block pattern to pick up any police surveillance, I noted an artists' framing shop. It looked familiar. I called in.

The owner came forward. "Any help I can give?"

"Have I shopped here before?" I asked. "These frames look like my kind of thing."

The proprietor tilted his head, then nodded. "Come this way." He took me to a back room.

There, stacked against one wall and revealed as he drew away a large white sheet were twenty 4'x5' framed and glass photographs. They were mine, pictures I'd taken with a Linhof 8"x10" camera.

"You might recall the special non-reflective glass," he said, perhaps thinking of the cost.

"Yes," I said to fill the air as I looked through the pictures. Huge photographs of the sides of old, mostly empty buildings. I'd brought him the prints almost a year earlier.

Clearly, the framer was pleased at my appearance. "We kept them here, thinking you'd be back, too beautiful to forget."

Indeed, unless you were living my life.

If I was distracted and contemplating retirement, a couple of hundred grand and a quiet life was not for Michael. He was looking for trouble and using his cash to find it.

Michael was buying his dope from some slime ball (it was cut with citric acid) and selling it in bits through the even greater toad, Duncan.

Within a week, Michael's ill-hidden safe house (a nearby flat) was robbed of the half-kilo of heroin – unfortunately with Michael in it. There was a tussle, and the thief got away, a screwdriver in one hand, the cling-film wrapped Tupperware bowl of brown dope in the other.

"People must have thought him an angry cook," I suggested as Michael sat in my kitchen, nursing a shallow screwdriver wound.

"It's not funny," Michael said. "That's the only dope in town right now."

It wouldn't be for long, if my new plan was any good. As it was, Michael wouldn't accept Duncan had anything to do with the robbery.

Perhaps so; from Michael's description, I guessed the identity of the pea-eyed, curly-headed loud mouth: a small-time crook with no link to the dope world. I sent him a message.

The next day I was sitting in the beat-up van of the thief, a block from the now-useless safe house. He'd brought the dope with him. Even though I'd agreed a return fee for the heroin, I was thinking that someone along the chain didn't want unmasking.

"There's an extra thousand for you if you spill," I said as those beady eyes seemed to narrow an inch closer. He spilled.

"Okay. Enough, enough!" I said as he gave me names. "None of those people are in our world. The address must have passed through a few hands. I'm surprised you didn't find a queue outside Michael's door."

Later, Michael was showing the usual paranoia of someone who's been saved.

"I thought the days of being robbed were gone," he said.

I shrugged. "You said you wanted your own gigs, Michael. Just be careful. I know you want everyone to be happy but don't show people expensive things you just bought unless it's a warm up to a gift. People think you're stealing their luck and they'll want it back."

Marie was newly pregnant and nervous. I brought in a London minder to look after them. That was simply to make them relax. The real safety came from my telling others that Michael was once again with me.

My saying this is not some prideful boast, just strategy. I'll explain.

As I've said, when I was introduced to Michael, he was plagued by those masked robbers, arriving at his house at night with shotguns. They took what they found. The fact that they did not try on some sort of ongoing protection payments says they were fearful of making, well, scheduled appearances. Still, it was a problem.

I'd never had such a problem. I supplied some major players, and since any attack on me would be an attack on the supply line to the majors, no villain worthy of the name would risk becoming the object of the anger of people who were supremely frank when expressing an injustice. I suppose I was fortunate in that my earliest connections in the business were people hardened by careers in armed robbery and safecracking. This meant I could be at risk only by halfwit newcomers, and if I kept my business to myself, not at risk at all.

I sometimes wondered if my chosen career might one day place me in a predicament where gunplay is the only option. Yet shooting people surely is just an admission that you haven't been thinking clearly.

Some friends once successfully staged the daylight robbery of the warehouse belonging to a big wholesaler of (legal) firearms. Of course, I made a point of buying a bucket load of the small-arms haul. Once that story filters out amongst the crooks, the chance of being robbed for household cash becomes small. In the minds of would-be plotters, they must contemplate becoming murderers for a few thousand dollars. Or becoming dead.

I've noticed that in Britain, where crooks rarely keep guns at home, robbing drug dealers is relatively common. That's not advice for dope dealers to carry guns. Anyone thinking so has missed the point: it is that which your enemy imagines that is the key element in safety.

One of the most successful gang-less gangsters I've known was routinely accompanied by a Lebanese cutthroat hitman who looked the part. A sharp dresser, thin from hyper-activity, eyes darting and alert. His boss put it about he'd met the kid in some refugee camp in Beirut. I'm sure the young man was, indeed, fast on his feet and good with his hands – after all, he'd been a waiter in a busy restaurant since his teens where Mr Big-enough had found him. The only time he'd been in Beirut was to visit his auntie. The mobless mobster had taken him from the restaurant when he heard from the boy he wanted to be an actor. When I learned the truth, apart from fresh admiration, I never looked again at any sushi chef without an employer's eye.

A last few words on prevention for those who've been bothered by amateur thieves. If you're wondering who it was who betrayed you and let them into your life, the answer is close to home: it was you. You've not only advertised that you are an easy target but your vanity has fuelled resentment.

How was it that Duncan Connor, a small-time dealer, was such a regular visitor to Michael's house? Because Michael wanted the extra money from gram and ounce sales. Now, it's possible to be greedy and safe, but never lazy. Michael should have met Duncan away from his house and gone through the charade of pretending the dope had come from someone else, and that he was just the honest broker. Drive to a block of flats to disappear for five minutes and come back bitching about the guy and what a hassle it is.

Duncan would visit Michael's house around three times each week, a house of growing wealth at which Michael would boast of his latest purchases. When I advised Michael of these flaws, he seemed hurt.

"But I've always been so fair with him. I've trusted him, it can't be?"

"Fair?" I said. "You've let him know of a world he can never be part of."

If Michael – and you, dear reader – choose to tell people what a wonderful life you have, be prepared to accept the consequences.

Despite the fact there was no sign of any police surveillance, I felt the cops wouldn't be gone long. I'd played my recordings of their radio transmissions and heard one say, *'Is that him? I've only got the passport photo.'* This told me that they were working from one of my passport applications, but was that identity a pick-up from my travels or something deeper?

The passports I used were not phoney photo-swaps of stolen documents but genuine issue from the Australian Department of Foreign Affairs. To get them I needed the birth certificates of people who were not ever to travel. The most reliable group of people who don't travel are those who are dead and who died before passporting age. If you're not squeamish (and without scruples) the certificates of those who've died in infancy are ideal. In those days, and even today in many places, the records of death are not linked to their birth. I'd go to the State Library to read old newspapers – small-town is best – for the years either side of my own birth. I'd then give Secretary Sue a wad of search requests to take to the records office. She'd also have some phoney ID from a firm of lawyers and she'd spend the day getting certified copies of the birth certificates. I remember using the name of Gray & Gray, Solicitors and Notaries. The phone number she'd leave was the direct line to her desk at the accountants' office where she worked. The office of Births, Deaths and Marriages is a busy place and doesn't call applicants when, say, there is no record found. Besides, law firms readily accept a note saying, 'no record', so any call would be a warning in itself.

If earlier surveillance had burned my passports – all of them somehow – I'd need new ones from a different source with new backgrounds. I chose interstate, using the Sydney records office, and made a special and very careful trip to get the certificates myself. I was touchy about Sue, anyway. She had declined another dope run the previous year. Nothing wrong with that but since her work for me went well and paid better, I couldn't understand her declining the work. Especially as I knew she needed the money. She'd sold the typewriter I'd given her to fill in certificate applications without asking me, a sign she needed extra cash. She'd had ex-boyfriend trouble (punchy, she'd said; also, stolen from her) though he seemed plain stupid the afternoon I wasted seeing him – though men who hit women often act all fluffy around other men. She'd said she didn't want the trouble but I wanted to check. There were echoes of something no longer spoken around her so I cut her out of my new arrangements.

My caution was justified. I got a call from my travel agent, Glen, who later told me the following story.

"There's a girl I'm seeing. She works for a big-ticket consolidator. We get half our tickets processed through her office. Maybe twenty airlines. Anyway, a couple of policemen arrived at her office this week. Plain clothes detectives. They gave a list of people. Passengers of interest. I've got the list."

Glen met me at a hotel near his office, producing a handwritten copy of the list. He must have been close to this girl. There were more than thirty different names. I was twenty of them.

The transformation of a person taking routine precautions to one who must guard against a certain enemy is a harsh change. On the uninhabited island in the Caribbean, I'd decided to go back and fight. The fight was exhausting. Every move I made demanded layers of complications that drained away energy that I needed for forward scheming.

I had to accept that every process I'd used was possibly tainted; that the police might know every name. Suddenly, passports and tickets already held might be worthless. Not only must everything be made fresh but acquired in absolute secrecy. Just one example: a careless hotel receipt could place me in another town, the room lead to its phone records, the call to the travel agent, and the moment to a name of the traveller. For, in today's world, the knowledge merely of a name could crush months of planning and endanger the lives of the participants. By 1981, Thailand had resumed executing drug runners.

Even the trip to Sydney for documents demanded accounting for my location. I called from my tapped phone to arrange a night staying at my mother's high-rise apartment, so those listening would know. I left my car parked underground and then walked out after dinner to take a cab, a couple of blocks away, to the airport. Buying a ticket on the last flight north, then to spend a night at a hotel, alone. There would be many nights alone from that time onward. Clelia had to become what she liked the least – the wife that stays at home, and I'd be deprived of her comfort and advice. I was close to abandoning all operations.

In Sydney, I arranged passports for myself and Peter Dale, using fresh certificates I'd collected at the time. I was short of one name. As couriers for the Bangkok-Europe sector, I would employ John, the London minder, who had grown bored with the needless task of looking after Michael and Marie. I'd been given the birth certificate of a dead relative of my mechanic, Paul Sigg. Memorably, the name was Moriarty. John had to have a new passport in case he'd been spotted by Australian police as he moved in and out of Michael's house.

When under heat, it's essential to let go of standard operating procedures. I had to abandon a new system that had just been perfected. The trick took advantage of the fact that long-haul aircraft became domestic flights once they'd landed on Australian soil. Of course, they didn't encourage domestic ticketing but in rare cases, an international passenger might begin his journey travelling Melbourne – Sydney to then board an onward international flight. I'd used QF6 (Qantas) frequently as it landed in Melbourne from Bangkok before flying north to Sydney to return once more to Bangkok. Peter Dale would fly in to Melbourne on his way to Sydney, staying in transit. I would board the same plane, but starting my journey in Melbourne with a ticket that was to see me connect at Sydney for an onward flight to Auckland in New Zealand. The transit time for me at Sydney was four hours, so when checking in, I'd ask for my bag to be offloaded at Sydney where I said I had relatives waiting. All that was tosh. What I wanted was Peter and I to be on the same plane. When my bag came up on the carousel, it would be mixed with the bags from Thailand. I'd pick up Peter's bag (the one with the dope) and he'd pick up mine. As I approached the customs officers who sorted arriving passengers, I'd show them my ticket and a little 'DOMESTIC PASSENGER' coupon, and they'd wave me through. Peter would hold back to see me in the clear, then walk through with my bag. It was a smooth system, but one had to ensure that the long-haul passenger had a clean passport. If Peter got a tug and they looked closely at his baggage tag, they'd know it wasn't his bag. Of course, he could always claim he'd picked up the bag by mistake – we used identical bags except for a little sticker – but it would cook the scam for later use.

Such parlour tricks were no longer available to me. With my face known, it would take just one sighting to bring such a careful operation down. To be safe for this next deep-cover run, I had Peter change his appearance for the new passport, and I would keep my distance as he reverted to the simplicity of an uninterrupted SYD-LON-SYD itinerary. John and I would meet in Bangkok from where he'd run the next two kilos through to Europe. I'd take it from there to London.

Just to establish if I'd be missed while away from Australia, I set up an 8mm movie camera pointed from my office window toward the street. It would take one frame every two seconds with its intervalometer – around a week's worth of activity with a 200' magazine. What could go wrong?

I woke early, under the stripes of a dawn sun in the house at the edge of Bangkok. A breeze carried jasmine aromas into the bedroom of my Thai business partner, Lee. He and his wife had taken their kids' bedroom for the night as I worked on stashing and sealing. I'd taken extra care with buffing using polish and beeswax.

After breakfast, I packed the stereo in a padded suitcase. Lee must have sensed my extra concerns as I frowned at the bag.

"You know my wife prays for you when you leave," he said, as he picked up the large glass ornament from a table. A two-foot phoenix of differing colours. "Thailand has a bird like this as its sign."

"Its emblem," I corrected.

"You take this?" Lee asked, being careful with the glass bird.

"Why not?" I said, looking at the sun shining through its golden breast. "It'll bring me luck."

John was staying at the Montien Hotel not far from the river that snakes through the capital. Minders – or bodyguards – are a strange mix of strength and fear. John had wanted this job, he didn't need persuading, yet the force I'd seen him produce readily in a London bar fight seemed to fade as his big day approached. He'd stood a few staged bouts in the ring so his nerviness wasn't stage fright. It might be that fighters meet their fears with that violence that comes with a resignation to take it as well as hand it out. And is the ability to take a punch that much of an asset off stage? In operations that demand, above all, serenity, the absence of a physical contest seems to drain this complimentary strength.

John wasn't in good shape as I pushed him toward the economy check-in desk at Don Muang airport. If what happened next was due to his manner, an observer might blame it on his beaten expression.

As it happened, they were waiting for him. By *they*, I mean the Thai police who surrounded him at check-in – and before anyone had looked at his bag. There were six of them, almost as if they knew they'd have a welterweight to subdue. There was little subduing to be done. As I stood at Business check-in of the same flight, I saw him sag unsteadily, dealt a near knock-out blow as he was led away.

The Scandinavian Airlines clerk returned my passport.

"Smoking or non-smoking, Sir?" asked the clerk.

"Smoking."

How was it that John was targeted yet I ignored? Clearly, the police were working from names, not photographs. The events that led to his arrest became a little clearer as my flight connection landed at Brussels. The plane's captain made an announcement no smuggler likes to hear.

"Ladies and gentlemen, immigration formalities will be conducted as you leave the aircraft. Please have your passports ready."

Despite that which you might have seen, it is not possible to get out of an airplane through the toilet in a hurry. However, I did make a quick stop there to dump my personal dope. A sensible move as the police at the aircraft exit were ready to stop any Australian passport holder. The thing that first puzzled the Belgian police was that they were expecting an Australian traveller name Moriarty. No one had yet told them that John was face down in a Bangkok jail cell.

A year later, I'd be told that John had behaved suspiciously at an airport on his way over to Thailand. I'd never taken to that story. I'd sent him from Sydney to New Zealand just to avoid contact with those Australian customs police who make it their business to sniff at passengers leaving for Bangkok. For him to come under suspicion at Auckland would have been unlucky. For the NZ police to report an empty suspicion to Australia would be doubly unlucky. For the Australian feds to link an unknown Moriarty to me multiplies the odds again. Thailand, 1981, was the start of being force-fed stories of extraordinary bad luck and outstanding coincidence. That said, I don't like to underestimate the power of small flaws' ability to undermine complex schemes. And yet... what do the mob say as they gather round the dead body of an enemy? 'He should have seen it coming.' There could be no informer or I would have been stopped. And I'd told no one.

Yet even the cover story was unknown to me as I left Asia. From the departure lounge before leaving Bangkok, I'd phoned Lee.

"We have a problem. The cargo has been taken," I'd said. "You'll need to read the postcard."

The postcard was a letter I'd always leave well-concealed at Lee's house before I'd leave. It contained the travelling names of all those among us leaving the country as well as links to friends around the world who could help. As I sat in a holding cell at Brussels' Zavantem airport, I hoped Lee would get to the police station in time to have John freed. A two-kilo limit was within the negotiating range with Thai police. I knew there would be seven days before the first court appearance. Until then, there was hope. I remember wishing I knew more about the Thai legal process – and you know the fate of those who make careless wishes. As for me, under Belgian law, police have just twenty-four hours to play with their catch.

Police worldwide tend to treat foreigners as they imagine they are dealt with in their own countries, only more so. The Brussels cops seemed unsure if Australian police beat up their suspects or invited them for tea. So, they did both. They'd searched me and my baggage but found nothing. A big lump among them peeled the bubble wrap off Lee's glass bird and muttered something about smuggling Thai national antiquities but lost that angle when the smarter cops laughed at him. Yet the Interpol alert had said drugs. When they thought I might be connected to some smuggling ring, they put me in a coat locker and threw me down a flight of stairs. That was more noisy than painful.

After I'd been dragged from the steel box, a report came back that my passport was genuine. Still smelling of coppers' boots and damp overcoats, I was given an iced bun and a plate of sausages. Then, because I'd refused to chow down to a dish any Belgian would die for, I was sent to a hospital for x-rays. They suspected I'd had a meal of heroin-filled condoms before leaving Thailand. When nothing showed on the x-ray machine, I was left to stew overnight and released by noon. I flew to London.

I didn't want to head straight for the Charles Street flat. I checked into a hotel in South Kensington and cleaned myself up before calling Lee in Bangkok.

"Your friend has problem," Lee said.

"I know that," I said. "Have you seen him?"

"He has big problem," Lee stressed.

Lee made some calls and sent a man to the police station that takes airport arrests. Lee had been told that anti-narcotics people from the US embassy had taken an interest. I expected the Australians, maybe the British, but I dismissed the US curiosity. They had a large anti-narc force at their embassy with little to do. Perhaps they just liked to nose around. Lee would need a case full of money to fortify the Thais against foreign power. I told him I'd send someone. And I would.

I didn't return to the hotel immediately. I walked through the long underground walkways that fanned out from the station before cabbing to the Charles Street flat. I turned on the television and stood watching. Yet I couldn't take the lightness of its comedies or the empty promise of TV news. Sitting on the sofa, I tooted a line of heroin and sipped some brandy over ice. I couldn't enjoy either. I didn't deserve rewards. Even the comfort of the plush flat seemed tainted somehow.

I would need bigger guns to get John out. Sure, he'd asked for the job, against my advice, but he'd had faith in me, and I still couldn't figure the flaw in my secrecy. Besides, *'against my advice'*: you don't advise people one way or another if you're genuine and strong. If the advice is right, you tell them to do it; if it's wrong, you stop them.

Michael's sister, Norma, had contacts in Thailand. I'd call Michael, though it would have to wait as he had no emergency procedure for secure calls. I wanted to phone Clelia but knew that doing so would declare my location. Everything would be like this from now on, I realized. I wasn't prepared to walk away from my life.

I looked around the large living room. The Charles Street address could be compromised now. They had known John was a boxer, otherwise why arrive mob-handed at the airport? And who were they? What had seemed a deep yet brief Australian investigation was now operating as something else. In such situations, it is essential to fall back only on those things that are surely secret. The Interpol alert did not list the name with which I'd arrived in Belgium. Fine, that new source of passports was not infected. Peter Dale's new identity should be safe.

I took two cabs to get over to South Kensington, collected my suitcase, left an envelope for the hotel staff, then zig-zagged across town before borrowing a car from a friend. I drove southwest to Dorset to meet up with Peter Dale, who I knew would be disappointed with the loss. Disappointed mostly at the loss of the big prize rather than the loss of John. Of course, they'd never met.

Stopping at a truckers' service station, I called Michael. I wanted to know what influence his sister Norma's friends might have on Thai law. It was my second call to Michael – he'd promised to contact his sister.

"Apart from the usual complaints," I asked of her, "what was the first reaction?"

Michael had got through to Manila. He was lucky. Norma was sober.

"She says friends of friends have had this sort of trouble before. They usually make the fix on the lab report. They lose the field test and the lab reports the powder as caffeine."

I'd heard of such a move. The lab guys get paid for creative chemical interpretations and they keep the haul for recycling.

Back on the road, I recalled my first meeting with Norma in the Philippines. I'd arrived with a plan to land a container of five tonnes of Thai grass at the Manila port. I'd wanted it re-packed and re-labelled to go to Australia in a new box. This was 1979 and the man who was to do all the fixing was no small player. And he played a bigger game than drugs.

Anthony Moynihan had inherited a title but not much money in England as a young man. He'd fled the UK under accusations of fraud and set up shop in the Philippines where he put it about that he'd done some dutiful spying for England while in Africa. It was said (mostly by Lord Tony) that he was in thick with the dictator, president Ferdinand Marcos.

Tony had put on a big show when I arrived with Clelia but during our two-week stay, he nearly yessed me to death. Little focus on my puff-container enterprise while sharp on his own scheme. He'd heard I took an interest in electronics and had a proposition for me. He took me to a night at the local cockfights. These contests were not just a two-bird squawk behind some oily garage but a betting spree before two thousand Chinese-Philippine gamblers pounding out millions of pesos on the outcome of each fight.

If you've never seen a cockfight, it is brutal. The male birds peck each other's eyes and brains out – and to add colour, the feet of each contestant are fitted with razor-sharp, curved, five-inch blades. The fights rarely last two minutes and the reign of a champion is short.

Lord Tony wanted me to rig the fights, of course. Or, at least one. I'd explained that no amount of electronic skulduggery could ensure a winner – unless the winner was to be the other fellow's chicken. A day later, in Tony's family-filled office, I suggested it might be possible to set a small, explosive capsule in the sagging scruff of your own bird's neck, then detonate the jugular-bursting charge from ringside by radio transmitter, and so collect by betting on the opposition's chook through some secret punter.

Tony accepted my musings all too quickly. Within a few days, I'd been tipped that Tony's scheme was no more than a classic sting. He'd pretend to win a small test bet (others operating my transmitter) before persuading me to join him on a huge bet as a one-time killing. Of course, he would have made no bet. Simply pocket the money and deliver some – no doubt interesting, if not plausible – story of technical failure. I suppose that would have been the polite ending. An alternative might end with my arrest on some fake but expensive charge to distract me from the bet money heading out a back door.

At that stage of my life, I found cheaters no more than mildly annoying. They were rarely threatening, and so annoyance gives way to amusement at the, often comic, efforts to defraud. This condescending attitude, I would learn, is a dangerous piece of indulgence. For a fraudster is accustomed to a life endlessly scheming whilst mostly broke. He wants your money for the perverse pleasure of revelling in your humiliation. The conman is not content unless you ultimately know you've been cheated. And if the swindle fails to deliver the cash win, the fraudster will try for a second prize, gaining your humiliation by proxy. In other words, he'll get you arrested using any information he has. Such understanding for me was years away, still. I thought Lord Tony might save John in Thailand. But bribery was too much of an honest deal for his Lordship.

I was to meet Peter Dale at Bournemouth rail station. I stood away from my car as evening darkened. Given the importance of keeping his new identity secret, Peter had agreed to keep a low profile.

A gold Maserati slid to a halt with Peter's gleaming teeth from the driver's window lighting up the station. Heads turned.

Too many to study. He was grinning and tanned like a million dollars, which seemed to be a figure he was working on with the Amex card I'd given him. Peter got out, shook my hand and tilted toward me in confidence.

"The girls will be along any minute," he whispered loudly. "They think I'm the manager for the Little River Band."

As Peter drove us to the Grand Hotel, he outlined my character as a record producer. This charade added nothing to any smuggling operation. I suppose Peter was a method actor.

"And to think, I used to tell you who to impersonate," I said, regretting how little time now there'd be for these games.

I sent Peter back to Australia the following night before any further leaks sank the ship. He sailed through untouched. I held on another week in case some opportunity arose that would need fast intervention to help John. Nothing did.

Taking short flights across Europe using a passport in which I had no faith, I began the mournful journey home to Australia, knowing I must find home elsewhere.

There was a slow transit connection in Abu Dhabi and I found myself sitting in the Business lounge for three hours, without interest leafing through local papers. There, I shared a few minutes with a US senator from North Carolina. He was with his wife, although I don't recall her speaking. Over some general conversation of things happening around the world, the politician began using the pronoun, *we*, including me, that is, the British. *We*, the West, keepers of the flame of democracy.

I drove the conversation toward Afghanistan where the Russians had installed a puppet government. Afghan rebels in the hills were fighting the Soviets. Should we be supporting the rebels, I wondered aloud, the Mujahedeen firing at helicopters with rifles?

"My enemy's enemy is my friend, you mean?" said the senator. "I know that too well from a long political career."

That sounded less than practical, and the kind of phrase that sounds better than it applies. I mean, if the police were my enemies, then just about everyone should be my friend. As our flights were called to the gates, I kept the tone friendly by quoting Churchill on America's policy mistakes.

"You can always count on Americans to do the right thing - after they've tried everything else, isn't that so?" I suggested.

"Don't count on it," he said, smiling.

My entrance to Australia was uncomfortable. I'd flown from Tokyo to Auckland, New Zealand and once there, mailed my iffy passport. Unwilling to wait for bogus papers, I risked flying into Brisbane as a New Zealander with not a single identity document. That was unusual enough to have me held for brief questioning by the Federal Police. Sounds rash? Maybe. But you can't be held for nothing. Not for long, anyway. In those days, New Zealanders could arrive without a passport.

The feds kept me for a few hours in their office, trying to get me to admit I wasn't Carl Miles, a name I'd invented.

"Just tell us your real name and you can go," said the young detective, all smiles. "Just say you're not Miles, not Carl."

I held my ground.

Suddenly, and annoyed, he told me to go. If I'd wavered, he'd have had a charge. With a final try, he joked, 'you don't look like a Miles, more like a Zabaglione.' The Zablione brothers had been convicted a year earlier for importing heroin, sentenced to twenty years' imprisonment. My enemy's enemy in this case were not friends. Those ambitious Italian siblings had a butcher's shop on a notorious junkie networking street. They'd built a million-dollar business by brutality and greed. They were not my friends. Even so, this cop was letting me know, out of sheer petulance, that he knew who I was.

Everything was peaceful at home. Sascha, our German Shepherd's pups were racing and pooing around the house, and Clelia was all warmth. Peter Dale complained about his reduced fee, Michael fretted at the prospect of having to buy his dope locally, and I told my trading partners to be patient.

I cooked Italian food and Clelia set the dining table as though expecting *House & Garden* photographers.

"Are we in trouble, David?" she asked.

I opened some wine. "Trouble, how?"

"Money, I suppose. I know you'll take care of the rest." Clelia cast a glance toward the night through the window.

"We're fine, Clel."

Late at night, a few days later, I crept from our bed to the living room. On the mantle above the fireplace sat the ornate glass figurine, the phoenix in clear yellow and red, its huge breast flanked by outstretched wings. Clelia hated the thing but I'd explained it as a gift from Lee in Thailand. At least the small light set behind cast a warm glow throughout the room.

I lifted it down and took it to my tool shed behind the swimming pool. I pulled on some overalls. Using rubber-edge clamps, I gripped the statue in a vice before taking a one-millimetre diamond drill to make a hole in its shoulder. I peered through a magnifying glass to find the place where a tiny air bubble had risen to the top of an inner surface. After using a second drill to enlarge the hole, I removed the small pump from a poolside fish tank and drained the fluid from inside the statue.

The liquid I took from the phoenix's breast, wings and legs amounted to almost five litres of yellowish but clear syrup. I switched on a portable electric stove and set a double boiler in place. The water of the double boiler would keep the liquid just under boiling point and prevent any sudden fire. I transferred the paste in a glass bowl to a large microwave oven, giving ten-to-fifteen second bursts, turning the paste to a hardened cake. I chipped the flaky cake from the bowl and then spread the chunks across the trays of a fruit dryer, using all ten racks. I broke off a piece after forty minutes. It seemed the finest heroin I'd ever had. Or was that just pride in my kitchen chemistry?

The phoenix had flown through unexamined despite half its journey in my much-challenged care before trusting it to Peter who knew nothing of its true nature. It was so big and charmless that no one who'd looked at its transparent features guessed they were looking at a liquid I'd injected through small holes, and then sealed with resin. (It is essential to allow a small air bubble to take the pressure and temperature changes during flight by jet.) It had survived my tussle at Brussels and cooed under Peter Dale's showmanship. Now, it had given me a nest egg.

Clelia noticed it missing the next morning.

"Great. You got rid of that thing," Clelia said from the kitchen preparing breakfast. "It was scaring the puppies. I was going to give it away without telling you."

She came to me and hugged, speaking softly.

"It reminded me of the Ugly Duckling. You're such a sucker. You'll take anything until you know better."

But I saw from her smile she knew it had been a prop.

Three months' later I was in Baluchistan, that province in Pakistan I had explored with Lee in 1979. Not far from the place I'd spoken of when I began this story. This time our caravanserai was like those formations of traders of the ancient world and Clelia was with me, having reluctantly left the doggies in the care of her father. He had a large country house with a big garden where they could play.

We had three grand, bus-sized mobile homes along with two four-wheel drive vehicles to carry spares and extra water. Lee was not with us but friends included the woodcarver, our soap maker, a camera assistant to keep the trunk of Linhof large-format cameras, Clelia's school friend and now her dresser, as well as our new host and protector, Mir (Lord) Noor Jehan Magsi, his retinue of five, along with guides and translators. On this part of the journey, along the Rakhshan River, we gathered some officials and a few army friends. As part of the Afghanistan Transit Trade Agreement with Pakistan, traders are allowed passage to land-locked Afghanistan. We were not traders and had no goods for transit and for once I was not running an operation.

I suppose that elaborate vacation was an expensive whim but my pretext was to have the logistical problems understood for a long dreamt-of journey following parts of the Silk Road from southern China to Rome. Even a campaign tent was being stitched though it had not been completed by the time of this journey. With dictator General Zia al-Haq in control of Pakistan and tribes across the border enjoying friendly Western glances, this was no time to be setting up marquee tents at high or low altitude, yet it felt strangely safer to be away from the civilized world. Clelia and I were travelling on British and Canadian passports secured years earlier. With a new baby, Michael and Marie weren't game for travel. Money makes it possible to walk away from one life to another but the same wealth can hold us down.

I was sitting under a canopy with Noor Jehan while the womenfolk were preparing a cauldron of lamb stew and beans (with the local guys too embarrassed to add their field expertise), neatly supplemented by Fortnum & Mason preserves. Helpers were securing the staff tents against a wind gusting from the hills.

"You can live by me," Noor Jehan was saying. "I need ships for Dubai."

He meant we could live in Baluchistan provided I paid for his smuggling boats. That would not be a real investment, it would be tribute to his Lordship, and only tempting for its safety. My real plan was to sell up in Australia and buy houses in London.

"Maybe," I said. "Do you want to be rich? If Baluchistan becomes independent, what will you do?"

Noor Jehan laughed. "I am rich." He spread his arms as though to take in the horizon. Noor Jehan was a leader of a separatist group mercilessly hunted by the dictator general. The fact we had an army captain dining with us that night was just another of the surface contradictions of a country carelessly divided by British neglect.

My thoughts were blocked to any new business that evening. The week of my return from England to Australia, I thought I had a deal to see John freed from his Thai prison. Unable to travel safely myself, I'd given Paul Sigg (the provider of the Moriarty documents) $30,000 to carry to Bangkok. It was packed in one of the stereos, now that they would not be used for drug cargo. Paul returned from Singapore with some story about being followed; that he'd lost the money. I didn't buy his story and since John had fallen while traveling as Moriarty, there was a deep shadow over Paul Sigg. I'd taken his honour for granted as he had been trusted by the old safecracking crew. But had they trusted him or simply used him?

    A couple of days earlier in Pakistan, while at Larkana, I'd received news of John in Thailand. He was refusing aid or to see anyone I'd sent. More telling was a report from one of the customs police at his airport arrest. The police, upon John's arrest, had arranged the unpacked dope in a pile on a table for the usual triumphal photo. John had grabbed a handful of the powder, intending to swallow it as a means of suicide. He must have hesitated or he would have succeeded. Even so, I wondered if it would be possible to arrange an escape for anyone brought so low. Could there be any circumstances that might even drive me to take my own life? None, I concluded, then.

    Near Larkana, we'd stopped at Mohenjo-Daro, the remains of a large city more than four-and-a-half thousand years old. A guide showed me a dentist's drill of the time, as I stood over the drainage channels of a wide street lined with rectangular brick houses. The life of this city flourished before any such advances in Europe or indeed elsewhere in Asia. It seemed that changes in the flow of the Indus River had led to the abandonment of their city. It was not clear if they'd become established somewhere else and there was no sign of destruction through war. I set up my cameras and captured moments of the silent endurance of lost civilizations. I remember to this day the rich smell of the film emulsion contrasting with the dry air. How often had the potential of civilization skipped a beat and failed to take for the kind of eternity today we take for granted? As petty as my tiny empire seemed, I did feel a duty to survive, to preserve my images, and not be flooded by the massed ranks of the opposing forces.

Before leaving Australia, I'd taken a closer look at the list of names left by detectives with the travel agency consolidators. The passport names that, mostly, were mine. They'd left a contact number. I'd run a trace on the number and that led to an old office block. Plainly, they didn't trust police HQ. Heavily disguised, I took the stairs to its fifth-floor location. Dressed in a safety inspector's dust coat, I looked over my clipboard at the office space after hours. Desks and phones for thirty people. I came to know this was a federal-state police taskforce. But were these people directed at my destruction alone?

Night had fallen. I walked over to interfere with the cooking, seeking warmth. A lull in the conversations and music left only the low drone of a generator powering the refrigerators. The silence made Clelia look up.

"We're about ready for some fizz, David," she said as I frowned. "We'll need to be tipsy to eat this." I moved to our mobile-home cabin as Clelia added a last command. "And tell Mikey to put on some better music."

Our music master had been recording Sufi chants, which are beautiful and mostly so to our Western ears because they don't carry the social exclusion of that minority Islamic sect directed by Pakistan's Sunni majority. By contrast, soon, Mikey had Laura Nyro's *Mother's Spiritual* filling the air.

I must have been staring at the sky or daydreaming, as suddenly I felt Clelia's arms around my shoulders.

"You okay?" she asked.

"Sure," I resumed, unclamping the corks. "You remember when I swam out to that island in the Caribbean? Way back – oh, months ago now – and by the time I swam back I'd decided to fight on."

Clelia set the bottles aside and began to warm my hands with hers. "You're worried about John —"

"It's not just that. We're not getting any younger," I smiled. "I think I've had enough. You must have had enough. This is it. I'm retiring."

"Good. About time," Clelia said. Then a pause, and, "I thought you still had luggage here and there?"

Clel was right. I still had three kilos of dope in Thailand, and one in London for emergencies. Worth a million if traded, maybe a quarter for a quick sale. But:

"Clelia, I'm superstitious. When something tells you to stop, you stop. Not an ounce more. London stock can stay buried and Lee will find a home for the three. We'll go back to Australia and tidy up. And no one must know of our plans."

Clelia knew that included Michael. He should know after the fact.

Pleased now, Clelia chided, "You once said you'd fight to the end on principle." She stood, then turned away.

"You never married me for my principles," I called quietly as Clel walked over the soft ground.

I thought, the only people who take a stand on principle alone are almost always those with nothing to lose. And those few who do so, at great cost, are of course, mad.

Retirement made sense. Besides, I was then past my twenty-fourth birthday.

Part II

1

Back in Melbourne, I returned most of the rented properties to their owners, and very quietly sought buyers for our first home and the office building. At the same time, I made as much noise as possible taking a long lease on a large and expensive beachside house.

A recent conversation with a lawyer had not resulted in pleasing advice.

"But," I argued with the Harvard doctor-at-law, "how can I be arrested if I don't touch drugs? Apart from my personal stash."

"How much is personal?" asked Dr Law.

"Less than a kilo," I said.

"Then it'll be less than life."

Mostly, the advisers were worried about conspiracy charges. Conspiracy is the crime of making an unlawful agreement. You don't have to be caught with so much as a joint. Even so, evidence in conspiracy cases almost always relies on inside testimony.

"No one will talk," I said, as though saying it aloud helped. "Why would they? They'd be informing on themselves."

A silence filled the air with possibilities.

Despite my retirement, there seemed more surveillance than ever. I guessed that was to be expected. If thirty task-force operatives had a secret office in town, they'd want something to occupy their time. That was a point raised by the lawyers. Task-force operations cost plenty. The funding would have been approved by Big Police. If they got nowhere, how could they accept defeat? *'Sorry, boss. There's no evidence and they've quit. I guess we'll go back in uniform."* My lawyer asked, "Is that a conversation you can imagine in the real world?"

The cops – our cops – were taking greater precautions. I picked up the tails but I couldn't get a lock on their transmissions. Since they got a look at my radio room they were using encrypted radios. You could hear them but it would be just the beeps and burps of scrambled signals.

Three weeks after moving into the new house I found a bug installed in the kitchen. I was lucky to find it so quickly. For that, I can thank Radio Shack and our dog, Sascha.

I never used the $4,000 bug detector I'd bought in New York. It had been made so that it would *not* pick up transmissions on particular frequencies. Notch filters allowed four channels on VHF and UHF to go undetected. It was a Trojan-horse device to give false security. So, it was not a concern when I had a call from a well-known, mid-level dealer asking for a loan of the machine. What was a concern was Sascha's reaction when I met him at a car park far from my house. As Alan approached my car she went crazy barking. Unusual, even with strangers. Alan jumped back with fear even though the window was up.

"Alan, Sascha thinks you're a wrong 'un," I joked, with private seriousness as I got out of the car.

I kept the meeting short, gave him the useless device, and then drove to Radio Shack where I bought a cheap wide-band radio. If Alan was an informer, then his job this day was to get the detector away from my house.

At home, I put on headphones, ran taps into the bathroom and kitchen sinks and began tuning from one end of the VHF band to the other. I heard the kitchen sink splashing at 112 mhz. In the kitchen, I folded and retracted the antenna. That would mean I'd have to be on top of the bug to receive a signal. It was quick to find but slow to remove from the under-spaces of a kitchen bench.

How had I missed the sound of police installing the little device with its big battery? I put a voltmeter on the brick-sized 12-volt battery. It read 11.8 volts, so the bug must have been installed no longer than a day or two earlier. Over Clelia's objections, I left it operating, confirming the average battery drain the next day.

With so much surveillance, I'd continued the precaution of setting a voice-activated Dictaphone running in our house when we'd go out for the day, especially those days away that we'd announced during conversations from our most-certainly-tapped home telephone. I checked the tape for the previous week. Nothing. I listened again. Just the phone ringing a lot. But then, the sounds of the front door being opened by key. I had assumed, wrongly, it was simply Clelia and I coming home. Not this time. I heard bumping sounds, a clump from what could have been the kitchen door. Then, a voice.

"Say, Bob. What—?"
"Shut it, idiot, shoosh!"

The strangled conversation was between two policemen not wanting to make a noise in a house that they came to bug, owned by a man who bugged his own place. And, they had the key to our house. These people were serious. They did *not* want to go back in uniform.

I attached the light bulb from a car to the battery terminals feeding the bug. This drained the power within twelve hours. I didn't have the patience to wait the three weeks the device would have taken on its own. I figured the cops might think their circuit had a faulty board, shorting the current.

Clelia and I made arrangements, in clear tones, on our tapped phone, for a country lunch at her dad's place. I expected the cops would let themselves into our house to collect their dead machine.

Clelia's father liked his work as a restaurateur and spent long days managing the three eateries and four bars. He, of course, loved family life more, while showing a bashful reserve. With three daughters and a son, he'd have been pleased to see the daughters married, not only happily but married well. One of Clel's sisters was wedded to a workaholic house builder. Ferdinand Viganò gave him respect and work, building family houses, and the large country house for our Sunday lunch was the work of the favoured son-in-law. What could I do? Serve the weed for the New Year's Eve bash? Even so, in his eyes, I was a good provider, and in me he sensed the loyalty of the slightly mad.

After eating, I asked Ferdi to show me his *Testarossa* Ferrari in his garage. He seemed puzzled as I'd shown little interest in cars, so he half nodded to himself when I later lifted myself from the driver's seat and spoke – in outline – of our troubles.

"All my instincts tell me to dump everything and run," I told him.

Ferdi stood back and toyed with the switch of a huge pump, part of a whole-house vacuuming system. "Can you get out?"

"We've got passports. I'm not so happy with them, so I've an idea to leave from Lord Howe Island —"

"I mean get out of the business," Ferdi was quick to say. "I hear people have trouble."

I smiled. "There's nothing to that. I'll be missed by some, I suppose. There's nothing I do that works under force."

I went on to tell Clel's dad of a villa in northern Italy that we'd lease if things got hot in London. Ferdi was pleased I would be out of the business.

He said, "At least the police can't do anything with you out of that trade."

"That's what worries me," I said.

The difference was the lack of predictability. When I was running an operation, the opposition has a limited number of moves. This peacetime seemed a silent war with ignorance the unavoidable trade-off.

A pager beeped from my pocket, halting our conversation. I took it out and looked at the message, three sixes.

Ferdi gave me a doubting look. "Business?" he asked.

I shook my head. "These police I'm worried about. Right now, they're in our kitchen."

Driving home, I felt my efforts to tell Clel's dad I had matters in hand had failed. I explained that my pager had been set off by an auto-dialler that was activated when an infrared sensor in our hallway was passed. I should have kept my mouth shut. I told myself never to tell someone something alarming when the purpose is no more than a needless show of technology. It's a hard rule to follow when young.

When I checked the kitchen, the bug was gone. Clelia was relieved. I was suspicious.

"Sascha wants a pee," I said, pointing to the rear garden and touching my lips with a finger. Clelia's shoulders fell but she acted brightly.

"Come on, Sash," she said, then to me, "I suppose it was a long drive."

A radio check of the house revealed another transmitter, this one behind the wall oven. I had trouble convincing Clelia we should leave it in place for a few days.

That night, over dinner at our kitchen table, we read aloud from prepared notes:

David: *Those people ran into me at the pub last week. The pests.*
Clelia: *What did you tell them?*

David: *I said good luck to you – they've got some big thing going in a few months – but I told them I'm doing okay as I am. The hard stuff is a little dangerous, as you know.*

Clelia: *Good. And I've been meaning to ask – can I keep one of the big stones next time...?*

And more of that sort tosh. I didn't expect the police to believe it. Just to have a reasonable doubt.

I came to appreciate the obsession with technical countermeasures that consumed those in the Colombian cartels when pursued by the American Drug Enforcement Administration. They'd employ staff whose job was only to ensure safe communication against the DEA's growing sophistication. And it should be no surprise to know that police have told me that the challenge is the part of the hunt they most enjoy. An actual arrest can be a downer.

2

I don't want to make this story any harder to follow than its events demand. Rather than ignore background and important histories until the moment I became aware of them, you deserve the privilege of knowing all that I did not. More fun, then, to see me blundering about, if you know first.

So here is an account that will later take on a clear importance. You can judge if I could have acted in any other way if I had this knowledge in advance.

First, a Thai businessman and his uncle. An event that changed forever how American drug agents behave.

Of the three big heroin suppliers in the Golden Triangle in southeast Asia, one was warlord Khun Sa of Burma's Shan State, another General Lei and the third we'll call the Uncle.

It was the Uncle who operated from Chiang Mai in the north of Thailand. He was famed – and loathed – for having introduced heroin to serving US soldiers in Vietnam.

Naturally, all things Uncle were of importance to US Drug Enforcement Administration agents stationed at the US embassy post in Chiang Mai. The processes of the trade made investigation difficult. With around three harvests each year, the seed pod of the *papaverum somniferum* – the opium poppy – would be tapped before flowering. Farmers striate the one-inch, spherical pods to let the sap ooze out overnight and then scrape off the thick resin early morning. Around a tenth of the goo is morphine. That goo is either dried for smoking - quality opium - or mixed with an alkali to make a paste for the manufacturer of heroin. In the Triangle (Burma–Thailand–Laos), an old French recipe is used, resulting in a high-quality powder (I can smell it in my mind as I write) despite the simple refining and conversion process. If a wholesaler in the north expects orders for, say, twenty kilos of heroin, his agent will first order two hundred kilos of paste from the village headman. When that's ready, the wholesaler will then arrange donkey transport to take the paste to one of the independent field laboratories. The dope cooking is a family trade, passed on from father to son, and a set fee is charged for the work. That's their thing. Neither farmers nor lab cooks are in the employ of Uncle; they, like the transport people, are independents. But it is Uncle who protects them. He takes a cut from payments between all three, often in the form of the finished product. So, when Uncle is arranging a load for someone in town, he's not close.

  The DEA staff at Chiang Mai would gain intelligence, or interesting falsehoods, from the Thai anti-narcotics police but they'd never conduct any direct investigations themselves. That is until one ambitious agent, unimpressed with the reports on his desk, decided to go into the field. Agent Mike Powers visited a village ripe with poppies. Through his nervous interpreter, he pressed the village headman for information on Uncle. Of course, the headman had never met Uncle but he knew better than to talk. Yet he had no choice but to listen.

  Uncle was told of the agent's interest but there was a delay in the headman coming forward. As an object lesson to the agent – and, to me, a pointless and harsh message to the village – the village headman's head was cut off and left boxed near DEA headquarters. My understanding is that the maverick agent was cautioned by his boss at the US embassy but he heeded not. The agent, not content with the damage done, let it be known that he'd not rest until Uncle was brought to justice.

  Now, you'd think that Uncle's history with the Royal Courts of Thailand would provide a lesson. Around a decade before agent Powers, information was given to the DEA saying that Uncle's Volvo, loaded with three hundred kilos of heroin, was on its way into town. The car was intercepted by Thai police with the Americans looking on. Uncle went off to jail. But not for long. In one of the most expensive decisions ever paid for in the Thai Supreme Court, Uncle was acquitted while the driver convicted, claiming the quarter-tonne of dope was his own. I guess the driver had something of a drug problem.

That history didn't deter the fearless and foolhardy DEA agent. And to give the agent a clear lesson, Uncle arranged a frightener. The agent's wife lived with him at the US personnel compound and his kids went to the local American school. That alone, if I were he, would keep me in my office but Powers had a mistaken idea of Thai independence and relative fear.

The lesson – which I've always thought misguided and grubby – was to have the wife of the agent kidnapped for a few hours and then released. Had it gone off neatly, I'm sure it would have seen the agent sent home – but then, so would have a nasty letter bricked through the office window.

The wife had a Thai driver from the embassy who would take her and a nanny to pick up the kid from the school on afternoons. On the day, the Uncle's men (not regulars) tried to intercept the Americans as they stopped at the shops in Chiang Mai. This got messy, with the chauffeur shot, the nanny getting away and mom with the kid bundled into a VW minibus.

The van didn't get far in peak-hour traffic, especially with a screaming Thai nanny keeping up close enough to alert a traffic cop at the next intersection. The cop walked up to the van to ask questions. The kidnapper answered with gunfire but before the cop hit the ground he'd taken out one of the kidnappers. Next, the engine of the van failed. What is it with cars and crime? Surely, it's a false economy to take a broken-down car just because you know it'll be dumped.

Soon enough, the street corner is all police cars, emergency vehicles, Americans and the press. To avoid being killed immediately, the remaining gunman let the kid go while keeping a bead on the agent's wife, Joyce, next to him. To make his intentions clear, he'd taken wire from the broken VW, and tied back the trigger of his revolver, keeping it cocked with his thumb. The idea was that with just his thumb keeping the gun's hammer from springing, if he caught a bullet, then so would she.

Uncle was informed and was not happy. His men in the police force tried to trade places with the wife. However, the value of a Thai policeman is not especially high and the gunman refused. He would accept only one proxy victim, a TV-celebrity monk. Still, his thumb was getting tired under the pressure and he was keen on a deal.

The Americans at the embassy were enraged. And they wanted the gunman taken alive since they'd guessed who was most likely behind the snatch – Uncle. They saw the Thai SWAT-team was in place yet called in favours and issued threats to some top Thai generals. Uncle had his own man, too. A sharpshooter commando on the SWAT-team had been told to kill the gunman as soon as the wife was safe. Unfortunately, the weather interfered with everyone's plans for the day. It was hot, especially in the van.

The amount of sweat on the gunman's thumb reached a critical point, and bang! The DEA agent's wife takes a shot to her head, and among the chorus of 'No!'s there is a silent 'yes' with the sharpshooter ending the gunman's life and with it any chance of a link to Uncle.

It cost Uncle quite a bit to keep clear. In fact, he spent a year out of the country hoping the echoes would subside. Yet there's a cultural difference I've noticed between Asia and the Anglo-Saxon West. Our police forces are staffed by men and women who, generally, are not personally fussed with the outcomes of the organizations for which they work. We can suffer corporate embarrassment. While most transgressions in the East are forgotten once the people have moved on, that is not so in the USA and the world of English law. As though compensating for a relaxed attitude at an individual level, our police never forget and certainly never forgive. It takes a full Presidential pardon to be forgiven in America, and even that is seen as a political stunt, not true forgiveness.

Uncle returned to Thailand and his business continued, some of his family taking up the reins. On a morning, some years after the death of the agent's wife, he drove into the countryside beyond Chiang Mai, his driver at the wheel. The driver came to a stop just over a hill in the road, complaining of a flat tyre. The chauffeur moved to the rear of the car, lifting the trunk to fetch tools. Perhaps he called to Uncle, who gets out from the rear seat – unable to see the road behind. At that moment, a truck barrels over the hill swiping the side of the Mercedes and ending Uncle's life.

Later, the driver is questioned, as is the truck driver. The questioning is done under the control of the second in command of Uncle's organization, who is Chinese-Thai and most inscrutable. Perhaps the second-in-command knew what was to come.

Vengeance by the DEA? Almost certainly. But the accounts are not settled. Not by one life. All of Uncle's kind and kin are cursed. Then and forever.

I was enjoying my retirement. Despite the company of police, I was carefully relocating those things of quality I had built up. The art: the paintings, sculptures, fancy cameras – everything I wanted to preserve I moved into the new house so they could be boxed, hidden and then transported to safety. As for the cops, I was hoping to outspend them. I figured that since they were some kind of dedicated taskforce, focussed, as far as I knew on McMillan & Sullivan, they would not be able to spend forever without delivering the goods.

I'd go into the large State Library and allow the police to follow before tabbing atlases and chemistry books. Similarly, at registry offices, noting lists of names in ballpoint, leaving an underlying blank page in view. (They used an electrostatic device to read what I'd written from the indentations.) I'd make airline bookings in names that were new but meaningless. I'd drive to apartment blocks, getting lost in the corridors; walk up to houses and leave coloured paper in letterboxes. Make calls from payphones to companies around the world. All things that would generate a lot of pointless hours of office and legwork for those watching me. Soon, somewhere, the police paymaster at headquarters would call a halt.

Or so I thought.

About two months before Clelia and I were due to relocate to London, Michael invited me to dinner.

He had a problem.

He'd had problems before, and as we four sat at a corner table at a Chinese restaurant, I expected to hear of the usual problems that had arisen since he became an independent dealer. That's why I'd wanted Clelia and Marie with us. Since my retirement, Michael had lost his short-lived taste for international travel. He did what most dealers do: bought locally and sold locally. Yet he still had that tendency to show off in front of people before whom he made no attempt to conceal his sense of superiority. Reacting, his little helpers would turn on him. Soon enough, visitors with masks and guns would arrive at his door. That night, I wanted Clelia and Marie to see that while I'd help if Michael was under direct attack, I wouldn't go so far as to sell his stuff for him. Friend, I might be, but retirement would mean nothing, and during a delicate period of relocating, everything would be at risk – especially as I could have no appreciation of the source of Michael's dope. I'd be one step removed from people I couldn't assess. Local dealers run greater strategic risks than importers who have the luxury of secrecy. The girls were there to see me fairly, reasonably, declining to become unpaid partner. Unfortunately, the new problem was not so simple.

A month before that night, Michael had paid for a connection to a Thai businessman who would deliver to his door just about all the heroin Michael could handle. More than he could handle. The stuff came, usually, concealed in elaborate cutlery boxes, sandwiched between the lacquered layers of the large, flat trays of heavy and ugly knives, forks and spoons. Michael had given me a small lump. It was good.

Tommy, the travelling Thai, had arrived on a second trip a couple of days earlier and was staying at a modern inner-city hotel. Michael had yet to collect the boxload.

"Why's that?" I asked.

"The police are all over him," Michael said. "And he's not someone who'd normally notice that."

This Tommy was effectively a travelling salesman with contacts in Europe and the USA (I winced inwardly) whose fat address book kept him airborne year-round, stopping at Zurich to stuff banks with his millions. He didn't use couriers.

"He doesn't trust them," Michael said.

"He doesn't like to pay them," Marie suggested.

I had to know. "How much does he sell it to you for?"

Michael hesitated – I insisted.

"Two thousand an ounce," Michael looked to the Chinese waiters as though they might be spies. They were not.

I was wondering at Michael's rare piece of good fortune. That price was only a fifth of what the dope was worth.

"Michael," I took on the most serious expression I'm capable of, "how much did this Tommy cost you?" I meant, how much had Michael paid for the connection. Again, Michael hesitated. Clelia was becoming irritated.

"Tell David if you want his help," she said. "Or sort it out yourself."

"Fifty thousand. I've already paid."

"Who sold him to you?" I wanted to know.

This time, Michael wouldn't give.

"David, I gave my word I'd keep his identity secret. I promised. Imagine, if I'd promised you something…"

Michael droned on about honour but I wasn't listening. I was thinking, and there was no reason not to think aloud.

"So, some guy comes to you and says, 'Here, take my delivery man. He's worth millions to me but I don't want him anymore so I'll give him to you cheap. I just can't stand the thought of any more money and I love you so much I want you to have a long and rich life.'"

"He said he wanted out of the business," Michael quoted, suddenly not liking the sound of it so much. I continued.

"And one extra thing he tells you, Michael, *'Don't give anyone my name'*. Like who'd he mean, I wonder? Did this generous guy think you'd tell the Chief Commissioner of Police? Was he thinking you'd chat to passing strangers?"

Clelia spoke. "He told you not to tell David, didn't he?"

Marie's face confirmed that.

I paused, recovering. Tommy's hotel was a five-minute walk from *The Golden Duck*, our restaurant. I needed to meet this golden goose.

"Michael, you and Marie walk up to his hotel. You get on the hotel's house phone. Marie, get a house plan of the rooms from reception but don't make a fuss. Either way, bring him back with you for coffee. Don't let him bring dessert."

When Michael and Marie had left, I tried to answer Clelia's concerns. For sure, Michael had been sold a pup, although as yet I didn't know what kind of mongrel. Our options were all bad. If the feds were all over this Tommy, they'd want to hit just when the dope was changing hands. As it was, the dope was in one of the cutlery boxes in Tommy's hotel room. If Michael walked away from the deal, the cops would arrest Tommy, get the heroin and arrest Michael because of the communications they'd had. If Michael arranged a meet, picked up the stuff, he'd be arrested. Forced to arrest Michael, they'd collar me and hope something would give. In drug arrests, police go with what they have. My only hope was to try to pick up the dope, keep Michael safe and get Tommy out of the country.

Clelia probably tuned out as I thought aloud. In fact, she was thinking ahead of me.

"David, you know how I met Michael and Marie?" she said. "It was through Peter Howard."

Peter Howard was that low-level yet irritating dealer with an ego at home in the gutter despite his pretentions to class. He got his start in the hippie communes at Scotts Head along the New South Wales coast where carelessness tie-dyed with greed. He moved south to Melbourne where he married a squeaking midget whose choice of husband confirmed her wealthy Jewish parents' view of her poor judgement.

Although Howard had built some of the stereo boxes I'd used for smuggling, I knew he'd cheat at any opportunity. If Clelia's guess that Tommy had had been sold to Michael by Howard was true, the link would make sense. Howard had done a lot of travelling through Thailand and Tommy owned a guest house in Chiang Mai as well as a Thai-silk emporium.

What didn't add up was why a chiseller like Howard would ever sell on a prize connection like Tommy. There had to be a reason why he'd approached Michael.

What I didn't know then, and what you should know now, is this:

Sometime around the winter of 1981 – that's July in Australia – federal police landed in force upon Peter Howard's house. Tommy had just left the premises. They caught Howard trying to flush half a kilo of top-grade Thai heroin down the toilet bowl. He was bailed as he was a man of property. That is, his wife's big house. Howard was in the kind of trouble you can't get out of nicely. To get out of it, he made a deal to help the cops with a case that seemed to be drying up. I was that case. The police were not impressed by Howard's detailed account of what bad guys Michael and I were. They told him he'd have introduce a little poison into our world without letting me know.

Two other things I didn't know on the night of the Golden Duck. Tommy had an uncle in Thailand. He was *the* Uncle, the man the DEA had vowed to destroy.

Secondly, as we all sat eating lychees and plotting our next move, the feds were in Tommy's hotel, room 601. They'd just extracted a drill bit from the base of a large cutlery box. The white powder adhering to the drill tip confirmed to task-force Operation

Aries that over a year's work was about to reach a conclusion with mass arrests. Such was their hope.

Michael and I left our houses just after noon on Saturday, thirty-six hours after taking Tommy to the Chinese restaurant. I'd abandoned a plan to make the switch from Tommy's room by taking a hotel room below his. The Southern Cross Hotel was tight as a drum. That made sense – it was the hotel used for government conferences and his room was one reserved for government targets. Another clue Tommy's arrival had been anticipated.

The night before that Saturday, Michael and I had shaken our tails and picked up two superfast but plain-looking vehicles that we parked near the rendezvous point. That point was the large Mercy Hospital located in East Melbourne alongside a park near the city centre. The hospital had a useful geophysical feature. The park had been formed around a hill with the hospital in an effective gully. The ambulance entrance was on the far side, blocking signals from the transponder-mast atop police headquarters. As well, the tree-filled park acted as a giant earthing core, soaking up any reflected radio signals. It would be difficult for the police to talk to each other.

For our communications, I'd collected, that morning, a set of hand-held radios with frequency generating crystals specially cut to resonate between two standard frequencies. Imagine watching Channel 5½ on TV. We would not be overheard.

As it happened, we'd need all the edge we could get. Again, on the day, Michael and I had lost the police surveillance cars but Tommy had brought the cops straight to the meeting. He'd had to take a taxi from his hotel.

As I waited in the hospital lobby, I kept in touch with Michael using the microphone pinned under my jacket.

"Keep your engine running but stay off the streets," I muttered. Michael had positioned himself in a car park under a block of flats.

Tommy walked through the glass-door entrance of the hospital. I stood and drew him over to the lobby chairs. He sat.

"Tommy. You see the police today?" I asked.

"No police – I look hard."

Near an information counter stood a flower stall. I directed Tommy's gaze.

"See over there? There's usually a young woman selling flowers. Today it's a big lump of a man. And look at the guy over in the waiting room. He's sitting but talking to his knee…"

I went on pointing out two other certain surveillance operatives until Tommy got the point. Had I known more, I could have told Tommy of the suite of eight interview rooms and a dozen holding cells that had been booked for the day by Operation Aries detectives. Arrest warrants had been prepared for twenty-two people, including family and friends not connected with the smuggling operations. The sides were drawn.

I gave Michael the radio signal, counted to five, stood, then swiftly guided Tommy to the rear entrance – the narrow internal road where ambulances arrived with the injured. I heard a screech of tyres and hoped it was Michael's Lincoln. As we reached the footpath, I saw Michael's car speed up to the ambulance bay. At the same time, a large van backed over the rear exit; the exit Michael would need. The cops must have guessed this would be our exit, too.

I grabbed Tommy's shopping bag containing the cutlery boxes and dropped it through the opening window of Michael's car. He was already throwing the car's shift into reverse.

"Hi, Michael —" Tommy wanted to chat.

As Michael sped backward, almost skittling a couple of pedestrians, I took Tommy into the nurses' entrance of the hospital – a quick walk to the staff car park. Michael hit the side street and spun his wheels into a controlled one-hundred-and-eighty-degree turn.

The flower seller had given up his interest in horticulture and had stepped out to the ambulance bay. The knee-talker abandoned any secretiveness and was punching at his handheld radio. Tommy and I skip-stepped to the car park where I'd left my car the night before. It was a controlled car park with a glassed office controlling a boom gate. A woman was running into the car park office.

Tommy was keeping up now. "She policeman, too!"

"She wants them to stop my car," I said. "But we've a fence to jump."

We walked straight past my car and stepped over the low brick wall that surrounded the car park. The policewoman and another were in pursuit. Of course, Tommy and I had given the dope to Michael but police can't help themselves chasing everyone who runs. From the roadway, I just saw the tail of Michael's car about a half-mile away as he turned into another residential car park. Within two minutes, he'd be in one of the supercars but still within range of pursuit.

Tommy and I got into the fast Ford. I started and gunned the engine.

"We go to Michael?" Tommy asked.

"No hurry."

The wide tyres gripped the tarmac and I surged ahead, too fast for police yet I saw a tweaked Monaro turning in behind to follow me.

"We have to protect Michael," I told Tommy.

Within seconds, I was into the residential street Michael had just left. I sped to the T-junction and stopped. "Covered," I announced into my radio but I guess Michael had other things on his mind. I got out of the car and stepped to the middle of the roadway.

Weekdays, this road had two metal poles that blocked commercial vehicles from cutting through to save time on the main roads where during mornings, they'd be clogged with traffic. Weekends, the poles were folded flat into channels in the road surface. From my pocket, I took out keys and unfastened the holding locks. The previous night, I'd changed the padlocks for my own. This allowed me to raise the poles and block the end of the street. There would be no fast way out for the police cars. Before getting back to my car on the far side, I threw the padlock keys to the sidewalk. Just in time to see the pursuit cars heading our way.

They'd go no further.

I drove at moderate speed to the one safe house I'd kept on. Michael had keyed in the all-safe signal before, as agreed, he'd turned off our radio communication. We needed to let our police calm down for a few hours. They'd missed the dope, and I didn't want any rash arrests while their blood was up.

Police don't like it any more than we do when our plans don't work out. In civilized society, both sides return to their corners and prepare for the next round. Sometimes, though when one side or the other is listening too hard for the sound of the bell, they react to any sound at all. And that's just what the cops did.

3

With Tommy safely out of the country, I again stepped back to the life of a retired gentleman. I advised Michael to see Tommy offshore as soon as possible before the end of the year, then just a month away. Tommy was due money, and if unpaid, would be making spontaneous contacts, careless noises, sure to be picked up.

"Meet him in Hong Kong," I suggested to Michael. "Just set the date with him, that should hold him."

Michael, I could tell, didn't want to ask me for a new passport, or make any moves that might involve me to the point of equal partnership. He seemed relaxed now that he'd stashed the cutlery boxes. "Well, it's not like Tommy will fly in with more tableware until he's paid." Michael thought he had some time to rest.

On the chance that these loose ends might entangle me and Clelia, I brought forward our exit arrangements. Instead of a calm disposal of property, I made a transfer of title deeds to a businessman who would quietly file the changes and pay the taxes without the fuss of a public sale. Publicly, I made enquiries about investment portfolios and made noises using my tapped phone getting insurance on life and property. None of this seemed good enough. I had no control of the Tommy business, yet it was exactly that which posed the greatest threat.

The standard rule gave me few options. If you're close enough to a deal to get hurt, take control, and if you can't take control, get out. Our new documents would be ready in January.

Christmas and New Year celebrations were full, colourful and all family. It was a hot summer in Australia and everyone was at peace.

As Clelia's three sisters and their tiny children made lots of fun noise running through the glitter of New Year's decorations at her father's mansion, not everyone we knew was enjoying the season.

Tommy had heard nothing from Michael. Michael had given his reassuring messages to Marie to pass on, and she'd called her sisters in Colombia to pass on. And they had phoned from Bogota to Singapore where another sister lived. This was because Michael didn't want to be recorded over his phone. Instead, Marie was recorded speaking in Spanish, most of which had been intercepted by the Americans.

Why them? You recall the story of Uncle of the Golden Triangle? The Uncle whom the DEA had put to the sword? Well, as that man was the uncle of Tommy, he and all his links were on their list.

Tommy, who'd been making deliveries to the loathsome Peter Howard. Howard, who'd been caught flushing a platter of Tommy's dope as the cops kicked in his door. Howard, who'd then dealt his ace card to beat the rap. An ace in the form of, 'Sure, I'll give you McMillan-Sullivan.' Howard, who'd sworn Michael to secrecy. *'Whatever you do, don't tell David,'* and Michael who'd fallen for it, too flushed with the promise of his very own delivery boy and his own show, at last.

We had survived the Christmas of 1981 and the police had been patient. But Tommy, without clear word from Michael, had not.

Two days after Christmas he flew into Australia, landing at Perth in the west and taking a bus overland where he picked up a tail so blatant, even he noticed. He phoned Michael.

"Two men," Tommy announced. "They back me."

Michael freaked. Manfully, Michael told him to go away. He didn't have far to go. Having heard that conversation, the police felt their pursuit had gone as far as it could go. They arrested Tommy at the state border and held him incommunicado.

Of this, I knew nothing.

I'd had trouble sleeping that night. As Clelia dozed beside me, I sat up watching *Scott of the Antarctic*. Captain Robert Falcon Scott, making final, tragic diary entries as he froze in his tent. I'd been troubled by trivial events since the weekend. Most Sundays, we'd spend the day at Clelia's dad's place. Sascha, our dog would be with us, of course, and keen to jump in the car for any journey. That last Sunday, she wouldn't get in the car going back. I had to push her in. Spooked, I drove back at a crawl. Arriving home, I left Clelia in the car while Sascha and I checked out the place – I with a rifle in hand; Sascha with her nose in the air. I looked at our dog.

"What can you smell?"

She didn't answer but there was a scent she didn't like. I felt the police had been in. Yet a scan revealed no new surveillance electronics. So, what were they doing?

Tuesday morning, just as I flopped into sleep, I heard the rasp of a key in our front door lock. The door opened but jammed against the chain. A pause. Then, the slow rhythms of a sledgehammer shattering the glass and frame of the door. I looked at my rifle but knew from the steady, unrelenting pace of this attack it was police. Sascha looked at me as she stood. *'I told you so,'* she seemed to say.

Clelia was dressing in haste. A SWAT-team appeared; stomping into the bedroom in heavy boots. I was thrown to the floor by one as another stood on my back. Sascha had disappeared. Clelia sat down on the bed. We exchanged a look as though resigned to a bad day. *Men with guns came to our house* – the phrase was in my mind from an old conversation with Michael about night raiders. Did it matter who they are? They're still men with guns.

Within minutes, control of the house passed to Operation Aries task-force police, ten of them anyway, who fanned through the house carrying wads of empty plastic bags marked, EVIDENCE. Confident. The bags should've been labelled OPINION. The faces I saw knew me from covert viewings and countless photographs. Oddly, they didn't speak at first. How do people who know so much about each other from secrets make that formal introduction? Like uncomfortable relatives at a family funeral.

There was nothing at the house that deserved the name, 'evidence'. In fact, I was puzzled by the timing of their arrival. After the hospital switch, I felt sure they'd make their move next time Tommy arrived. Of course, he had, though I didn't know it. The day had come when the police wanted to do their police stuff to me. I was twenty-five and had defied them. It was time for me to pay. For Clelia to pay, perhaps. For all those of my world to be taught we were on the wrong side.

Clelia was kept in the bedroom. I wanted just a few seconds with her to say, *'It will be alright'*; I would make it alright, somehow. I looked around the room: at the furnishings, the pictures on the wall, at the tech spread, photographs and finally to the clothes I was wearing, everything with a story. Goodbye to all that.

I was questioned for two days and declined to speak. The cops had moved in panic. When they'd listened to Michael telling Tommy by phone to go away, they believed Tommy would never come back. Now, at least with him in the bag, they'd have something prejudicial to parade in court.

Police moved into my house as I moved into the old Melbourne prison, Pentridge. Australian law is British law, which is to say, like American law without the safety of strict procedures for admitting evidence. In any jurisdiction, the chances of freedom following arrest are slim. Sure, we had lawyers, technicalities, but in a calm way, I merely wondered, like a doomed animal, if the massive jaws might slip so I could escape. They did not.

The police were not kind to our house. While living there, they barred entry to family and partied hard. They burned paintings, stole things of interest, got drunk and shit in the pool. I was dragged around town as though on a tour to my office and houses for a final viewing before destruction. A court confiscation order soon took hold. Accounts seized, property held before faked auctions saw titles change to friends and family of police.

Everything that was not destroyed went to police. I'm not sentimental about objects. A pity about the art, though. And the cameras, those icons of Byzantium. The long rolls of film torn from their canisters before processing. It was enough I could keep the specifications in my head, and should you ask I could detail all that was made and touched. Well, not quite everything. And, I would have to find a way for Clelia to be freed.

A problem appeared for the prosecution because of the hasty arrests meant that no drugs had been found and of course no one would confess. There was no one who could testify to having seen any drugs, and no idea how they were sold. To shake the tree, dozens of additional arrests were made. All the couriers were questioned. They didn't talk. So, the police turned on families. Clelia's sisters were questioned, my mother and even my school friends were arrested, although soon freed. Still nothing. Bail for Michael, me and the girls was refused and we were sent to the city's hundred-year-old prisons. For the first days, I'd contrast the horsehair mattress, steel bed and stone walls of my cell with the last comfort of my linen sheets and pillows. I dumped those thoughts. Tin plates, tasteless food and open showers were my life now. A metallic sound from prison talk radio and endless clanging of steel doors replaced selected music. Survival demanded forgetting any thoughts of restoration. There was the trial to consider, and one with no useful evidence or testimony for the prosecution. I wondered how the police would deal with that after having spent so much on the fruitless investigation.

About that time, I was trying to make a difficult pitch to Michael.

Our lawyers thought we had a fighting chance in court. We'd all been charged with conspiracy to import drugs. We might win the case, and certainly Clelia and Marie would be acquitted even if Michael and I went down – yet for the girls, it would still mean two years in prison awaiting trial. I was prepared to take a plea if the charges were dropped for Clelia. Michael wanted, perhaps sensibly, to be patient. I wasn't. I was selfish about Clelia. I would do almost anything to see her free. Once she was safe – the plan was that she'd go to the villa in Tuscany – I'd be able to take care of myself without any limits on my actions.

Not only did I fail to sell the idea to Michael, I couldn't even sell it to the police. They'd agree, they said, only if I agreed to rat others out. That would've been, simply, ill-mannered.

I would soon care nothing for the law, the trial or for myself.

A psychopathic street girl had been recruited by the police to get information from Clelia and Marie as all three, along with half-a-dozen others, shared a small dormitory in the women's prison. The use of cellmates' testimony in trials is desperate but not so rare.

The cell-dormitory of the women's prison holding Clelia and now the informer Danielle was a wooden building locked within iron bars and mesh. Danielle was promised her freedom if she extracted useful admissions from our girls. She wasn't having any success. She became frustrated and set fire to the cell.

That part of the prison burnt to the ground. Some of the women were saved. Danielle, the hopeful informer was dead.

So, too, were Clelia and Marie.

Clelia and I were best friends before we became anything more. Through laughter, we told each other of all those we'd known before. We came to see people through the same eyes, the colours of our world through the same lens. She was a tough girl to the outside world, shy in private silences, yet embracing everything living. To us, the Earth without each other would be an alien world.

Clelia's father was generous. He forgave me my crime in allowing his daughter to be taken and held by such a dangerously determined enemy. I have never been so forgiving. The loss of any human life is the loss of the irreplaceable. That must seem trite until one thinks carefully of how much in our world is, in fact, replaceable. Just about all of it transforms and is evolving. And to love someone truly, it must be that you know that one truly, so the loss is not mere absence but unrepairable damage.

The deaths changed everything. For the police, an opportunity to make up for the deficiencies of the case. They puffed out a mist of rumours. To distance themselves from any culpability in Clelia's and Marie's deaths, talk arrived at newspapers, prison authorities and lawyers on all sides that we – mainly, that I – was having all potential witnesses killed, presumably starting at home.

Here is part of a conversation (relayed to a lawyer after the trial) between the DEA agent, Bill Shenkmann, flown in from Washington, and the head of the Aries taskforce. I paraphrase, but:

"The girls' deaths are a real asset for us," said the Australian. "We get McMillan and Sullivan put in high security. It won't be easy for lawyers to see the bastards once they're in there, and anyway, we can hear every word from the prison tapes."

"Is there any truth to the fire being a drug killing?" asked Shenkmann.

"None. But the advantage is that it'll spook these couriers who won't talk. Not only that, they'll say they're in fear for their lives, or they will after we talk to them. McMillan will be in supermax for years and there'll be no trial for a year. No committal, either."

"A what?" Shenkmann hadn't heard the term, committal.

"What you'd call an arraignment. Without that, we go straight to trial. They won't have time to put investigators on anything we say."

Shenkmann had doubts. "You've found no drugs, have you? I think we can help you on that. Lots of stuff on the uncle and plenty of finds."

"No need to worry," said the Australian. "We'll fly in a few kilos. Put it in the courtroom so all can see."

"We'd never get away with that in a US court. We wouldn't want to see your boy McMillan hook up with Marchandat." That was Tommy's family name.

"This is not America," the taskforce head stressed. "Besides, we'll have one of our own on the jury."

True to the policeman's prediction, the couriers folded. In exchange for testimony, seven of my former co-conspirators were given a guarantee of immunity from prosecution by the federal Attorney-General.

Michael and I were hurriedly transferred to the new supermax prison, built for terrorists but filled with domestic psychopaths.

A funeral was held for the girls. Michael and I were termed too much of a risk to attend, even if shackled. We were refused representation at the coroner's inquest. Clelia's dad's lawyer was there, but under police threats, he caved in. The coroner allowed the fix: Clelia was accused of murdering Marie. As for the prison, jailers pointed out that the alarm bell was usually set off by troublesome women. Prison officers were given medals for bravery.

I can't see much value in detailing every day of my trial. What's the point? Trials are often little more than democracy's clumsy formalities along the path of sending people to jail. Talking too much of it recalls 1960s comedian Lenny Bruce in his final days on stage ranting about his obscenity charges – a wad of courtroom transcripts in one hand, his microphone in the other.

Still, there's a few things of the trial important to this story of the hunted.

As the trial date neared, we had lawyered our way out of supermax and squeezed into the ramshackle squalor of the old prison. Who were we? Michael, I and Tommy, of course, and a new co-defendant, Brendan Healey, a hippie hauled south from Scotts Head's communes. Brendan had met Tommy in Thailand while backpacking. Peter Howard, true to form, had secured himself immunity from prosecution as a trade for testifying against us all.

In a move I couldn't help but salute for its ruthlessness, Howard expressed fear from Tommy's Asian links and so had 24/7 protection, with a team of police living in huts in the large rear garden of his house. This gave him cover for the year until the trial to deal as much dope as possible, knowing he couldn't be busted. The cops would drive him to Melbourne's red-light-district where he'd peddle his stuff in the cafés while his police kept watch, looking on ruefully.

So, it was just the four of us remaining as the accused, facing a dozen charges in the trial to be held at the state Supreme Court. All conspiracy charges. The conspiracy charge is one loaded with advantages for any prosecutor. Rather than the difficult charge of proving some crime happened, it's necessary only to prove the players agreed that they might do something illegal. If that sounds vague, it's because it is meant to be. The charge allows hearsay evidence, accusations by people not in court, and, importantly, a drug charge without any drugs. Like a murder trial without the body and, in this case, a maximum penalty of life imprisonment.

Still, a drug-free trial is something prosecutors don't like. It sounds thin, and after the deaths of Clelia and Marie, the police wanted some pre-trial publicity.

For a year after Clel's death, I'd been unable to take an interest in the case. Even so, in the weeks leading up to the hearing, we were in a good courtroom position. Sort of. Unfortunately, my diamond dealers had been scared into silence, and you can't call witnesses who won't co-operate – unless you are the law.

Days, Michael and I would work in the prison's number-plate factory; nights, we'd work on detailing defence witnesses who wouldn't mind earning the lifelong hatred from the cops. The police, however, had been active, too.

Three weeks before the start of the trial, Michael's friend and accountant, Max, got a call from a visitor. The man said he was in contact with Michael's sister in the Philippines. He said he'd been sent by Lord Tony Moynihan. You might recall him as the English expat and fraudster who'd tried to tangle me in that cock-fight betting sting in Manila.

The visitor said he was a commando formerly in the British Army. That he had come to free us from prison. By helicopter. He said the chopper would airlift us from the exercise yard of the prison. Then, he'd hide us in a specially rigged interstate truck, and take us to Sydney from where a yacht would sail us to the safety of President Marcos's Philippines. All for the modest fee of $250,000. Oh, and could we kindly provide $50,000 upfront now, in cash?

You might think that when awaiting trial in jail, the offer of a helicopter escape from professionals might be unusual. Not in our case. In fact, if every offer of a helicopter escape made to us were true, the prison would've had to refit the guard towers as air-traffic control centres.

In the early days after my arrest, I might have gone for a helicopter escape just for the hell of it. But not then. Especially from someone referred by a notorious fraudster. We passed on a polite message: thanks for your interest but we'll play out the trial before panicking.

Yet there was more to this helicopter offer than a simple confidence scam by Moynihan. Not only was Lord Tony a scammer but he'd been an informer for police and spy agencies for many years. It was no offer at all. No sooner had the 'commando' left Manila for Melbourne, Tony Moynihan called the Australian Federal Police to tell them the next phase of the operation could go ahead, giving commando Percival's flight details. From the moment he landed in Australia, police logged his every move.

Lord Tony had told him, *'Percy, we can scam these druggies for a fortune. But they might have people watching you, so make some very public moves checking out dockside transport – I'll give you a connection for the helicopter.'* The connection was another of Tony's scammers. Percival Hole, the commando (in fact never in any army) was too busy drooling at the prospective dollars to wonder why he had to put on such an elaborate charade. Tony knew: the cops would want impressive evidence of a real escape attempt.

In fact, all the experts Percy met were policemen and policewomen. Even the de-bugging expert was a policeman who put in a bug at the hotel where Percy met Max the accountant, rather than taking bugs out. Percy was a fall guy, too. A day before a disappointed Percy was to leave Australia, police – in uniform this time – steamed into the hotel room and, as planned, arrested Percy and poor, honest, Max.

The pre-trial police publicity machine kicked in to high gear. Six days before jury selection began, the following headline splashed across morning papers: DRUG GANG IN JAIL CHOPPER BID above a story that claimed machine guns would take out any interfering prison officers. Michael, Tommy and I were slapped, kicked and punched across the prison compound and back to supermax. Brendan, the hippie – as hippies sometimes are – was spared, for now.

The trial began.

It would run for six months, Monday to Friday. Saturdays reserved for lawyer's visits and Sundays to worship the Lord and all His works – though remarkably few in the supermax prison.

The charges? Nine of my courier runs, the Mercy Hospital switch and the supposed delivery of a cutlery box to Brendan. A SWAT-team would stage an elaborate show taking us each day to court in chains, in which we'd remain while in the dock. A fundamental difference between US and English (as with Australian) criminal trials is that the accused remain in the dock – a wooden box – rather than seated by our lawyers. So, it's important to match lawyer with client. Michael had a smarty-pants, good on technical points; Tommy a nervous, puffy loser while Brendan had a Catholic. How's that matter? Well, your Catholic lawyer puts his soul out there on your behalf and Ian Hayden was willing to take on Brendan's sins. He didn't so much as defend him as absolve him. I mention this – and the points below – just in case you find yourself facing a life sentence in court. Couldn't happen? No, of course not.

Now, your lawyer should be a better version of you, your flaws demonstrated as virtues. If you are then acquitted, it is as the person you could be, not as you are. For example, a thief is best represented by a lawyer who shows generous spirit. I was matched with a tall and noble Abe Lincoln type. Regardless of what that says of me, when Stratton Langslow spoke, the jury wanted to follow his lead.

Until recently, those accused were permitted to challenge potential jurors without stating reasons. This meant having just those seconds between a name being called and before the juror walks to the jury box. One man, when called leapt to his feet, grabbed an overnight bag at clenched between his knees, and almost ran with excitement to take his place. My lawyer, by my side (the only time he's allowed so close) felt we should stop him but we'd exhausted our twelve peremptory challenges. Yet, despite his alarming enthusiasm, he would become the often-neutral jury foreman – more interested in playing lawyer than lawman.

The police had their way with at least one of the panel. Although serving police cannot sit on juries, that hurdle was overcome by sneaking a trainee policewoman among the twelve. In fact, the trial had later to halt for a day as she took her exams.

Prosecutors take their chances when using an indemnified witness who is, by admission, party to a crime. Their characters start out bad, and don't get much better. George the Greek seemed impossibly slimy, complaining of his losses in coming to court, despite keeping free by dodging a prison sentence if what he claimed was true.

The police had dressed Secretary Sue down for her day in court but even pale make-up and a dowdy print dress couldn't conceal her past. I, too, was surprised that she'd had a conviction for prostitution in her late teens. How best, then, to paint her as a liar?

First, Stratton set a price. The value of avoiding a few years in jail – certainly worth something.

"So, you wouldn't lie for money?" queried my lawyer to Sue. "I'm asking – if you had a client who asked you to pretend. To pretend you're a milkmaid, a nurse, the schoolteacher, perhaps. Would you play along?"

"It never happened," said Sue, adjusting her dress, almost against her will.

"But if it did, would you play along? Say whatever words were needed to be convincing?"

"I suppose so," said Sue.

"So, if the money was right, if you were getting your side of the bargain, you'd use the words the situation demanded?"

There could be but one answer. Yes.

Peter Dale, the courier extraordinaire and fabulist, was less successful as witness for the prosecution. The police had drawn on Peter's chameleon nature to transform him into a perfect witness. Yet, like the other indemnified witnesses, he'd seen no drugs and could testify only that I'd *told* him he was carrying dope. Yet I'd never said so, in precise terms, and the absence of a memorized text proved his undoing. That, and Peter's odd new transformation into a fantasy undercover cop. Stratton Langslow, my lawyer, focussed on the words exchanged.

"So, how did David tell you?"

"He said we'd be taking the product out of Bangkok," Peter gripped the witness box like a sea captain his helm.

Stratton, "He said, *product*?"

"No, the heroin."

"What exact words did David use?"

Peter rolled his head and looked to the police detectives in the gallery, his new pals, ruefully as though – all coppers together now – he'd want to say, *'These damn lawyers'*. Then spoke, "David said we will take the heroin from Thailand. That's what I told Bob and Phil. I mean Detective Inspector Henderson and Sergeant Phil Cramer. We were trying to nail this down," Peter, now in *Miami Vice* mode, "—these drug guys don't make it easy."

Unhappy with the performance of the couriers as witnesses, the prosecution brought in the one insider the police had owned all along: Peter Howard. Although Howard had been arrested along with everyone else, he'd agreed to testify – his name was mud around town anyway – but surely, he'd have to give up the dope trade he loved. In fact, Howard's real passion was for getting the edge over people, and his deal with the cops ran all Howard's way. On the stand, he spoke of swindles and scams, of tax frauds and money laundering. Knowing he could never be prosecuted for any crime to which he then admitted, he cleaned his past, his present and made no attempt to lighten his thoroughly black history.

The jury had known of the immunity deal, yet were puzzled that anyone could confess on oath to such infamy yet keep clean. The foreman, halfway through Howard's testimony, raised the question.

"Your Honour, is this witness already sentenced?"

The trial judge moved uncomfortably in his chair. "The state, for better or worse, has agreed this man will never be charged," Judge Murray straightened himself. "Sometimes in the interests of justice, some are punished while others go free. That is not your concern."

The jury's concern, the judge seemed to be saying, was to keep the accused in prison. And the jury didn't cotton to being side-lined.

A long trial can take on a life of its own, and this trial ran for half a year, the jury taking it on as adopting a troublesome princeling. From our point of view, there's nothing wrong with dragging out a complex trial. Never act in haste. The more time goes on, so onward amount the errors prosecutors are likely to make, errors only the now-educated and capricious jury is likely to punish.

Before ending these trial notes, just two examples of the reaction of self-schooled jurors.

Witnesses, especially professional witnesses such as police and forensic scientists, come to court, pick up the bible, swear an oath and, if they wish, lie their heads off. The jury had heard old-school police tell fibs out of corporate loyalty while others, like George the Greek, swear oath and lie to suit their purposes. Some, without professional interests, even told the truth. Yet even lying witnesses had the courage to tell their whoppers by swearing on the holy bible.

One policeman took the stand and immediately distinguished himself from all the others – there would be one hundred and nineteen witnesses – by saying that his ethics would prevent him swearing upon the Good Book. He was an atheist. The jury seemed offended. Not simply because he was a declared godless heathen – he, after all, swore some limp promise to tell the truth – but because in doing so, he appeared to hold himself above everyone else. Somehow purer than his porkie-spouting police colleagues in that he wasn't willing to dishonour the King James version. I remember his evidence related to the hippie on trial, and was sniffed at by our jury, I could tell.

Brendan had another piece of luck, jury-wise.

Brendan's mother, a gentle, grey-haired woman, was called to testify. It is with reluctance that any prosecutor calls upon the mother of anyone on trial. A risk. The question was a simple one of whether a car belonging to Howard had been parked in a driveway. The senior prosecutor wisely spoke softly, apologised for bringing her to the court, asked his question and then left her alone. I'm sure if Mrs Healey had answered, 'Aliens abducted my son!' that this most experienced lawyer would have nodded as though that were a perfectly rational answer and sat down.

By contrast, the QC's junior prosecutor couldn't help himself. He got to his feet, beaded an eye at the lavender-scented lady and demanded of the mum, "Mrs Healey, your son kept some odd company, did he not?"

The jury were horrified. Brendan's mother stammered and flushed; she didn't know what to say. The jury was plainly disgusted that the prosecution – the government – would ask any mother to assist in sending her child to prison. The senior lawyer pulled roughly at the young prosecutor's gown, but it was too late. In time, Brendan the hippie would be acquitted of all charges.

As I say, that jury became owners of the trial. As it should be.

The prosecution had put on a show – the jury knew of the great (yet fake) helicopter escape as nightly news ran dramatizations using police choppers. And each morning the spectacle of Michael and I rattling in to court in chains. Yet the show still had no drugs.

As a remedy, federal police flew to Thailand, bought two kilos of heroin and brought it to Australia before introducing it as evidence. An expert witness testified that just this type of heroin was used by smugglers. A special table was erected in front of the jury box, and the bags of white powder were set in place each day, staging an impressive display as an armed police team marched it in talking in military codes under their black Kevlar armour.

This theatrical touch was arranged by DEA agent Bill Shenkmann who had flown in from Washington to testify to Tommy's villainy and my opportunities. From the stand, Shenkmann looked at me as though he knew me. He did.

When I was starting out as a smuggler, I'd begun with smuggling runs of hashish from New Delhi. That financed the ambitious plan to load a tonne of Thai marijuana from Phuket, refuelling in Malaysia and the Cocos Islands before landing in Western Australia. This was an overreaching scheme at any age, and one that violated a basic rule: never invest more than a third of your assets in any one plan. In case of failure there could be no trading back from the loss. The money went to Thailand but the buyer disappeared. As a warning, my apartment was completely gutted, every possession taken, every stick of furniture. Even my clothes. Apparently, my little importation would have risked exposure of a secret American operation that, in the mid-seventies, used Australia as a transhipment point. It was this DEA agent who'd hobbled my financier. I was eighteen and bounced back but Shenkmann never forgot me.[5]

All but two of my diamond traders had been scared off, so I supplemented the weakness of my defence by speaking to the jury from the dock for three days. As the trial grizzled to an end, everyone was exhausted.

The jury left to deliberate. The following day they returned, announcing that they were immovably deadlocked. The judge wasn't having it. He sent them back out to think again. They went out – and stayed out. On the third day, they asked for two of the

---

[5] For details of my early misadventures, see *Escape: The Past*, 2011, Monsoon Books

exhibits: $80,000 in cash taken from my office desk and the two kilos of heroin brought in by the DEA as an 'example'. As the judge squirmed over their entitlement to handle any of the exhibits, Michael shot me an impressed look.

"I'd do the same in their shoes," I said.

His Honour persuaded the jurors not to play with the exhibits, and the week ended with no verdict, despite an extra day of deliberations on Saturday. Around 5pm, the foreman advised the tipstaff he had something to say.

"Your Honour," the foreman spoke, "we're tired. We'd like Sunday off."

That, they got. A bus was arranged and the twelve took to the countryside for a picnic. Our Sunday jailers allowed our lawyers to order us some Chinese takeaway, minus the chopsticks.

Monday afternoon, the foreman seemed to have another question. Everyone scrambled back into court. In fact, the jury had an answer: the verdict.

Michael, Tommy and I were acquitted of all charges except one. Brendan, the hippie, was freed. And for Judge Murray, even a one-charge conviction was enough.

The three of us were sentenced to a minimum of fifteen years' imprisonment on different counts. Michael and Tommy for the hospital switch with the cutlery box while I was convicted of the courier disaster where John – the London bodyguard – had been jumped at Bangkok airport. This meant ten years' prison time before parole. Perhaps I'd earned the punishment for being careless. During the trial, I'd learned that Paul Sigg – who'd provided John's identity – had secretly shopped him to the police before he left. And it was to Sigg that I'd entrusted $30,000 get-out-of-jail money for John. As it was difficult for me to travel, I'd sent Sigg to Thailand with instructions to use the money with my contacts. He'd later told me he'd been picked up by the police in Singapore and lost the money. In fact, he was never under surveillance. He just pocketed the money. None of this he admitted to the police, yet they knew. Although the traitor had come with good credentials it was careless of me to allow anything to prevent me freeing a fallen courier. Despite the courtroom betrayal by the couriers, I still held that duty of care. After all, most people are weak, and if that frailty harms those who are stronger, who is at fault?

We were kept in the cold supermax prison within a prison in Melbourne. Looked upon from the air the complex - built to house forty-eight – looked like a giant spider, scaled walkways leading as legs to each section, six cells to a branch. Communication with guards by intercom yet no space anywhere that was beyond the eyes of prison officers who operated electronically closed doors. Even the shower was in view within bullet-resistant glass. Inside my cell, all the fittings were steel bolted over concrete, including the bed, a solid block. The sink and toilet, icy steel. My first transfer from there, to the old prison, had felt as some kind of release. Now, again in supermax because of the phantom helicopter escape, the place smelled depressingly familiar – of machine parts and brick dust. An isolation exacerbated by the madness of the guards who would enliven their nightshifts by steaming into the cells in the middle of the night, utterly trash the place, then leave inmates in the darkness trying to refold plastic blankets into a memory of comfort.

Months into the sentence, I still had the case papers and a pile of cassettes taken from the surveillance bugs and telephone taps. All else was gone. Houses, money, photographs, even clothes. I'd sit in the cell wearing compulsory white overalls listening to the audio fragments that amounted to echoes of my lost life.

Using a cheap tape player, I could reconstruct days when I was away from home, clicking between the bug in our kitchen and the voices from phone calls. Of one such lost day, I listened to the tape in the bare cell: Clelia was walking through the kitchen, whispering to Sascha the dog. I couldn't make out what she was saying. Her sister then phoned. At one point, Clelia's sister asked,

"What's wrong? Are you crying?"

Clelia paused before saying, "No. I'm okay."

"Is it David?"

"No, it's nothing."

I wondered then, and over the years, just what had upset her. But of course, I will never know.

During the first year, I was returned to court for another trial. The charge was elaborate: conspiracy to pervert the course of justice by not attending the previous drug trial. And the evidence of that conspiracy? The helicopter escape plan. Sure, the prosecution accepted that there was no helicopter and no intention by the conman that there would be any escape; that it was just a trick to extract money. But, said the judge, we *might* have thought it real.

The trial was an extraordinary parade of bad law and prejudiced lawfolk. I note that just as someone who's been in a few trials, not a just a whining defendant. But as mad as it was, there's nothing worth saying other than this advice given to me by a top lawyer: 'There's no law when it involves drugs or druggies'. I was sentenced to a further year in prison. Michael and Tommy weren't charged – I was younger and some thought I should have extra time in prison – and we were quickly sent to different sections of the supermax prison.

The Jika Jika facility, as the supermax complex was called, was intended to house terrorists. Australia had a shortage of terrorists so the place was filled with madmen. The inmates were even crazier. Of the five other prisoners on my block, four were murderers and one a failed killer. He'd detonated explosives under the bed of an inmate in the old prison. The bed had been blasted to the ceiling of the cell, deafening the man but leaving him alive. The explosives had been triggered by wire from beyond the cell window. It was the ingenuity of the device that had brought the bomber to supermax. More successful killers in my block included a Yugoslav immigrant who'd stabbed his bank manager for failing to approve a loan for a journey to Rome. When asked the purpose of the trip, the Macedonian announced, 'I want to kill the Pope.' I wondered if His Holiness had ever thanked the manager's family.

Another inmate had knifed to death a point-duty policeman before calmly walking into a bar and announcing that he was Jesus Christ, while a less religiously observant fellow prisoner had thrown a farmer down a well while working the outback.

Each day, after the electronic doors were released, we'd move from our cells to a dayroom to sit on plastic chairs in front of a plastic table. That would be it. A day's activity. Like all prisons, time out of cell is set by the time of a single shift of the staff.

Most days were bad, some days worse. Early in the sentence, I'd met a man who was serving thirty years for kidnapping a busload of schoolchildren. Ted was easy to talk to because he'd been a teacher. We passed each other some mornings as I'd walk down to the concrete, high-walled and caged yard to secretly water the tiny weeds that grew through a few of the cracks. The yard cage was heavy mesh but in some years, the wind would blow seeds over the walls.

"Watering your garden, Dave?' said Ted as he mounted the steps to return to his side of the block.

"Coming along fine, Ted," I said. "I think one's a dandelion."

Ted was carefully cutting his hands with a hobby-knife blade, making sure to miss his veins. I noticed, then, the feet of one of his block-mates poking out from a wall corner of the yard.

"Dandelions are hardy perennials, Dave." Ted threw the blade to the ground. "Should grow year-round."

I raised my plastic teacup. "The screws probably know I've been watering," I said, "but to hell with them."

"My thoughts exactly," Ted said as he entered the building, wiping blood across his white jumpsuit. The effect was to look as though he'd been fending off a knife attack.

A couple of minutes later my time in the yard was cut short.

"McMillan," said a raspy voice over the loudspeaker, "back inside."

As I turned to step inside, I saw Ted's companion, lying on the ground, dead. The veins of his neck had been carved open. They'd been friends until recently.

When my court hearings ended, I began serious thought of escape. A real escape, not falling into phoney stings as with the helicopter con. While the old jail had potential, the supermax would be difficult.

Among those in the high-tech prison, there was a few still sane enough to make worthy attempts. The essential tool for any escape is a steel-cutting hacksaw blade. Getting the blades past the metal detectors was possible if sealed in the rubber soles of shoes where they wouldn't be scanned but visits were restricted to one prisoner at a time in a special room, often with one or two guards watching.

When a fellow inmate, Colin, told me he was planning to make a try, I followed his progress with great interest. He'd managed to persuade a visiting friend to sneak in a dozen six-inch lengths of hacksaw blade. Colin then got through the after-visit strip search (explaining away the blood in his underwear as haemorrhoids), and got to work on his plan the following week.

Over two nights, Colin cut the bolts of the floor rails that secured his sliding cell door. Then, on the night, after 9.00pm, he simply tilted the freed base of his cell door, and crept out beneath the corridor camera. The view by camera of the last cell was only partial. The guards patrolled once each hour, yet that allowed time to cut loose a bar from the door to the dayroom. He used the bar to smash through the layers of toughened glass of the dayroom door. Squeezing through, Colin cut his chest on glass fragments but still managed to clean up and hide himself in the corner of the dayroom before the next patrol. There was a movement sensor in the dayroom but the guards had come to ignore it as it seemed oversensitive. In fact, I'd set up a couple of devices to trigger the sensor between 6.00pm lock-up and 9.00 pm. (One device used a laundry basket balanced on the edge of a bench. The basket was held in position by two shoestrings tied from the basket to a sink top. I'd twisted the strings and frozen the join in a block of ice, made in the dayroom refrigerator. When the ice melted, the basket fell off the bench to the floor. The guards had taken ten minutes to respond. Finding nothing suspicious, they left.)

From the dayroom, Colin then began work on another glassed and barred dividing wall that led to a corridor which in turn led to the exercise yard. Colin later reported that he was so drained by his efforts to that point, that he ate a dozen oranges whole, fruit that had rolled to the floor from an earlier alarm-triggering device. It took him until 4.00am to cut and smash his way to the darkened exercise-yard corridor where he faced another barrier. A steel roller door blocked the exit to the yard, and he ground down three more hacksaw blades to cut the hardened steel of the padlock that secured the roller door at its base. Yet he was through to the yard by 5.00am, hands bloodied from gripping his blades.

The next obstacle was the heavy wire cage that covered the exercise yard. Colin climbed to the top of the concrete and glass observation pod that jutted into the yard. From there, with only five inches of effective blade remaining, Colin worked on the steel clips holding the wire mesh shroud. Beyond the mesh, only passable barriers and grass fields separated the supermax complex from the outer wall of the old jail. Just one cut short of freedom, the last of Colin's blades snapped. By 6.00am, as the morning-shift guards arrived, Colin was spent. Exhausted, this man previously fit enough to jump from floor to table top hands-free, had no more to give. The guards had to carry his limp body from the pod canopy, in grudging admiration of the superhuman efforts made. A year was added to his sentence.

After Colin's failure, I began taking in escape stories. Mostly failures, and surprisingly few attempts considering the long sentences most of my fellow inmates were serving. Groups like to plot escapes but rarely act on those plans. It seemed that loners were more likely to succeed. There's a strong advantage in acting alone. You know your strengths and weaknesses and can act immediately on decisions made. Even so, with the right team, three could be better than one, providing added strength and reach by joining body lengths. However, the selection of potential accomplices in the supermax were limited and of poor quality. Mostly psychopathic murderers whose victims were always weaker, often cornered and surprised. And my friend Michael had been taken to a separate unit but he was holding to a faint hope for a High Court appeal. (That appeal would take seven years and came to nothing.) If I teamed up with psychopaths, I'd have to cut loose from them soon after the wall. They were not people who could easily blend into society. Besides, a manipulating, intimidating nutter would, by nature, hope to use my resources ruthlessly for his own benefit.

Another question: why escape? I could survive the ten years' imprisonment but should I sacrifice those years? Life on the run in the western world is a tough one. As well, Anglo-American law never forgives; never says, enough is enough. I'd be pursued forever. I had family I loved. Could I settle for the life of a recluse in some strange land? I was young and decided to stay. Looking back, probably a bad decision.

Even so, I knew that soon and forever I'd ask myself if I could have escaped from that anti-terrorist electronic zoo. If only there were some way to answer that question, perhaps I could serve my sentence at rest.

A few months later, I stood in the corridor of my six-man unit talking to the officer who, behind his glass bubble, controlled the sliding electronic doors of the cells, walkways and dayrooms of each side.

"I'm busy tonight," he said. "Everybody seems to want something at once." He nodded to the showers on my side. Four of us had taken showers in rapid succession. "I'm lit up like a Christmas tree." He was referring to his door-control panel.

I leaned into the intercom. "Won't your mate help with the panel?" I asked.

"He's a crossword nut," said the officer. "Only moves for his cup of coffee."

True enough, his colleague that night seemed screwed to his chair in the observation pod.

In the opposite unit, a mirror set-up of our own unit, five inmates sat playing cards at a table wedged against the near wall, which partially blocked a clear view of the players. Only their heads could be seen as they leaned in to drop cards.

Between the players' dayroom and the observation pod – itself a glassed-in control centre, shaped as a tram carriage – was a poorly lit corridor leading to the exercise yard. Inside the corridor stood The Artist – Trevor – working on yet another of his ugly, savage canvases. There was no intercom in the corridor, and Trevor had to tap on the window to get the guard's attention when he wanted something. He'd been given permission to paint in a space alone following complaints from other inmates about the oil-paint fumes.

"I don't blame him for not wanting to work in his cell," I said to the guard. "The smell's overpowering."

Trevor tapped on the corridor window to get attention. He mimed choking and suffocating.

"Just a minute," mouthed the guard before tapping a button in three short bursts.

The outer roller door was raised a few feet, letting in cool air. Only once the roller door was again closed would the guard briefly open yet another intervening door to release the strong odour of oil paint. The guard kept his eye on Trevor before re-sealing the corridor.

In the dayroom, one card player was standing, laughing ruefully as he threw down his cards. I suppose if someone chose to add up the combined sentences of the card players, their minimum term would amount to almost two hundred years. The Artist himself was serving two life terms for contract killings. Just one of the players was serving less than ten years, a bank-robbing acquaintance of mine. Still, the stakes were high.

"Sorry to be a pest," I said to the guard behind the control panel. "Mind if I duck into my cell to boil some water for tea?" The electric kettles had been banned from the dayrooms ever since Chopper Read had emptied a full jug over the face of another inmate to settle an argument.

"Yeah. Okay," the guard replied, a little flustered as he tried to keep track of his panel lights. "It's lock-up soon, hurry."

Just over the guard's shoulder, I could see Trevor's easel nudge forward, as Trevor reached to catch it with narrow-eyed annoyance.

I held the guard's attention. "Sorry, I'll be quick."

This guy was one of the few reasonable guards. The poor bastard.

One by one, the near-invisible card players were finding excuses to get into the cell corridor as the next man would call for the dayroom door to be opened. Trevor the Artist was a great coffee drinker that night, too.

And one by one, they crept low into the walkway corridor where Trevor was painting. Soon, four of them were huddled under Trevor's easel. When the Artist requested a change of air, they all moved to the roller door, and then into the caged exercise yard.

The trick to the breakout was in not having to rely on hacksaw blades, only distraction. As the last card player played to mop heads with great animation, the four climbed up the cage to where it met the roof of the main building. Although much concrete and reinforcement had been set above the cell ceilings and walls from the inside, the access to the utility space above – from outside – was through pop-riveted, thin aluminium cladding.

The boys, once outside, broke back into the prison building above the interior ceiling, working their way through the crawlspace to the thinner exterior cladding. A solid kick put them outside the supermax. Yet, they were astonished that the plan they'd been told about actually worked.

Of the four, one was a well-known escaper linked to my business friends. Another, a halfwit called 'The Ant', inside for a clumsy murder. The remaining two's murders were, respectively, drunken and nasty. Nasty climbed back down to the roller door. At the crack, he whispered loudly as he dared.

"Trevor! It's all good. We'll go tomorrow."

Trevor looked over to where I stood, now at the dayroom glass. We'd each developed a shorthand sign language through so much glass and over so much time. Trevor signed to me:

"They want a delay."

I signed, interlocking knuckles and a T. *'Lock them out.'*

With no chance of returning, the four belted their way out through the roof, scaled the inner razor-wire fences using a blanket and tripped across to the old brick outer wall. Lifting each other, they locked at the top a frame of a dayroom chair, bent tight and tied with five twisted sheets. Since they'd had everything they needed for the jump, any postponement combined with self-destructive nerves would have brought the plan undone. I would learn later that with most group escapes, the transformation from entertaining dream can be too much for some, and often one of their number would subconsciously (or blatantly) let the plan be known to the enemy just to get them off the hook of having to face the real world with all its uncertainties.

As expected, the four made a mess of the job once they were over the wall. My friends had provided a house but of course the heat was intense. Ignoring instructions, the Ant just had to wander out to make a call to his brother from a nearby payphone. The police swooped the next morning. Robert Wright, the double murderer, got away, only to be cornered in a highway shootout the following day.

The Artist spent years more in supermax. No suspicion fell on me. Of course, I came to regret not joining the group, even though I knew I couldn't trust most of them for a minute. Escapes should follow electoral advice. Vote early, vote often.

The taste for escapes from supermax was peppered soon from added security combined with the administration's careful mixing on units of the capable with the barking mad. Never again would a unit be without an informer and at least one lunatic.

Staff, too, would often crack up. An officer leapt up from behind the staffroom sofa one night firing his .357 revolver at his workmates. He was firing blanks but some of the officers never recovered.

The new inmate mix included a half dozen women deemed troublesome. As a prisoner, there is little worse than having to hear someone else take a beating. The sense of helplessness is heart-breaking. More so, I found, in proportion to the frailty of the victim. A girl of around twenty – a kid tearaway – had been chained for the night to the steel toilet of her cell. From time to time, big, sweating officers would make a slow and foot-clacking walk to her cell before having the door opened where they'd take turns kicking her in her stomach and legs. Come morning, we all agreed we'd rather take that kicking ourselves than hear those pitiful sounds again.

By my second year, I was in a unit of three multiple murderers and two others kept in high security for their own protection. I'd become isolated and took every opportunity to lose myself in a book or radio play. I shielded myself from those around me by draining my true personality from the surface. I recall the afternoon that I realised I must move on.

I was at a dayroom bench rubbing stale slices of bread together over a newspaper. This was our way of making flour. The prison food was almost inedible. It was bad to begin with fresh from the distant kitchens, but rendered cold, fatty and solid after being left on trolleys in the supermax corridors for hours before being pushed into the dayrooms. Once each month we could buy eggs and milk. I used these and my reconstituted flour to make pancakes on a bench-top sandwich maker.

My back was toward two others in the dayroom. They were Barry, a long-haired, near toothless wreck at forty-five, and the younger, heavyset Cypriot Alex serving two life sentences for killing his business partners. We were all wearing the standard-issue prison white jumpsuits.

They were at a table talking about some music on Barry's record player. Alex was at the far end behind Barry stitching large, soft animal toys for a charity, and gluing leather patches on an overstuffed bear. I imagined nightmares any child might vibe as the recipient of one of Alex's bears.

From the reflection in the window glass, I saw Alex stand and calmly walk behind Barry, carrying the two-litre tin of contact adhesive. He emptied the tin of glue over Barry's head, taking on a thoughtful expression as though decorating while ensuring the volatile liquid spread over Barry's shoulders, back, and then began to pool in Barry's lap. Oddly, he didn't leap up.

"That's not nice," Barry said, still calm but now standing as the glue – a texture of thin honey – seeped into his jumpsuit.

Alex stood back and produced a fat bundle of matches held by rubber bands from his own jumpsuit. Barry swore as his eyes stung from the draining glue. Alex lit the torch of matches on a striker. As Barry stood, Alex threw the flaming wad of matches and turned him into a walking pyre. Barry made little choking sounds, trying to bat away the flames as though a swarm of flies. His hair fluffed into a ball of flame, finally gaining the attention of the guards who'd been in their pod playing their usual of game reading our mail.

I looked around the dayroom. There were no towels. Alex backed toward the sink taps, giving me a warning look. Barry was twisting around trying to find air from beneath the flames which were beginning to blacken the cream-coloured ceiling. There was nothing I could do except wait.

The guards seemed to take forever to override the door lock's normal one-at-a-time sequential opening. By the time they reached the dayroom they met Alex who was at the door ready with his guitar to bat away the guards as they tried to get to Barry who was, by then, crouched on the floor, head pushed between his legs and surprisingly still.

Alex stood aside, pleased with his work. A guard snapped into action as Barry seemed to come to life and begin to writhe. The flames, now smouldering, were patted out easily by the fire blanket, sheets of blackened fabric and skin flaking away at each lift of the silvered blanket. Alex ran out of the dayroom as half-a-dozen officers arrived in response to the fire alarm, wearing equipment for which there was no purpose.

I leaned to Barry's side as he was taken away. His eyes, cooked open, were locked in position as he spoke to me.

"Don't let Alex fuck with my stereo," he said. He was, beneath the black crust, naked, testicles swollen to apple size, adrenalin staying, briefly, the unbearable pain that was to come.

Barry died in hospital three hours later.

4

Ten years had passed, and jail life had changed.

I was transferred from supermax following what must be called a successful protest by five inmates along one unit. The authorities rarely respond to protests but this one had been unintentionally spectacular. Each man in the row had scooped out the water from his steel toilet bowl and covered his head with wet blankets wrapped tight around the bowl. This would allow them to breathe as each had set fire to his foam-rubber mattress. The idea was that the smoke in the sealed unit would make its way to the guards' pod to show how vulnerable they might be against determined prisoners. Black and green acrid smoke filled the cells and seeped into the corridors.

Unfortunately, one of the prisoners wavered in his determination as he lifted a lip of his blanket to check on the flames. The suction tore the poisonous smoke through the interconnected pipes. All five died within minutes. One of them the recaptured Robert Wright who had escaped with the help of the oil painter. Their deaths brought the annual death rate in the supermax to forty out of a maximum population of forty-eight. Of course, it was only the threat to the staff that resulted in the closure of the supermax.

I was first transferred to the old prison. At first bad, then better. Then, after a few years, to a country prison surrounded by wire. Eventually, a year before my release date, to a country house on a farm. There were no walls.

The big house had been built as the mansion for a retired doctor in the 1880s. Located near a small town in agricultural Victoria state, it later became a girls' school and then a prisoner-of-war camp during World War I. Mostly German soldiers were held there and they'd carved tunnels in three directions in failed escape plans. Days, they worked the farm.

By the 1990s, as a state open prison, most of the eighty-six prisoners occupied dormitories made from the large upper rooms. A half dozen prisoners lived in self-contained huts outside. Murderers all, completing twenty-five year minimum terms. Except for me, as I, too, had one of the well-fitted cabins, complete with a bathroom. My job, as a prisoner, was to operate a staff café.

Not long after arriving at Dhurringile Prison, the governor-superintendent took me to a pre-fab house beside the old mansion. It held a kitchen and dining room as well as two bedrooms and a laundry. He gave me a bunch of keys and a cashbox.

"You'll find you're a one-man show here, McMillan," he said. "Now don't let them at the keys no matter what they tell you. And never let 'em have credit. This officers' mess is meant to run at a profit. And it does."

The maligned *them* the governor spoke of were his own prison staff. His stress on profit – which paid for televisions, kitchen equipment and soon a pool table – told me that the guards wouldn't be too nosy as to how the profit was made. I could take a staff driver to the nearby town twice each week for supplies.

As the governor left me to my new enterprise, he added, "Guy Maclean is the head prison cook here. He seems a good fellow." The old guv had seen a few prisons in his time and knew good head cooks in prisons combine secrecy with ruthless acquisitiveness. Some can even cook.

Although busy, I enjoyed the most valued luxury, so rare in prison: time alone beyond prying eyes. Afternoons, I'd walk through the wheat fields to feed some of the half-dozen tired horses carrots. Nights, I'd walk off my special meals strolling the low hills surrounding the car park. Yet with relative freedom, guilt returned. Not for a day had I forgotten the carelessness that had allowed Clelia's death. Toward authorities, my feelings were simpler. They remained a dangerous enemy, without forgiveness. I presented none of this wariness. I appeared polite, humble and almost caring. Over the years, bitterness had dissolved beneath the surface courtesies of a servant. It was not as though I had any grand plan for my release. I just wanted to be anonymous, forgotten.

For three years, until I ran out of money, I kept paying the lease on the villa Clelia had found in Tuscany. I'd remembered she'd sent ahead some luggage but I had no recollection if it had been delivered. Clelia's dad had died of cancer, as had a sister. There was no contact and no reconciliation.

Saturdays, I'd take a train to Melbourne where my mother still lived. She lamented my lost years.

In the eleventh year of my imprisonment, around three months before my parole date, two policemen arrived at the jail. The governor phoned the café.

"Send them down," I said, removing my apron and putting on a pot of coffee.

They had been mid-level investigators during Operation Aries. Now, senior-ranking officers of the state police. Their excuse for their visit was to return – after a decade – a pile of dated electronic equipment. Scanners, transmitters and special lenses.

"Thanks," I said as we sat on the café veranda. "I'm sure these toys are all quite useless these days. Oh, and congratulations, I suppose." One, in uniform, showed a chief superintendent's rank.

"We don't get to chase crooks these days who put in your kind of effort," said the CS.

I supposed the promotions were in part due to early success. Yet I couldn't figure if this trivial and top-heavy property return was indirect warning or a sop to put my mind at ease.

"Just think," I said, "if my jury had held out we'd never be here, enjoying the sun together."

The governor was busting with curiosity after the two cops had driven away.

"Don't ask me," I said in answer. "A long drive for a coffee."

"Did you ask for your stuff back?" asked the governor.

"No," I said. "And there's the point. In whose office did my name come up first?"

The next day was one of many distractions. I'd booked a car for a trip into town to shop for supplies. In reality, I filled the café's supplies almost entirely from the prison food stores. An arrangement with the prison cook provided a hundred dollars' worth of groceries, meat and fruit for twenty dollars' worth of delicatessen specialities unavailable in the jail. The cook had given me the keys to the storerooms to be copied in town so we could make after-hours transfers.

The day started well enough. My driver was an officer named Maria, married to another on the staff – both became active Christian fundamentalists out of country boredom. Her beliefs didn't prohibit taking off at every opportunity, and I left her at a hair salon. After racing through the supermarket, I had the keys cut and grabbed a few things on the never-ending list of extras fellow prisoners asked of me. A few minutes at a bank and a betting office, then back to the salon. No Maria.

I was running out of time. In fifty minutes the lunch break of the prison kitchen officer would end and he'd find himself locked out. As I knew the despatcher at Dhurringile, I got on the car's two-way radio. The radio operator sounded nervy.

"Don't worry, I got to the shop for you," I said. The officer was a racetrack fan and I put on his bets.

"Maria's not here, Dave," he said. "And the governor's with me."

"Don't come back without her, McMillan!" he screamed over the radio. "And don't forget your temporary pass ends at three."

I ignored the governor's threat, drove back to the prison hoping I wouldn't be stopped by local police – I was in a chef's outfit – tossed the keys to the prison cook, and drove back to town to look for Maria.

If I hadn't been searching faces, I doubt I'd have picked out those that did not fit the dry and quiet town. As I stopped in Main Street, I saw two plainclothes detectives halt their sedan and back into a parking space for cover. When I moved on, so did they.

They were from out of town and I felt sure I was their target. A rush of minor misdeeds raced through my head. No, my pale mischief didn't warrant their presence. It could be worse, I thought. A couple of detectives weren't a surveillance team.

I found Maria at her home on the edge of town. She'd fallen asleep. We drove back to the prison to face the governor. He ranted a bit, mostly at me.

"What if you'd had an accident?" he asked. "No insurance cover..." and complaints, too, about using the official radio. I wasn't listening.

I was thinking of my post-release plans. A release then just two months away. First, I wished simply to breathe out. I'd been holding my breath for over ten years. I'd need to shed the armour I'd grown over any true feelings. For a decade, I'd never reacted to anything as myself while being held by my enemy. Now that brittle armour was thickening its shell toward my core. I hoped to spend the first six months in masterful inactivity. Breathing free air, walking happily without borders. Then, there was a book of short stories on my computer, some physics studies (dull stuff: particle effects in protein folding) and some elaborate wooden boxes I'd made over the years and intended to show. Still, these things that amounted to an occupation were not of the most importance. I was more interested to meet the self that would arise from the ashes of that twenty-five-year-old.

"… and you keep an eye on her from now on…" the governor droned on, talking about Maria, the most troublesome of his officers. "Or I won't let you take her out again."

He sounded like some irate father listing boundaries to a risky boyfriend. I didn't particularly want Maria on my shopping trips. I preferred the older, male officers who could be relied upon to quietly drink in a pub while I did my business. I was too tired to argue, just kept my head tilted in repentance. Such role reversals were not uncommon at that open prison. Often, senior prisoners would be sent looking for other inmates who'd gone AWOL or fallen into a drunken stupor while on a work party.

That night while collecting my dry goods stacked for me by the head cook, a familiar voice of panic called from a window of the big house.

"Dave, you'd better get back to your cabin," said a tame officer I'd befriended. He was one of only two night staff. "Looks like there's a ramp on. I can see their cars coming up the drive."

He was warning of one of the infrequent security searches that arrived unannounced by a special squad from the Prisons Department. The wannabe SWAT teams never found much. Usually beer in the dormitories. This time was different. They headed straight for the cabins and called everyone out.

As I stepped from my hut, I noticed something odd. The search officer who stepped up to my door was wearing new, navy-blue overalls. So what? Well, he also wore a pair of polished Florsheims. The search crews always wore heavy black boots. Looking into his eyes, I recognised a customer from my visit to the bank that afternoon. He'd been part of a team following me.

As I sat with my murderer friends in the dining hall of the big house waiting for the search to end, my heart sank. I was a target again. When I was allowed back an hour later, my computer was gone, along with a box of letters and project files.

The next day, the duty officer from the night came in alone for lunch. I asked him if the searchers had reported finding and taking anything.

"Not a word," said the old guy, half-smiling.

I felt as though the endurance of the past eleven years had not been an ascent to the mount of freedom but a foolhardy expedition to the precipice of everlasting despair.

5

"Don't you think it looks a little... plain?"

That was my mother as we stood in the living room – the only room other than a bedroom of a flat I'd taken just outside the central business district.

"It's just fine," I said. "It used to be a motel before they built the airport freeway. All ground floor and the bedroom's quiet, at least."

Rosie gave me a maternal hug. "Are you settling down okay?"

I wasn't. I'd chosen the ex-motel site for its position. There were no tall buildings overlooking the flats and with the new freeway walls at one end, parkland running west and a railway line east, there was only one way in for vehicle traffic. If I were to be followed, I'd know it.

This might seem as though I was set for conflict without giving peace a chance. Not quite so.

Before leaving the country prison, I'd packed all my years of woodcraft – including a reproduction from memory of the timber gearbox – into large bubble-wrapped boxes, and booked a pick-up by a commercial courier van. This was for delivery to my new office – just a room in the old terraced house used as office space by my friends, Max and Jenny. The package arrived a day late, torn and roughly taped together. All the delicately carved and beeswaxed cabinets inside had been hacked to pieces with a coarse saw. I almost marvelled at the time-consuming effort that must have been made to do so much damage. I left the kindling with the BBQ firewood in the office yard. I decided, without conviction, that objects made without immediate practical need amounted to childish sentimentality. I should attach myself to nothing. What was disturbing was the personal venom of these new investigators. Were these next-generation police, the crueller children of the old?

My days rapidly became routine precautionary movements. I'd take a run mornings, lunch with friends in town, and spend a few hours in the office afternoons soaking up the new-born online world. Unfortunately, I saw everything in terms of defence against my old enemy. Especially as I was being followed by a small team of clumsy shadows, a number I hoped meant they were underfunded and with a limited mandate.

In the first weeks, I had to report Mondays and Fridays to a bothersome parole officer. A twitish bachelor who wanted to talk books and movies, drawing out what should have been brief sessions. Looking from his window, I noted the registration numbers of the cars in the surveillance team.

"Have you had thoughts of your old life?" he'd ask from time to time.

It would have been satisfying to tell him that his building was surrounded by hungry police. To suggest that he, too, might find himself soon under suspicion. But I said nothing. Telling him of that which surrounded us would have spooked him. He assuredly would have panicked and revoked my parole.

A check on the surveillance cars revealed only that they were listed as unassigned, so I had to follow one of the drivers. To do this normally requires at least two cars of your own. I was, at first, lucky. After parking my car off-street at home, I sneaked out to where I knew one of them had plotted up – intending to follow their surveillance car as the shift ended. This was around 11.30 pm, and I'd parked a friend's car nearby for the task. In a dark, padded jacket, I watched the sedan and its two occupants, a man and a woman. At midnight, instead of driving away, a new car pulled up, a shiny, white coupe. The driver got out to allow in the two watchers, who simply locked up the surveillance car and left it. A smart move. If I saw a car parked and empty, I'd assume it was owned by some harmless local. Perhaps someone else would take over tomorrow. On the hunch that the coupe was owned by one of the team, I took the number and went home. This paid off – the new car was a private registration to a man living in Melbourne's outer suburbs. I'd gone to the registration office, and, posing as a clerk for a law firm, gave the story the car's driver might be a witness in a car accident. I took the address and managed to get away and out there two days later. A mailbox check showed insurance due from the Victoria State Police Insurance Co-operative. This saved having to do more.

So, seventy-two hours to establish that the operation was one by the state police. That meant they should run out of money within weeks as they'd have nothing to tell for their efforts. I could live with that.

Michael had been released a year earlier (he'd dodged the helicopter-escape trial) and earned a quiet living dealing speed bought from friends in the Hell's Angels (remarkably placid in serious business matters), who had a near monopoly with the amphetamine trade. He'd never recovered from the death of his Marie. I don't think he wanted to. He'd spend afternoons playing electric guitar until his fingers bled.

Nights, he'd drink.

A couple of weeks after the state police dropped their surveillance, I drove out to Springfield cemetery. Clelia was buried there. I parked, enquired at the gate and began walking to the assigned plot. It was a sunny day with a warm breeze. I paused at some of the older headstones, admiring the histories of the grateful dead. I was almost alone.

Through the columns of an elaborate mausoleum, I saw another visitor. I stopped and made some noise with some loose stones. He didn't look up. I resumed a curved path to my destination. Halfway, I saw another visitor. A woman in jeans, around thirty-five. Almost at once, I knew that she was a policewoman, and that, again I was being followed.

I had not yet reached Clelia's grave. I slowed, feeling smothered by my distant observers. I backed away. Breathing in shallow draughts, I felt like a wartime child who, having crept from hiding to gather food, returns to find the Gestapo are bundling his betrayed family into a truck. Helplessness and fear. Survivor's guilt. Anger, too, at the intrusion. I would not visit Clelia's grave that day, I determined. I would not stand before her with my enemy, bring them to her final place. I have never attempted a return since that day.

I managed the next days in secrecy, when secrecy was hard to come by, alone and searching until I established my new companions were federal cops. I knew, too, that they'd have money and time to burn.

The era into which I'd been released, 1993, was the beginning of the age of advanced electronic surveillance. I noticed that when I'd get clear of the shadowing undercover vehicles, they'd reappear twenty minutes later. After taking my car deep into an underground car park, I ran a scanner for the usual transmitter frequencies. Nothing. So, I pulled the Toyota to pieces. I found what I'd been looking for. Cut into the padding beneath the dashboard, my suitors had implanted a stripped-down mobile phone, a coil and wires linked to the electrical system. It would run forever. And this was all that was necessary to locate the position of the car to within a few metres. The little phone's speaker had been removed while its microphone was extended to the edge of the padding. So, they could listen, too. Except in an underground car park.

The next day, I drove my car around, with the tracker taking power from the cigar lighter, until late afternoon. Four cars followed in relays. When they became jumpy, they'd drop back for a while. I led them to a multi-storey car park in the city centre. Then, after drawing them out on foot – something they hate – I bought a black scarf from a department store, finally losing them in the walkways of the big building.

Back in the car park, I wrapped the tracker in the scarf after attaching batteries, walked to the exit boom gate where three cars queued, and wedged the scarf-phone into one of the idling cars. It would take the police at least thirty minutes to catch up and see they'd been chasing the wrong car.

On foot and temporarily free, I walked to the City of Melbourne building, raised in 1888 and still with its original fittings, despite partition in the 'sixties into small-room offices. Half-storey landings divided the stairway, and I climbed to the third-and-a-half floor. There, a carved-wood centre column held a small hatch. Through the gloom, I unclipped a rear panel inside. This left me with a one-inch board, about two-feet square. Made to last. Keeping my ears alert for footsteps, I slid a side panel and tapped out the contents. Although the $100,000 in mixed currencies looked impressive, a third of the money had been withdrawn from circulation. Soon, all Australian banknotes would be printed on plastic. The older notes could only be exchanged at a bank, and new cash laws had made larger amounts difficult to explain. There were two passports as well. Out-of-date.

When I had sealed this stash, I had said to myself, "Well, if I don't get back here within ten years, I must be dead!" Never dismiss a precaution on the assumption death will save you from the consequences.

Over some reluctance on my part, a girl was introduced into my life in those few months. Single men under forty were thin on the ground in the nineties, so it was difficult to venture out in mixed company without risking entanglement. A restaurant party of twenty-five for someone's pre-wedding bash presented a scattering of women cleared from bad marriages or looking to trade up.

Sharon, seated next to me at the large table, asked of my occupation.

"Gun-running, narcotics. A little white-slavery," I answered before realising that in the 'nineties, such glib answers wouldn't be a deterrent.

Still, we made ready friends and became close. Sharon ended her affair with her boss. I was warm and courtly. We had weekends in country retreats and ate in all the new restaurants as – until my old enemy had appeared - I'd planned to open an eatery under the guidance of my stepfather. On the surface – and even privately – it appeared as the bright beginning of a new love affair. Yet, inside, I held a deep sadness that hugged the ground like the poison gas of the Great War.

The surveillance became more intrusive. Each evening before leaving my office, I'd snap a Polaroid photograph of the room, and repeat the process upon entering the following day. A mismatch quickly led to a large chest of drawers. Set in the wooden base, I found a battery-powered transmitter. Its sophistication proved its origin from within the federal government. The bug was the first I'd seen that digitised its signal, transmitting by a new spread-spectrum technology, undetectable by scanners. I disconnected the device, knowing that to the police, I'd appear completely on the defensive.

"Will I see you on Christmas day?" asked Sharon.

"It's a family day, but I wouldn't be surprised if I make an appearance," I said as evasively as I was driving, losing my tail on the long streets. In fact, I would have been very surprised, for I was making the most secret preparations to leave Australia. I'd need passports and money and above those, the certainty that buying the tickets would go unseen. I pulled up to the kerb and stopped.

"What's wrong?" asked Sharon.

"Nothing," I ran my hand through my hair in frustration.

There was no point in telling Sharon that my new world had become the worst of the old. The world of cops and robbers was new to her. Besides, the rule was to tell no one of my plans, if I wished to succeed I must at least hold to the rules.

When I'd returned home that evening, there were obvious signs police had been searching. They'd cleared my phone of new messages then left anonymous, childish and obscene messages of their own. Making almost no attempt to hide their visit. I didn't think much of these new-generation cops, even knowing they could be more dangerous.

"Let's eat at your place tonight," I suggested. "We'll pick something up from the delicatessen near the beach."

The days of obtaining false passports using the birth certificates of the deceased had gone. As predicted, the records office had finally computerised their entries, and made links between the living and the dead. The only safe method was to assume the identity of someone who had yet to apply for a passport. This, I did. I asked a friend to prepare his application papers – including the countersignature on his photo – and then do nothing. That would give him a way out if things went bad. What I did was to simply duplicate the entire application on a fresh form with my photo – the countersignature copied for smoothness over felicity. If the passport office phoned the dentist over the photo (my friend's dentist as reference had been my choice), of course, he'd say he'd only that week signed one. My friend would still have plausible deniability by saying he'd abandoned his travel plans and thrown away the application in a temper.

As a backup, I applied for and received, a New Zealand passport posing as an expatriate living in Australia. For that, I used a black and white photograph posed on a different angle. New Zealand passports had yet to be scanned for biometrics, as all are now.

The elaborate rules and demands of slipping in and out of visibility combined with the certainty that the smallest error would end my freedom had the effect of draining every minute of each day of even a moment's pleasure. Michael sympathised, yet, since he was not a target, could only watch as I planned my escape. Sleep had become a process of numb waiting, food fuel without taste, and air inhaled only for the scent of danger.

6

Aboard QF7, at 22,000 feet, the seatbelt lights pinged off. From the window, I could see the dry heartland of Australia below.

The weight that had become intolerably suffocating had begun to lift as I passed through passport control at Sydney without a tremor as Immigration stamped me out. In Business Class, I noticed how comfortable was the chair. During the brief Melbourne months, I'd tempered my lightly Spartan existence with one luxury: that every object that touched my skin be of the highest quality and comfort. In the last weeks, even that small but personal concession had failed to stay the itch of surveillance. Now, I could feel again. Being airborne of course took me back to my old days and trade. I told myself to keep a distance.

I had, before leaving Melbourne, arranged the location of my car and the trail of transmitters to suggest a visit to the countryside. I'd hinted as much to my mother – her phone, too, was tapped. I'd booked restaurants and services, left dry-cleaning – done everything to suggest a return within a few days. The truth was, I would never return, and felt guilty about the necessary deceptions. No one other than Michael knew I'd left.

For the first time in fourteen years, I was free.

London was my ultimate destination (London born, I have British citizenship) but first I would land at Bangkok, Thailand. I'd invested a small fortune there, and after over a decade without one word of communication, I needed to know what, if anything, remained. If Lee was true to character, eleven years' silence would alter nothing.

Looking across Bangkok city from the balcony of my hotel, pale pink fumes clouded the horizon. Not a living soul knew where I was, nor who I was. It was glorious.

Thailand, though, remained the most dangerous point of my journey. The police in Australia should never suspect my location for the Thais were notoriously compliant with western police agencies.

The day after my arrival, the Australian Federal Police – having tapped my mobile phone – intercepted a call. Listening in, they heard Michael calling me from a number they knew to be a payphone in Melbourne. There, I answered; we spoke for a few minutes, nothing of consequence, after which I hung up. My cellphone transponder indicated I was somewhere in the outlying hills. They were certain I was still in town.

The reality was that Michael had stopped at a payphone and dialled my number. In his free hand, he held my cellphone, set to silent mode. When it rang, he opened the phone and placed it next to a tape player from which spoke both sides of a conversation we had recorded earlier in the week. The police were sure they had a lid on everything. My secret was safe.

The American diplomatic presence in Thailand was unbalanced by the numbers stationed there to observe and intervene in military, spying and security matters. Just in one area, as Bangkok was a hub and loading centre for illegal immigration, over one hundred and sixty staff were in place to check the thousands of Chinese hoping to travel east to Hawaii and mainland

USA. The numbers of Drug Enforcement Administration operatives were even greater.

As I would later come to know, DEA agent, Bill Shenkmann, was in Bangkok that December of 1993. He was the agent who had volunteered to testify as an expert witness during my trial in '83. He had later expressed dissatisfaction with the covert assassination of Tommy's uncle by road kill. The death did not destroy Uncle's north Thailand heroin network, and as Shenkmann saw it, was no compensation for the killing of a fellow agent's wife. You might recall Tommy was the man who brought cutlery boxes of dope to Michael, and disaster to us all. For all that, I liked Tommy, yet continued to blame myself for not preventing any predictable failures. Shenkmann, however, quite wrongly, saw Tommy as heir to the dead Uncle's drug empire.

That December, Shenkmann, now promoted to Special Agent, was pleased with the interdiction figures for drugs to the United States but less impressed with the method.

An arrangement had been made with the bosses of the scores of Nigerian heroin smugglers in Bangkok. The Nigerians, in a naïve deal that kept the DEA from interfering with their Asia-Europe operations, had begun framing their own US-bound couriers after their usefulness ran out. As soon as the couriers – mostly white Europeans, a few black Americans – arrived at the doors of Don Muang airport, the Thai police (with DEA agents watching) would pounce. In operation, this was less of a burden upon the Nigerians than it may seem. Only around one in three US-bound couriers would be given up, and of those all had carried bags for the smugglers previously on other routes. Usually, the hand of arrest would fall on a courier's fourth run, particularly when owed money for previous jobs.

Each week, at least two poor slobs were arrested before check-in. Fallen couriers would tell of staying at the same Bangkok guesthouse, even given the same taxi driver to take them to the airport. So notorious were these set-ups, that regular taxi drivers knew the places, people and pattern and would refuse to take even these sap passengers, since they were loaded with drugs.

Shenkmann had no reservations about all this despite its artificiality or quality of arrest (the drugs were always of low quality); he objected because he felt it made the agency complacent and failed to target the independents. 'Mild' Bill, as he was known, used almost irrational quantities of resources hunting the independents. Why – who can say? Perhaps the demands of political statecraft hindered his fight against the major players, and the indy who rubbed shoulders with a major was as close as he could get. I don't think so. In my life, I've encountered so much hostility from agency people, it must be personal. You'll probably know better than I before the end of this book. This misdirected rage once reminded me of one of the traps my kid brother set for me when I was nine. A rubber spider. I'd stepped barefoot from my bedroom to land on the rubber tarantula. When I leapt off its black legs, it jumped a bit (Simon knew his plastics from a tender age). Climbing down from the ceiling, I battered the joke-shop with everything I could lift. Here's the point: I kept hitting it, pulling its legs off, and jumping on it long after knowing it was rubber, a fake. Only when I began to laugh at myself did I stop. What's the connection? I am that spider and people like Bill Shenkmann have no sense of humour.

However, something of which Shenkmann did approve was the recent installation of a secret telephone-snooping network. As Thailand upgraded its phone systems, it took crucial elements of the switching control systems from American suppliers. Without the Thais knowing, this system allowed the US National Security Administration to listen covertly to almost every phone in the country. That December, the process was being tested.

My reunion with Lee had gone well. Although his old number had long been disconnected, I had a firm memory of his house. Unfortunately, the landscape had changed in the years of Thailand's property boom, so I drove a couple of taxi drivers slightly mad by trying first one street and then another. When I found the place, Lee had moved on. Luckily, neighbours directed me to his new place, an elaborate clutch of linked tree houses, even further out of town. Lee seemed both shocked and pleased to see me.

"I knew you'd come back!" Lee yelled as he climbed out of his four-wheel drive as I stood by his grinning wife.

That night, as we watched a tape transfer of some 8mm film I'd shot with Lee years ago, he told me of his success.

"There, that land," he'd said as the screen showed a younger Lee walking enthusiastically around some very scrubby hills. "You'll see tomorrow. You have a supermarket. And many houses and apartment blocks."

I explained that I was on my way to England, and that I'd return soon.

Tommy was in Bangkok that day, too. Before venturing out to find Lee, I'd met him for breakfast. Tommy was nervy, I thought because of meeting me. Sensibly, our meeting was at a hotel far from my own.

"Are you in trouble?" he asked.

"Not now, I'm invisible," I said. "I'll call you from London – maybe your wife's number here is better than your office up north." I gave him my room number and hotel. If he did not hear from me within two weeks, he should find out if I checked out okay. Lee was my old friend but Tommy was the man to pull strings if there was trouble. At least, according to Tommy.

"Don't worry," Tommy said, with a reassuring smile. "This is my country."

The following day, after lunch, I was ready to leave. Lee had given me $US50,000 in cash when we'd met near Sukhumvit Road. I'd not asked for anything.

"I'll be back," I promised.

As I was about to leave my room, the phone rang. It was Tommy, wishing me well. He'd called from his office. That bothered me but within two hours I'd be on my way to the airport. If there was one thing I could rely upon, surely it should be the creakingly slow pace of investigations in the East.

Bill Shenkmann took great pleasure in teasing his counterpart at the Australian embassy. I give his voice from his later colleagues' reports. He'd phoned the Australian.

"I'm guessing you've still got your eye on David McMillan," Bill said, with the pride of insider knowledge.

George Chalk was stuck in traffic, as usual, on his way to the Australian compound.

"Yes, we're waiting for him to make his move."

"Yeah?" said Shenkmann. "Well, he's here and he's making moves."

For three hours, the Australians did not believe the Americans. They were convinced only when two liaison officers were taken to the communications bunker at the US embassy. There, they heard a tape of Tommy's call from Chiang Mai.

I was stuck in traffic that afternoon, too.

And forty-five minutes from Bangkok airport, the Americans had been given my travelling name – courtesy of security at the Oriental Hotel. A discussion followed as to what, if anything, to do next.

"But he hasn't done anything yet," claimed the Australians, hoping I'd return to Australia so I could be arrested there.

"He'll be at the airport soon," offered the DEA crew. "Our people there are checking names against flight lists."

The Australians hesitated until Bill Shenkmann spoke.

"This might be your only chance."

Airports radiate the most confusing and always alarming vibes. When I walked into the check-in zone, I felt bad. I dismissed that. The sight of the Scandinavian Airlines desk took me back in an instant to the unexpected arrest of courier John thirteen years earlier. Dead John, who'd been consumed by AIDS having shared needles after picking up a drug habit in the Thai prison. If I'd not been imprisoned myself, could I have prevented his death? No, all superstitions smoking around time and place, should be dismissed. Besides, I knew that at any given hour at Bangkok airport at least two hundred people would be carrying drugs, sweating it out. Vibes enough to overload the most insulated wiring.

I had a few minutes, so I bought a soft drink and looked around. It did not take long to spot the four certainties and a dozen maybes. Even one fellow I knew well as a freelance drug runner. I didn't think much of his body language, gabbing to people in his queue. He's carrying, I thought, but travelling economy, nothing big. He was safe, though, his manner wouldn't seem out of place at a Bangkok airport, they only jumped people they were expecting. Knowing I would be better off in the safety of the Business Class lounge, I moved on.

Only when second in line at check-in did the accumulation of images come together in my mind. I began to identify the spooks, the watchers. Two on an overhead walkway, a third by the immigration desks. A couple of out-of-place uniformed police near the glass entrance doors seemed somehow connected. Who were they expecting? They all looked too rigid for a drug bust. Some terror threat, perhaps?

So confident was I of my own precautions, I'd blinded myself to what I would see in the next instant. Only as the girl at the check-in desk took my passport and read the name, did I register her return look with the faintest flicker from her eyes, and know, with absolute certainty, that it was I. They were all for me, and they wouldn't want me to get away.

"I'm not familiar with this passport," said the girl. "Please just give me one minute."

And please just give me two, I thought.

I backed away as she left her desk. The smuggler guy I knew read my face at a distance and disappeared. I felt the illusion of a ripple running through the terminal. I went into automatic flight mode. With my carry bag over my shoulder, I walked to the drinks machine, shot left and down some steps to the Arrivals Hall. It was usefully crowded and I knew, just outside, massed ranks of taxis waited their turn in the queue for pick up. I strode into the mass of cabs, rather than put myself on show in the line. Then, I plucked one from the herd with the best chance of getting through the ranks. Though surprised, the cabbie nudged his way out of the pack over the rasping complaints of his fellow hacks. Within five minutes I was heading back to town.

I had no doubt as to the source of the leak. Tommy's phone. Yet the speed of arranging the police at the airport suggested I'd walked into an operation that was underway. I didn't then know that the Americans had plainclothes liaison officers on duty at that airport round-the-clock. What, in any case, did I have to do with the DEA?

I took two more taxis around town, a motor rickshaw and then walked to a big hotel, taking a drink in the bar. On the way, I found a payphone to warn Tommy. He didn't want to accept that the heat was on him - though he offered me no sanctuary. The second purpose of my call was to distract the enemy. I made it plain I'd be taking a train south. In truth, I knew I'd be safest with Lee. I didn't want to stay in the city longer than essential, so I grabbed a motorbike taxi (the fastest transport during rush hour) and rode pillion to Chinatown where I'd left my back-up passport with an old friend at his travel agency. Large Raj had run the place for years after his deportation from Australia following a stretch for dope running. He wasn't active in Thailand, just hopeful, I suppose. I'd had a close call but at least I'd got away. I stopped again to phone Lee to make sure he was in. After he heard the tone of my voice, he kept it short.

"Just come my home," he said.

"The Thais say it's not worth chasing him for a phoney passport," announced Australian fed-pol liaison Chalk as he was admitted to Bill Shenkmann's DEA office in downtown Bangkok.

Shenkmann leaned back in his chair. "Do you want him?"

"It'd be nice to see him in a Thai prison cell," the Australian replied. "Explaining back home how he got away twice is not something I'd like to do."

"No problem," Shenkmann pressed a button on a tape player. "Listen to this."

A scratchy conversation in Thai came from the tape machine. Chalk looked puzzled.

"It's a phone intercept. Little Tommy talking to the owner of a travel agency. Warning him to be careful because your boy just got away from the airport and might be headed his way."

"Is there time?" Chalk thought he'd never convince the Thais to assign – what? – half-a-dozen men on a mission of such little importance. And, of course, foreign police have no arrest powers in Thailand.

Shenkmann assured Chalk that their friends with the Thai Narcotics Suppression Division were always helpful. Most of their money came from America.

"Besides, the chase is on!" stressed Shenkmann, reaching for his phone. "It's infectious, isn't it?"

I left my transport and continued on foot, cutting through shops and arcades. I felt exhausted. As soon as I finished with Bangkok and found a safe bed, the sooner I could think through the day's improbabilities. Perhaps fate was letting me off the hook provided I learned the lessons of this close call. The communications rules are tough ones. If you worried about everyone sticking to them, you could end up talking to no one. I should have adopted the rules for escape as soon as I accepted I was on the run from Australia. Not a time for leaving a trail from some social catch-up with old acquaintances. At least, that's how I saw the lesson just then.

As I stepped into the arcade where Raj's agency was located, I was half-congratulating myself at surviving, painting a fanciful mural of life-lessons and destiny. Coming out of this reverie, I noticed a small hill of cigarette butts on the pavement near Raj's shop.

Seconds after, I stepped through the office door when four plainclothes but armed Thai police walked through behind me.

Instantly surrounded, I breathed out all my air, and for a minute, as they spoke words I didn't hear, knowing I was hopelessly caught, I tried to breathe in.

They took me away. Their car was nearby in an underground car park. The engine was cool; they must have arrived some time earlier. I would come to know of a dozen reasons that would have prevented them from responding to the Americans' call. The chances of arrest that day were almost incalculable. Seeming to know this, they had little to say, simply leading me from place to place in handcuffs.

As I was taken through their office doors, along corridors, we passed a small room in which two white men sat. The boss of the arrest team halted us, and then went to speak to the two palefaces. To announce and display his prize. The younger of the two appeared sheepish. He was the Australian. The other, older, with a drawn, hawkish face was familiar to me. This was Bill Shenkmann. He was not so shy. He stood and walked over.

As I remembered – from my trial a decade earlier – I expected some gloating remark of victory. As he neared, he slowed, grimaced and managed a half-shake of his head. Shenkmann then waved his hand dismissively and returned to his table and an open file which he pretended to hold a greater interest. It seemed the human person under his pursuit and technology was, for him, irrelevant, and with proximity, quite uncomfortable. I was less than a pawn in his game; at least a pawn can strike, however briefly.

The combined effects of initial exaltation, having escaped Australia followed by twice being crushed in one day robbed the last of my dwindling reserve of will; a will held as sacred embers for so many years. I was soon in a dark and damp pit of a holding cell within the Thai Narcotics Division. From a small, blackened grill high on the wall I could hear busy street sounds, passing music from cars, often Christmas jingles. I had cellmates: a snug group of Chinese, a Nigerian and a Swiss. The young Swiss guy, two mats away, attempted suicide with over one hundred sleeping pills. I wished him well, only mildly curious. He was unconscious for two days, then woke unable to move until, on the third day, thirst drove him to crawl.

The events that had brought me to ruin were so unlikely I abandoned any attempt to give them probability. That my enemies were so unreasonably determined, and with such extraordinary luck against what I believed were my more-than-adequate defences utterly overwhelmed my spirit. The Thais – perhaps goaded by the Americans – had scraped up a few grams of heroin from the little packets abandoned daily by nervous travellers at the airport. Twenty grams was enough to ensure the death penalty and they added that to my charges. The money went missing – and my boots. "You won't need those where you're going," said one of the bored policemen. I cared for nothing and death by machine gun was cluttered by years of law and so seemed a distant promise. I would lie on my mat and listen to my heart making one beat follow another, a blind machine of complete ignorance, I thought.

I've written in detail as to what happened next.[6] Of my two years in Bangkok's biggest prison, and the difficult escape just before conviction and sentencing. Even so, it is important in this account of the hunting that I offer just a chapter of those events to describe the costs of survival.

---

[6] *Escape*, Monsoon Books, 2007

7

Despite all my precautions, I'd betrayed myself through an intoxication with freedom although I doubted any player could predict such unreasonable misfortune. I'd spent a week in the utter depths of wordless, timeless despair in the black jail of Bangkok's Chinatown. After a thirty-second court appearance, I was remanded to the huge Klong Prem prison.

For weeks, I was immovably under the weight of depression. Even so, a tiny pocket of what was left of me took in what I saw with a view to escape. Nothing I saw made it look easy.

Klong Prem, the Bangkok Hilton (the name is sometimes used for the smaller Bangkok jail for lifers, *Bangkwang*, which is known locally as *The Big Tiger*) holds almost 8,000 people in eight prisons, all walled together in a huge square. It can be seen from the International Space Station. It includes a women's prison, a remand jail (called *The Cure* by Thais), a prison for the dying, for children, for transvestites, and three meaningless distinctions of adults. A prison city, surrounded by a twenty-meter moat, with high outer walls strung with electrified wires and posted at intervals with guard towers. Talk of escape was rare among the Thais, common enough between foreigners but almost never attempted.

Conditions were bad inside for those without money, charm or talent. (And you've got to be in a pretty rich country to live in comfort without any of these, eh?) Cells packed, sleeping like tinned fish on concrete floors; just a few hours out of cells each day, mostly spent chasing food since the prison ration of brown rice and cucumber was, most days, rotten. Even so, the prisons were self-contained communities with industries run by the guards, shops and street trading. Of course, some lived better than others. Ate well; had a little mattress and a ceiling fan. But no money could buy your way out of prison – especially a foreigner with nosy embassies. Early, I wondered why some of the Thai street gangsters did not try a breakout. I soon understood.

Four Thais and a Singaporean had, with great luck, managed to cut out of their one-hundred-and-twenty-eight-man dormitory without any fellow inmates blowing the whistle. That last literal, as each dormitory had a trusty sit up all night with a drum to sound hourly 'ALL'S WELL' and a sports whistle to sound an alarm. The five crept to the outer wall and halted. They'd deceived each other as to their respective abilities to scale the twelve-meter wall and supposed friends waiting outside. They decided to turn themselves in. I doubt that they'd have done so had there been any survivors alive of the few historic attempts to speak of the treatment they were sure to receive.

They were put in heavy chains and shoved into individual punishment boxes – half-size coat lockers with no more than crouching space. Suffocating in the heat, they'd be given a bottle of water and a bowl of rice each day. Starvation was not a cause of death. Four died within weeks from internal bleeding caused by daily beatings with heavy sticks. The Singaporean lived but never spoke again.

I was in *The Cure* – the drug-case remand prison – when I witnessed this failure, most of my day on a rented square of cardboard in a huge, stinking dormitory. I wasn't put off escape. Yet it was there I surfaced from despair and found reason to go on.

An Australian policeman newly posted to Bangkok station arrived one day, soon after my arrest. He was young and arrogant. He asked a couple of questions: of who had my cellphone in Melbourne, and what I'd done with their transmitters. When I answered unhelpfully – as he must have expected – he seemed miffed.

"You won't have any assistance from us without a full and frank confession," he said as if he had anything to offer.

I pretended not to have heard and spoke as if thinking aloud. "Frankly, I've often wondered about your diplomatic status in foreign lands," I said. "I mean, are you protected from arrest with one of those blue passports? Unlike, say, those poor hippies on the islands who are busted here and milked of their parents' savings."

I shouldn't have given away my anger. Pointless. So, in return, I was treated to a long gloat about my future.

"And, even if you slip through a death sentence," he was staring up through the mesh as to blue sky. "What? Twenty years or more here? Then what's left of you back to Australia on fresh charges, and more prison."

I didn't answer to his wish list. From within, finally from the heart rather than the head, rose a surge of fresh blood that I took pleasure in concealing.

"Best of luck," I said as he stomped away.

No one had ever escaped and lived from that prison. A few Thais had got over the wall but were set upon almost immediately. Certainly, no foreigner had so much as made the attempt. Walking back from this visit, I looked to the wall. That, in the end, was their only real barrier and could be overcome. Had I known then that I was looking at just one of seven lower internal walls, it wouldn't have made any difference. To the novice policeman, and even my friends who thought me destroyed, I vowed to show that, importantly every so often, the world is not necessarily as it seems.

As soon as I found a reliable fixer I bribed my way onto the transfer list to the large, older Klong Prem prison complex. People awaiting trial were not usually part of the population of this more settled core, but it had advantages. There wasn't a great shift in numbers, so inmates and guards had, effectively, working relationships. There was still much cruelty, with around two deaths each day, almost always the poor. To bring the moneyed class to the surface, newcomers were packed on arrival into small cells, with little air. After a night hunched and sweating, kept awake by the need to kill the waves of lice and bedbugs, those who could afford better accommodation soon came forward.

The Thai guards didn't see their taking money as corruption, they were simply helping the prisoners. And the ones to help were those with money, for they were lucky. Luck is an almost sacred factor in Thai society, so best to associate with the lucky. I'd managed to keep hidden since arrest a few thousand Thai baht (there's about thirty for each US dollar) but that was running out. How to spend money when I arranged some? Instinctively, I knew running around the jail throwing money at people would be disastrous.

This big sub-prison had a quite complex economy. There were six large buildings, each of around fifteen hundred inmates. A Building Chief in each, the boss. He would assign the territories within his building to each guard. In Building #6, guards ran an umbrella factory, an army boot factory, a dim set of warehouses that made brightly decorated – though cardboard – gift boxes used and burned at Chinese funerals. The least abusive factory was that of sheds where prisoners made portraits of royalty in simulated mother-of-pearl inlay. Tonnes of mollusc shells were laboriously broken, glued to large boards, ground down for the picture base. Rows of artists with black ink would pen the images before another team would apply thick resin and later buff the surface. Guards could sell these heavy artworks for over $100 each, and naturally the Building Chief took his cut, as with all other industries. His biggest earner was the Coffee Shop, as the general store was called, making profits of over $5,000 per month selling food, operating a hair salon and restaurant and, importantly, running a bank from one window of the thatched hut, where inmates could, for a 25% fee, take money from their official accounts.

Despite this organisation, only fifty or so in the building lived and ate with minor comforts. Most prisoners were worked hard and lived in squalid conditions. After a couple of months, I'd had some ATM cards mailed to me – in fact, to the home of the accommodation-block guard who seemed the most useful to have in hand. For an honest ten percent commission, he would bring me enough cash so I could rent some space in one of the art-factory huts and to take control of my own cell. I had to appear settling down for the long wait as my trial dribbled on with one-day appearances every six weeks.

However well a little cash could improve life in the prison, there was one thing money could not buy: freedom. Even from the outside, buying freedom was difficult for all but the most well-connected. Especially if there were eyes on the case. The Thai former chief of police was held in jail connected to a couple of murders after jewellery belonging to the Saudi royal family had been stolen. The major-general kept a cellphone, his own rooms and the ability to drink himself into a coma each day but could not find any judge willing to grant him bail. My case had little press, yet was watched keenly by the DEA and Australian police, who were actively helping the prosecution.

From the inside money was even less helpful if escape was the prize. Even at night, there were more than a dozen guards between cell and gate. They would never co-operate. Besides, they made a good living with their daily take. If a prisoner walked from the gates, most would lose their careers and a lifetime's income. It was better to keep a paying prisoner inside for years where any golden goose might be bled dry slowly.

In my first year, at least twenty plans for escape were examined and some initiated; yet all with insurmountable flaws as each demanded strong and well-executed help from outside. Lee, my old Thai contact, offered $50,000 to find a judge prepared to grant bail based on a fake doctor's report. The money disappeared in the pockets of middlemen.

Another plan was based on a snatch from the court as I would be taken from the holding cells. It was a sound plan as the court was one of many in a multi-storey high-rise building and prisoners were taken, one at a time, by special lift and through a passage out of view of the courts' corridors. Some heavy security-van robbers flew to Bangkok to investigate. One, unhelpfully, did a count of armed police throughout the court buildings. He reported over one hundred and thirty-five over just one hour. All the professionals returned to what they saw as safer ground in their homelands. While it was true that some years earlier a gang tried to free a prisoner from a court-bound van and had botched the job (all seven were later massacred by an army commando unit), I still felt less of my self-styled heavy friends.

Several schemes were detailed for escapes from the prison during the day. One plan asked for a special van to be built and taken to the prison's auto-repair workshop, which happened to be in my building #6. I was to hide in a prepared cavity while the van was repaired and later driven out. These schemes had to be abandoned as they required the aid of prisoners. I found that not one of the inmates in key positions could be trusted to keep a secret. All daylight plans I discarded.

Despite these setbacks, I had a great advantage over the other prisoners. I had friends. Real friends. I'd met a couple of Swiss nationals, a half-dozen Americans, many English as well as dozens of Asian foreigners. None of them had any real friends, and so were quite helpless. Even the most self-contained person needs help. After many months, I finally got the use of a phone. It was a cellphone, and I had five minutes among the rice sacks of the coffee shop. When Michael picked up, I began to detail a summary of what had happened.

"Don't explain," interrupted Michael. "Just tell me what I have to do."

Whatever the expression of heartfelt intentions and loyalty, I learned, slowly, that the nature of Thai prisons made the best plans fail.

Eighteen months after arriving at Klong Prem, every scheme had collapsed. I gave up on outside fixes after an American expat disappeared with $80,000 after early promises. I was left with a core of fellow prisoners who began with noble promises to escape but slowly lost confidence.

There was Swiss Freddie, who had become disheartened, pleaded guilty, and was sentenced to forty years before being transferred to Bangkwang, the Big Tiger. Then Theo, another

Swiss. He was careless with his health and died in agony in our cell from a brain haemorrhage. I was left with Sten, the Viking Swede, who was enthusiastic almost to the end.

I was in my office – the open hut in the art factory – one afternoon trying to convince my butler, little Jet, to stop hiring staff. I had a cook, two cleaners, a team that collected the ice each day to keep the food from turning in the heat, water bearers, and a table of carpenters who ate a lot but never seemed to make anything. Jet, about four-foot-six high and glorying in the power of being the boss of all servants, had found another orphan he wanted to feed. The kid, who looked Persian, spoke no language well and didn't know the name of his country of birth. He'd lived on Bangkok's streets for years after he returned to his uncle's rented house to find uncle had moved. The police arrested him on a charge no one knew and he hadn't been to court for five years. We took him in as a chimney sweep, despite the absence of any chimneys.

The water carriers ran into the office shouting, "New white men. Broken white men!"

Although I'd been learning Thai, I didn't understand. Until I saw them. They were two Israelis who'd been arrested up north in Chiang Mai on drug charges. They'd been held in the local lock-up for a couple of weeks. Before they were transferred to a secure prison, they broke out through their tiled roof, scaled the wall and were free in that city of around 250,000 people.

Getting out was as far as their plan went. They had only one contact. The owner of a local guest house, a man who'd arranged their dope purchase. He reluctantly hid them at a cousin's smaller guest house. They had around $12,000 in cash. I interrupted their story there.

"Why didn't you two split up and mingle with the tourists? Buy suits? Keep to limos?"

They had reasons. Their host had accurately reported that the Thai prison guards had put up a reward for their capture. Half the tuk-tuks in town had photocopied mug shots of the pair taped to their little motors. More pictures at the bus station and airport.

When the guest-house owner had drained them of their money (promises of passports and truck drivers), he shopped them to the police. The cops crashed in early the next morning. Amazingly, one got away, although cut with glass. He was grabbed at the Chiang Mai bus terminal twenty-four hours later.

I was so distracted thinking about what they might have done to get clear, I forgot to ask about their appearance.

I'd conducted this debriefing as we sat around the base of the one big tree in Building #6. I fed them ice-creams from the nearby coffee shop as they tried to get comfortable on the circular concrete surround. Both Israelis' legs had been broken in several places. The breaks had never been set properly and had fused in odd shapes. Their legs looked like twisted drinking straws, mashed by an angry kid.

After their second arrest, they were taken back to the prison. Tied up and dragged into a dungeon. While helpless, the irate prison guards smashed their legs with iron bars before dropping a pile of rocks over each. One was in a particularly bad way, and owed his life to the care of the other. Time in the Israeli army had toughened them, and one dragged himself painfully from the rocks to provide water to his friend.

"They've still got their sense of humour," I chirped to Sten, my Swedish escape-mate, later at dinner. "Still joking about their luck."

"Yeah," said Sten, lifelessly toying with his chopsticks as we ate on the mat in our cell. Manservant Jet began clearing the dishes.

"The thing is," I said, keeping it light, "they didn't have any plan beyond the wall. What would you have done?"

Sten paused with a look. "And I'm sure you're gonna tell me."

I did my best to sound confident but I knew I'd lost my last potential partner. If I was going to escape, I'd be escaping alone.

Gaining an understanding of the layout of the prison was difficult. These were the days before Google Earth, so without public aerial images I had to rely on the few walks beyond Building #6. There was a Sunday, open-air church meeting in Building #10 that at least gave me a view of the outer wall. Already substantial when extended during World War II when the Japanese were locking up their Thai allies, another three meters had been added as well as five feet of electrified wire strands.

At least I'd chosen the best building to live in. The cells there had bars less than two inches thick. I'd kept away from the so-called foreigners' building where the cell bars were fat slabs of thick steel. There was one major hurdle in #6: foreigners were not trusted in ground-floor cells. My cell, number 57, was on the third level from the ground, and just above a cell full of trusties.

Thai jail trusties are a breed apart. Wearing ludicrous navy-blue service-style uniforms and batons in holsters, they were more than just informers, and took pleasure in administering brutal punishments. Those under me had taken three days to kill a prisoner they'd condemned as a junkie. And this from the same trusties that controlled and taxed any heroin dealing in the building.

Michael had ingeniously sent me four tungsten-edged hacksaw blades, concealed in the tubular ends of a poster, packed within a giant box-load of groceries. Rope, I could get from the army-boot factory where one-hundred meter rolls of heavy nylon tape were cut for webbing. Concealing the roll would be difficult in my cell. The idea for the ladder came to me in parts. One of the factories dried sheets of coloured paper folded over long poles of bamboo. The poles were over sixteen feet and strong. Most of the builders' scaffolding used in Asia is made from tied and clamped bamboo poles. How to turn these poles into a ladder in the night in minutes was not so simple.

Sharon, the girl from New Zealand I'd met in those last months before leaving Australia, had flown over to see me a few times. I hadn't expected that. The prison staged grand open visits on a grass field within the jail a couple of times a year. She'd sit there at our table picking at the food she'd brought while expressing absolute confidence in my ability to get out. I tried to be realistic.

"How many gates did you go through to get to this spot?" I asked her.

"I dunno. About five."

"And the gatehouse," I went on. "How many guards there?"

"What's the gatehouse?"

But nothing mattered. She was certain I'd free myself.

Someone with less confidence was Charlie Lao. Charlie had been an inmate when I met him. A Chinese-Laos national, he held Australian citizenship and was finishing a thirty-year sentence for a little dope when pardoned by Thailand's King. Royal pardons had been common for foreigners until the time of my arrest. Pressure from the Americans had all but stopped such reprieves except for the dying.

Charlie was that exception that proves the rule about not trusting anyone you meet in prison. Charlie was gold, and I knew it the moment I saw him haplessly trying to train new arrivals of foreigners at Klong Prem. The foreigners refused to learn the Thai words for left turn, eyes front and forward march, and just wandered around.

"Please guys, the boss is watching," Charlie would plead. "You can pretend just for one minute."

Charlie had good connections with the Chinese in Bangkok, and so was well-placed to get a passport for me. Now he was out, he would visit me every time he returned to Bangkok. I'd arranged for Charlie to have a copy of my radio-operator's licence. It had a photograph in one corner I hoped to use for a passport.

"Is the picture okay?" I asked on his penultimate visit.

"Not so good," said Charlie. "The wrong size. Too small. I can fix, I think."

Charlie didn't want me to try an escape. He knew of all the failed attempts and their consequences.

"You'd have such a small chance," Charlie said. "And if you stay, I'll come to see you every time I'm here in Bangkok."

I shook my head despite being moved by his friendship. "We have to think of someplace to hide the passport when you get it fixed."

Soon, there was little time to get anything fixed. My Thai lawyer looked humble and sad at my next court appearance.

Almost whispering, he said, "David, the court will end this trial in two weeks. It might not go well for you."

"A life sentence?" I asked.

"Maybe," said Montree, even sadder. "I'm sure we can manage that. Before the end."

He'd meant that I would be sentenced to death. I asked why the judge was in a hurry to end the case. He told me it wasn't the court.

"It comes from the foreign agencies. They are not your friends."

I knew that already.

When I returned to the prison that afternoon, Sten from Sweden announced he'd decided not to try for the breakout. I'm sure it was because of the Israelis' recapture. He made his excuses – the hope of a prisoner-exchange transfer to his home country – but the sight of the two soldiers' twisted limbs must have weighed on his mind. He promised to help me on the night.

On what would be, one way or another, my last day in Building #6, I held back until everyone else had left my space in the large huts of the art factory. Little Jet had left with the water bearers for my cell in the main building and the guards had wandered off their dayshifts. Beyond the huts, the trusties were preparing the beds under canopies for the night staff.

I looked around at what had been my office for the last year. A desk, some cupboards, an electric cooker, tables and a big ice chest full of food from the outside markets. Moving to my desk, I raised the top surface-lid. Beneath, I looked at the matchstick-model plan of the jail I'd been making in secret for six months. As the light from the setting sun struck its contours, it was plain most of the prison was still unknown to me.

After clicking open the padlocks of the cupboards – I didn't want to be fumbling with noise-making keys in the dark – I walked outside and up to Cell 57 for the last meal from our cook.

On a blanket in the middle of the cell, Jet had set out the food from steel tins. The four of us ate quietly, the slow rotation of the overhead fan making most sound. Perhaps my distracted mood had killed conversation. Calvin, new to the cell, was an American from Oahu and hoped for transfer to the USA within four years. Sten, the Swede, was the only one who knew of my plans. He wished me well but knew there would be hell after I was discovered missing. The fifth man was Miraj, an Indian who was serving nineteen years for a false passport. (The US Immigration Service suspected him of facilitating hundreds of illegal immigrants, and so had settled the score with Thai help.) Miraj, a notorious miser, ate alone on his bed mat.

After Jet had cleared our plates, we unrolled our bed mats and sat back against the walls to read. Calvin wrote a letter home. My bed was different from the others. Below the two-inch thick foam mat was a bamboo bed frame only a few inches high yet cross-woven with strips of canvas webbing. Other than I, no one in Cell 57 knew that the strips were made from a single one-hundred-meter roll of nylon ribbon taken from the army-boot factory below in Building #6.

In a corner of the cell, I'd built a concrete shower stall. Screens of plastic sheeting gave privacy surrounding the hole-in-the-floor toilet, and showering was more a human bird-bath, scooping bowls of water from large buckets. Earlier in the day, after my morning run, I'd removed four tungsten-edged hacksaw blades from the device in which they'd been smuggled, and hid them within the shower screen.

A few months before this night, some of my friends from around the world had met at a dinner in my memory. A wake, I suppose, dining with the certainty that I'd never be seen again.

Michael did not attend. Instead, he was putting the final touches on what appeared to be a religious scroll. It was the parody of the *Desiderata*, renamed *Deteriorata*. The poster was supported by 2cm dowel rods top and bottom. Michael had used a radial-arm saw to cut slits into the wooden rods, into which he'd wedged the hacksaws before filling the gaps with sealant and over-painting with gold and lacquer. I'd recognized Michael's fine calligraphy immediately on the scroll when it appeared among a huge boxful of food stuffs sent as a care parcel.

Stepping on the high concrete steps of the toilet block, I looked from the single high window of the cell to the yard three floors below. It was large; an acre among the four otherwise taken by factories and workshop huts of Building #6. The ground below held a long, open-sided hall. This was used for meetings as well as the feeding of one meal each day to prisoners who had no money to feed themselves. They were given a lump of rancid brown rice and half a spotty cucumber. This night, it was empty. With some alarm, I saw that a trusty had prepared a hammock bed, chair and mosquito screen for a night-duty guard. He was known to be gun-happy, according to his servants. If he was on duty, I'd need to keep some edge on him.

With five in our cell we had space for relative comfort. Most of the small cells held fourteen; even the trusties' cell below mine held eight. In 57, Calvin, Jet and Miraj were asleep or trying to be. Just after eleven, I stood and moved to the light-switch, the only such in the prison, a privilege bought at a cost of five thousand baht ($150). I looked at the Viking Sten, propped up and pretending to read a book. I nodded, *'It's on!'* and flicked the cell into near-darkness.

Just before midnight, I stepped into the shower and split the wood frame cover holding the hacksaws. Freeing them made some noise. American Calvin was now awake and Jet, peering from under his blanket. I bent to Sten.

"The others will be fine," I told Sten. "But that Miraj needs watching."

Although I'd muffled the sound of splintering wood with a towel, almost everything seemed noisy. I moved the low table I'd built beneath the window and unfolded its interlocking parts to form the stairs needed to reach the window. Although I'd accounted for some sound, I'd underestimated how much keeping quiet would slow me down. Although it was not yet 1:00am as I removed the insect screens from the window, I felt I was, already, working against the clock.

Calvin sat watching with fear and some resignation, certainly imagining the consequences come daylight of an escape attempt by a foreigner.

Jet looked on but did not speak. As I unclipped the frame stays from my low bed and began unthreading my escape rope and winding it around my arm, my little head butler looked at the fittings around the cell. He saw, before any other, that everything had a concealed purpose. The shower fittings, heavy wall hooks, bookcase and cupboards all unfolded into specific tools.

I stepped up to the window and began cutting low on the first bar with a hacksaw blade. Given free reign, it might have been cut in ten minutes. Yet a full pressure draw yielded a shrill vibration that seemed, in the night, to carry throughout the building. I wet a towel, wrapped it around the bar. Then, wiping the blade with oil, I made slow strokes. Sten and I took turns, as I glued my face to the cell door watching for any disturbance to the accommodation building night guard who was sleeping in an open room less than a hundred feet away. Forty-five minutes later, the first cut succeeded. On the last stroke of the blade, the bar – under massive tension from the decades-slow drift of the building's brickwork – sprang away from its cut base with a loud '*sprong*!' We all froze for long seconds, ears straining to listen for any outside reaction. Miraj, the Indian prisoner with sixteen years still to serve, moaned softly. Sten and I quietened and calmed the others.

As Sten went to work on the second cut of, still, just the first bar I knew I'd not have time to play around further in the cell if I was to have a hope of getting away before dawn. By 2:45am only half of the second, top cut, of the first bar was made.

"Dave," Sten said, "maybe leave it for tonight. Get going again tomorrow night?"

From beneath Sten's feet, propped on the artificial stairway, Miraj moaned loudly. To ensure his silence, I crouched low to his ear.

"Miraj," I whispered, "I know you can't wait to call out to the guards. I don't want to upset the others in the room but have no doubt I'll kill you if you make another sound." That seemed to work.

I stepped up and looked closely at the cut bar.

"No, Sten," I said. "I'll go tonight. You think you can bend that fucker inward?" I tapped the bar.

Sten, who was big when he came in and bigger now from working out, looked doubtful but determined. He clamped both hands around the towel that held the bar and heaved. It moved a few inches and then sprang back.

"Good enough," I said to his surprise. I got ready.

I pushed through a pigeon-hole cupboard mounted on one wall. I'd fitted fake rear panels made from balsa wood. Through the hole, I removed a few tools I'd need this night. As Sten strained on bending the bar – supported by Calvin from below in case he fell from his perch – I noticed something different about Jet.

Jet was standing on his sleeping mat in the gloom. He was wearing his best clothes. In the top pocket, he'd jammed a plastic bag with what I knew were his family photos and a few letters. At four-foot-six he looked like a child ready for Sunday School. He wanted to go with me.

I gently persuaded him not to go. Jet had only four years remaining of his sentence. My arrangements were for one, I said. I gave him four thousand baht and my good watch. He sat down with sadness. Sten had earlier promised to take care of him, and I'd left money in preparation.

"Can you get through a six-inch gap?" Sten asked as I turned off the overhead fan. It might have struck the escape plank if spinning.

"I'll have to," I said.

Stripping down to briefs, I put my clothes into a soft shoulder bag. Sten helped me take down the cell's eight-foot bookshelf. It was a builder's plank we'd carefully stolen months earlier. By the cell door sat a wooden footstool. It was made like a Chinese puzzle box: with a few twists, it turned into a strange, angled contraption like a giant key. This had a purpose. It would jam in the still-intact part of the cell window bars to hold firm the bookshelf plank. We slowly pushed the plank out through the bars, keeping its flat side at a ninety-degree angle. The footstool key held the short end tight within the bars. The plank now poked out into the night air, turned sideways, with only a couple of inches remaining in the cell.

"You sure this'll hold?" Sten asked. "You'll be dangling off the far end."

"Sure," I said. "It worked on paper."

Sten knew I'd have to clear the masonry awnings that were between each storey of the cell blocks' outer walls.

It was 3:15am according to the cheap but rugged digital watch I'd strapped on. With a few curt goodbyes, I oiled my torso, and took a last look for guards. None.

Stepping up beside Sten, he gripped the cut end of the troublesome bar. For him to get a better purchase, I shouldered him high to the ceiling of the cell, at which height Sten could brace both feet against the edge of the window's base. If the bar snapped, Sten would fall back.

Sten strained and grunted to lever and hold the bar a few inches, allowing me to angle my head through the small gap now between his fists and the outside world.

"Take your time," Sten sarcastically rasped through held breath.

I'd draped a towel over the cut stud of the bar that remained fast in the concrete to spare my exposed back as I wriggled through. I'd squirmed through backwards, face to the heavens, grabbing the outside top section of window bars to lift myself out. Once my groin and knees were through, I told Sten to relax. He was ready for that. The bar eased back to its previous two-inch gap. Considering the force Sten had used, I'd easily imagined Sten crashing back into the cell with the entire window bar assembly falling with him. I would have thundered down fifty feet through two tile awnings followed by a plank. That did not happen.

With my shoulder bag over one arm, I clung, half-naked, to the outside of the cellblock. I was out, give or take seven inner walls and a moat or two. Yet the sensation was odd. Whatever happened next that night, my life in Klong Prem prison as I'd known it was over. Looking through to bars to which I clung, back to the gloom and the moving shapes inside, I knew those people were gone to me now, come death or success. My feeble comforts, water bearers, cooks and carpenters must fend for themselves now. My elaborate office and its web of complex services essential to survival in this prison-city of decay, effectively destroyed. I quickly shook off this dangerous reverie and got moving.

Dangling with one hand from the tip of the upturned plank, with the other I groped in my shoulder bag for the 100 meters of army-boot webbing that was my rope. My hands were full of splinters after sliding hand over hand to the end of the plank. I'd not wanted it to wobble through any swinging.

Still one-handed, I found the mid-point of the rope and looped it over the plank, looking down to see it clear the awnings. Those angled roofs were cracked and crumbling. Earlier tests had shown that even a thrown pebble would dislodge a broken tile that would noisily fall to earth.

My idea had been to slide down the rope to a series of tied-loop footholds. Abseiling was out because I couldn't trust just one strand of the webbing for strength. Anyway, I'd need the rope for the walls ahead and had to avoid knots. My foot-loop plan failed immediately. As soon as I slid down to the first set, one foot held, the other flailed while I had to grip hard on the overhead loop to keep from sliding to the ground. That would have been okay, I suppose, had I not found myself wildly swinging in a figure-of-eight pattern facing the trusties' cell beneath. Their overhead fluorescent light was on, of course, and they appeared to be sleeping, mostly. My rope below my feet was caressing the broken tiles of the second awning. I had to hold fast until my swinging ceased.

When still, I loosened my grip, knowing the slide would not be kind to my hands. It wasn't but at least the skin that was stripped from my fingers and palms removed the wood splinters. I padded softly to ground and rolled back, rope still gripped, to clear those damned awnings. I flipped the rope clear of the plank. As the rope spaghettied into my arms, I saw Sten's arms draw the plank back into the dark cell above.

I scrabbled flat against the cellblock wall to the prepared gap in the factory complex fence that allowed a hidden path to my office. By the light of my digital watch I opened the cupboards as quietly as I could. It was 3:45am and I'd just been through the easy part, although I'd not have wanted to know that then.

Peering through the open sides of the factory hut, I saw one of the guards. He was sleeping in his hammock, about forty feet away, shoes off, still in brown trousers and his fat gut stretching a dirty vest.

In slow moves to keep quiet, I took from a cupboard seven heavy rectangular picture frames. Each 18 x 24 inches. Sten had made them while pretending an interest in oil painting. They would form the struts of my ladders. I packed them into a second bag, and put on a pair of black trousers I'd had hidden. Long pants are forbidden in Thai prisons. Prisoners must wear shorts to distinguish them from guards.

I carefully stepped my way out and over to another factory, worrying about walking on the noise-making shell fragments that littered the factory floor. Arriving at the Chinese-funeral-box factory, I found the hole in the mesh blocked. It had been repaired the day before with a large plywood panel secured by nails. Fretting always about time – and being visible then in one of the Building #6 internal streets – I took a pair of pincer pliers from my kit and began extracting a nail. It squealed against the plywood so I had to soak the nail in machine oil to quench the sound. More time lost.

Inside the factory, it was completely dark. My tiny penlight torch gave little light but my tasks were simple. I had to make two ladders from the fourteen-foot long bamboo poles that were set on racks in the factory to dry coloured paper used to fold little gold gift boxes used as cheap offerings at Chinese funerals. I lifted four poles of the tapering two-inch thick bamboo to the floor, laying them in two double rows. After positioning the picture frames lengthwise between, I took black duct tape from my bag and secured the frames to make solid rungs.

This gave me two good but heavy ladders and the problem of getting them out of the factory unheard and unseen. I couldn't go back the way I'd come to the internal street so lifted them to the rear of the factory which I knew abutted the auto-repair shop. There was a mesh vent at the top, so I used one ladder to climb up, tore a flap of mesh with pliers away from the supports, and lifted the second ladder up and out to the auto shop. With difficulty (noise, again) I hauled the remaining ladder with rope up to the mesh, through and down to the auto shop. All this, and I was still not free of even Building #6. It was after 4:30am just over an hour before dawn. I would have to speed things up. Later, I would wonder at movies that seemed to show the time taken for cutting and climbing in escapes taking place in minutes. The real time is always much slower.

I saved a few minutes by pushing my ladders under the far gate of the auto shop and then climbing over. Just as I moved beyond the coffee shop to the laundry-drying lines where I planned to scale the first inner wall, a fresh problem arose. Guards walking around. I spotted fat-guts padding towards the open, ground-level water tanks sixty feet away.

I should say that over the last two years at Klong Prem prison, two (highly doubtful) opportunities had arisen with offers of a working gun and ammunition. I felt sure then that I would have been informed upon had I taken either offer. As the guard neared the water trough, I hugged low against a factory pillar and carefully took out a device I had in my bag. I attached the fat silencer to one end and switched on the red laser pointer. Tranquil in his safety, the guard splashed his face, shook his head, and then staggered back around the corner, presumably to where he'd been sleeping.

I'd spent months thinking about the value of a weapon before realizing a real gun would be no asset. If, on the night, I saw a guard at a distance, I need only hide. If I rounded a corner to meet, unexpected, a guard within a few feet, a weapon would be slow to take in hand and pointless. Face-to-face, I could – however unpleasantly – silence him by hand. The only useful purpose for a gun would be in the range of fifteen to fifty feet when what he sees is immediately capable of keeping him quiet. Yet to fire a real weapon at night would risk a scream from a wound, a miss or misfire, and the sounds would surely bring others. My fake gun was made from carved wood pieces, tubing and a shampoo bottle. Painted black it appeared big, fearsome and more impressive than anything I could have smuggled in. The red laser sight was merely a laser pen pointer glued to the top. I was sure the sight of a red dot over the heart along with a command to halt and kneel would be enough to close the gap and tie up any guard. I'd packed cable ties and extra tape for such an event. Luckily, I saw most guards in advance. This would not be the last time over the next years when guns would prove useless.

A four-meter concrete wall topped by rolls of barbed wire marked the perimeter of Building #6. A quick inspection of the bolts that secured the barbed wire told me there'd be no time for fussing around with them.

I'd brought an extra bamboo pole. This allowed me to grab the wire with an s-hook taped to the pole and simply pull the wire clear of the top so I could set the first ladder in place and haul up the second. Once sitting atop the wall, I brought up the ascent ladder and carried it down. I was then out of Building #6. I knew there were five or more inner walls to go before reaching the massive outer wall. I crouched in the mud below behind some weedy plants and looked at my watch. I'd never make it before sun-up.

Ten minutes later, any pre-dawn observer would have caught an unusual sight. A man in black with his head poking through an absurdly long and floppy ladder as he ran while trying to keep both ends of the thirty-six-foot-long ladder off the ground. I'd taped my two ladders together as one. It was heavy and awkward, smashing both shoulders with every step. Each time I approached a new inner wall, I'd tilt the front end high, catching the wall's top. Then, I'd run back to where the ladder touched the ground, heave it high until its midpoint (where I'd taped the two together) reached the wall's top of curve and barbed wire. I'd scramble up the long ladder and scramble down the other side, my weight lifting the far side. Once over, I'd drag the ladder down to ground level before hoisting it again over my shoulders and making for the next wall.

This was exhausting. Several times I had to re-tape the joins along the poles as barbed wire tore at the duct tape. Michael Sullivan had been a pole-vaulter and had explained the trick of carrying an oversized flexible rod. "Lope," he'd said. So, I loped.

I used this see-saw action to move through buildings #7, #8, #9 and #10. I got lost twice until I recognized the smell of the old hospital – now used as a hospice for hundreds dying from AIDS. Passing the open windows their waxy faces looked at me but they were beyond speaking.

After running blindly into another inner wall of twenty rows of stretched barbed wire, I dug underneath taking the ladder with me. After a difficult crossing of the seven-foot inner moat, I was finally at the outer wall. It was over twelve-meters high and topped with an electric fence – the limit of my double ladder.

I climbed to the top to see dawn's first lights.

I cleaned myself up with a bottle of water from my bag. Then hastily dried and put on a fresh shirt and trousers the colour of the guard's uniform. I left my phoney gun floating in shit creek, the inner moat. Its effect would be comic in daylight, however menacing it seemed at night. The acrobatics over the electric wire were tingling – I hadn't dried myself well. I used my last length of rope to slide to outside ground. Outside, yet not safe. A twenty-five-meter moat ran on all sides of the prison. On those sides beyond, except for the front gate, were guards' houses and their kind. It was just before 6:00am, suddenly morning. The dayshift would be arriving at the front gate. Along the outer wall, spaced two-hundred feet apart, rose watchtowers. The armed guards within, now alert after a night's half-sleep, were rising and curious. With no more darkness as cover, a moat-crossing would fail. The sky held a tropical grey of clouds giving a few specks of rain.

I reached for the last trick in my bag: a black, pop-up umbrella I'd taken from one of the factories. Under its shade, I walked along the wall path towards the front gate. There, a wide bridge crossed the moat. Beyond, shop stalls were opening for the morning trade of coffee and breakfast rolls. Peeping from under my umbrella, I saw guards look down from the tower. I hoped they'd see me as a late-arriving fellow officer creeping to work.

As I crossed the bridge, I recognised the shoes and stride of some of the guards from Building #6. There, soon, trusties would be unlocking the cell doors. My cellmate Miraj would quickly tell of my escape. As I walked the long two-hundred meters of parkland in front of the prison to the six-lane highway beyond, I thought of my crazy home-made ladder propped against the wall. Surely, some guard was looking at it now – or do we only see things when accompanied by a moving human?

At the highway, I collapsed the umbrella, and ducked through traffic and climbed the divider to cross the road. As soon as I reached the far side, I knew I was safe. Safe from the prison, perhaps, but not safe from Thailand. Images of the shattered limbs of the two Israeli escapers who were caught prompted me to move. Yet I couldn't resist climbing the stairs of the nearby pedestrian overhead crossing to take a last look at Klong Prem prison, still packed with its eight thousand suffering inmates. Why did they remain? Within the mind of the creature that I'd become, this hated prison-city was no more threatening than a postcard, and already a memory.

Two taxis took me to a nearby suburb. A large complex of flats whose address I'd memorized. Just after seven, I stood before the door of flat 187. From my bag hung a decorative wood and lacquer tag. I twisted it to shatter its shell, revealing the front-door key to the flat. It had been so hidden in case I was caught and tortured – otherwise my questioners would want to know what the key was for. Inside the flat, I'd been told, was a small bathroom. Behind a wall-mounted mirror, I'd been assured, an envelope held a British passport. The passport had been sold to Malaysians in Jakarta a month earlier; my photograph had been substituted and a visa stamped in. I let myself in, went to the bathroom, and found the envelope behind the mirror. Within, to my profound relief, the passport was all as promised. And all that from someone I'd met in the Thai prison. He was a Chinese crook, and certainly, the Chinese are the most reliable among crooks, but I wondered then if I'd ever achieve the wisdom to know on sight and at first meeting those who will do as they say and those who would find reasons to fail.

At the airport by ten, only forty-five minutes ahead of a posse of guards from the jail who were guessing a foreigner would head for the Bangkok airport.

A friend had left an overnight bag for me at the airport's long-term luggage storage depot. I pulled the receipt from my shirt collar, then moved to a bank of ATM machines. I had two bank cards. One failed while the other paid $500 – enough for the one-hour flight to Singapore. Even if I had money for the long-haul, I didn't want to be trapped on board a plane eight hours after police and embassy officials had been scanning flight records.

On board the airliner, I assessed damage. I looked at my hands. The skin from the palms would grow back quickly. Fingerprints never forget. I was thirsty, and that was about all. I could continue my journey interrupted two years earlier.

I landed at Singapore's Changi Airport, took a cab to the town centre, then another to a mid-level hotel on the fringes. After checking-in, I went straight to the rooftop swimming pool and dived in, swimming below water end to end. I lifted myself out to stand in the warm breeze as the water drained from my body, and with it the handprints of death that had held me for two years. I took a deep breath and jumped back in.

Part III

1

Standing on the balcony stone of a minor mansion in a small town near the coast of Baluchistan, I had a clear view of the Arabian Sea. This was the residence of tribal chief Mir Noor Jehan of the Magsi clan. Again, close to where I began this story. Baluchistan is a province of Pakistan, although it is not that to the Baluchi's. They'd been fighting for independence before British India; before anyone there knew the idea of independent government. Or, perhaps, simply always fighting. I had arrived just weeks earlier.

My time in Singapore was necessarily short. Once I'd convinced my friends I was out (without voice contact they viewed messages by any medium with suspicion – such had been the ruthless persistence of scammers), things moved fast. A fresh passport was sent from Paris along with matching credit cards. Those I kept in reserve, taped as usual to the underside of a plastic chair on the small balcony of my first-floor hotel room.

My friend in France who'd passed on the documents was an adventurous lady of sixty-two with family connections. Josette drove to Luxembourg to allow me to make a brief but important call. I'd asked her to link two payphones together, holding the handsets head-to-tail to re-route the call and block any trace. I wanted to phone the Australian embassy in Bangkok.

"To hell with them," complained Josette, adding a stream of French curses. "Just come to me. You'll be safe."

"Humour me," I said. "There's something I need to know."

A day later, from Singapore, I made the call. It's worth knowing that since the 1980s, any call on a modern network can be traced in an instant. As with caller-ID, the originating number is transmitted even as the call is attempted. All that nonsense in movies with, *'Ah, we didn't have time to trace the call!'* is simply a dramatic device (based on 1930s' technology) from unimaginative writers. When I phoned the first payphone at the Luxembourg train station that night (European Central Time) and Josette dialled the Bangkok embassy using the adjacent payphone holding the handsets together, I knew the call would show Luxembourg on the embassy equipment.

"I called to thank you for those Christmas lunches," I said when I got through to the vice-consul. Some embassies put on Christmas or thanksgiving feasts in the Thai prison. Morbid yet charming. Never the Brits, of course.

"Yeah, well, Dave," the vice-consul began, seeming to choose his words carefully. "I guess we won't see you this year?"

"Perhaps not," I said. "You think anyone will miss me?"

A pause. "The Thais, maybe. I suppose you'll keep moving," said the voice with a shade more echo.

"Like a rolling stone," I said. "Or one of them, anyway." I cut the call short a minute later.

When Jo came back on the line I spoke briefly. "They already knew. They didn't' buy it," I said, meaning the Luxembourg trick. "The Agency knows where I am."

In those days – this was 1996 – it was still possible to buy handwritten tickets. From a one-man agency, I'd bought a return ticket to Karachi, Pakistan – not that I'd be coming back. I jumbled the names of my passport, allowing the surname 'Charles'. The precaution was essential as Singapore would have sent me back to

Thailand. They execute their own drug runners. The Australian embassy official had made no attempt to probe my location and his tone was of a man glued in something bigger than his usual function. The only way my travelling name could so quickly have been unearthed would've come from comparing outgoing passenger lists against stolen or lost Western-country passports. A major task just suited to a large, often idle agency with a taste for the hunt: the DEA.

I landed at Karachi after just five days in Singapore. A cousin of Noor Jehan was waiting at the airport with his car. The tribal lord himself was in town, attending a court date for what would be an interminable trial. The case was known in the newspapers as the 'September 30 Massacre', an attack in Hyderabad with 250 casualties, and Noor Jehan had been implicated. I didn't like the idea of a meeting on the courthouse lawn, however curious I might be about the workings of a Pakistan court.

"How about we stop for tea?" I suggested to cousin Iftikhar, pointing to an open café nearby.

"No. He won't –" began Iftikhar, before announcing, "We'll eat when we get to the house."

I soon saw why Noor Jehan didn't like eating outdoors. As he crossed the main street from the court building, at least three of his men blocked the lines of sight from most angles to the road. At the car, Noor Jehan let himself in the rear seat with me. He hugged me briefly with traditional greetings, then looked at me carefully. I still had my life-saving umbrella – the black pop-up under which I'd strolled from the Thai jail - its handle jutting from my overnight bag.

"You're a lucky man," Noor Jehan nodded. "A good man. Come, we meet some friends."

I spent the next three months in Pakistan, visiting old pals in (relatively) green Lahore, dusty Faisalabad, and in Karachi, a massive urban growth where tilted, crumbling buildings seemed held up by the tangled knots of makeshift electrical wires. Yet always returning to the peace of Baluchistan where I was protected. I'd wanted to drive north into Afghanistan, though my host warned against it. The Russian occupiers were out and the Taliban were ascendant, while the Americans were beginning an attempt to buy back the Stinger anti-aircraft missiles they'd given to the Mujahedeen opposition. At that, they failed. I recalled then some words of the retired US senator I'd met in a transit lounge. 'We Americans, one way or another, always arm our enemies. And, in the end it makes no difference.'

One night, during my third attempt to impress with European cooking, Noor Jehan told me some people in Karachi had spoken my name.

"Who were they?" I asked.

"Karachis. Sindhi spies," Noor Jehan said. "They take foreign money." Sindh is the province surrounding Karachi. It has its own independence movement.

"What kind of foreigners?" I wanted to know.

Noor Jehan shrugged, smiled. "Who knows? They don't get out from Karachi. Not now."

The time was near when I should leave. I had passports enough and money was running low. My host was not rich. His business was local smuggling from the Gulf states. High tax goods, mostly, and a little alcohol distilling. But Noor Jehan had many to feed beyond his immediate companions. Along two benches outside the walls of his house, each day a dozen poor and mistreated petitioners would sit seeking justice, which by any method, cost. I'd seen enough of his land and position to understand the possibilities. I was unsure if I should return to trading. I'd been twenty-four when last I made any major move. Now, I'd turned forty. Only my fate in the west would tell me. Still, I'd need to be prepared.

2

In the tall-tree parks surrounding Stockholm, I felt weightless in the cold air. I finally had the long-imagined freedom of anonymity. I felt as though gentle ocean swells lifted me as I walked. Even so, I tightened my scarf and turned to the city and my hotel. But I'm getting ahead of myself.

My landing in Europe a year earlier had been problem-filled. The passports I had were not of the best quality as the photos had been substituted in Pakistan. So, I had to avoid any close inspections. I'd flown long-haul to Oslo, then transit on a back-leg to Athens. An unexpected difficulty was finding credible winter clothes in Pakistan. In Oslo transit, I wished to appear as a European, yet even the best tailors in Lahore somehow made ill-fitting shirt collars that advertised third-world. My tan hadn't helped. Eventually, I found a supplier. An enterprising Ali Baba (who had over forty thieves) had a massive warehouse filled with donated European clothing purchased by weight. Donations that had all but destroyed the Asian manufacturers whose few had re-tooled for cheap exports. I climbed twenty-foot stacks of numbered bales in the dim warehouse tugging out overcoats and jackets.

The owner's office held loot from passing travellers. Wedgewood plates, carved ivory and lacquer-ware set with jade. Some of it seemed genuine. On one wall, above some silks, I noticed a wooden plaque. It was a set of gold-disc CDs with a brass plate saying, 'Awarded to Atherton Studios for sales of over 100,000 copies of The Three Tenors.' I tapped the plaque.

"More donations?" I asked.

"They're not real gold," the boss said as if once, unforgivably, he'd made a bad deal.

"How much?" I asked. "Including the clothes?"

From Athens, I'd flown to Rome – by then effectively a domestic flight under the Schengen agreement. I would then avoid airports by travelling overland to England. I tested the strength of my top credit card by renting a car to drive to the French border. It held.

Driving north away from Tuscany, I began to think of those years at the close of life in the 1980s. Less than two months before Clelia's death in the prison fire, we'd leased a villa not far from Torino. I wondered if the place was in use. It was on my way; I could drive by. If the original owners were around, would they recall communications of a couple that never arrived despite a half-paid, twelve-month lease? Of course, not a moment of this was spontaneous. Over the previous fifteen years I'd often thought of this place I'd never seen. It was to be the escape for Clelia and me. And who but the driven would memorize the address of a forlorn keep?

That November, there was some snow on the high ground but a sharp wind kept rocks around the hills bare. The villa was empty, but built on three levels of a rise, it would have been fine in summer. I looked through the windows. With curtains drawn there was little to see. Stepping down the path, I saw a stone cottage, probably part of the property. Smoke drifted from a chimney. I knocked at the door. When I saw the old man who opened the door, his wife by the fire, a chill of fear gripped me for some reason. In patchwork Italian, I explained myself. He looked to his wife, perhaps not understanding, then moved to close the door yet stepped nimbly outside as the door closed.

"Come," he said. He called himself caretaker and gardener. He'd lived here with his wife for twenty-five years. The old man took me to a woodshed built on the side of the cottage. Beyond wood, in a dusty corner, were stacks of boxes. Efficiently, he moved tools and sacks to reveal a suitcase beneath. He lifted the heavy case with ease and brought it to me. He left it at my feet as though collection was perhaps just a week late, rather than fifteen years.

I fussed for a minute giving him money, as though I might not take the case, though I knew I would. The old man stayed put as I lugged the case to my car, watching but declining to help further, despite the money. I drove for an hour before halting to look inside. I'd crossed the French border not thinking about the rented car. I went off road a little, stopped, then opened the case. Musty, of course. Clothes, some new and unworn. Familiar jeans, much worn by Clelia. Oddly, just two of my shirts. There was an envelope, marked, 'David', and I hesitated to touch it. As I lifted a long taffeta dress, I saw Clelia twirling in it, turning to me – I stopped immediately, and folded the dress back into the suitcase with my shirts before tearing open the envelope. A single page, hardly faded in its sixteen years.

> David, darling
> I know you always case our homes before I'm allowed in. I hope you know I'll always be with you no matter where we are. Richer or poorer — though richer is nice.
> I love you so it hurts.
> C

I put the letter back in the envelope and closed the case, for there was nothing else I could do. I'd passed a river a while back but it was not deep and the clamshell case would float. Instead, I drove along a track until out of sight of the roadway. I took the case to some wooded ground that looked beyond the plough. There, I dug a hole and buried it. Fortunately, I had a shovel. My first business partner Rocky once advised, 'Never drive cross-country without a spade', I heard his voice often, Rocky, even by then among the dead. 'You never know when you might need to bury something.'

Josette's house near Autun was heavy with snow when I arrived. I'd returned my car at Lyon, then taken a train south so Jo could collect me from the station. The house she shared with Simone was large, warm and comfortable with two basset hounds completing the family. I slept well at night and ate forgotten foods. I'd walk the dogs to the village bakery each morning.

Within a week, I'd arranged for Sharon to fly from Australia to meet me. I was overcautious about the Interpol alerts – at the level of a Blue Notice, they would stop me only if travelling by air using my own name – and insisted Sharon fly to Switzerland from where Jo brought her by car from Geneva to meet me. Sharon and I had a week in Annecy. First in an *hôtel du charme* then at the *Impérial Palace*. One evening, near the end, after Sharon had sung on impulse in the large salon while I sat at the piano with a drink trying to keep up with one hand, I knew the time had come to say goodbye.

Although we were close, I could see no future with Sharon. I could not, and didn't want to live in Australia. I have never retuned, publicly. For Sharon to live with me would mean burning everything behind her. I supposed we could meet as we had from time to time. Perhaps selfishly, I saw that as a security flaw. More truthfully, I wanted a cut from the past, and anyway enjoyed being alone. As much as I appreciated the company of friends, I'd been solitary for so long that time with people could be exhausting, something I limited to a few hours every other day. Even then, I'd hold a nagging doubt that I was neglecting something more important. I knew that this was an effect of long imprisonments in which, at each moment, I needed to watch my enemy's every move in search of weak points. Yet, in the real world, surely this was no better than window watching.

For a few days more, Sharon and I travelled north together. Near the security barrier at Copenhagen airport, we parted, Sharon to the air while I melted back into the crowd.

I'd been living on other people's money. By the time I reached the United Kingdom, there was not much left. My friends there had families and regular jobs, and while pleased to keep secrets, they were people from whom I'd never ask money. In France, Josette had pleaded a ten-thousand-dollar crisis, and I'd spent more again with Sharon. No matter, I thought. Would not the bank accounts, hidden treasure and the two flats I'd bought in the late '70s in London's Earls Court provide all I needed? Well, no. The long dormant accounts were sequestered, documentation lost. The woodlands and buildings that once hid my cash convertibles were now inverted: shopping malls on greenfields and brownfields on former town shops. After fruitless searches of utterly transformed landscapes and faced with a year's work to duplicate historic documents, I gave up. Sixteen years are too many to leave anything unattended; in modern times, even five years is too long. And what of my beastly trade? England was where I'd spend money, not make it. Most of my European contacts had moved on or seemed away for the Christmas season.

On a bleak Thursday, halfway into December, I walked through black rain to my cheap hotel in Paddington. Poor heating, tiny bath towels so scratchy that they'd strip bark from an oak, and with that tradition of dark hallway carpets that never quite dry. I sat on the lumpy bed and laughed at myself.

Friday, I left London for a ferry to Belgium. From there, several trains through Germany, Denmark and on to Sweden. In Malmö, I called a number new to me.

"Hello, Tomas?" I asked.

"Yes."

"I have a message from a mutual friend." One can rely on the Swedes to understand English perfectly. I was posed to cut him short, for although it was Sunday, I'd broken the phone rule. Fortunately, Tomas wasn't gabby.

"Okay."

I said I'd call by early evening, and ended the call after Tomas gave me his address. I resumed the train journey to Stockholm and cabbed to Tomas's apartment block. I let myself through the security door. Two floors up to the apartment. As soon as Tomas opened the door I knew I'd come to the right place. Tomas was a small man, neatly dressed, rather too thin and with a demure smile that would have sat as comfortably upon a doctor from *Médecins sans Frontières* as upon Dr Joseph Goebbels. The apartment was over-warmed, well-furnished and walled with pictures and artefacts that spoke of continuity, honesty and reliability. Tomas being what I'd hoped was just as well. I had less than twenty dollars to my name and even the name would soon expire. I'd left a trail and the passport was due for a change.

We chatted about travel and the wicked world for fifteen minutes before I came to the point.

"It was a pity about your friend," I began. "Before he died he gave me your number, as you know." The friend had been a courier, tangled in an Asian triple cross. As with many, he had died in the Bangkok prison due to the lack of medical treatment. I continued, "He said you had certain interests and some interesting friends." 'Interesting' translates well into Swedish; intriguing.

Tomas seemed relieved. Then cautiously hopeful.

"You have cargo? Here?"

"I do."

Tomas made a brief call using a second handset he took from his bed. Ten minutes later we were in Tomas's guest room, newspaper spread on the floor, as I used tools to reduce the gold-disc plaque of The Three Tenors to splinters. It was an inch thicker than when I'd bought it from the clothing wholesaler in Lahore.

"The best devices are things that can be used just once," I said as I slid free the plastic pouch of Helmand heroin. "And, of course, help yourself."

That, Tomas did.

After Tomas's friend had arrived and saw that all was good, he promised to return the following morning. In fact, he returned after two hours when I was settling into the guestroom. By midnight, I was abed, sleeping the untroubled sleep known only to children and to the truly guilty.

It took a few days to turn the Swedish kronor into UK pounds, over a hundred thousand of them. Bulky, so I had to return to London at sea level rather than by air. At least I was back before Christmas. Now all I needed to do was make a home.

3

Over the next year, I would return to Sweden often. Not always on business. Stockholm is perhaps the most civilized city on the earth. It is open and calm, caring in detail and populated by citizens who know they've got it good, and the fact they don't want to be somewhere else makes a perfect tonic for the visitor. Sometimes, I would fly from London midweek for no other reason than I don't like Tuesdays.

Business had altered, too. The Taliban had stopped opium production in parts of Afghanistan to unload the huge stockpiles that were affecting the black market. It was more profitable to tax travellers and traders rather than poor farmers, who suffered most as usual. Even in the border tribal areas near Peshawar in Pakistan, dope prices had tripled. I felt there was unfinished business in Pakistan but decided to let it be. I turned to South America.

Colombia had gentrified over the years, less Spanish colonial; touches of Spanish modern but a look of Californian sprawl. The big cartel players had been killed, imprisoned or were hunted. I had no ambitions of doing anything big. Relatively small trades over a year would be enough.

The home I'd taken for my own was a three-level mews house in Chelsea, newly renovated with the comforts of deep fabrics and deep cover. The cover provided by a new identity with no connection to my travelling names or places of business. I kept a separate flat elsewhere for guests, official mail and the few meetings unsuited to public space. I'd stopped running, finally, by my second year.

In London, I undertook all the things a gentleman of leisure should do. I found a good tailor, attended concerts and the theatre; took two days at Tower Records recreating and enlarging a record collection, and fitted one wall with bookshelves and filled them. I'd entertain friends, although sparingly, avoiding entanglements. Those who might ask me to invest in their businesses received instead a single cash gift to support them as they pursued their goals. Sometimes, rarely, I would take a girl to the flat to pass an afternoon carelessly. I'd give implausible explanations for my future unavailability – foreign legion call-up, hat-blocking conference in Iowa, a beatnik hunt in Brooklyn. Spoken with kindness, nonsense is often accepted.

The mews-house garage I equipped as a workroom with plumbing tanks, lathes and precision saws to create magic boxes and places of concealment. For transport, I'd take on a large car with a driver for perhaps two or three days each week. Private cars, like telephones, are a surveillance gift to potential investigators, their movements easy to follow. Having a driver is a useful reminder that in a car there's always someone who knows where you're going. I'd look out from the insulated padding of the rear compartment to the streets. So many strained faces, mothers overwhelmed by cares, older people defeated, younger people hastily dressed pushing hopelessly through the competition. People enmeshed through family, colleagues of work and liaisons scorched by miscommunication. We were all born to the wrong century, it seemed, a couple of hundred years too early. The brevity of life and its weight bears down in our times. I'd return to my folders of new ideas or contemplate the satisfaction of a lunch ahead.

So, Stockholm. I walked from the park to one of the two hotels into which I'd checked. The walk in the park broke the connection with the Grand Hotel where I slept and the lesser hotel where I had work to do. I'd taken the largest room on the top floor so I'd be least disturbed as it was an attic conversion along a narrow corridor and up another flight of stairs.

From a big suitcase, I took out the equipment. A small microwave oven, a portable two-plate electric stove and a coffee grinder along with bowls, funnels and glass dishes. From my shoulder bag, I unwrapped two dozen ceramic dinner plates. They had little Danish flags at the edge of a white surface. In fact, they had been created from solid cocaine partially dissolved in pure alcohol to form a thick paste. Then, scoops of almost microscopic black nitrate-polymer fibres were stirred in (those used before in a suitcase run), turning the paste grey. Pancakes of the paste were shaped in a warm press after which a spray of white paint gave an enamelled appearance. I had added the Danish flag decals before leaving Colombia. I'd previously bought a matching box for the dinnerware at the Copenhagen airport duty-free shops, duplicating the till receipt of the day of my arrival in Sweden. If I'd been stopped by customs at Stockholm it would appear I'd simply been shopping before my brief flight.

Reversing the process was comparatively easy. In my hotel room, I broke the plates in a towel, used the grinder to reduce the shards to a powder, then poured the granules into a beaker of alcohol. As the cocaine is entirely soluble in alcohol, while the nitrate fibres and polymer paint flakes are not, the coke becomes a separate solution. After filtering the liquid (a coffee filter will do if chemical filter is not available), the particles are left in the filter while the yellowish solution is ready for evaporation. I'd brought a few bottles of Polish *Spiritus*. At 195° proof (97½% pure), carrying the labelled bottles was less suspicious than a jerry can of flammable liquid. A one-hour cook of the solution in glass bowls on the electric stove - again, careful of those alcohol fumes - left a creamy paste that ten-second bursts in the microwave oven rendered as lustrous white flakes. These I packed in black plastic bags. The kitchen equipment went back into the suitcase. Just in time as a wide-bodied Eastern bloc ogress was banging on the door with a trolley of small towels and tiny soap bars. She'd come to dirty the room with long grey hairs and wart droppings.

Outside, I opened the suitcase into a construction-site dumpster and let the microwave, stove plate and grinder smash the glassware. A taxi took me into town where I left the coke in a safety-deposit box at a bank. Well, almost all of it.

The major difference with the change of source from Asia to South America was the difficulty of a safe entry into Europe. While thousands of flights each day landed in European cities from all over Asia, the number of transatlantic flights over the Caribbean and the Gulf of Mexico was in the hundreds, and most of those via the USA – a transit connection with grave inherent risks for the smuggler. Even without a US stop, smugglers bound for Europe are funnelled into the two dozen direct flights where they are routinely met by a wall of customs officers. And that's assuming they can get away unscathed through the exit points at Bogota, Lima and Caracas.

One solution was island-hopping, something that cannot be judged alone by reading maps and comparing flight schedules. The wise underground tourist will make test flights and test connections, arrive early and observe what happens at check-in and security. An example: an early route was from Colombia's seaside Barranquilla to Dutch Curaçao; then to the French-Netherlands shared island of St Martin. However, it was essential to know that at Willemstad, the pre-flight walkthrough metal detector was over-sensitive. Even the brass zip on a pair of Levi's would set it off. And if so, the operator would demand the passenger's shoes x-rayed following a pat-down search. I had all-plastic belts and nylon zippers made especially for Curaçao departures. The St Martin-Paris journey was (and is) the safest Atlantic crossing from the Caribbean despite several plain-clothes narcotics police who await the landing at Charles de Gaulle airport. The trick is to transit hold baggage to another European city, and once off the bus, take the ground floor corridor from Terminal F to G. Again, the point of this is not to come to attention. Even the most elaborate packing will not survive deeply suspicious narcs. Just once I've been caught at an airport with drugs, and that due to ignoring these rules.

I would leave Stockholm the following morning. As usual when I was in town, I called by the evening before to see Tomas, though there was no longer business to be done. By then, I dealt directly with his contacts. Tomas opened his door to let me in and returned to rest on his bed – the bedroom was the largest room – while I loaded groceries in an alarmingly empty refrigerator and stacked cans of food for his cat. Tomas had become increasingly cadaverous. I then took a comfortable chair by his side. Was he okay?

"I'm well, David. I feel sick, sometimes."

"How are you going for dope?" I thought he might be using the low-quality brown heroin that was taking over Europe. I took a twenty-gram sealed pouch of clean-white powder from my pocket. "Don't go spending your money around town," I said. "And eat first. Get stoned second." I wasn't about to lecture Tomas on cutting down. Although I hadn't used heroin for over a decade (other than test snorts), I wasn't about to take the oath on other people's behalf. I'd long accepted that some people, fortunately less than one in ten, lack the happiness gene, and only misery would follow any interference with their chemical compensations.

In passing, I mentioned a beggar who'd approached me on my way to Tomas's home. Around thirty years old, his clothes were of good quality yet uncleaned.

"Did you give him money?" Tomas asked.

"Yes," I said. "He was a doper, I'm sure. So, I gave him a hundred kronor."

Tomas raised his eyebrows. "Why? Did you feel guilty?" As elsewhere, Swedes usually give coins to beggars rather than ten pounds.

"Not guilty at all." I was surprised at Tomas's suggestion. "It's just that since he wanted to buy drugs, he'd need more than a few pennies."

I left the apartment twenty minutes later as I had a ticket to Art Garfunkel's concert. I'd offered a seat to Tomas but he'd declined. It was rare, and sad, to find someone of good nature in whom no event or substance could inspire joy.

Before my flight home, I visited half a dozen currency exchanges and swapped kroner for wads of British pounds that UK travellers had unthinkingly left in foreign hands. Most of these I packed in flat boxes, posting them to mail-collection services I rented in South Kensington. I was still wary of UK border officials. When the eyes of Englishmen meet, often too much is transmitted for comfort.

Life in London had settled into an easy pattern. After rising at seven, I'd walk to a well-equipped health club to work out and swim a few laps of the pool. Trotting homeward, I'd stop at a French patisserie for breakfast breads. At home, read the papers, under a cloud of music. Once dressed, I'd walk and underground tube to the flat, then switch on five cellphones to collect messages or make calls. I'd take the music with me. An early taste for progressive country and acid funk had morphed into the more mournful modern works for orchestra. Those, and the voices of the rare, perfect singers. Usually, I'd have lunch with a friend with a profession other than my own. Sometimes, a photographer, an artist or, at best, a someone with scientific interests. Worlds beyond mine. I soaked up their lives and was grateful for the reminder of how hollow was my trade, however dependent I'd become for its Zen simplicity.

Towards the end of 1998, I switched on my phone one morning to find a dozen message alerts. Nothing of urgency, just contacts getting chatty. Listening to them, I saw there was no reason to remain in business any longer. That week, I'd collected two new full identities with passports, driver's licenses and background documents. One, in the name that would allow control of the old properties, and the other for a secret exit should events turn bad. I had enough cash and stock to pension off all those who had helped me in the last two years. There was no reason to keep taking risks, no matter how calculated. I think I even told myself that I was then virtually un-arrestable. Not out loud, of course. No one, not even the most innocent flowers, can say that.

Searching for something difficult to take on, I found myself at charitable organisations and think-tank institutes. I didn't want to do something good, you understand, just to find something interesting. The old cause of fighting to legalize drugs seemed doomed, for the world seemed more puritan with every year. *Puritan*: defined by H L Mencken in the 1930s as, 'The haunting fear that someone, somewhere, may be happy'.

As well, I'd not long read a DEA flyer warning America about those involved in changing drug laws. Such people, the DEA warned, were the paid stooges or manipulated dupes for the drug lords and must be watched. I couldn't figure what advantage the dope kingpins might gain from a legal market that would cut their profits and destroy the black market. The report had the tone of some 1950's anti-communist campaign.

Anyway, £50,000 lighter, I was coming to the end of my tour of worthy organizations. As I was standing at the reception desk of an outfit called The New Economics Frontier, an old story came to mind. In Wilde's *The Picture of Dorian Gray*, the ever-youthful Dorian wonders at the source of his immortality, testing for any moral order. Could he slow the decay and corruption of his portrait by acting either sinfully or virtuously? In the story, nothing makes any difference. No matter how he behaves, his features in the picture continue to rot, while he remains unchanged.

"Mister Petersen will see you in a few minutes if you'd care to wait?" This was the receptionist, interrupting my thoughts.

"Ah, no. I've another appointment," I said. This place was not for me. Economists as greens were yearning for Nature's Armageddon and are as hopeless as academics at predictions. "I'll send a donation." I took a card from the desk and walked to the stairs. As I was about to descend, I passed a young woman and we exchanged automatic smiles.

Sitting at a nearby café on a footpath table, I decided to keep my life as it was, an early retirement. Controlled, peaceful and happily solitary. Besides, there's nothing more dangerous than a cause. I looked up from my table to the faces of passers-by. Did they look like believers?

At that moment, a girl walked out from the headquarters of The New Economics Frontier halting my self-absorbed reverie. She turned walking in my direction. It was the girl I'd passed on leaving. I looked at my watch. It was 4:36, and close along the street was the underground station. She walked as a dancer might. Lithe and smooth, head held high yet eyes downcast with occasional glances to the treetops as though a level gaze might reveal something frightening. Slim and long-legged with a sweet face, familiar somehow. The kind of face you might imagine seeing some now-aging actress as she was in her younger days. I laughed at the picture – after all, every actress had a youth, seen or not. Unfortunately, this laugh coincided with the Frontierette passing close to my table.

"I'm sorry," I said, standing. She stopped, frowned, an expression immediately dissolving to unreadable. "I wasn't laughing at you. You work at the Frontier, don't you?"

"Oh, yes," and nothing more but she didn't move. She seemed to tilt, to adjust her height. I was no taller than she.

"We passed as I was leaving," I said. I lifted the NEF card from the table next to my phone. I looked at it narrowing my eyes as though it were written in Hebrew. "Perhaps you can help me," I gestured towards a seat. "Just a few minutes."

She half-looked around at the people moving past before carefully – gracefully, I'd later think – sat. Her name was Eloise Morse; she was twenty-six and had worked there for two years. She spoke of the Frontier's work. I wasn't taking that in. I was listening to her voice. London voices are very specific to groups, maybe twenty of them to my ears.

Eloise's voice held the diction of a private girls' school, a learned puff-pout of intimacy (the generous plosive, the swallowed fricative) at odds with her manner. She'd pronounce 'book' like a Russian princess, and much of what I said was simply to elicit repetitions of the word. The people moving behind her were making her uncomfortable. She sure was skittish. Would it help if I shot them all? No, that wouldn't work at all.

I must have been stifling another laugh, for the frown reappeared, with, "It's a serious organisation, Mr Russell."

"David," I insisted, though I wanted to leave. I gave her my visiting card. Name, address and land-line on heavy stock with heat-raised print. Given only to the city's merchants before that day. I left her with an enquiry that would provide her an excuse to call, and then ended the conversation, paying and standing. I hailed a cab and climbed in. Could I drop her somewhere? No. As she walked toward the station, I wondered why she left work early, probably three minutes after I'd sat down. "Idiot," I said aloud, thinking it foolish to apply motive to random events.

"What's that, mate?" asked the driver.

"Nothing." Unlike that London hack, my own driver was accustomed to me talking to myself.

Eloise phoned two days later in the evening. We had lunch. Then, a dinner: the restaurant at Blakes. The food fine, but the dark Byzantine décor made her fret at the leather straps of her bag at her side. Eloise had an impressive list of phobias; birds, nightfall, the use of umbrellas, dark spaces under bathtubs, travel by air and the rear seats of cars. This last, I noted when I tried to make her feel pampered one night in the Bentley. Instead of cosseted, she felt trapped as we were driven from Leicester Square.

"I can tell Igor to take a taxi," I offered. "And you can drive if you like."

"I don't drive," she said. "Is his name really Igor?"

I shook my head, darkened the car's glass partition with a switch, and gave her a small history of the London streets we passed while taking her home. Eloise snuggled and held my hand. After leaving her at the flat in Fulham her father had bought her, I went home, smoked a joint, took half a Xanax, and slept. The next day I left for Saint Martin.

On the island, I kept a small beachfront house, rented for most of the year. I'd arrived late and woken early. Before breakfast, I padded out to the water. My neighbour was already on the sand. He had a bucket of golf balls at his feet and a number-four wood in his hand.

"Morning, Dave," said Bobby Junior. "I thought I heard you get in last night." With his feet, he squashed up a little mound of sand and set a ball on top. Bobby Junior was the son of Bobby the mafia captain I'd met in New York in the seventies. His dad and I had kept in touch despite difficulties, and I'd recommended the island. I had no business with the family but I've made it a rule never to lose contact with anyone who might prove useful. Bobby Junior had sworn loudly and often that he wanted nothing to do with family business. Dad's money was another matter. He'd bought his beachfront villa just before the world woke up to the fact there is only so much coastline.

Bobby J whacked a ball far out over the breaking waves, barely looked at its fall, and began setting up another.

"Try not to brain me while I swim," I said. I swam out to where I guessed Bobby's golf-ball reef was forming, ground zero usually the safest place to avoid hand-aimed missiles.

The few days on the island were to decide how best to treat friends and business associates now that I was to retire permanently. The trading businessmen could be introduced to each other should their interests fit; the two remaining couriers matched to those who might care for them, but it was the orphans who might be a problem. Orphans were all needful but come in two flavours. While both fear their one piece of luck might never come again, those like Tomas in Stockholm, are low maintenance. Others were like big Billy, who'd gained contacts by being drunk in the right places, still with one eye open. Billy was a failed boxer, arrested in Asia for running fake US dollars for the Malaysian syndicate. He'd managed to source a couple of passports for me when I was pressed, and he'd been a pest ever since.

Wading out from the water, I dried standing beside Bobby, who was now using a dead Portuguese man-of-war jellyfish for a golf tee.

"You still retired?" Bobby asked.

"You still the outsider to the mob?" I replied before asking a question without expecting an answer. "What sort of retirement plan does your dad's company give its loyal workers?"

Bobby eyed me a look older than his twenty-seven years, adding, "Pretty much what I'm doing now," then slamming a ball and a few tentacles into the Caribbean Sea. "Unless they retire themselves to prison." Orphan tentacles in the sea.

From the patio of his villa, Bobby's girl appeared in a bikini and loaded with towels, a striped umbrella, a foam ice-chest, an air mattress and more. Enough to claim a small country on the beach. I waved a hello.

Bobby nodded at Libby, picked up his golf balls and asked, "You still a free man?"

"So far," I said. Eloise's face framed at her door shot to mind, unbidden.

Five days I'd planned for the island. I left after two. In Europe, I tore around the capitals making generous settlements with helpers. To dope connections, I pretended concerns that the heat might be nearing. I'd get fewer calls. There was no heat. British police won't bother you unless you tap at their window.

In Copenhagen, there once was a place called Freetown Christiania – although attempts to close it permanently have failed. A former army barracks, it had been taken over by hippies in the seventies to make bicycles. In a square, there was a circle of wagon-stalls. Hendrix lookalikes there sold hashish from many lands, as Victorian tobacconists might offer private blends. That open commerce in *Pusher Street* has since been closed by the New Right. I'd just left a meeting at one of the Christiania pubs and was selecting a fistful of Lebanese reefers (individually sealed in plastic tubes) when my phone rang. It was Eloise.

"What are you doing?" she asked.

"Shopping," I said.

"That's all you seem to do. Shopping for what?"

"I'm in Denmark," I said. "Looking for some kind of publication, an edition."

"A book?" asked Eloise at last. I said I'd be at home the following day.

Now, please have patience with me, fellow travellers. There will soon be strong substance to the story of Eloise. Before I'd left London, I'd had an afternoon with her at the Portrait Gallery. Too morbid for her and another phobia. Pictures of dead people, after all. Once in the open, she held my hand as we crossed the road, she cantering ahead, still attached. In Green Park, I'd made enough jokes to steal a kiss, and it did seem like cat burglary. With a hand lightly at her neck, I lifted the dark waterfall of hair at the opportune kiss. However, it was the smell of her as warm air escaped Eloise's neck that struck me unlike anything before.

Unsettled, I stood back, knowing I'd sensed an intoxicant against which opium was a stumbling amateur. I leaned back in but she averted her head, again shy. That moment, no matter how often dismissed within the folds of reason, soon enough drove each footfall at a faster pace.

But Eloise was not easy to capture. With feline flexing, she'd be in my arms at one moment, curling away at another. I guess I've been lucky with women. Long accustomed to warm hunters, I was lost with this unreadable enchantress.

Tested stagecraft did not seem to work. I sent food from Harrods as lunch to her at the New Economics Frontier. She said it was too much and left it for her co-workers – who argued, of course, on the ethics of packaging and eating small birds. I determined to buy Eloise jewellery. Earrings, perhaps; a watch, better. Time slipping by.

I had quite a conversation with a girl at the jeweller's shop. Eventually:

"So, you want to impress her?" she asked.

"No, I've impressed her already," I said. "I want to sleep with her."

The girl produced a cute blue and gold watch surrounded by tiny diamonds.

"How about this?" she said. "It's expensive."

I showed my doubts. "Mm... no, I don't mind the cost – that's as nothing. But for my girl, she'd panic when she comes to know the price – and she would – and the strain of keeping a balance. I mean, for you, the watch would be perfect. Your fair hair, outgoing nature..."

That night, I slept with her. The girl from the jewellery shop, that is, and at the flat, not my home. I bought a suitable watch elsewhere. I gave it to Eloise the evening I was helping her through an interview for a new job, boxed, wrapped and ribboned. She felt its weight and became uneasy, and took to the trains.

Eloise phoned me at home around eleven. Would I come over to her flat? Yes, I would. The basement flat was certainly a singleton's place, no sign of even an insignificant other. She had painted soft murals on her bedroom walls and halfway along the hall. Ghostly mermaids and Mediterranean coastal ruins. Quite a few shells.

Eloise was barefoot, wearing knickers and a light vest as she answered the door. We talked as we sat on her bed. She held her knees as her hair draped her shoulders. Soon enough, we were in bed together. For warmth. Under torture, I doubt I could tell of what we spoke, although, through my discomfort, I recall her saying:

"I really know nothing about you."

"What's to know? What you see is what there is."

"For all I know," said Eloise, "you could be a drug launderer or money trafficker."

"I think those involved find it works better the other way around," I said.

There was no natural conclusion that night. We kissed rather late.

"Kissing is so intimate," she said. "More than sex, really." She wriggled away. It was a large bed. I was confounded, and when Eloise slept, I went home.

With some humility, I'd say, I know my way around the sports field. I can be persuasive. I've talked timid clock-punchers into risking their lives as couriers. Certainly, I'd do my best to keep them out of jail, and if caught I'd get them out. That's the heart of it, telling the truth: I will get you out. I won't leave you. Could I risk my real history before Eloise?

That week, Michael phoned from Australia when I was lunching with Eloise. I gave her the phone.

"Convince Michael to come to England," I said. "It's been years and I miss him."

Eloise was doubtful but they spoke for a few minutes before she excused herself to go to the loo.

"She sounds quite special," Michael said.

I agreed. "She's a doll but I've got out of supermax easier than I can get into this, well, superminx."

"Does she know who you are? "

"No," I said. "She'd freak. She freaks at nothing as it is."

Michael paused. "Tell her the truth. Then you'll know if she'll stick."

"Would you do that? Tell the truth?" I asked.

"Did once."

"And?"

Michael, ten years older than I, sounded a growl of regret. "I haven't done it since."

So, I fine-tuned transmissions. I met her parents. Had dinner with Eloise and her dad. He was a genial fellow, if a philanderer, and gave me all the breaks. I think he was in the wine trade. Mother didn't attend. They were separated. Mum had been in a nuthouse. (Oh, I don't think I mentioned Eloise saw a headshrinker Saturday mornings.) I made it my business to be at

Eloise's flat when her mother was visiting. Aloof, like a deposed royal. She was ageing well, despite stress lines.

"Why did you want to meet my parents?" asked Eloise later.

"I want to see what you'll look like in twenty-five years." Another warm, but chaste, kiss.

It was time to bring out the big guns.

"Say, Eloise," I said by phone the next day. "A girlfriend of mine is in town. Let's put together a dinner. You bring this boyfriend of yours." I figured I could deal with the slob at the same time, if there was one. She'd hinted at having one.

I arrived at the hardwood Italian eatery in Fulham Road with Sylvia Troy. She was a stunner. Tall, too. Worked at an image-processing outfit in Soho where they digitized old film stock. We'd get together for laughs sometimes.

"Syl," I said, "hang on to me a bit when we're eating tonight." I explained the gambit to Sylvia.

Then I saw Eloise approach the glass door of the restaurant. She was alone.

"Are you sure this will work?" Sylvia whispered to me.

Of course, I was sure.

In the distant past, I'd been part of a show staged by some out-of-work actors – literally working for their supper – and for the benefit of an office loser – Joe – who had a crush on an in-house honey. A dinner with a group of old friends, he was told to say. The girl and Joe appeared ill-matched on arrival but things got better. At the table, a war-torn vet claimed, "I would never have got out of 'Nam if it wasn't for Joe." (I'd later hire the actor for a court trial – he made a bulletproof witness.) A nerdy type, posing as a cosmologist, engaged Joe in an admittedly one-sided conversation about the many-worlds theory. "We took on your idea about electron position, Joe. And, dammit, none of us could see a flaw!" The dining room even had a couple of phoney group photos – interesting people with Joe in exotic places.

But the killer of the staged evening was a curvy brunette who spoke using a Spanish accent and made it known she'd had a torrid affair with the schmuck. As the object of Joe's affection returned from the bathroom, the actress as senorita collared the girl, exclaiming hotly, 'You take him, if you can. He'll ruin you like he did me!' Joe got his one night with his desire. Within a week, it went badly, a loser to the end. I hadn't told Sylvia any of this. I didn't want her overplaying her part, not that it mattered.

With Eloise arriving alone, the plan was weakened. I had no one to undermine and Eloise seemed distressed rather than showing any fresh resolve. I ended the night within an hour and put her in a taxi home.

I paid the driver and then closed the door.

"I'll call you," I said in a hurry.

"All right, David," Eloise replied as though I'd announced that I'd had to put down her cat.

Back in the restaurant, I ordered panettone and champagne to lighten the mood.

Sylvia, an American, was consoling, sort-of.

"Those are some lips she's got," she said. "Is she like that all the way down?"

"How the hell would I know?"

The following week was busy and I didn't see Eloise. Or call. One of the orphans was stressed out. As well, I'd received a message from Dubai. Lord Noor Jehan of Baluchistan was in trouble.

The orphan first: Billy the ex-pug was in his forties, from Liverpool, and had kicked around Asia for years after drinking his way out of well-paid jobs on the oil rigs. Over time, he'd met just about every scallywag Brit expat who sweated out the musty bars of Pattaya. This meant he could always find someone to do those burn-immediately-after-single-use drifters I'd never employ. For all that, he'd found a bent lawyer able to get me the passports essential for my safety. I'd paid Billy well and offered a £10,000 gratuity that I hoped would close our accounts. That wasn't enough for his ambitions. Over my coffee and his beer at a cheap restaurant in Earls Court, he explained why.

"I've got this girl in the Philippines," Billy said. "I want to set up shop there. Maybe have some kids."

He showed me photographs, as though I might demand proof. A chubby woman in a village setting.

"You didn't meet her in the sticks," I suggested.

"No. In town." Billy meant a bar. "But she wasn't there long."

Not long after you walked in, I thought. I asked, "How much do you need?"

"Fifty grand, somehow." Billy looked hopeful and devious at the same time.

"Sorry. Can't do it," I said.

"I could do one of those jobs for you. You know, travelling."

"Billy, you're not cut out as a courier." I'd already had one bad experience taking on a former boxer as a courier. Minder John Alford had been arrested in 1981 with a couple of kilos at Bangkok airport. This Billy was a fan of true-life crime-boss books. Read them grinning. A dreamer, and in the slow-changing language among crooks, a 'gangster's moll', which nowadays only applies to wannabe males. Such people can flatten out very straight if things don't go well.

"I'm out of the business," I said. "There's only one group who pay high rates for couriers. Five times over the odds is what you're asking. I'll see if I can hook you up. You'd best get others to do the actual runs. You can be boss," I ended brightly, yet hoping to put him off. He wouldn't be, I knew, and I felt uneasy at passing on to someone else that which Billy had made my problem.

Noor Jehan's difficulties were less easy to comprehend. From a call-box shop in South Kensington, I phoned cousin Iftikhar. His uncle had been ambushed in Karachi by three gunmen. For the would-be assassins, the attack had resulted, in that famous wartime Japanese capitulation-phrase, 'events not necessarily to our advantage'. Their bodies were found decorating Clifton Bridge. Noor Jehan had been on bail for a decade-old carnage, so would have trouble getting bailed again.

"But surely if they shot first – some kind of self-defence?" I reasoned.

"It's complicated," said Iftikhar. "When will you be in Pakistan?"

"Not for a long time," maybe never, I thought. "I'll send some money. Give your uncle my best wishes."

Two days later I tubed to Wall Street Forex in Piccadilly and transferred £20,000 to Iftikhar. The foreign-exchange office was owned by Dubai-based Pakistanis. It was no more than a glass booth in an easy-to-miss recess of the station. Yet behind the wall was an operation that probably handled over a million pounds each week in cash at this one office. No banks are involved directly, and the transfer fees are low. That's because the cash doesn't go anywhere. At its simplest, the system works like this: many people in Pakistan have cash in rupees they want to exchange for pounds their friends can collect in Britain. Income tax is rare in the Islamic Republic, and there are very restrictive currency-export laws to evade. Conveniently, there are many people in the UK with cash earnings they want paid in rupees to their families – not just support money; often cash to buy property. If the balance is right, no money need move. The money for Iftikhar comes out of the cash left by customers in his town. The banknotes I left at the station would go to recipient customers in London. If one accounts for trade in Asia, and all of Europe, that balance is not hard to strike, week on week. The business involves often no more banking than a set of daily registers in Dubai. It works on trust, and it does work. Iftikhar said he'd call me from Quetta. With this transfer system, it's as important to nominate the city as it is the payee, who can be given a code word to collect where regular ID might be unwise. Today, the system has been forced off the High Street, pushing up rates.

For Billy, I'd found someone who was desperate for couriers. A Dane.

"Where's he supposed to go?" I asked when I phoned Copenhagen.

"Karachi."

Somehow, I didn't like that. "What's wrong with Phuket?"

My friend chuckled. "Haven't you heard what's happening in Thailand? The government is sick of truck drivers driving into people after a week on speed. *Ya-mah*, they call amphetamines, horse drug. [Now, *Ya-ba*, crazy medicine] Police are shooting dealers on sight. The broke ones, anyway."

"I've been out-of-touch." I closed the call on a confident note. "He's not too clever, but he'll do what you tell him. He does for me, anyway."

On Friday, I gave Billy a ticket for Manila, his pension, and pointed him to the platform for the express train to Heathrow. He wasn't required in Karachi for a couple of months.

"I don't have to tell you the rules," I said. "But I will anyway. Leave all personal papers at home. That goes for you, too, not just the runners. Nothing bad will happen – Christian knows what he's doing – but it's the old cab-driver-gave-me-the-suitcase story. Tell them nothing. I'll always be contactable." I gave Billy a message-service number.

His eyes seemed to glaze over.

"Are you sure you're up for his?" I asked.

"A hundred percent," though he pressed upon me the details of his woman in Manila. "Take care of her please, Dave."

"Will do," I said. I'd seen wrecks like him make it through their chores plenty of times, I told myself. "Billy, it's just like going into the ring. You hear the bell and come out fighting."

4

London was cooling. I was in the Strand having concealed pockets fitted to an overcoat when Michael phoned.

At some point, he asked, "You still seeing that girl?"

"Which girl?"

"That girl," Michael insisted.

"I've abandoned the Eloise project," I said. "Hopeless."

"I see," Michael didn't sound convinced. "So, a virtuous life then. Just you and your other intoxicants?"

"Actually, no." I'd neglected to keep my private larder stocked. "Can't recall the last line I had."

"Indeed?" Michael throttled a laugh. "Remember young man, he who shuns a vice risks the inevitable punishment of the righteous."

Yet it was true. I'd stopped even cigarettes the week my mother was visiting London. And just a little wine with dinner.

I took the weekend in peace with music, all phones unplugged. Monday afternoon, I checked for messages on my home phone. Eloise. She sounded strained. I'd call in on my way to a concert that night. *Talk Talk,* I think it was.

Outside Eloise's basement flat, darkness had fallen when I arrived. I told my driver I'd return within minutes. Inside, the place was dark, too. Eloise was wearing a dress with cape-like folds against the chill. She returned to the edge of her bed where I guessed she'd been sitting.

"I haven't seen you," she began, then halted.

"Been busy," I said, standing; formal. "Winter coming and all that."

After a few minutes of distance, I saw the marks on the inside of her forearm. She'd been hurting herself. Without saying anything, I sat next to her and took the arm in both hands to look closely. Not deep but probably scarring; a fork used, perhaps.

"Darling," I found myself saying. "I'm sorry," and I kissed the wounds, the stigmata. "The one thing I'm supposed to be good at. I've allowed—" I stopped talking then. I kissed Eloise's face, all over. "No," I was saying.

"What, David?" she said. "No, what?"

When I was a kid, alone in a big house at night or even a spooky low-lit church with a friend, against fear I'd call out to the devil and dare him to rise before me now so I could fight him. I'd sometimes stand on the altar screaming defiance, sending my little friends running. Whatever demons possessed Eloise, I would destroy.

"No, I won't let this go on," I told her.

I lifted Eloise from her bed in my arms, turned and walked to the door.

"Where are you taking me?"

"Home," I said. "Close the door behind you."

My driver must have had his eyes on the mirrors. He got out of the car, puzzled, as we reached street level.

"Domenico," I called. "La porta!"

But Eloise said, "Let me stand, I can walk you know." She took a moment to loosen her grip. I set her down.

On a second thought, I told Domenico to leave for the night. I drove to Bedford Mews with Eloise at my side. Impatient to be indoors, I left the car on the cobbles. Not even Dom knew the exact address.

Later that night, in bed with Eloise naked, folded around me, I asked, "How are you?"

"Happy," she said, her face, for some reason, at my armpit.

Although this night had been so desired, it was not without the unexpected. After I had drawn Eloise upstairs and undressed her, I saw she was wearing the underwear I'd sent her months earlier before knowing what it would take to get to this day. Another thing, although she'd spoken of experiences with men from an early age, she had no sophistication in sex. I'd best explain that.

The first fuck with somebody new is inescapably experimental. However, it must be close, bonding. Eloise almost immediately returned to the position she'd taken as I'd removed those knickers, face down. She raised herself to her knees, not looking toward me.

"No, golden girl," I said, sliding underneath her and smiling, turning her over and holding her tight. "Not that, first." I lifted her at the waist, sliding a pillow beneath her, though never letting go. I held all of myself against her while keeping my weight just above our surfaces with skin touching head to toe, moving slowly. Just as I began to move inside her, Eloise averted her eyes, looking to the wall. Shy still, perhaps. But I suspected her mind was someplace untouchable. I kept the slides with slow motion, and was rewarded by her flow, a sensation that compelled me to withdraw briefly.

"Don't stop," Eloise said almost inaudibly.

"You're – you're all this world can be," whatever I meant by that. I locked words away in their lair and sank deeply into the ocean of surrender.

It should not surprise you men and women of the world that there followed, from Eloise:

"You certainly took your time," which I misunderstood. Then, "You could have had me a long time ago."

This, I knew not to be so. She'd dodged kisses, lowered her veil only to tighten it at her hips, and squirmed away at other times. Eloise was a kitten in a world of snapping dogs.

That Tuesday, since Eloise had left for work, I was having lunch alone at an Indian restaurant in Brompton Road. I had not wished her to go but didn't stop her – the bachelor in me standing firm. As well, I wanted a few hours to rinse my brain which was sticky with Eloise. I couldn't shake it, didn't want to. When we were reduced to stillness, I held tight; I wanted nothing beyond this woman. The city, the country, five-thousand years of civilization amounted to museum dust. For me, that had never happened before, and that a true conquest again nature. Even when young and in love, after sex I'd be contentedly daydreaming worldly possibilities, intricacies.

Michael rang as I was about to leave the restaurant. I told him of Eloise and her effect on me.

"Congratulations, David," he said dryly. "But of course you feel that way. It's all so daisy fresh. For now."

I grumbled, "A cynic never experiences joy, you shit."

"Perhaps. But he is seldom disappointed," Michael said with no satisfaction.

We ended our call, as ever, friends. As I stepped to the street, I remembered something, and it could not wait. I phoned Eloise at the Frontier, asked her to make excuses and come to me.

"Tell them anything," I said. "Say there's been a life in the family. And taxi, no trains. I'll be waiting."

"What's wrong?" she asked.

"Nothing. Everything's wonderful."

The night before, when I'd seen the marks on Eloise's arm, I was so enraged that I failed to take in her words at the time. "You understand, don't you, David?" she'd said, then something more I'd missed. I'd been thinking of Eloise as a woman but she was a girl, a slightly crazy one at that, and many parts a mystery for me. How much of my scheming to seduce her had worked? Perhaps it had, as an accumulated effect. Or perhaps I hadn't a clue. None of that mattered. At least I was clear-headed enough to know that I must prevent the idea taking hold in Eloise that harming herself would produce a good result. As her taxi pulled into the mews, I knew that if it were any other girl, I'd run away, and run fast.

After I locked the door – I'd installed some impressive locks on a steel frame – Eloise was sitting on the sofa unwrapping her scarf.

"Make yourself comfortable," I said.

"Why did you want me to come here now?"

I sat beside her. "Because right now this is the safest place on Earth." As long as I'm here, I added to myself. Then, "You asked last night – the wounds on your arm – you asked, did I understand? Well, I don't. I don't have to. I love you, and I'll make the pain go away."

Eloise was making herself so comfortable, as every article of clothing dropped away, some time passed before I could ask, "Who was it you said also understands?"

"Patrick, my psychologist."

"A psychologist?" Right, I thought. Some Pat Picklehead, and not even a proper doctor of Nuts. At least, no pills. That figured. Eloise wouldn't even take aspirin and could barely manage a glass of wine. Hated cigarettes. I wondered if this Patrick nursed filthy designs on my Eloise. Of course he did – if not, he'd be the crazy one.

"Patrick understands, does he?" I said softly, matter-of-fact. I kissed and stroked her. "Maybe there'll be a time when you don't see him anymore."

I was making some bold promises for a wanted man.

When Eloise wasn't swimming through my head, concerns of attack from within and from without circled as sea beasts in that pacific lake. From within I feared the crestfall experienced always after achieving something difficult. A prison break or a border checkpoint considered impenetrable. 'Is that the worst you can do?' I'd asked in Bangkok once free; 'So what?' I'd thought at Montréal driving away from the airport, case and kilos in hand after winding through the forty-man team of customs officers called by the

Nigerians the 'Smugglers' Wall of Death'. Many times, I'd had the same feeling after winning a reluctant woman.

I no longer saw Eloise as some project or peak to be conquered. There was no end game, and I wanted no end. A victory, again, only over my own nature.

And attack from without? I sensed nothing. I closed most of my phones, rarely travelled, ended the lease on the big car, and sent Domenico back to Italy ("Let me be your hands", he'd pleaded when I first found him). I sniffed the air like an animal; there was no danger. Really.

With Eloise, life only got better. She had no interest in science or history; for the arts, a mild fixation on the painter Frida Kahlo. I didn't care. An innocent in the breadth of sex – though I thought a perfect natural beneath. Yet, around other people, Eloise remained as nervous as a long-tailed cat in a room full of rocking chairs. Lunches or nights out with company, I'd select only the most generous and open-hearted among my friends.

One night, late, with streets almost empty around Convent Garden, a trio of loud young men approached. One was plainly drunk and all wanted to make themselves brief stars. When brotherly greetings failed to move them on, I had to sit Eloise on a bench out of harm's way as I dealt with the imbeciles.

"Close your eyes, Kiddo," I said. "I won't be a minute."

The idiots were already wheeling around when I had Eloise seated. I closed the gap, walking fast towards them, still smiling but eyes narrowing.

"Aw, here he comes," said the middle pin, a smartass.

Stopping just out of arm range, I reached into my overcoat breast pocket, leaving my hand inside.

"Now, you boys just fuck off quietly," I said. A double-click sound could be heard from my coat. "Now we all know London's camera'd-up but rest assured I'll take my chances leaving you kneecapped. Just for the hell of it." I was speaking in a hoarse whisper, effective, but really to prevent Eloise from hearing an alien accent and tone.

The drunk made as if to move forward but his right-side mate held him in check. They shuffled around yet edged back and turned. One muttered, "Nutter," quietly as they found safety under a street lamp. I nodded at them but held my ground. A releasing clack could be heard from my coat, and I stepped back slowly until they stopped looking back at intervals. There was nothing in my pocket other than a large hobbycraft clamp whose sound struck me as interesting in my workshop. The trick is to look like you shoot people for fun. It's true about London's cameras though, and I think, lesson #4 upon the uselessness of actual guns.

When I returned to Eloise, her eyes were open. She was not more relaxed at my preventative success.

"What did you do?" she asked.

"Nothing, I just made them listen." Eloise was shivering.

This would've been worse if the gun-illusion hadn't worked. I'm not a big man and against three the scene would have been nasty, brutal and perhaps not so short. (Fortunately, although my private school had useless and eccentric teachers, the evening classes – politely named Karate – were given by the psychopathic streetfighter who ran the boiler room.)

We walked to the nearby car park quietly and climbed aboard the new Audi. From there until the house I felt more the object of fear for Eloise than were the louts. Only the safety of home and touch calmed her. The possibility of opening my past to Eloise receded farther into darkness.

It is necessary to halt our London story for a moment as, in the interests of synchronicity, I must tell of another event from the many things I would later come to know.

Ahmed Baboosh was born to a wealthy family in Karachi, Pakistan. As is the practice of families whose money demands no greater attention than a vice-like grip, a lucrative government job was procured for the younger son. Other than milking governmental contracts, few jobs are as rewarding as those in the customs service. Ahmed was angled into the narcotics division and became Superintendent Inspector of Karachi ports. A large man with a calm voice but a cruel manner, he did his best to ensure that no drugs were exported without his knowledge or consent.

At this time, he was in Washington, DC, having been invited for twenty-one days to experience the scope of the Drug Enforcement Administration and its dedicated officers. One of the DEA's senior administrators was Bill Shenkmann, last appearing in my story in Thailand driving another nail into my coffin. Ahmed Baboosh and Bill got along well, although Shenkmann held deep suspicions of all officials in Pakistan. Ahmed would have been pleased to assure Shenkmann that he could be bribed only by hashish smugglers. Though this fact made him a model of rectitude in Karachi, it would not impress the rigid DEA chief. Instead, Ahmed told Bill that compared with Mexico, not much heroin moved from central Asia to the USA, and that he would grind to powder all those involved. Not those, Ahmed failed to mention, who served the interests of Pakistan's intelligence service, which included almost every armed group bordering Pakistan, including the Taliban.

Shenkmann was no stranger to Asia, he told Ahmed. He'd been on that battlefront since the '70s. The conversation then turned to people they did not like. After speaking of major drug runners and the difficulty destroying those woven through power politics, the talk arrived at small but persistent irritants. Ahmed Baboosh had none that came to mind; such people found themselves dead in Pakistan.

"You ever heard of David McMillan?" Shenkmann said. The name meant nothing to Baboosh. "He was Daniel Westlake in Thailand when we had him. He slipped through."

"Is he important?" asked Baboosh.

"Well, no, I guess. Not in the great scheme of things but he's connected with the death of an agent in Thailand." [Connected, I should note, only by the degrees between the queen of England and a rice farmer in China.] "We've got information that he's operating out of Pakistan." Shenkmann showed Baboosh a thick file complete with photographs. Baboosh flipped through the pages looking for Pakistan references. Finding none, he lost interest.

"What sort of quantities are we talking about?" Baboosh wanted to know.

Shenkmann shrugged. "We'd like to see him caught."

It must be – and today more than ever – that there are always people somewhere in the world wishing you harm. How can this possibly matter? Without knowledge of place and time, nothing can happen.

At the wall of a modest villa near Cap Sicié in southern France, I took in the evening air of the Mediterranean in September before returning inside. The modern house was open plan, and I could see Eloise on the kitchen phone. While she spoke, I sat in a chair by the fireplace looking at a map I'd marked with places of interest.

Convincing Eloise to travel was difficult. For just five days away from London we'd driven to the coast, then ferried to France where the faster train service took us south. Domenico flew in from Firenze just to drive the Audi south to us for the following day. I kept him in a hotel in Toulon in case he was needed.

I looked at my marks on the map, folded it and threw it on the fire. Eloise was by then sitting on my armrest.

"You've memorized the map?" she said.

"No. I just figure we'll never go further than a restaurant," I nodded back to the phone before asking, "You tell your friends you're having an awful time?"

"If you were listening you'd know it was my father. I said you'd kidnapped me," Eloise smiled and kissed me.

She was trying, I had to give her that. She hadn't said anything jokey to her dad. Cool, really, and evasive in using that causal sophistication to mask her new relationship with me. I was learning to discount most of what Eloise said while decoding her little sounds, movements and invented phrases. After I once suggested an African journey with all its unknown safety, she wriggled next to me in the dark and said,

"No— no, – I'm too fatsy squeak for that!"

I pictured a chubby mouse shrinking back between some grain sacks.

Only when back in London at my house did Eloise fully relax. Even so, not once had she hurt herself during my brief absences. Patrick Picklehead, the plain-wrapper shrink, had free Saturdays now. (By the way, I found out that at twenty-three Eloise was seeing a proper doctor psych who did put the hard word on her. The old tosser was nearly my age. No wonder I'd had my work cut out.)

Anyway, Eloise was mine and I intended to keep her forever.

A couple of times each week I checked messages from cellphones I kept at the flat. Mostly greetings, though often veiled pleas from the needy or greedy. In early October, I received a message from Noor Jehan Magsi's family in Baluchistan. Perhaps cousin Iftikhar had managed to free his uncle? Not so. On calling, I was told that Noor Jehan was still in prison and Iftikhar had disappeared somewhere along Pakistan's North-West Frontier Province near Afghanistan. Could I help?

Should I? Well, yes – Noor Jehan had protected me and probably saved my life more than once. I'd already sent money, which would have been eaten on many plates. I knew that sending more would help only those who first received it. If cash were to solve anything, I'd have to be there to ensure it reached the right pockets. I had passports to burn, so there were no security considerations other than possible kidnapping. Still, the bagman is rarely snatched and I was confident I could strike a deal.

Though I had no wish to leave Eloise even for the week or so I'd be away, I thought this might be a time to see how she coped. I was only just appreciating how isolated she felt most of the time. At work or in familiar London she was with company yet alone.

And without company, I suspected there was some underlying terror that she hid. Or, is that only something I believe now?

"But why?"

That was Eloise, sitting in the middle of my bed.

I draped my jacket over a chair, kicked off my shoes and held her narrow frame. "Because he's a friend in trouble," I said.

"Where are you going? No — don't tell me, I'd only be alarmed."

Kissing the gentle curve between ear and cheek, I spoke softly. "You're all the world to me. But what would you think of a man who deserted his friends? Would such a coward be any use to you?"

"I adore you," Eloise said as though to herself. "Here, this is magic."

Magic aside, it must be possible to keep a promise to the one you love as well as a friend.

I'd never held men in high regard. Only a dozen or so are real friends. Growing up in a household of variously abandoned women saw to that. Even so, I'd strike the deal with the few men I'd found worth knowing: if you're there for me, I'll be there for you. In practice, it's 'If you unquestioningly do as I ask, I'll help you no matter what.' One of life's valued certainties or a tragic boys' game, depending on your luck.

That night I was very careful with every touch upon tender Eloise. My hand flat on her tummy, I could feel tiny contractions of nerves. Her breath at my ear in pulses. My lips at her neck lifted by the rhythm of her veins. And later, inside her yet without movement, encircling, holding through twists of arm and hand, each whisper overlapping, I layered promise upon promise. Protection and eternity. Clear as I remember that night, sharper remain the vows.

5

Airborne at 33,000 feet almost alone in First class, I listened to Joni Mitchell sing *Amelia* through headphones while on the upper deck of a decaying Pakistan International Airlines 747. A song of aviation and false alarms.

Before leaving Europe, I'd paid my rent for the year ahead, extended the terms of the safety deposit boxes, and hidden cash and documents in places just about immune from detection, but also safe from flooding and any renovation or re-wiring that might take place. This may sound overcautious for a ten-day return journey, but my luck has never proved reliable, and I had a lot to lose. Eloise. Everything else could be replicated. While I knew that if I wasn't back in, say, three weeks, it would mean I was dead or shackled in some dungeon, I took comfort in the idea that elaborate fall back plans are rarely needed if, and only if, you've already taken the trouble and expense of putting them in place. In truth, there's not a shred of rationality in this proposition, but doing so made me feel better.

More logical preparations included travelling to Paris on one identity, then on another to Oslo for the PIA flight. Although there are bundles of direct flights from the UK, I didn't want my countrymen to know my destination. In Norway, I mailed my first passport to a post box drop in Stockholm. (These were two services available in Sweden at the time, one operated from a corner tobacconist's shop by an ex-Nazi informer. He'd read you mail and phone increasingly irritated police with his findings. He's dead now, bless him.) That left me with three solid identities for the journey. Does any of this matter? Sure, it does. I don't want you thinking I was stumbling toward death thoughtlessly. I had two thousand dollars sewn into the waist of my trousers, and another fifty hidden in my luggage.

My first stop in Pakistan was at the house of Adnan and his family in Lahore. Pakistan is not a place where you stay at a hotel unless you want the curiosity of many agencies and opportunists. To use the word 'crook' doesn't convey useful information in Pakistan. There's an old joke in Urdu (the compound language understood by most) that Pakistanis tell each other. A Pakistani man dies and goes to hell. He's shown around by one of the devil's demons. Huge, boiling cauldrons of shit steam for acres in the fiery cave. Each is labelled with a nationality. The demon explains that each sinner must suffer with his own kind. The newcomer sees that surrounding the lip of every massive vat, little imps have spikey tridents with which they jab at those desperately trying to climb out. When they arrive at the cauldron marked 'Pakistan,' the man notices there are no devil's helpers around the edge. 'Don't tell me I'm the only sinner for the Pakistani pot?' asks the new arrival. 'Is it empty?' 'Not at all,' says the demon, 'It's full to bursting, but we don't need pokers – the Pakistanis pull each other down.'

That low view of the people for each other was not one I shared, I've always felt relaxed in the country. After the grasping desperation has burned itself out, there's a good nature on the ground. It is necessary to think beyond the fact that a westerner is richer than everyone he sees, and take no superiority from that. So, what if the poor cheat and swindle at every opportunity? What do you think us pale Northmen would do if we woke up to find ourselves barefoot, hungry and cleaning out a black man's turdpan? Well I know my devil's cauldrons too. The response would be genocide and annihilation, quick as lightning on account.

We're all so co-operative and civilized, so they'd not see it coming. Simple larceny is beneath us.

I awoke in my bedroom refreshed, then borrowed the family car, honked my way to the only biggish supermarket in Gulberg, and returned to cook breakfast, only to find the electricity fused out along the street and houses. My host Adnan shrugged and told me blackouts occurred every second day. He then asked his wife to set up the gas burners.

"I'll just take a look outside," I said, mostly from fascination at the tangle of wires at every lamppost. Climbing up the narrow metal skeleton (there are few wooden lampposts in Pakistan) I saw that almost every house had hooked a second power connection, all dangerous twists of wires. These were to bypass their meters. As well, in the fuse box, the high voltage one-inch diameter fuses had been replaced with cut sections of plumber's tubing.

Over breakfast, I suggested to Adnan we drive to the local electricity sub-station to find out what was going wrong. He looked at me as though I were mad, yet with nothing else to do agreed.

I visited the neighbours along the street to gather support. Most knew of me from previous visits to Lahore. They were positive something should be done. It's worth noting that the suburb of Allama Iqbal town is what we'd call solid middle class with straight roads and the houses built over twenty to thirty years. That's not so obvious at first sight. The homes appeared as grey concrete blocks of two or three floors with painted iron gates. The street had been made with footpaths but every house was built with its front wall bricked to the road edge or beyond. The road itself probably once had a thin layer of asphalt, but was now rutted earth and stones. The builders and the residents were all respected townsfolk. My neighbours, mostly civil servants, including a low-ranking customs officer, two teachers and a land office clerk. Standing in the street looking at the tangled mess of wires, my neighbours joined my call for action, most with passion, yet each made excuses of time and work when I brought out the car.

Adnan explained as we drove to the Pakistan Electricity Commission office: "Everyone has something to hide in our street. None of us pay the correct money for electricity. For gas, we each pay cash to the man who comes to check the meters. I don't think he knows how to read a meter." Adnan bumped the car into the ruin of the local electric company office. It was once a solid colonial-era structure but now not even the original window frames remained. Our car suddenly lurched and dropped to one side. "Manhole covers," Adnan hissed as a curse. "All gone. Iron, you see. Top-dollar scrap."

We walked into the office to find a single chair and a dust covered desk. Not a pencil. A lone employee came in to see us. Looking at me, he became apologetic. Of our enquiry as to the failures, he spoke in English.

"Load shedding."

To which Adnan replied abuse in Urdu. Soon the man's family gathered. Had I come to fix everything, the young ones asked. Who was in trouble, the older among them feared. Adnan and I left within minutes.

In the car, Adnan began again. "And you think anyone pays water bills? Not one. We've mains pipes, but there's fifty illegal pumps going down five hundred feet in bore wells. Five hundred feet! Sucks the aquifer dry..." and he went on, clearly enjoying himself.

Not long after I'd arrived, when we were alone in the living room, Adnan had produced an old browning 9mm automatic from beneath his sofa. It had been locked solid with dust and neglect. This next morning I'd tapped it apart and was oiling its sliding mechanism and springs with many sighs and tut-tuts. "I keep it if people attack the house," Adnan said.

"Yes, you could throw it at them." I suggested. "Then get away while they try to get it to work."

This seemed a good moment to hint at my purpose in Pakistan.

"Is it true what they say about kidnappings here, that you're invited for dinner, then to stay overnight, then all the overnights?"

"That's the polite way," said Adnan. "It only happens if they know your family has money or land. You know, the rich families in the country areas all keep their private jails. It's only in the cities they buy the police."

I'd finished cleaning the reassembled gun. I offered it to Adnan. "Keep it," said Adnan with a look of understanding. "For your travels."

I began my journey south the following day to the Baluchistan capital of Quetta by air. A branch of the Magsi clan lived in an old house with fine gardens, but so heavily draped and carpeted inside, the old uncles and aunties seemed entombed. I'd begun in Quetta because that's where the money I'd sent had landed. No-one seemed to know where that had gone after Iftikhar had collected it.

"He went to see Noor Jehan in the Karachi jail," I was told. "His uncle sent him to Peshawar. He's been taken into Afghanistan. They want money to give him back." Did I want to visit Noor Jehan in prison? No I did not.

For all of Noor Jehan's virtues of loyalty and determination, I knew him as a man who would manage defeats by encouraging new schemes, and unlikely alliances with a ruthlessness that might obscure the truth behind the Iftikhar kidnapping, and his being imprisoned would add a false urgency to those new plans in which he'd surely want assistance. Besides, his information could only come from his visitors, people I could talk to myself. It's easy in this part of the world to become entangled in private ambitions when pursuing an independent goal. Before I left the house in Quetta, I asked who was negotiator for any ransom payments. I asked only so I could add another name to my list of those not worth talking to.

I gave the relatives some housekeeping money and then flew to Faisalabad in central Punjab to meet Kamran, one of Iftikhar's drivers, who was staying with his own family. From the air, the early life of the city reveals itself. Faisalabad was called Lyallpur (after Charles Lyall, a colonial administrator) until '79 when Saudi money brought its new name. The original city street plan, based on the British Union flag can be seen at altitude. On the ground, road encroachment has produced a jumble of streets narrowed by extended stalls and shops.

I'd met Kamran years earlier when he was among Noor Jehan's most trusted hands. Speaking to him while sitting in the tiny walled courtyard of the modest family (by marriage) home, I wondered why he was away from the clan action in the south. He seemed reluctant to provide details of Iftikhar's capture, even though he'd been on the scene. "Noor Jehan had some trading across the border," Kamran said. "He wanted Iftikhar to complete the business."

"What business?" I asked.

Kamran paused. "Guns. A dangerous thing."

I didn't believe that for a minute. Especially when Kamran added, "It's possible I could get him back if we gave money."

Firstly, there wasn't much room for extra gun-running across the border since all sides were flush with weapons, and Pakistan's ISI Intelligence Service fed the Taliban with many of its toys. Secondly, Kamran spoke in a tone that suggested he might have been party to Iftikhar's disappearance. I convinced him that I'd arrived without a lot of cash, and so extracted by the deceit the details of Iftikhar's drivers on the border zone.

I returned by road to Lahore to prepare for a crossing of my own. I left two good passports at the house, kept a disposable British passport (that is, an original issued to someone else, but with the photo substituted), and a matching Pakistan passport. I'd bought it a year earlier when local-office issued passports were going cheap. You might think a *gora* (a white man) presenting a PK passport in an English name, and with a feeble grasp of Urdu at a checkpoint might seem suspect, but there were over twenty thousand left over sons of the British Raj with just such documents. In my large shoulder bag, I packed a couple of shalwar kameez, the Persian baggy pants and long shirts favoured by overweight Pakistanis since the '70's, one set in dazzling white. I also took Adnan's browning pistol as it's clip holster nestled firmly at the small of my back. I'd tested it on some kites flying over the flat roof of our house during the loud call to Friday prayer.

I set off at night with a Punjabi driver and a Japanese car heading for the Korean-built highway connecting Lahore with Islamabad, the national capital. The only smooth highway in Pakistan, it was funded when a former prime minister (and back now as the current chief) used to commute between those cities. The link road to the highways was a glorious mess, best seen evenings as a million dim yet multi-coloured lights decorate the trail of jangling haulage trucks that bump and lurch through town like painted circus elephants kicking up dust. The roadside was lined with stained, leaning shacks, kerb-wobbling barbers' chairs, phone call offices, tiny chewing tobacco and *paan* kiosks (whose munchers of the betel-nut concoctions cover anything below three feet with gobby, eternal patches of brown), signless shops between the food-fires drum-and-grill cookers, while behind every hut and cramped office, no matter how narrow, a hundred-or-more people lived in hope of meeting someone with the right connections.

My driver and I stopped in the capital for an early breakfast, before completing the last seventy miles to Peshawar, the large frontier town before the tribal areas. I took a room at a guest house and sent the driver home. Iftikhar had two local helpers when he'd passed through. One didn't want to be found, but his local guide was still in town. I was in luck; the man was an Afridi. Those of the Afridi tribes are often called the Jews of the North West Frontier, and what an Afridi doesn't know isn't worth knowing.

Naveed was pale skinned, well-built and keen eyed, not a simple driver for hire. As he sat taking tea with me in the garden of the guest house, I knew that everything I said must make me worth helping, but not worth targeting. Naveed was frank about the reasons for Iftikhar crossing into Afghanistan.

As Afghanistan has no sea port, a transit trade agreement exists with Pakistan for goods arriving at Karachi port though bound for Kandahar or Kabul. Containers are sealed and trucked without the need for customs duty payments until entering Afghanistan. In practice, often goods cross the border only to be smuggled back into Pakistan. Noor Jehan had arranged a container load of air conditioners to cross, then brought back in small consignments through the border at Spin Baldak. The goods had been paid for but not the Afghan-side smuggler's costs. Iftikhar had been sent to negotiate a settlement.

"Did Iftikhar know how much was owed?" I asked.

"Maybe," said Naveed. "I know he didn't bring money."

"Well there's nothing I can do to settle the business," I said. "I only want to see him so I can tell his sister in London he's okay." There was no sister in London. I didn't want to seem a negotiator for Iftikhar's family.

Naveed didn't want to take me across the border but would arrange for passage through the tribal areas that were forbidden to foreigners, and then on to the Khyber Pass border crossing at Torkham. There was more Naveed could say but when I declined the offer of a phone call with Iftikhar and insisted on crossing immediately by the side roads, I knew better than to invite complications by involving him more that I had to. It's best to be satisfied with small steps.

Thirty-six hours later I was approaching the border crossing in a car I didn't like with a driver I didn't trust. I had the driver stop before the lights became too bright.

"I can take you across," he said, "We have to pay. You have cash?"

The car we were in was a newish Subaru sedan. Ahead were perhaps fifteen trucks parked in a line by some shops. To me, the border posts on both sides looked closed.

"I tell you what," I said, "I'll meet you on the other side where the lights are." The driver didn't like the idea. He shook his head saying, "I still need cash for petrol."

The word 'money' is rarely used by new English speakers up north, as it carries the sound of twat in Urdu. I gave him a thousand rupees, about thirty dollars, before climbing out with my bag. He drove forward at a crawl to keep me in sight. I pointed ahead and repeated, "Over the other side, by the lights," before moving quickly to the kerbside of the trucks. I was dressed in a less than white salwar kameez. It was nearly 8pm.

Once I was safely out of view from the driver, I called in at a shop with a phone and racks of music tapes, and lots of curtains. The phone meant cab drivers in plain cars would be nearby. I found one with a nicely beat up local make.

Within minutes we were at a huge hole in the wire fence, where a single officer in the remains of some uniform sat on a chair listening to a portable radio. Through the car window, my driver held his chewed up ID card in his hand, as well as my Pakistan passport, with a five-hundred-rupee note poking out. The guard, if that's what he was, simply plucked free the banknote. I slumped in the back seat looking sleepy as we were waved through. My new driver seemed alright, and of course there was no sign of the Subaru, so I had him take me on to Jalalabad.

The crossing I'd taken was not ideal. Tradition and tribe, as well as the Taliban made the area a patchwork of controlling forces – control being loose or lunatic depending on mood, weather and the dispute of the hour. The area I'd passed through to the border, Mohmand, had been proudly pagan for two thousand years since the time of Alexander, the forced conversion to Islam less than a hundred years earlier in some places. That's less important than it sounds: it is tribe and clan that matters most. The same applies to the Taliban, a term meaning pupil, young people from the madrasa schools. Their village outlook was strong as any unifying spirit of Islamic orthodoxy. Bad borders didn't concern me here, and anyway I wouldn't slow my schedule.

Jalalabad: at the time a busy junction; Taliban from the south hanging about like gunslingers from the wild East, waiting to collect the latest batches of Pakistani kids fresh from the halfwit schools of the mullahs in the tribal areas of Kurram and Waziristan. They would be bussed north to take on the Uzbek and Hazara militias where the Taliban had scores to settle.

The large movements of people inward with smuggled goods, and opium heading out, kept most prying eyes on their business rather than on a stranger without much of a beard. (The Department for the Propagation of Virtue was still a year away from enforcing the minimum-beard-length edict.) I'd arrived late the day before, found a bed for the night thanks to my departing taxi driver and was now in the morning light and dust of the bus station trying to be invisible yet seen by expected friends. They found me quickly enough. I recognised one of them, just.

"What's with the beard?" I joked to Syed, a very distant cousin to Lee, my former partner in Thailand.

"My name's Abdul now," he said as soon as he could.

I'd met Syed– now Abdul – when he was seventeen during that final grand journey to Baluchistan in 1981. He had crossed over from Afghanistan's Paktika province to avoid the Soviet Russian army that had launched a major campaign in the southeast. He was beardless then. I walked with Syed and his friend to the very plain restaurant at a nearby hotel so we could get off the streets. Even a simple egg with bread tasted gritty, though the pool of oil disguised the dirt.

"Syed, you were joining the Mujahedeen back then," I said. "I guess you're too old now to be called a student." I looked around the room at the long beards and dark tunics.

"Mister David," Syed spoke quietly. "You can't make funny talk like in the old days."

"What, no laughs?" I leant close, "That's a big price to pay for peace, if that's what this is."

Yet there was some truth. The Taliban were humourless and savage but welcomed by most outside the capital Kabul as peace enforcers. Still plenty of killing, though stability when compared with the factional wars of the post-Russian rebellions.

Syed, and his friend who spoke no English, had long cloth sacks at their feet. The barrels of their Kalashnikov rifles were plain to see.

"Why bother with the bags?" I asked, pointing to their guns.

"Everyone has a gun," said Syed. "In a bag tells people we don't use them here."

I was about to say a visible gun, if made slow to operate, is worse than none since it is a gift to enemies and filling even friends with doubt. Instead, I explained why I was in Jalalabad. I passed to Syed the phone number I'd been given in Peshawar. We then moved a couple of blocks to a quiet though spacious PCO. Public Call Offices were everywhere in central Asia before cellphones reached the poor. From tacky huts with one line to the multi-booth offices of the cities, they were meeting places and service providers for form-filling, photocopying and information hubs.

Syed had his Pakistani cellphone but had to use the PCO line to call Iftikhar's captors. (In 1998, there was a cable through to Peshawar from Jalalabad and a couple of attempts to set up a pirate transponder. Only those who frequently crossed the border kept cellphones to use on the Pakistani network.) They'd be over to see us in an hour, they said. We retired to a large room with hard chairs to wait.

"Now Syed, listen carefully," I said. "Please translate for me just what I speak, whatever you think. And politely stop them every few minutes so you can tell me everything, and that includes what the number-two man says. How many are coming?"

Syed shrugged a don't know. So, we waited. Syed and his friend unbagged their guns, leaving them at their chairs. An hour passed, then two. More calls made, then Syed returned and held up a finger.

"One hour," he said.

There was a small annexe behind our room. It had a woven jute daybed and a corridor that led to a hole-in-the-ground toilet. I stretched out for a nap.

Just as I thought I was near sleep, I heard sounds of people arriving. I got up, left my bag out of sight beside the doorway – a bag is too interesting – and then saw Iftikhar's kidnappers at the table in the next room. There were three. I didn't like the look of them but didn't show it. I gave them the reserved smile given to room service. Watchful yet with the promise of a tip. The three newcomers set their rifles by their chairs, too. Syed was less careful with his expression. Despite the handshakes, hugs and heart-touching all around, even I could see that Syed would say, 'After you,' to them at a bungee-jump and knife-sharpening contest. I suddenly wished I had Iftikhar here to translate, but of course that was the point. He wasn't. The PCO operators had left, closing the metal shutters to give us privacy.

Here's the conversation, though I'll edit out the translation process from Dari, the Afghan Persian. More than once I had to tap Syed's knee to stop him adding his two cents as we sat at the table, particularly as I could tell he was challenging what was said. Our three guests were certainly smugglers but to look at them, they didn't appear so. Unified by black tunics and a manner that told of having co-ordinated themselves as a team. The tall one did the talking. I got straight to it.

"Young Iftikhar is not with us," I said. "Why didn't you bring him?"

"He is safe," said tall one. "Have you come for him?"

I dismissed that with, "No, I'm here on business. I just want to see him. You know his family have no money. I'd like to talk to him for a few minutes, that's all."

Looks of uncertainty passed between the visitors before the tall one said, "We can bring him tomorrow. Not here."

"That's no good," I said. "I'm leaving for Kandahar early morning."

"When will you return?" asked the second man before his leader cut in.

"Maybe tonight is possible," from the tall one. It sounded thin.

I shook my head. I took from my loose shalwar trousers a wad of afghanis, the local money, patting my thigh to show that's all there was.

"I'll give you five hundred dollars if you call whoever looks after him now so I can speak to him," I said as though that would be enough to end my business.

"There's no phone. He's in a small village."

I leaned forward on the table, hands clasped under my chin.

"You don't have him, do you?" I said. I picked up the money. "There is nothing you can do."

One of the sidekicks whispered briefly to the tall speaker. My Syed became agitated. At the next words from the kidnappers Syed began to bark back. I stopped him. Syed turned to me.

"Just translate," I said.

"They are saying that maybe you want to join Iftikhar where he is. I don't like—"

"I understand what they mean," I said, interrupting.

I smiled generously across the table, stood and held out my arms, palms open. Do what you want, I was suggesting. Knowing I was in a lawless land was not frightening, it was liberating. Here, there were no cameras on lampposts, no forensic scientists would sift the ground, no dedicated investigators seeking evidence. One could settle accounts in full at any moment of one's choosing. I sat down, telling Syed to find out who had Iftikhar now.

Soon enough, it became clear Iftikhar had been sold on, a common practice when a hostage fails to yield ready money.

"Fine. How much did they give you for him?" I asked. Then, "No, don't tell me, I'll never know. We are all businessmen. Just call the new people now to check he's still alive and with them."

The tall one fished out a cellphone from his pocket, and checked a number. He then went to the call-office phone. After a couple of minutes of phone talk, Syed, listening, leaned to me.

"Iftikhar's in Kabul, alive," he said quietly.

"Okay," I said. "I'm going out back to change into my English clothes. Tell them I'd like to know what else they can do for a businessman in their country."

The earlier tension seemed to ease, so I stepped into the back room to change, picking up my bag. I supposed that the three original kidnappers would make sure they were along for the ride and, ideally, they should buy him back. Syed had said he'd heard the word 'army' spoken. Well, there wasn't a proper Afghani army in Kabul beyond the Taliban.

I'd changed my clothes for two reasons. Firstly, there would be no secret now that I was an outsider but also, I felt slow and confined in the traditional dress.

As I was putting on my shoes, I heard laughter from the front room. Then, the completely deafening sound of gunfire. They must be showing off with celebratory shooting through the open windows. I'd heard plenty of joyful machine-gun fire during my time in Lebanon. But there, at least they shot into the air from outside. Now they kept at it and my head was ringing – I was deaf and annoyed.

The firing stopped and I tied my shoes, still deaf. As I walked toward the front room, it occurred to me that there were no windows from which they could have fired, just a small square window high on one wall. Inside, I saw no one. No one standing, that is, just bunches of red rags on the floor. In less than a second, the reality became clear. Five bodies on the ground, shot up, and not moving. A mist of gun smoke and powdered walls falling slowly from the ceiling. On my side, Syed and his friend were plainly dead. Syed with lifeless half-open slits as eyes; his friend's frozen open in surprise or shock. One of the Kalashnikovs on the table, the other guns on the floor. On the other side, the tall one looking sideways under the table, his legs bent underneath. I walked around to look closer, and movement snapped my attention to one of his companions. He was the only one without head wounds but from the look of his torso, blobbing blood in lurches, he wouldn't have long. Even so, I slipped free the Browning from my belt at back so he could take that in – if he was capable of seeing at all – as I had to turn my back on him. I kneeled to the body of the tall one. A bullet had driven through his nose near the cheek. Wherever it went, it had left a deep hole with white cartilage lifting through the red. I had to resist a temptation to poke a finger inside to see how far it would go. I was looking for his phone, and found it in a pocket of his pants that was bearing his weight. The screen was damaged and messy. I wiped it on his clean arm and put it in my own pocket.

    I stood and looked properly at the composition of the room so I might later figure who shot first. Whoever did, that wouldn't matter now. I'd used two days already and gained nothing. My hearing was returning. I could hear some voices and a rattling of shutters outside. I moved to the rear doorway, aimed with the 9mm through the gaps and fired a couple of rounds into the PCO's landline phone on the office bench. The rattling stopped. Turning, I picked up my bag, trousered the gun and walked swiftly to the rear exit. This led to a narrow alley. There was no one visible as I moved out until I reached a side street.

    I took a taxi toward the bus station at the west side of Jalalabad where air-conditioned buses leave every fifteen minutes for Kabul. With the picture of the PCO room in mind, I had unhappily to conclude Syed had shot first, or tried to, before the others opened up. That didn't mean he started the fatal dispute – one that might well have surfaced later as the three kidnappers wanted any spoils to themselves – but Syed should have held back. Too many guns in the room; all it takes in a confined space is just one wise-guy. And the only point I'd scored all afternoon was when I was open-armed yet unarmed. That's the downside to lawless lands. *Everyone* is free to kill.

    On the bus to Kabul, as evening drew night, I criticized myself for having brought in Lee's family. Distant family, true, and killers I'm sure before this day, but beside the point. I'd used no street savvy. Building a local base. Bringing in hired guns because I was in a hurry was no way to win. Anyway, hired guns are no better than a playground game of war.

I woke in a room of the passable Park hotel. There were a couple of American oilmen as guests, too. UNOCAL had hopes of a gas pipeline from Turkmenistan through to Pakistan. The deal would collapse within months, after Bill Clinton ordered cruise-missile strikes on Osama bin Laden's outpost at Khost. At breakfast, I saw one of the Americans eat, surrounded by his local and pricey warlord mafia. He'd never penetrate his personal *cordon sanitaire* to see the truth.

Outside, I used the morning to wander around. I went in search of Scribe Street. There was a time when, near the old court building, a row of tables was open for business. At their small desks, scribes sat with antique typewriters to complete forms, typed petitions and provided stamps for those unable to manage paperwork connected to officials. The row of street clerks had disappeared along with central government but I found an assortment off the main drag behind the half-wrecked courthouse. To be publicly literate was out of fashion. I looked at the faces to make a selection.

The one in a shirt and jacket had a woman in a burka as a customer. He seemed to be a stickler and making her needs difficult, so no. Another looked at me, then ducked his glance. The third was an overweight slob who had few papers before him. He'd be more of a greedy bribe negotiator than a clear translator. The next man was in a clean and simple local dress, around thirty, and looked bored yet active at the same time. At his side he had a couple of paperbacks with bookmarks.

"What's your name?" I asked after a couple of minutes' conversation to assess his English.

"Daoud," he replied.

"Really? Same as me. I'm David."

Daoud had graduated from the university in 1992, the last year of the Soviet-backed government, in most ways the most progressive era since the 1920s. He'd lived through the US-supported Mujahedeen warring that destroyed more than half of Kabul. Importantly to me, he spoke not only Dari, Pashtun and English but also Urdu and Tajik. I asked him to come to my hotel for lunch. Everyone would soon know of me there, and that was fine with me. I just needed a cover story.

Leaving Daoud (who, I noticed, packed up his table and left for home quickly), I made some calls from a teashop payphone. With difficulty, I called Lee in Bangkok to tell him of Syed and his friend.

"How are they?" Lee asked.

"Slightly dead," I then told of the unseen argument and its aftermath.

"Oh. I see," said Lee. "But you're okay?"

"Same as ever," I said, admiring Lee afresh.

Next call was to Eloise.

"Do you know when you'll be coming back?" she asked softly. "Doing your troubleshooting, or whatever it is."

"Troublemaking more like it. I think I'm making things worse."

To which, no response. Then,

"My tummy hurts."

"I'll be home soon," I said, knowing I'd have to bulldoze a forest to knock on enough wood to beat the curse of uttering a promise out loud.

Daoud was relaxed enough at the hotel. That was good. At least he had no immediate enemies, and he responded observantly to things going on among the guests.

"A question before we get started," I said. "If a man from Kandahar meets a group from Jalalabad and they speak Dari rather than Pashtu, what does that tell you?"

Daoud thought for a moment, then spoke.

"Maybe the Jalalabad guys were Pashai," he said. "But only a small chance." He paused. "Perhaps the Kandahar man was really from somewhere else. Or they didn't trust each other."

Daoud was a thinker. And Syed a fibber, though my protector to the end. His was the last Kalashnikov firing, judging from the smoke. So much for the Pashtunwali, the code of honour and hospitality.

"Okay, that makes sense," I said, and then moved on. "I've heard the Taliban plan to destroy a lot of artefacts in the museum. Is that true?"

"The Taliban don't believe in any past, not even their own," Daoud looked sad but resigned.

I told Daoud I wanted to buy what I could before the relics were smashed. He asked me where they'd be going. I told him somewhere safer than the museum. He looked sadder. I gave him a slip of paper. The note was the number of the last call checked by the dead kidnapper in Jalalabad when locating the holders of Iftikhar.

"Try this contact first," I said. "I think his name's Mansour." Or so Syed had thought.

Daoud hesitated, suggesting his own contacts. No, I insisted.

I realised I'd been taking the wrong approach to the armed players in Afghanistan. I'd been swept under by an eternal sunset of history, the claimed religious beliefs, the entangled political factions – even the costumes. A better mindset would be to accept the gun-bearers as fellow criminals yet with fewer scruples of restraint. Just like those I'd been locked up with over the years. I'd never be fooled by Mikey in cell fourteen who'd offer a cigarette while memorizing your home address from your kids' letters. Or Frank who'd conned his way into an infirmary orderly's job so he could plausibly sell syringes of palm oil as steroids to the muscle-heads in the weights room. Why should the Taliban be treated differently simply because of their pretentions?

As it happened, Mansour was not your average Talib or mullah stooge. We met outside the mausoleum in Zarnegar Park.

"I was given your number by some Afridi friends in Peshawar," I told him. I figured he'd not heard of the foreigner in Jalalabad.

"Really?" said Mansour. "I have many friends in Peshawar." He didn't press for a name or details.

Mansour spoke a little English, which would be useful. Now in his forties, he'd been a technical officer in the Afghan army under the Khalq communists, and since had changed sides almost as often as the colours of the Afghan flag. The Taliban needed professionals, especially in the air force, to operate the remaining military equipment. Although salaried, Mansour had a lot of downtime. He agreed to speak to friends at the museum. He didn't much like Daoud, which was as I expected. I pushed for dinner at Mansour's home.

Following a day of nothing, Mansour called. Daoud and I went to a rebuilt block of flats. We ate with Mansour's family in the well-furnished apartment. The fittings were mixed old and new, so no sign of a large income from black-market sources. But then, the entire market in Afghanistan was black, levelling out any easy judgements.

After dinner, Mansour produced a list of items he felt confident he could obtain from the museum's large collections. I marked a dozen from the pre-Islamic era. He then unwrapped from cloth a Bactrian coin from the reign of Diodorus II and a stamp seal from the Greco-Bactrian period at Ai-Khanoum. Daoud showed great interest and knowledge.

"I know of that site," he said. "Two years ago, the looters were using bulldozers for their excavations." And two years later the Taliban would use the same machines to level the site. Daoud was as unhappy as most at the destruction of the archaeological remains.

I agreed on a price for the seal and coin as well as for a small Gandaharan Buddha statue that Daoud thought 1st-century, CE. As Mansour and I took to the balcony for a smoke, I signalled Daoud to stay inside. I asked Mansour if he had a problem with my translator.

"Daoud's an honest man," I said.

Mansour nodded. "Sometimes a man is too much honest."

"I had a very good translator in Pakistan," I said. "He came this way. His name's Iftikhar. But lost him."

Mansour frowned, then smiled, tapping two extended fingers at the air between us. "Is two times now I hear this week."

I left it at that, moving on to our arrangements for the next day.

The three of us met at my hotel. Daoud translated. So, shall I. Mansour had made enquiries. He'd been told of the shootout at Jalalabad but the story had been garbled. He seemed to think six men had tried to capture and rob one foreigner.

"That was you," Mansour looked at me. "And you finished them all." He looked impressed, and I was happy to ride with it for the moment.

"They were not businessmen like us," I said. "Just thieves," I waved a hand dismissively. "Now, your list. I have arranged the money for the things you have now."

That morning, I'd visited a money-changer to exchange dollars for afghanis. It's always best to pay in local currency (if there is one); flashing dollars or euros leads to dark ambitions. The office was owned by the Pakistani Kahani brothers and known for international transfers. I knew the Kahanis wouldn't spill, so Mansour shouldn't know I had all my cash with me.

I then spoke about business possibilities. I wanted to know which factories were still operating, what load could be purchased, how bad was the telecommunications network and any problems with local construction. I hoped my enthusiasm would catch.

"And," I added as though dividing one lunch bill, "if you can acquire Iftikhar for me, I'd be pleased."

Through the wreckage of skeletal buildings in Kabul, a unique anomaly had appeared. Attached to the bullet-scarred telephone exchange, an optimistic European telecoms company had begun construction with planned fibre-optic cable. It was there, in a modern air-conditioned office among racks of unconnected machinery, that Iftikhar was brought to me.

When Mansour guided him through the glass doors, Iftikhar looked small indeed. He had faint healing bruises on his face and seemed to move uncomfortably. I was sure his new shalwar kameez hid other injuries. I hugged him briefly and drew one of the wheeled office chairs beneath him. Mansour had brought just one other man with him who held back, arms folded. His heavy jacket suggested that he was armed to the teeth. But it was all smiles.

"Iftikhar," I said. "Naughty of you to go missing. I've had to do everything myself." I went on about the business potential all around us, pushing from mind the wish to take names and end lives.

Daoud would later tell me of Iftikhar's refusal to volunteer for the Taliban army and the painful consequences. Iftikhar, of course, was too embarrassed to talk. The refusal notwithstanding, he would have been sent north within weeks to join the sacrificial mine-clearers preparing the revenge attack on Mazar-e-Sharif. The Taliban would massacre six thousand Hazara civilians as retribution for earlier losses. Even if he'd survived the taking of the city, Iftikhar would have been left damaged in other ways.

I paid Mansour four thousand dollars for Iftikhar and six thousand for a fine Kushan temple-scene carving with a Greek-alphabet inscription. By the end of the week I was ready to leave.

There was little Iftikhar could tell me that I hadn't already guessed. His uncle wouldn't have known for sure he'd be taken, but Noor Jehan had been thoughtless. I didn't know Iftikhar had been passed on to three sets of captors, none of them good company. He wanted to return to Pakistan through the southern border with Baluchistan.

"Let's do something unexpected for once," I said. "Anyway, never move in haste to a place of the heart, Iffy. Places of the heart remain forever. We'll go north."

After I checked out of my hotel, I took Iftikhar to Daoud's new rooms in a house on the edge of town.

"Do we still need him?" asked Iftikhar.

"More than ever," I said.

Daoud had the artefacts wrapped in cloth, paper and twine, ready for me to take.

"They will be heavy to carry," he said.

"Does anyone know this address?" I asked.

"No."

"Then I hope they're not too heavy to hide under your bed. They're yours." I was never able to keep safe artworks, no matter how precious. I thought with Daoud, the antiquities would be in good hands, and safer than in the Kabul museum. Their purchase had provided the smokescreen I needed. Two years later the Taliban would destroy over three thousand objects of pre-Islamic art – and early Islamic art, such was their iconoclastic zeal – as offensive for being images of people and animals. I kept a coin of Demetrius the First for luck. And a silver dinar featuring the image of the fifth caliph, Abd Al Malik ibn Marwan, his shaggy face and holding a sheathed sword, as though saying, *'Don't make me have to take this out!'* like a dance-hall bouncer.

I'd told Mansour I'd need to find buyers in Europe for the remaining items on his list. I asked him to keep them hidden for me. I hope he did since I had no plans to return despite all my talk. I was confident in his ability to change sides to the winning team. As far as he knew, Iftikhar and I were going grave-robbing in Surkh Kotal. In truth, I planned to cross at Arandu into Pakistan's North West Frontier. Daoud had bought an old Chinese-made sedan of the type as kids we'd call a 'rammer'.

We left Kabul, turning north east to join the Kunar River road to avoid Jalalabad. The snows of the Hindu Kush would close the crossing soon enough as we passed some blond-haired, blue-eyed Nuristanis moving sheep into the valleys. In the 1930s Nazi anthropologists hoped to peg them as descendants of their peculiar idea of Aryans. Daoud said their language was a poor fit for anything European.

We were soon in Tajik lands and would have been lost without Daoud's languages. We bumped through the crossing into Pakistan, winding back to the Chittral-Dir Road where I hoped to get a flight to Lahore. There were none, so we kept moving. At Mingora, we said goodbye to Daoud who was returning home using the good Peshawar road before the car collapsed. Iffy and I went the opposite way to the capital in a hire car. On the way, I asked Iftikhar about his journey into Afghanistan with his guide Kamran and Naveed, the evasive Afridi I'd met in Peshawar.

"Did you give him any money to safeguard before you met the smugglers?"

"Yes. I gave him five lakh rupees," he said, a touch apologetically. "I had to pay some other things before I left."

That was about five thousand pounds from the twenty I'd sent from London. And I was sure much of the rest went to his uncle.

"Kamran's no good outside your uncle's control," I said. "But don't go chasing the cash. Noor Jehan will know what to do."

We separated at Islamabad. He on a flight to Karachi, I to Lahore. I gave him my lucky coins at the airport.

"Keep these for me," I said. "I'll be around to collect them some time."

"You have enough money?" he asked.

"I'll eat my pants if I get hungry. Give my best to your uncle." I was going to say something to Iftikhar about any further trade missions for Noor Jehan but I stopped myself. Family and tribe, after all.

6

My time in Afghanistan had subtly changed how I felt about this part of the world during my last two days in Lahore. To stroll through a video store and stop for fresh juice before driving to visit friends in Model Town seemed the height of sophistication and civilized living.

Adnan took me to hear some musician friends play creaking instruments while an aging but vocally agile 'playback' singer performed. Playback singers provide the voices dubbed over actresses (and often actors) miming in Indian movies, and have their separate fan base.

"How long before I see you again?" asked Adnan during a pause.

"Quite a while," I said. "Unless you come to London. Part of me doesn't like to travel."

The old airport at Lahore was cramped and shop-worn, with an unusual mix of domestic and international travellers at check-in after security screening. Those due to board the long-haul flights had to volunteer for checks at customs desks as local passengers sorted themselves out with their bags just a few meters behind at the opposing wall. This apparent advantage for the underground traveller is deceptive. The effect on the ground is that the few enthusiastic staff look for international passengers hoping to be mistaken for short-haul flyers, so view everyone with suspicion.

I'd had Adnan keep one passport in reserve while I had another for the exit from Pakistan, having added the necessary entry stamps. After being on such public display in Kabul, I wanted to break any link with earlier identities. Outside the airport, I insisted Adnan stay until my departure. He stood at the glass entry doors with his friend, an off-duty but senior immigration officer, waiting for me to go through to the boarding gates.

As I passed through the security check, I wondered how much of these last weeks might I safely tell Eloise. Of caged and harmed friends, the freshly dead or merely of the essential need of millions betrayed by millions more, tramping to bare earth already broken stones? No, not a word to Eloise. Keep all hidden with gifts of a fetching scent from Zurich and that Parisian hat I saw with the black lace veil.

When I turned from the check-in desk I saw two officers from the row of customs men looking at me and whispering to each other. With my bag, I immediately moved to the most dopey-looking inspector. Unfortunately, the two I didn't like joined us. I was asked for my passport. They weren't interested in what I might be carrying. The two went to a desk where their eyes told me they were looking at some A4-size document and conferring, disagreeing.

Whatever was going on, I'd need Adnan and his official friend. I couldn't see them through the glass. The customs pair returned, the eager one still holding what I saw as a large colour photograph of a face. The face was mine.

Should some beneficent genie grant you exemption from just one unwelcome surprise in life, you could do worse than select this: that never may you find yourself at an airport in Pakistan where two officials stand before you with a poster bearing an undeniable image of your face. (Unless you're a cricketer, I suppose.)

Undeniable, yet deny it I did. And I demanded to see the topmost officials and police at Lahore airport, all the while hoping to see Adnan appear. As new officers assisted, I'd assess each for bribability. I managed to get outside – although surrounded – to look around. Adnan and his friend had disappeared at the first sign of trouble.

I was taken to an office within the airport. An incident at Karachi was mentioned. Unspecified, yet I knew Pakistan well enough to know that taping someone's picture beneath desks at airports was a rare thing. Not for terrorists, not fleeing dictators, and never for criminals. What did that make me? As well, I couldn't think of anything I'd done bad enough to warrant the hunt. Afghanistan wouldn't count, the border rivers wash away all sins. I was making good on the bribery front. My passport was standing up and the airport chief was talking only of a similarity between me and the colour photograph.

Then a couple of creeps arrived. Dressed in safari suits, the unofficial uniform of Pakistan's spy networks. I was to be flown to Karachi. They took me to a local police station while tickets and escorts were arranged. I was locked in a small cell already occupied by a youngish Lahorite accused of theft.

"At least you know why you're here," I told the terrified man. It didn't make him feel better.

"What are the police like here?" I asked.

"They torture," he said as he might say, 'the sun rises at dawn'.

"And if you give them cash?"

"Then, only a little torture."

The cell seemed to be the only one in use that Sunday. It was built on the side of the small police station. A dirt floor, low ceiling and thick mud-brick walls, with a steel frame holding the iron-bar door. A door that faced an open courtyard to the road. The courtyard was deserted.

"What's your name?" I asked my cellmate.

"Mahmood."

"How long until they move you?"

"In the morning, I go court."

"Good Mahmood," I said. "It's your lucky day. We're getting out of here. You'll be free."

I knocked against a wall to test it, freed the clasp of my belt and plucked out a thin tool from the hinge pin. One end was a flat-head driver, the other a standard handcuff key. With the screwdriver, I pried free from my boot heel a ceramic headstone-shaped plate. The curved end was serrated for scraping and cutting. Whatever was waiting for me in Karachi was not something I wanted to meet.

I kept Mahmood as lookout while I began scraping and digging a gap beneath the centre section of the wall that faced the yard. He squawked a couple of false alarms before I too could hear footfalls approaching. Less than fifteen inches had been excavated. I dropped the cutter into the tiny pit, covering the gap with Mahmood's towel-sized cotton blanket.

The safari-suit spooks had come for me. I never found out if Mahmood made it out. I hope so.

At the airport, I was kept in a small, poorly furnished office awaiting the flight south to Karachi. The guard left to watch me was a bored nobody but the office was four-corridors deep with few windows, all barred.

After a few minutes, the door opened and three men walked in. A Pakistani official of some sort with two palefaces; one young, one old. The older man had aged grimly in the five years since last I'd seen him. He was the American DEA agent, Bill Shenkmann. A thread linking cause and effect tightened around my neck. Shenkmann spoke to his younger confederate, wagging a trembling finger at me.

"This thing here just won't die," he said. "He'll find things won't go so well in this country."

I lifted myself in my chair as a kind of shrug. The younger man looked to me for a response.

"The villain always gets the first line in a situation like this," I said. "Do you think he did well?"

"He does very well," said the sidekick, defensive of his boss.

I spoke to Shenkmann. "Bill - I hope we've known each

other long enough for first-name terms – I can't imagine there's any real work for you here. Why bother?"

"There's plenty to do, David," he said. "People come to *us*, you know."

"Well, you seem to be where *I* am," I said. "You don't look well, I must say."

The younger man began to say something but Shenkmann cut him short.

"Mike, forget it. Everything's arranged."

The two men who escorted me on the flight to Karachi were plainclothes officers of the Anti-Narcotics Force. They didn't know much, or simply weren't saying. I couldn't ask many questions without adding to their knowledge, so I kept it general. I asked if they'd known of anyone else whose picture had been posted at all airports.

"Never," said the talkative one as I sat sandwiched between them during their flight. "Also, you were unlucky. The officer who kept the picture was certainly the exception."

I'd become exhausted over the years at hearing how often my misfortunes were matched to a series of unlikely events.

In Karachi, I was deposited by my escorts at the customs' Narcotics Division, a separate agency. Once inside, a uniformed guard attached a manacle to my right forearm linked to a heavy chain and end-ring. The manacle key was a museum piece. A cone-shaped threaded screw of a type I'd never seen before. He led me down a flight of stone steps to a basement corridor. We passed under a short iron bar that had been fitted to the ceiling. It could only have one purpose: a device from which to hang people in excruciating positions. The manner of the guard was disturbing, too. He didn't look to me for reaction as jailors often do. He was performing a daily routine, processing an object that had been brought to this place.

I was taken to a large office in the basement. Fluorescent lighting and high, barred windows. A man sat behind a desk reading papers in a folder. I was chained to a chair in front of a desk. The chair, I noticed, was bolted to the floor. I assumed I was here to be questioned prior to being returned to Thailand for execution. The only clue to my arrest so far was the photo on the improvised wanted poster, a picture that I knew had been enlarged from that in one of my passports. But how?

The man at his desk closed his folder.

"What have you to tell us?" he asked.

"Not much," I said. "Nothing at all really. Can I go now?"

The man smiled to himself, shook his head a little and said, "Then you must see the doctor."

He collected his folder, rose and left the room. I turned to see that the first guard had been replaced by a small and grubby *muktadar* – a kind of soldier – with a rifle who now sat on a chair by the door. The rifle looked old and unreliable but I was trapped. Against one wall was a row of long canes of different thickness. Next to the desk was a 24-volt truck battery.

I'd always understood the application of torture as an unpardonable act but not known enough to specify why. And I damned myself for not having solved the problem of vulnerability at airports. So completely reliant on others to get me out. This was not the time for what-ifs. The 'doctor' arrived at the office door. Doctor: a filthy perversion of the word in this context. The man was a big bruiser born with hands so large they were bound to lead to trouble. He sat at his desk. I locked Eloise deep inside me. A tiny capsule no one could find, even in a corpse. Whatever happened, not even a stray thought of her should be allowed and so harmed in the places of my mind where she lived.

Ahmed Baboosh leaned back in his chair, then dug in his pockets. He took out his Zippo lighter, not what he was looking for. The lighter was engraved with the crest of the US Drug Enforcement Administration, a memento of his time in Washington. He opened a small packet of *paan*, taken from another pocket. He offered me some of the aromatic spice mix.

"You chew it, don't swallow," he said.

"No. Thanks," I said. He shrugged.

"You might like to try it sometime," he said. "Even my wife likes it."

While Baboosh was working himself around to a question, I was inventing an itinerary for the last ten days - the date shown as entry on my passport – complete with places I went to, where I slept, ate and who I saw. Baboosh stood, walked around to the front of the desk, leaned against it, and looked down at me.

"What would you like to know?" I asked, keeping my head down.

"The truth," he said.

I saw his feet take his weight, and braced myself. His slap to my face was hard but well-aimed so not head-spinning. Wake up, it said. The guard with the rifle came over quickly and grabbed the ring end of my chain. As I looked behind another slap less well-aimed. My ear was ringing.

"Be careful with the *muktadar*," Baboosh said, gesturing to the guard. "He's a village man. A peasant. He'll shoot you."

"Do you want money?" I asked.

His response knocked me off my chair. As I lifted myself off the floor, I looked to Baboosh sideways.

"A simple no would have been enough," I said.

I wasn't playing this right. I knew that as a weak European, I should act terrified and answer all his questions. Trouble was, I wasn't in the mood. Besides, he wasn't asking any.

At some signal I missed, I was dragged by the guard over to a long low table, who after pushing me face down on the table, pulled off my boots. I looked to Baboosh standing with one of the canes from the wall. He'd selected a medium, I recall. Annoyingly, I was getting slapped by the guard, crouched at my head, for looking around. There was a protocol to this business, I was learning. Baboosh swung his cane with a batsman's skill, striking both soles of my feet at once. The blow to the arch tendons sends an impressive jolt of pain through to the knees. He kept at it for a long minute during which - from the guard's tugging on my chain and slapping - I was not meant to speak. Yelping was permitted.

Sometimes Baboosh would miss and strike the toes. From the fifth blow onward the effect is that of having the feet crushed.

Baboosh seemed to bore quickly at this. Or perhaps he had something else to do. He gave a final and vicious strike across my Achilles tendons, and then had the guard take me to a cell.

"That was nothing," he said, "You wait."

I hobbled into the cell and waited.

How far would he go with a British citizen, I wondered. Not as far as with locals, but that still left him plenty of scope. And my Bangkok history would strip several layers of restraint. I figured I'd best give him some weak story of my activities in Pakistan, then let him have another go at me before appearing to break down and give him a name. No one real, of course. But I'd have to make the breakdown convincing.

As it happened, Baboosh gave me all the help needed for that.

I was brought back to the office. A tea trolley with wheels had been moved beside the low table. On top of the trolley sat the truck battery. I was again pushed face down on the table, my bare feet hanging over the edge. The old soldier with the rifle over his shoulders wrapped my arm chain around a table leg. Baboosh was giving instructions in Urdu. I felt a rubber mat of some kind dumped on my upper legs, then the weight of the guard as he sat on it, forcing my knees to the table.

"What do you want?" I asked Baboosh.

"Shut up," he said.

I felt the bite of the alligator clip from a jumper lead clamp my right-foot big toe. Instinctively, I jerked a little. That got a good laugh all round as the battery was not yet connected. A second clip was fastened to my left foot.

I've had major pain before then. Kidney stones blocking the ureter. Nature's version of the medieval water torture. The pain of that, as the kidney expands is wild, brain-tearing and unendurable. Yet there is a gulf between the shrieking pain that the body sometimes inflicts upon itself and pain inflicted by another person.

The stone is neutral. It did not set out to cause pain or harm. Your torturer does.

And nothing surpasses electricity for pain. As Baboosh attached the second lead to the battery terminal, a thousand-clawed fire-dragon tore and ripped up through every fibre of both legs to meet at the groin. Not in the waves of pain brought by injury but ruthless, instant, constant, matchlessly penetrating and complete to every nerve. Since the victim cannot breathe, only scream and suck air in high-pitched chokes, the timing of a torturer is important. I suppose the first shock was only seconds, yet Baboosh had the twisted art of knowing how devastating is each increase in connection time. Injecting hopeless despair to the control and abuse, he would wait until I could speak and then start again the moment I began to plead.

The phone must have been ringing. Baboosh stopped and took the call. While he spoke, I prayed that any god of mercy would provide the gift of death where man-made instruments exceeded a biblical hell.

Baboosh told the guard to disconnect me. I didn't move. I was obedient now. The guard then unwrapped the chain and tugged me towards the door. I had trouble walking. Baboosh pointed a finger at me.

"I've been called away for a while," he said. "But I'll be back and we'll start again. Then you'll tell how you gave the stuff to your man and where you got it."

My cell had become a place of safety. Noises of any kind in the corridor were the sounds of impending danger. It was by then almost 9:00pm. Within twenty minutes I was leaning against the door listening to interpret the scrapings and shuffles, grateful each time the footsteps passed, terrified when they paused. Would Baboosh return or go home for the night? He'd told the *muktadar* to have some tea and wait. In Urdu, of course. I couldn't conclude anything from that.

There was no way out of the cell, even if I had the tools from my boots. The only quick way out would be death but there were no secure fittings in the dark and narrow cell. As time passed, I found myself walking around in tight circles. The wait is the third ligature to the torturer's cruel bow. Soon, after a dozen misleading noises at my door, I sensed my brain distorting itself to the new reality. If sessions such as I'd had were repeated often, who I was would be rewired as something else, a craven living autopsy.

Maddeningly, I couldn't fathom what Baboosh had asked. What stuff had I given to whom? This had nothing to do with Afghanistan. Thailand hadn't been mentioned directly. Although Baboosh had said something to the guard like, 'he likes to escape'. By midnight, I realized that sooner rather than later I'd be talking – if that's what Baboosh really wanted – and talking a pack of lies. By 3:00am, I was almost sure he wasn't coming back this night. Maybe. By 5:00, I thought that eventually some truth might be mixed with the lies, however unintelligible.

I've detailed this dark treatment not as entertainment but because in recent years I've heard people of our kind speak favourably of torture. Terms that include necessity, enemies never encountered and ticking bombs as though bombs really tick and bad people have just been invented. When torture is called, 'enhanced interrogation', you know there's already a funded department.

Torture is utterly different from any other torment. Subject to hunger, humiliation and random acts of violence, victims keep their minds as their own. A place of refuge, rationality and – however imperfect – control. The torturer strips that control away, in truth fully possess all control. Completely helpless, staked out and naked, brain exposed, a core of the mind is replaced with a knotted tumour of fear. A black growth that, under repeated torture, grows unending tentacles permanently rewiring the damaged mind. It is accepted by many that psychological torment is a torture. I'm sure it is, yet there is a radical difference when violent pain is the conditioner. We are creatures of bone, flesh and skin. Our minds are built from the sense of touch more than by any higher form of learning. Touch something often and your mind will create a replica of the object. A stone and its wall; the flow of water through fingers; a caressed face and body. In cold terms, the brain has no choice other than to form pathways from tactile input. Sight and sound are poor cousins in that construction, and reason little more than a coat of gloss. The torturer makes all touch a revulsion while the brain, a slave to physics, builds a deformed creature from pain and fear as solid as bone and more deeply etched than any mortal scar. Nothing will undo the perverted tangle of signals left twisted by the torturer.

We might pardon the murderer and forgive those who act in uncontrolled violence. Such mercies cannot be granted to those who, worse than ending a life, create a broken child as a living trophy to their monstrosity.

An hour after dawn I decided I would not allow Baboosh to implant some corrupted changeling in me. I'd seen enough of other's misfortunes to know they should've acted while they still had the strength.

The rifle the guard carried had a magazine that holds five rounds. Perhaps it was loaded with less. As soon as I was taken back to the room, I determined to break his windpipe and take the gun. I'd need just one shot for Baboosh. The plan from there was all unknowns. The only people who run toward gunshots are those with guns of their own. My slim chance of getting out of the building alive was not improved by daylight. The night before would have been the time, if ever. Still, I had nothing to lose. And if you're lucky, one gun begets many when you strip the dead.

It was close to 10:00am when a key turned the lock of my cell door. As it opened, a fat hand held my boots. The hand belonged to a new guard. A big blob though in a relatively clean uniform. He produced a manacle key and gestured to my arm. He removed the chain, turned and threw it in a box of others in the corridor. As I put on my boots, I wondered why no rifle. My plan was looking shaky. This new guard would not go down with one punch, no matter where placed. And without the gun, there'd be no second act. I was guided to the office by this strangely deferential guard.

Inside, I saw Baboosh standing behind his desk. The tea trolley and battery had gone, although the canes were still on display. Sitting on a faded couch, on the opposite side of the room was a large man, a European, in a suit with a leather diary on his knees. He stood. I looked to Baboosh who turned away. The suited man introduced himself, at the same time offering me his card. He spoke with a Manchester accent. He was Geoff Macintyre a police liaison officer attached to the British High Commission in Karachi. He had come to the Narcotics Division on other business and heard – not from Baboosh – that there was an Englishman in custody. Baboosh excused himself grudgingly, and left us alone. I sat on the couch. Macintyre seemed unprepared.

"I'm surprised we weren't told you were picked up," he said.

"I'm not," I said. "I suppose you'd have heard in a week or so." Or maybe never, I thought.

"The boss here says you haven't been very helpful."

When I told Macintyre how Baboosh was doing everything he could to prompt my recollections, he didn't get it.

"Just like English coppers when they take you out back and give you a bit of a thump?" he suggested.

I then made clear the distinction. When I probed for information as to how I came to be in Karachi, Macintyre expressed mystification.

"I don't really understand the how. Wasn't us. And I can't see these guys –" he trailed off. "But I sure know why."

Macintyre had come to the Pakistan narcotics police to see a British national who'd been arrested at Karachi airport a week earlier while trying to board a flight to Copenhagen via Frankfurt. A couple of kilos of heroin had been found in the luggage of the man from Liverpool. He was still in the customs' holding cells in the next building. His name was Billy Green. The same Billy I'd last seen two months earlier getting on to a plane for Manila, and who was to organize couriers for my Danish friend Christian.

"And this Billy had the dope on him?" I asked.

"In the sides of a pilot's flight case," said Macintyre. "But that's just the beginning. I've seen a man spill his guts before but the Pakistanis never laid a hand on him and they said they thought they'd have to knock him out to shut him up."

The story Billy told the British officer was that he'd run up large gambling debts in the Philippines to a casino owner he knew as David Russell. This David had escaped from Thailand after a death sentence and was in big with the Calabrian mafia, and kept a personal Russian contract killer. Billy had been forced to meet dangerous (unidentified) contacts in England to obtain false passports for the villainous David. Billy was in fear of his life, he'd said. If the British would help him in Pakistan, he'd help them even more.

"Billy had a half-dozen passport photos of different people in his suitcase," Macintyre said. "He gave Ahmed Baboosh that colour snap of you. And he gave us your London addresses."

I was quiet for a minute trying to absorb all this. For one thing – among many – I'd never given Billy extra passport photos. I showed some disbelief.

"So, Billy is travelling around with photos of this mister big, just on the off chance he'd need them?"

"He'd made photocopies of everything that passed through his hands," marvelled Macintyre. "And kept a note of papers and letters he'd seen – or opened – at your flat. Just in case you tried to blackmail him." Macintyre couldn't help smiling.

I massaged my temples. Maybe lack of sleep was jumbling my thoughts. I muttered, "The idiot can barely write his name yet he kept notes."

"Never underestimate the truly stupid," said Macintyre.

"Did you believe a word of this crap?" I asked.

"Not much," he said. "Especially as he had a receipt for an identical ticket he'd cashed in with the name of an expat we know in Manila. And we already know you don't do business at home, so his claim about UK trafficking is nonsense. The Pakistanis want to send you back to Thailand. They're quick about it, too."

"Nothing else you can say to cheer me up?" I couldn't accept easily that Billy would have so destroyed the one person who might help him.

"Just one thing," added Macintyre. "When Baboosh told Billy they'd lifted you at Lahore airport, Billy told the Pakistanis that you'd have them all killed by hired assassins."

I suspected there must have been a reason why Baboosh kept a special place for me in his heart.

Karachi Central Jail has held some prominent Pakistanis over the years. The father of Benazir Bhutto had been imprisoned and hanged there. Zulfikar Ali Bhutto had been a prime minister before his daughter held the same office. He'd been executed at the hands of General Zia-ul-Haq who'd taken power, until he too had been blown to bits by his own agencies. KCJ had been built during British rule on huge levelled grounds where the cellblocks appear as isolated buildings. The spaces would allow great mobs to be corralled until riots were quelled. In quiet times these wide spaces between the internal prisons were to help the army rangers who manned the wall towers aim at their targets if prisoners broke free from the cells and surged to the walls. That has never happened. Remember the joke about the Pakistani in hell?

After three days in the newer section of the customs' holding cells, I was sent to the jail. Billy Green had been moved the day of Macintyre's visit. Baboosh ruefully dismissed me as I left.

"You don't know how lucky you are," he'd said. "If that embassy man hadn't arrived, you'd be a bloody smear across my wall by now."

Baboosh's neat turn of phrase was thanks to a good education at Pakistan's top English-speaking schools.

At Karachi Central Jail, the superintendent (the head warder or governor) was unsure how to treat me. On the one hand, foreigners were usually good for cash extortion, while on the other he'd been told of my Thai escape. In the reception office, I picked up on talk of being sent to the punishment block despite concerns over embassy visitors. The solution was to send me to a section controlled by one of the many imprisoned political factions where I could be watched by compliant inmates.

The walled compound within the prison housing this set of activists held two hundred men. I could readily distinguish the leaders from the troops. I was welcomed by their English speakers and given my own cell and a meal, cooked within the compound. The cell was built from concrete slabs yet was clean though windowless with a thin foam layer cut wall-to-wall and covered with dyed cotton. Despite relative comfort, my first night was troubled. Billy had rewarded me for his care by destroying almost everything I'd made for myself since leaving Thailand. He must have sifted through my mail while staying at my flat to clock the mews-house address. The only reason he would have been running the dope himself would've been to keep all the fees Christian would pay, rather than hire a courier. It didn't look like I'd be free any time soon, and within weeks, bank statements would arrive through the mews-house door. And there was Eloise. I shuddered in the dark.

The following morning after breakfast of chapatti and egg, I asked my hosts if I could explore the jail while under their care. Cells in special sections were locked between six at evening and seven in the morning but otherwise open. This internal compound had ten-foot walls and only a narrow entrance that was always open to the prison grounds, with people coming and going most of the day. Still, I couldn't see beyond. Rarely would a guard come in. My request to roam was met with uncomfortable murmurs.

"We're sorry," said one of the group's jailhouse lawyers. "It's not good for you."

I understood. "You mean you've been told to keep me here." I made a point of looking a little sadder about this than I was.

Sometime in the afternoon there was the sound of English chatter outside my cell. I'd not long taken a shower and shaved. I'd dressed in a shalwar kameez from my suitcase, which that day had arrived. Everything missing but the clothes. The young translator of the group removed his sandals and stepped into my cell with enthusiasm.

"Mister David," he said. "We have gone to much trouble for you. We have brought a companion for your room here. He was in the place where they keep the shit people. But he is Englishman."

The young man smiled, stood aside from the door and extended an arm. "We bring you a friend," he announced.

Under the shadow of the veranda outside, a lumpen shadow appeared. The eyes on the losing boxer's face avoided mine. It was Billy Green.

7

Quickly enough, I was charged with a conspiracy concerning the heroin in Billy's luggage. The crime would be heard first in the customs court where a penalty of ten years' imprisonment was possible. A second hearing was to take place in the special anti-narcotics court set up by former prime minister Benazir Bhutto. There, the penalty was death. I was long past any concern about death sentences. Billy, strung around my neck like a rotting albatross, was in a panic.

"You think they'll hang us?" he asked that first week. Us? Having brought me to the prison, his yearning to share was deathless.

"What are you worried about, you big slob?" I said sizing his weight; put a necktie around the top of a sack of potatoes and that's Billy in formal attire. "With your gut and fat ass your neck will snap like a pretzel. Me, I'll just dangle there 'til nightfall until the scavengers start tugging at my boots."

The casual reader might be wondering why, after a week in Karachi jail so full of cheap cut-throats, Billy was still alive. Put such murderous thoughts aside for a moment. I would soon begin a trial in which the only evidence against me were the statements of a co-accused. If Billy met with an accident in the jail, the usual suspects would be rounded up, charged and another trial set. Suspicion would fall upon me, regardless of any evidence. Billy had already told consular staff at the British High Commission that in jail, he feared for his life. Of course, to me, at first, Billy made all the expected denials.

"Dave, this wasn't in the script," he'd said. "They knew everything. And I didn't know you were in Pakistan."

"So, if I wasn't here, it was okay to cook up a story and dump me in it?"

"I'm sorry," he said. "I didn't know what to say. You're the biggest villain I know. Punch me in the face. Go on, please!"

"How many professional fights did you ever win?" I asked. "I told you to keep your distance here. All those couriers you obviously didn't want to pay for? Hear the bell and come out fighting, I'd said. You could have told me you got knocked out every time."

There'd be no more satisfaction in punching Billy's face than driving my fist into a cowpat. He was an insufferable coward, and a yellow belly in a big man's body is the most treacherous of all. I had no choice but to keep him alive and under my eye.

Another unhelpful thing: once imprisoned, I acted in haste attempting to save the life I'd made since leaving Thailand. Nothing worked, of course. I was trapped but it was tough to let it all go. I wrote to Eloise. I said sorry, using too many pages when a note of three words might have been less hurtful. I promised nothing. How could I? An image of Eloise sitting at the side of her bed alone in her subterranean flat formed as a small but sharp-edged and painful metallic implant to my head.

And, too quickly, I had £5,000 sent to a Karachi lawyer on no more recommendation than that of the British consulate. That was eaten two-handed without a napkin, although the hack did attend one hearing. Other lawyers loitering at the court said, 'Well, look who's got a new suit!', and I saw immediately that he'd have to go. Within weeks I realized that no experience in Pakistan had adequately prepared me for the hunger and appetite of Karachi Central Jail. There were no honest brokers, advice from the most respected inmates simply a trap, and I'd have to learn this new world as would a street urchin, shoeless and wiping the dust from my eyes.

The task ahead was exhausting to contemplate. I'd hit the ground running at eighteen, been smashed at twenty-four, and been at war for nineteen years. The gentle rain upon that black umbrella as I walked from the Bangkok prison for which I then praised the heavens I now saw as mere spittle from the gods as they laughed, knowing I'd live a year sublime before again being crushed. Without will I let slip from an empty hand the memories of a life that no longer had substance or place.

Before parting with more cash – especially so as every penny was now coming from long-tolerant friends in Australia – I needed to understand the way the prison worked. With a little persuasion, my inner compound hosts took me for a tour under watch. I left Billy in the cell.

KCJ held around 6,000 inmates, most of them in the cramped accommodation of the *Chekka*, named for the circular layout of its five blocks of cells. The men there were C-class prisoners unable to afford better. Yet even within the *Chekka* lived a poorer class: the men and boys without visiting family kept in massive dormitories of bare floor, and compelled to eat the prison food of a scoop of beans, flat bread and water. The cells were open for two hours each day, the dormitories never. Beyond the *Chekka*, spread about the jail, were compounds separating the political prisoners – the A-class. Such prisoners were entitled to individual cells with raised frame beds, a bathroom and two servants chosen from the lower ranks. These privileges were also granted to B-class inmates, whose claim under the law to better conditions could be based on higher education, social class, being a taxpayer (a very rare group), and those 'accustomed to a higher standard of living'. If this sounds like a very British accommodation, that's because it is. The prison law has held from the days of the Raj, and even in Britain was applied at London's Holloway women's prison until the 1950s (although without the servants). In Pakistan, a more active legacy of the British system was the near-absolute power given to prison governors, there called a superintendent.

In practice, the political prisoners held court in large rooms with their deputies. Only the top layer was A-class, while their followers – as many as thirty – would be titled as servants. In 1999 there were nine such groups, including four splinter groups of Bhutto's PPP, the MQM leaders and a Sindhi nationalist party. The bosses of self-styled sons-of-the-soil factions slept on the floor with their men, although on thicker mattresses. Regardless of court-ordered class distinctions, money had to be paid to prison staff to implement the orders. To me, the first sight of these groups seemed a visit to the cave of Ali Baba and his forty thieves – during a very lean period. Hold that thought, I said to myself.

Before reaching the best accommodation areas, our little party was intercepted by a slim young man dressed in a lightweight shalwar kameez. He was a westerner with fair hair and he had emerged from some official's office.

"I'd heard there were some new Brits here," he said, extending a foppish arm. "I thought it would be good to see you as soon as possible. Perhaps it's better if we go to your block so I can speak to your friend, too." He looked to my guides as though they were spoiling something, though greeted them in flawless Urdu.

"I do all the talking for my friend," I said. "Here and now is good."

"As you wish," said Mason, as he soon introduced himself. His east-coast American accent reminded me of Dean Reed in Bangkok, the eerily relaxed Bostonian in Klong Prem prison. A man who had charmingly fleeced me of $50,000 with bogus quick-release schemes.

Young Mason was acting as go-between for the prison boss. He was selling the prime real estate of B-class accommodation. Two cautions came to mind. I knew the amount I paid then would set the price levels for all future dealings. As well, Noor Jehan was somewhere in the prison but I knew better than to mention his name before I'd established contact. Yet I was in no mood for bargaining, only haste, and settled quickly for $3,500.

"And that's for each of you, of course," added Mason. "For your friend, too."

Although I'd have readily paid twice that to see Billy in some Z-class pit, I'd yet to extract from him the full extent of the damage. Besides, I'd have to keep him close to control any courtroom pantomime.

"Okay, the superintendent, and you, have a deal," I said. "But I want him in a separate cell." I realized I could not stomach another night in Billy's company.

The first trial began in the Karachi customs court. Hearings took the Asian pattern of a day's listing with a session of less than an hour every six weeks. Yet the procedures were very British. In the small courtroom, the language was English, as were all documents. No witnesses appeared on the day but I learned that statements from police concerning any confessions of the accused were not admissible. Too many had been ruled in appeals as extracted by violence. This did help explain why inquisitors were not fussed with their victims' answers, although not why they became torturers.

As time inside the court was brief, I spent most of the morning in the dusty grounds of the customs buildings. I looked carefully at the lawyers coming and going, hoping to replace the timid fool I'd paid for. Despite their dark coats and white ties, they all appeared desperate or trivial.

The C-class prisoners were held handcuffed in a broiling iron van, while B-class had no shackles and an assigned guard who was happy to be sent on errands to buy food and medicines. Although this seemed to present opportunities for escape, I held back, wanting to learn why those with more money and power than I settled for prison life.

Jeremy, a vice-consul from the British High Commission, arrived and took me aside to the shade to hand me an envelope containing Rs 20,000 (£200) sent by friends.

"I guess you'll, ah, secure that about your person before you're taken back," Jeremy said. "Unless you have some better way."

"Five hundred in the palm usually stops any intimate search," I said. Jeremy gave the impression he enjoyed anything cloak and stage-dagger his job might offer.

"You sure must have annoyed someone," said Jeremy who knew of the DEA's part in my arrest. I wondered aloud if the agency was still directing events.

"Do you think they've moved on?" I asked.

"Probably, although the Thais have been asked if they want you," said Jeremy before nodding toward Billy who was squirming to get within earshot. "But he's the one I'd worry about."

"Yeah," I said, then held my tongue. Billy was babbling Liverpudlian nonsense to our uncomprehending guard. Would the guard shoot him if he tried to escape? Maybe, though my judge would surely look to me for answers.

My large cell at the jail was one in a row of eight in a small compound in the B-class section. My neighbours were all wealthy and included the former chairman of Pakistan Steel, Usman Farooqui, imprisoned on charges of fraudulent contract kickbacks. This came about because he didn't share, and his miserly treatment of his servants spoke of the attitude sure to bring him to grief.

For a moneyless prisoner, assignment as a servant provided many benefits. I had two attendants: a *dhobi walla* (a clothes washer) and a *bardashi* – a valet. They would make my bed, fetch water, iron clothes and cook meals. I'd give them a shopping list each day with a little extra money for their own needs. They'd eat after serving my meals. So valued were these servants' jobs to the broke prisoners, they eagerly saved hard for the five-hundred-rupee bribe to the guards for a position. Gentlemanly protocol (rarely followed) demanded that I should have them freed after six months' good service. Freed not from domestic servitude but from the jail itself.

Like most of the poorer prisoners, my valet had been imprisoned for years without once having attended court. Boss-eye (his nickname after losing an eye during interrogation) had been dumped at the jail five years earlier. The charge concerned the possession of a pistol, an offence that carried a two-year sentence or a fine. Boss-eye would've denied the charge had he an opportunity at court, and the evidence was nothing more than a photocopy of a photograph of a gun. The grainy image was clearly from some shooting catalogue. Over twenty prisoners at KCJ had the identical image (same serial number) stapled to their charge sheets.

The problem of getting a hearing was that a small bribe was needed to have the matter listed at court. Then, another fee to be listed by the jail for court transport, money for the guards and then a few notes to the court clerk to have time with the judge. The judge himself, another matter: by payment or whim. Boss-eye had nothing, and his family could barely feed themselves. So, he fed me.

Another neighbour was, of course, Mir Noor Jehan Magsi, just two doors away. Assuredly A-class for his place in the Baluchistan independence movement and since the September 30 massacre of which he was accused (where over a hundred people lost their lives), a political force rather than a merely ruthless killer. That is, if numbers elevate the event.

I almost walked past Noor Jehan. Although now in his fifties, he never kept still, and swam at speed from meeting to meeting among the conniving party chiefs, his gold watch and neck chains loose, and tribal dress struggling to keep up. He was surprised to see me.

"No!" drawn long and ending deeper.

"Yes," I said, letting my face tell the rest.

In private, I did my best to explain how I was brought low. Noor Jehan ducked out to look at Billy, as ever lurking about when I was in conference. He returned shaking his head and sat.

"Tall people," he announced. "They live with fear of all uniforms."

Noor Jehan couldn't understand the extent of such a thorough betrayal. I'd put him into retirement; and that his childish resentment exploded upon his arrest. Noor Jehan gave me a stern look, and I thought of Bobby Jnr clubbing jellyfish tentacles into the Caribbean.

"No," I said to the implied offer. "Let him be. For now."

During the first months at Karachi Central Jail, it was difficult to understand why those with money and friends stayed put. The poor had no choice. They rarely left their fetid pens. Yet A- and B-class cells were more like rooms with a heavy grilled wooden door locked at night by bar and padlock. Although such doors could be broken, but once outside the internal compounds, the probability of a whistle-blower was strong. Prison guards dozed often during the day and were more active during the cool of night. The perimeter walls were high and without electrified wire. In compensation, the frequent wall towers were manned by alert army rangers who looked as though they'd enjoy an opportunity for moving-target shooting. I would later realize that this security was more to protect our high-profile prisoners from outside attack than to prevent breakout.

Any night-jump from the prison was quite unnecessary given the lax arrangements for us special prisoners at court. No more than a team of three could pick up any B-class prisoner from the customs court. Jeremy from the embassy had described what lay beyond the thirty-meter drive open to the streets, and two minutes would allow a small car to disappear into the Karachi traffic.

So why didn't anyone try? For those with political pretentions, being imprisoned by the supposedly oppressive state was almost an honour. That aside, their careers were by nature in public view, so a hidden life on the run was not for them. The B-class prisoners were mostly scammers and cheats but not – as they saw themselves – of the criminal world. Almost all in KCJ were unconvicted, and actively delayed any conclusion to their trials for as long as possible. The reason was simple: under Pakistan law, no person could be held for more than two years without being granted bail. Once bailed, they would drag out their cases until the prosecution fell apart with age. (Noor Jehan's September 30 trial was already in its tenth year of sporadic hearings, only a new charge was holding him.) For some reason the simplicity of this process was never expressed clearly by lawyers or inmates, and had to be gathered in fragments. Not at all unusual when comprehending Asia. Perhaps unlucky to speak of it. Life inside for the wealthy or influential was restricted but almost as slothful as their lives outside. However, I could find no example of a foreigner granted bail. And a gamble on a two-year wait seemed unthinkable.

In London, Eloise had received my letter. It made little sense to her. After a month of many visits to the closed house at Bedford Mews, the door was finally opened by the owner.

"David?" he responded to her question. "He's been arrested in Asia with two tonnes of cocaine. We won't see him again."

I knew none of this at the time. I thought my little London world would go into sleep mode as I'd planned in the event of a fall. Of course, there was no sleep mode for Eloise.

8

My Sunday custom, after five months in Karachi Central Jail was to have lunch at the home of Younis Habib, the former director of the Mehran Bank. Younis Habib was accused of swindling $250 million through phoney loans from the bank he controlled. On a tree-lined street within the prison, his house had been constructed over six months. Air-conditioned and with satellite television, his was one of three private houses within the jail.

Lunch was elaborate, with many servants bringing food from the kitchen to the large table in a well-manicured garden. Around the table, the dozen guests included some very creepy police chiefs, secret-agency heads and government officials. They were all held on murder and kidnapping charges. The conversation was in a refined English, even though I was the only foreigner. They didn't want the servants to be enlightened. I asked Younis Habib why his case was taking so long even though he was at the special Banking Court four days each week.

"Why should I hurry?" he said. "I have my days out. I can meet my friends. What more should I want?"

On his days out, Younis kept as his office a large and comfortable judge's chambers where he would hold court. While there, he could keep some distance from a grasping extended family and the legions of would-be kidnappers who saw him as a prize. His court listings were only on prison records – no hearings ever took place since the prosecutor was paid to keep away – and Younis provided his own guards as escort in an armoured Mercedes.

Not everyone was so content in the garden. A chief of Pakistan's Inter-Services Intelligence agency declared he would soon be free. In his fifties, he was immaculately groomed with an air of sophistication wearing a cashmere pullover and discreet cravat as though stepping from a golf course. It was a rare event when anyone from the ISI was named, rarer still to find one imprisoned.

"My friends have questioned many so-called witnesses," he said mildly beneath black-glass eyes. "They can tell us nothing, I assure you." I guessed their speaking days had come to an end.

I left the lunch well fed though uninspired by these top-ranking prisoners. For my own ends, I wanted to understand how the highest levels of Pakistan society viewed the political groups that were imprisoned and challenged; especially, Noor Jehan. And to do so without any direct questions.

After many Sundays, I learned that the factions were seen as rebel scum with their followers as ambitious dupes or mere cut-throats. Noor Jehan was not spared this judgement, although he was respected as a dangerous man.

About a week after Boss-eye was released by a court (through gritted teeth, I had to bribe again the guards at the front gate an additional Rs. 500 to see him out by nightfall), a tall newcomer with a smiley face and white teeth joined us in our little B-class oasis. This was Zahoor Baloch, a practicing advocate in the Karachi courts and those of his hometown, Hyderabad.

Zahoor was affable and immediately blended into our eight-room club where English was the language of sorrow, Urdu the talk of laughter and Sindhi the speech of hope. Sometimes, all at once. Zahoor was held in prison on corruption charges. An unhappy client had filed a complaint with the police (Rs. 5000) and then lodged a statement at a court (Rs. 10,000) accusing Zahoor of property fraud. So, only $250 to have a lawyer thrown into jail. Release on bail was a problem for this advocate. He was too well known for bail orders under his hand arriving at the prison on documents that had never been before any judge. Over lunch on our veranda, I explained my own case. Zahoor was dismissive.

"I can tell you, David, there is nothing to keep you," he said, stretching his arms wide. "You must walk free."

"Great," I said. Then in a lower tone, "In two or three years."

"Not at all," Zahoor waved away the years. "If someone stands for you, bail is easy."

Zahoor was ambulance-chasing, of course. Still, if he managed to free himself, he would have me as a client. He might be a scoundrel but at least he was no sleepwalker.

I'd just returned from a hanging when Billy loomed at my door, suspended in the sweat of another panic.

"Dave, we've got trouble," he said. "They want to know about the satellite, and they've taken away the bardashis."

The *bardashis* were the servants, and the satellite was nothing of the sort. Billy meant the terrestrial-link dish atop the cell of the Pakistan Steel boss that relayed a score of television stations poached from unencrypted international feeds. P. Steel had allowed his servant and my *bardashi* to split the cable to provide CNN to other cells. Informers had seen them on the low roof. I ignored Billy's announcement.

"You should have come to the execution," I said as I began changing from jeans and shirt into my whitest shalwar kameez. "I had to give your seat away to some guy without a ticket. And the kid on the rope was a skinny little thing. Couldn't have weighed more than fifty kilos."

Billy's putty face greyed. "I couldn't go," he mumbled, trailing. Then, "We might be in trouble. Soon as I heard, I tore all the wires out from my cell."

"The thing was," I continued, "the boy – twenty years old, someone told me – didn't weigh enough for a clean drop. The hangman had to strap some sandbags to his ankles. They keep a row of green little canvas sacks for just such a problem. Inventive, don't you think?"

"What are you going to do?" Billy was plaintive.

"Well, the kid's dead now," I said, pretending to be confused. "Innocent, by all accounts."

"I mean about the satellite. They'll make the servants talk."

"So? You just blame them. I'm sure you can do that. All their idea," I said. "Cheer up, Billy. It's Pakistan. The usual suspects get it every time. Anyway, it's nothing to me," I pushed past Billy at the door. "Easy to get more servants, eh?"

I wouldn't waste time talking to P. Steel about the fate of his servant. He'd never help, even though tiny Shahid was a thoughtful and educated young man from Swat who had served him well. P. Steel had Shahid sleep on a mat at the foot of his bed.

I knew well that if I charged over to the deputy chief's office waving money about, I'd only find myself held hostage to any kindness. No one along our cellblock could be expected to take an interest, and I guessed the story of my freeing Boss-eye had leaked out. He must have cursed me with unthinking praise.

Instead, I went to the enclave of the political followers of the assassinated Murtaza Bhutto. (Murtaza was the brother of former prime minister Benazir, herself assassinated a few years later.) Outside Karachi Central Jail, the Lebanese-born wife of Murtaza was nominally the head of this secondary party, while the jailed activist was, I suppose, the sergeant-at-arms. Aging and respected Khaled with his crew were held on tangled murder and kidnapping charges, but however ruthless, they seemed tight and loyal. I was ushered before their boss in the large hall that was now their communal cell.

As I explained my problem, I was somehow distracted by the many recesses along the walls of the hall. Although bed rolls and carpets took the floor space, there was a raised platform before a bricked-in arched window. I realized that this barred and bolted old house was once a Christian church. (I learned later it was the chapel and former residence of a Raj-era Church of England prison minister.)

"I need your advice," I concluded to Khaled. "I am sure they are suffering now."

"We go!" announced Khaled, springing to his feet despite his years.

A bunch of Khaled's boys had moved to join us but he patted them down. We didn't talk as we strode to the deputy chief's office. With someone of less substance, I often float words to keep the mood buoyant. There and then, this was unnecessary.

When we climbed the steps of the stone veranda surrounding the deputy's small building, I saw my new *bardashi* sitting crouched at the wall by the office door. He hugged his knees and looked miserable. I gestured for him to rise. He did this in silence, head down as though in shame. Khaled moved to the open door. We could hear the solid claps of the *chitta* striking flesh. A *chitta* is a six-inch wide leather belt. I touched my valet's shoulder, bidding him to wait. In the office, face down on the floor lay Shahid, where two of the deputy's prisoner stooges held him at each end. A third, long-armed, was raining blows across the boy. He stopped when he saw Khaled. The fat deputy superintendent looked up from behind his desk.

Other men might have made enquiries before acting – given cursory respect to the deputy. Not Khaled. He tore the *chitta* from the hand of the now terrified trusty, looked at it with contempt and held that look as he bellowed at the deputy. I noticed that the wide belt had words in several languages carved and stamped by hand on its surface. 'I will love you always' and other pitiful jokes. As I helped little Shahid stand, Khaled threw the belt through a window.

"Don't let me see this again," he told the deputy in guttural Sindhi.

As we left, the deputy shot me a vengeful look. There might be a price for that morning's work, I thought, but surely a lesson worth the cost. None of the other political bosses I found had Khaled's honesty. I later paid for the TV-feed to be reconnected. I gave the bribe to that deputy's nastier rival who oversaw our section. Even though I'd sided with a strong faction, I could still be isolated, and should not now reward the defeated.

It was a rival deputy who called me to his office in the compound that held the Shia Muslims. I took a seat before his desk.

"Look out there," he said, pointing to a chubby white man with a red-tinged beard sitting along on a low wall. "You see that man? You know him?"

"No," I said. "Should I?"

"He is rich. He has millions."

"I am very happy for you," I said. "What do you need me for?"

Since the young American Mason had been released (after three years; drug case), the senior KCJ staff were without a credible negotiator to help extort cash from new arrivals from the West. The deputy raised a finger and eyed me a conspiratorial squint.

"One lakh rupees," he said as though the $2000 gambit would allow me plenty of scope to add a fee.

"I'll speak to him," I shrugged with doubt. "What did you say to him?"

"Nothing. I cannot understand one word he says."

As I left his office, the deputy pointed to the poor boys sweeping the dry earth of the yard with bunches of twigs. "Tell him! Or, one lakh."

Robbie, still sitting on the wall, seemed relaxed and introduced himself. He was wearing a loose shalwar kameez to cover his paunch, and a woollen vest. I sat next to him and explained my mission.

"The deputy says if you don't pay he'll have you sweeping the grounds," I said. "I suggest you don't pay him for anything you can't eat in one day." I meant that any contracts are short-lived.

"Oh, I don't mind paying," said Robbie easily. "I've been living in Pakistan for a year. I know their ways." Robbie spoke with a strong Edinburgh accent.

The press reports of Robbie's case made his negotiating position difficult. The local papers had him as a financier of an £800-million gas pipeline project running to the Arabian Sea at Gwadar. Raising loans was Robbie's skill. Unfortunately, some careless practices with local banks had raised concerns with the correspondent European banks, and Robbie's name landed on the desk of the City of London police. (The thread of doubt began with a single line of text appearing faintly upon just one fax transmitted with the Pearl Continental hotel's name in the header rather than the bank's machine.) All of that would not normally penetrate the barriers of misdirection that protected Robbie. His misfortune was that two visiting London policemen happened to be in the lobby of the Marriot Hotel as Robbie sat reading and taking coffee. They joined him, chatted politely, and then left to make enough fuss to see him arrested on bank fraud.

"If I'd had coffee in my room, I wouldn't be here today," Robbie lamented cheerily.

"If there were no extraordinary coincidences, there'd be no extraordinary stories," I said. "I'll tell the deputy you can manage twenty-five thousand. That's a quarter of what he's asking but he'll take it. You can move in with me if you like."

I left Robbie, and went to the deputy's office.

"You've got it wrong about the new man," I said. "It's all newspaper talk. He's got nothing. Twenty-five thousand."

As I left the compound, the deputy was making fierce broom-sweeping gestures with his arm. Yet he couldn't hold back a smile.

Jailed lawyer Zahoor Baloch had been released on bail by his wife. I then gave him a few thousand pounds to see what he could do. At a district court, he produced a couple of bail guarantors for me holding phoney title deeds in trembling hands. Zahoor failed to secure the judge, who was having none of his tricks. I read the results in my room without great interest. Those months had been bad for me.

Carl Parker, a Canadian friend who lived in Luxembourg, had flown to London where he'd assessed the damage Billy's debriefing had caused. I'd lost everything from the house and the flat but he'd found my keys, as directed, hidden in a false drain that ran from the roof. Carl then flew to Karachi with money, and attended Zahoor's courtroom efforts. Although he sensed the divisions between judge and lawyer, Carl was new to Pakistan and so could not follow the play. With a stack of warnings, I sent him back to Europe to extend the rental on safety-deposit boxes, and to advise my contacts I might be held in Pakistan for as much as another year. This would not be so. The journey to freedom would be unexpected, with many misleading paths.

Robbie the Scot had alerted me to the arrival from Hyderabad jail of someone unusual even within the exotic mix of Karachi Central. Andreas was the leader of a gang of minor Moscow villains during the Soviet era. Minor yet tough. All twelve had been imprisoned for robberies, then immediately split into two groups sent to different jails beyond the Ural Mountains in western Siberia. Although Andreas would accept prison, he'd not tolerate any division of his crew. With five of his men, he broke out of his jail, drove to the local airport in a stolen military vehicle where they hijacked an Aeroflot Tupolev jet. Instead of promptly fleeing the Soviet Union, the fugitives flew to another Siberian prison-city where they exchanged passengers for the remaining half of the gang. Once whole again, Andreas ordered the aircraft to Pakistan.

This could not have been easy. I recalled something of the approach to troublemakers by Soviet security forces from my time in Lebanon in the late 'seventies, and an incident in 1985. In the decade of the civil war, the factional anarchy allowed rebel groups to kidnap locals and foreigners at will. Hezbollah used these snatches to make money but also to restrain world powers from intervening in the larger conflict. When some Russian diplomats were kidnapped, and one killed and dumped, the Soviets had spoken to Grand Ayatollah Muhammad Fadlallah. He didn't comprehend the position. After a month, a posse of KGB operatives flew in to Beirut airport. After a brief stop at their embassy, they drove with hired Lebanese to the political offices of Hezbollah. (There was a thin divide between Hezbollah militia and the public face of its political leaders.) There, the Russians snatched a relative of a top Hezbollah boss, castrated him, then shot him dead, and sent the little package of testicles back to headquarters. The Russians made it clear that more bundles of nuts would follow. The next day, the remaining three Russian captives were released unharmed. I suppose the Russian demand had gained force with the brutal contempt demonstrated to their shocked challengers.

So, against such routine brutality, for Andreas and his boys to have succeeded with their hijacking meant a plan executed without error. Or simply with ruthless determination.

However, at home with Soviet thinking, the Moscow gang understood little of the world beyond Russian borders. Andreas told me he'd selected Pakistan as their destination as (in 1988) it was controlled by dictator General Zia-ul-Haq. The general was dismissive of the Americans yet an enemy of the Soviets due to Russia's invasion of Afghanistan. Well, Zia might have acted as dictator but he was a military man in an army with a long history of conservatism and imagined nobility. Zia would never have sided with street criminals hoping to be viewed as political activists. After all, the country's jails were full of just such people the general had targeted.

Andreas and his men were tried in the Hyderabad courts, convicted and given life sentences. That term reduced to ten years following a quiet appeal. Those years had now passed. Andreas and his friend Alex were the first of the group set to be deported - separately - to Moscow, which accounted for their appearance in Karachi Central Jail.

The decade for the Russians in Hyderabad jail was not peaceful. Andreas and his boys were in no position to pay for comforts, so applied their Soviet-jail manners to get what they needed. This began with taking the lives of prisoners acting as agents for the jail bosses. Three were thrown from blockhouse roofs to their deaths. Two guards were hospitalized in failed attempts to get the Russians into their cells. Soon enough, Andreas adopted local ways. A tradition of hunger strikes still ran through Pakistan prisons as weakened threads from the days of the British Empire when imprisoned Indian nationalists would express their dedication with a willingness to die. In my time, activists with more personal causes proudly carried striped scars upon upper and lower lips from where they'd sewn their mouths to prevent forced feeding. Daily beatings would add pain to the effects of emaciation.

In his style, Andreas had taken his determination to another level. When I asked about the four symmetrical gaps where eight of his back teeth had been, Andreas told me the damage followed an attempt at force-feeding. He was tied to a chair by half-a-dozen guards who then cut the fishing line sutures from his lips. A steel contraption was then forced into his mouth so a tube could feed watery beans to his stomach. Rather than submit, Andreas crushed his own teeth against the iron. The Russian group had gained nothing material from their rebellions in jail, although I suspected the appeal that reduced their life sentences to ten years was to get rid of them as much as from any issues of law.

Now facing deportation and return to a Siberian prison, Andreas had been escorted to Karachi airport by police to meet Russian Federation officers who could guard him on the flight home. They hadn't arrived, and Andreas was back at KCJ trying to explain some pressing need through a mixture of Urdu, English and Russian. I sought a translator.

Robbie the Scot had met a Russian girl who was serving time in the women's section of KCJ. Robbie was arranging clients with his lawyer Rana Shamim to run a test case in the high courts for the benefit of thirty-five prisoners who had been tried, convicted and sentenced in the customs court. All were facing the second trial in the special narcotics court for what was a duplication of the same case. Advocate Shamim would challenge the prosecution on constitutional grounds that a second prosecution would amount to double jeopardy. For Robbie, as his own case meandered on, rounding up petitioners gave him something to do while hearing many stories. And that of the Russian girl was unusual.

Tatiana was from Krasnodar near the Black Sea. There, she had befriended a visiting Nigerian. He left her with child, although returned soon after the boy's birth. Tatiana was in her early twenties. She kept her blonde hair short and wore rimless spectacles that made her look like a pretty schoolteacher. Her Nigerian husband (the marriage gave him Russian residency) then had an idea. Not his first, since he had wives in several countries. He convinced Tatiana to take her baby boy to Pakistan, and then to return with two kilos of heroin. He thought the appearance of mother and child at Karachi airport would allay suspicion. It did not. Almost all young Russian girls visiting Pakistan were thought of by officials as working prostitutes. Tatiana's unscrupulous husband knew that to be so but even the dope was on commission, so he saw the plan as risk-free – to himself. Such behaviour, though mercifully rare, enamels the public perception of drug dealers. Yet Tatiana was far from timid in crisis. She had notoriously decked her lawyer in open court with one punch when unhappy with a mistimed application concerning her child. Eventually, the toddler had returned to Krasnodar with Tati's dad after the boy turned three. The mother's reunion now awaited settlement of the double-jeopardy hearing.

Through visits to Tatiana in the 'family room' at the women's prison next door, a clear picture of Andreas's current problem emerged. This followed his stalled appearance at Karachi airport when his Russian escorts had not arrived. More helpfully, the local airport police had no interest in the deportation. As far as Pakistan was concerned, Andreas could fly anywhere for which he had a ticket. And a passport. This meant perhaps two weeks to arrange those before the heavyweight Russian escorts might arrive.

We made every effort possible. Money was easy enough to put together; a camera less so. Yet within six days a fair passport photo was taken against a cell wall and prints made. Then, the usual traps opened as they do when trying to find solutions in

Pakistan while still imprisoned. Those outside seeking a European passport upon which the picture could be substituted fell to profiteering between the many exchanges. Ten days after the challenge began, Andreas was again taken to the airport. This time, two huge slabs in suits from Moscow were there to take him back.

Andreas was to survive his second Russian imprisonment, and gain release into the new Russia. Yet his Asian adventure also provided slow lessons for a stranger in a strange land: that fighting the prison would mean losses with no reward, and – despite relatively easy contact with the outside world – those working against time in Pakistan are sure to fail.

9

I left the house of Azif Zardari early, worn down by the prattle of treachery and my lunch-time host's stage-managed ill health. Zardari was the husband of former prime minister Benazir Bhutto. Imprisoned on (probably fake) murder charges – including a claim that he'd tried to assassinate his wife – he pretended a range of near-fatal and chronic diseases to help his bail applications. And, it seemed to me, to give his many enemies the idea that he wasn't worth the cost of assassinating on his own account as he was anyway dying. Zardari had a reputation, when in public office, for remorselessly demanding fees and kickbacks for every official act. But no evidence of wealth appeared in his walled fortress within Karachi Central Jail. Despite the roominess of his house, Zardari's guards were shabby and poorly tipped, the food miserly, his servants fearful and unhappy. The former minister's companions that day either pretenders or reluctant. However gloomy this 1990s snapshot, Zardari would one day become president of Pakistan.

I was a poor companion myself at lunch. I'd not long had news from Europe of my friend Carl who had disappeared for three months. He was on a mission to fetch a wad of bribe money for my troubles. Pretty much ignoring my instructions, he had removed all my papers and passports along with boxes of mixed currencies from their lockers and loaded them into a new stash rented under his travelling name. He then went to Stockholm to see my friends before his planned return to Karachi. I'd provided Carl with addresses and detailed instructions about arranging meetings. These included a Stockholm cellphone number to be used only in an emergency. By that, I meant a last call of warning, if required, should he have to board an express train out of town. I should have known better. It was the first call he made after arriving in Sweden. Carl was impatient. The uncertainty of waiting in the corridor of Tomas's apartment block for my contact to return from work at six would have cost Carl only an hour at most. Yet the call he made alerted the Swedish police a foreign visitor had arrived, as Tomas's phone calls were monitored.

Carl was picked up by Stockholm police the following day as he left Tomas's apartment. They had nothing on him but he was kept in solitary confinement (standard treatment for suspects in Scandinavia) for three months until a judge tired of police promises to produce evidence of wrongdoing. However, receipts in Carl's luggage led to his new storage vault in Luxembourg where most of my papers and some cash were held. Luxembourg city police took possession, and nothing more was heard or seen from that tiny Grand Duchy. Yet this meant the end of the reserve identities I'd created in London, and the close of that life. Even so, there was one strand of that life I was unwilling to abandon: Eloise. But for now, there was nothing I could do.

On my way back to the B-class compound from Zardari's house, one of the prisoner lackeys from administration stopped me on my path.

"Mister David," he said. "Maybe you can meet my new boss. A young gentleman."

"A young gentleman officer in here?" I wondered aloud. "Tell him I'll see him later for tea."

When I arrived at my room, Billy was on the veranda, looking anxious. Any time I spent away with people known to be strong or influential was, for him, a concern. In truth, I'd long passed giving him so much thought. Today was one of his routine fears.

"Dave, they want money," Billy said.

"They always want money."

"Yeah, but the chief says we have to get out of B-class unless we pay. They want to see you."

"I know that," I said. "Their boy collared me on my way home."

"So, the money's for both of us. So they know we're together."

"Oh, I think they know we're together," I said with exhausted sarcasm.

The new assistant sub-deputy spoke English very well. His uniform was tailored and shirt clean; a good family somewhere behind him. He'd been assigned this mission of polite extortion and was clearly embarrassed. He squirmed in the chair of the small, barren office. Often, he'd cast his eyes to the windows to look at the slothful despair of those passing. He looked at me as if I were an alien visitor unable to see in human colour.

"I've been here for three months," he said. "You have no idea – you cannot imagine how corrupt is this place. How low are my colleagues. At the highest level."

"That's all right," I comforted him. "I understand."

Taking a Rs.100 note from my pocket, I unfolded it flat on the table between us. I touched the head of Pakistan's founder, Muhammed Ali Jinnah.

"I would ask of your boss what would Mr. Jinnah say," I said, knowing the low value of the note (£1) would be taken clearly as a refusal.

That afternoon Billy and I were moved out of the prime row of B-class to separate, nearby cells sharing with prisoners of mixed fortunes. Fallen policemen, low-level civil servants and foreigners whose embassies cared nothing for their fates.

The compound along from B-class composed rows of small cells holding the odd loners and the abandoned who just might one day produce some money to feed the prison bosses. I'd been moved with haste into a cell with two others. A contrasting pair. One was young, neat and small who claimed he was a medical student. The other, a bloated middle-aged halfwit police sergeant whose drunken brutality had somehow gone beyond the pale of the near limitless excesses of a local police station. That would've taken some doing. Only after twice being the subject of complaints by lamenting families of those who died in his custody did he find himself in prison. He held only a dim memory of those he'd killed. Sober and eternally hungover, he now had only his cellmate to torment.

Within a week, another stooge from the superintendent's office approached me to ask – while pretending to be ever so helpful – if I'd come to accept reality and would now pay. I knew that my place in B-class was taken by a man who'd paid over the odds for those minor comforts, so there'd be no hurry to restore my position. Billy Green had moved in with a couple of Europeans who were always broke as they spent their money on coarse brown heroin the Africans had spared from confiscation during their arrest. (This was by re-swallowing the fat capsules every time they were sent to the toilet, only giving a handful to satisfy the charge.) As my loathing of Billy was well known, there was no profit to harm him as a way of putting pressure on me. Anyway, I'd had enough. That aside, paying was no simple matter. Getting European money from deposit boxes, then through friends to some trusted intermediary to Pakistan, and then rupee banknotes to my hands involved many steps and much communication. Steps made more difficult now after Carl's disastrous European vacation. All that, for what? Not freedom, certainly – and only to hold at bay the grubby attacks of some uniformed toilet attendants. I decided I wouldn't play anymore. Unfortunately, for captives, the terms of play are set by the captors.

Each night, in our cell, the fat policeman would go to work on the medical student. Having slept most of the day, he was refreshed for an all-night session of goading, growling and guffawing at poor Sohail, who would flop his arms over his head in despair. Tubby would then poke him from insensibility with his stubby fingers while musing loudly about gambling, women, drinking and the hard lot of a policeman. I couldn't follow his nonsense in any language.

"What's that idiot telling you?" I asked a weary Sohail after three straight nights of explosive theatrics from the murderous cop.

"Oh, I don't know," replied the broken Sohail. "He thinks he's funny. He eating my brain."

Around 9.00pm on the tenth night, our cell door opened. One of the chief's deputies stood with unfamiliar guards. Without explanation, I was taken to the Bund Ward. Bund means closed, although that high-walled compound at the jail's centre was more than just closed. It was the notorious block where difficult prisoners were taken for further punishment, away from others' eyes and recall.

Through the darkness of several doors, I was put in a cell with a half-dozen guys who had been set up or caught with trivial fragments of contraband – although most were simply on the losing side of jail-house disputes. Even on the winning side, the loser might have had a few rupees on hand to buy a reversal and see his victor taken away. In my cell, the boys spent the night trying to cadge tobacco from the bund-ward trusties before beginning a search for matches. This, despite their chains and shackles.

Early morning saw the arrival of selected newcomers to Karachi Central Jail. From our unlit cell, the light dimmed further by narrow corridors of slimy bricks, we could see nothing, yet heard the voices beyond. In Urdu, they sounded educated, middle-class and rising in tones of desperation. My cellmates explained: those from good families whose sons arrived at the prison were quickly assessed for worldliness and connections. Those who lacked an understanding of this nether world, whose eyes revealed fear and had family with any money would soon have their nightmares made real. Taken immediately to the bund ward, they'd be locked in leg-spreading ankle fetters, chained at the wrists and neck, and then beaten until they paid.

The low-browed oaf who oversaw the block had me taken from the cell mid-morning. I knew him from days he had substituted at the B-class gate, and had paid him sometimes for a few routine services. Now, I gave him my last Rs.500 with the suggestion he shouldn't annoy me while I was on his block.

The five-hundred wasn't enough for him. His licence to torment in the bund ward had doubly corrupted his values. He ordered his trusty to attach some heavy and ancient handcuffs behind my back. The mildest punishment of the ward was to leave inmates cuffed from behind and fettered around the clock. Using a toilet would be a challenge. I didn't think much of that, and began screaming at the guard.

"I know what you're worth, and it's not much," I yelled. "I'd only pay to give someone else your job."

And I went on. I had to raise the level of my tirade due to the sounds of a long beating coming from a nearby cell where more energetic trusties were working over a newcomer, a minor civil servant. Now, after an hour, his clothes torn away and the two untiring trusties whipping him relentlessly with leather belts, his wailing for mercy was reduced simply to wailing. This was the background to my conversation with the bund ward boss.

The guard moved to strike me. I tilted my head towards him with a nasty smile.

"Go on, try it," I said as the trusty needlessly translated. "You'll see where you are this afternoon."

This was bluff, especially when followed by references to the British High Commission, an embassy that would do nothing. The trusty behind me was still rattling the cuffs. "You can fuck off, too," I said, trading again on my status as an outsider. I added threats using the names of my political friends inside, though this was shakier ground. While I well knew that this guard could customarily rely on the betrayal and abandonment of those moved to the bund ward, he held just enough doubt. He spat curses but left me to return to my cell.

Not for long.

Within an hour, I was taken from the punishment block to the office of a deputy superintendent, a fat man in a grubby smock and worn jacket, despite his rank.

"There's nothing we can do with you," he said, sadly.

By which he meant, there was nothing more they could get from me. Before noon, I found myself alone in the dirty iron box welded to the back of the van bumping along the roads away from Karachi. My destination was Hyderabad prison, although there would be no record of my location on any register held by Karachi Central Jail. I was being disappeared, yet my true position was more like that of a hostage whose primary kidnappers had abandoned hope of extracting payment and so traded their victim to lesser – and perhaps more brutal – hostage takers.

From the outside, Hyderabad Jail looked big, judging from the vast stretches of ochre walls. I saw little of the inside as I was quickly taken to Hyderabad's bund ward. I came with nothing, only the shalwar kameez I stood in. No money, although a blanket an acquaintance had passed me at the gatehouse in Karachi.

This bund ward was a widespread compound of single-storey colonial-era buildings, mud-spattered over whitewash. Mercifully quiet. I waited for two hours by a wall, somehow enjoying the sun.

A deputy officer arrived, looking neat. He had the bund ward trusty bring two chairs. We sat chatting about Anglo-Indian history for fifteen minutes before he announced the demand from the superintendent of Hyderabad Jail.

"Twenty-five thousand dollars," he said. "For me, I want nothing."

"Of course," I smiled, then musing: "I'm guessing your superintendent doesn't get to see many Englishmen."

"You are our only one. A few Russians, but—", he cut himself short.

I explained to my new companion that his boss shouldn't expect to retire on the singular appearance of a foreigner. I added, "If I was worth anything, they would have kept me at Karachi."

Over the next couple of months, I had time to know the features of my solitary cell. Small, with a bare earth floor and jagged brickwork, the rusted bars of its narrow and low door faced a dank corridor. However, with no cell light, only between ten in the morning and mid-afternoon was there enough dimly shafted glow to allow vision through the gloom. Hyderabad's superintendent rarely applied Karachi's big-city brutality to those reluctant to pay (Karachi guards lived within the greater compound; the Hyderabad jailers liked to walk home at night), he simply wore them down by neglect and isolation. Food, in the form of watery beans, arrived once a day. A trusty would jam a section of metal roof guttering between the cell bars, and then pour a cup-sized dropping from outside. Until I was given a soft-plastic bowl, the sliding beans had to be caught in the thin disc of chapatti bread given to complete the meal. Water, from a muddy pot in the corridor, could be scooped with difficulty using the all-purpose bowl. A three-inch hole at the far corner of the cell comprised the drain and toilet facility. And that was it. No daylight, no washing other than a splash or two of the precious (and insect-filled) drinking water, and no exercise. Few sounds, although I knew when Fridays came because I heard the voices of other inmates as they were allowed out for the weekly prayers. I was the only prisoner in that corridor of cells. I was pleased that, at least, there was no one to whom I need talk.

There is much freedom in letting go of most things. Any once-lived life takes only a moment to set aside, with enough practice. Well, almost a moment. Without conscious effort, when in semi-darkness and isolation, all the images and memories of that former life soon appear as though on a screen, a presentation of someone else's history.

Without the benefits of natural light, I wanted to make a clock out of routine itself. Standing during mornings, avoiding daytime naps, and assigning different quarters of the cell – small as it was – and different sitting positions, to parts of the day. Also, limiting any repetitive pacing, exercising with moderation and always with some make-believe change of clothing. As I was not actually starving, thoughts of food could be set aside without much trouble, though I found useful an imagined picture of a bucket of rotten oatmeal in the corridor, next to the water pot. There was no bucket, of course, but the idea that there was something on offer that I had refused seemed to work to quell appetite.

After the third week, another thought mechanism became useful, perhaps essential. Although the cell allowed a separation of myself from my life, a sense of self would sneak in if I churned over disastrous events of my past – even the distant past – with some series of what-ifs. Only anxiety would follow. So, I'd trick away such unhelpful speculations by pushing the what-if to events before my time. What if Alexander the Great had been permitted by his companions to fight on into Gangeatic India? What if Byzantine emperor Heraclius had restored Arabian *foedorati* and contained Arab expansion? Working through such events and their consequences effectively blocked thoughts of my real life and current fate, those already overthought and pointless. Oddly none of the new, imagined scenarios had happy outcomes. A few Greek cities along the Ganges didn't prevent town pestilence or bring peace. And a Christian Middle East was more violent and restricted than Islamic and later Ottoman rule. And along another strand, even though sparing Archduke Ferdinand the assassin's bullet at Sarajevo certainly prevented the First World War and much of the second, the late arrival of atomic weapons in the 1950s risked nuclear annihilation on two continents. Almost every intervention to history seemed to produce suffering.

In the following month, I set aside thinking about people altogether. Turning to music, I'd stand in the centre of the cell and imagine instruments playing, adding one at a time hoping to put together an orchestra or at least a cover band. With time, I improved, although could not restore the childhood ability to hear imaginary symphonic compositions. Those efforts might have helped with the next phase, in which I tried to improve my maths with sets of problems that required a mental notepad. I began with shapes: glowing lines of vectors that could be manipulated as three-dimensional constructions, rotating and combining. These led to numbers; angles and surfaces. By the time I got to the problem of infinity, unsolvable to me anyway, I ran out of my limited mathematical knowledge.

In the third month, I was designing houses in places I'd like to live, cars for roads I'd like to travel, and ships for oceans I'd like to sail. To this day, I could tell you the position and number of every floorboard in a three-storey townhouse I imagined, including the position of each nail. No people in the house, of course; no passing cars on the roads, and sadly, the imaginary ship could be operated by a crew of just one.

At some unknown hour of an unnamed day in September, the bund-ward guard came to my door. I'd had visitors before. Every few weeks, senior officers would walk swiftly by, not silently (to me the swift walk past of three staff seemed a stampede), and move on. However, on this day, after some difficulty, the ward officer alone unlocked my door. Instinctively, I stood back, as though this was an unreasonable intrusion.

"Someone to see you," he announced.

I looked away cautiously from the door along the corridor to the daylight.

"No," said the officer. "You come with me. The superintendent office."

As we walked from the low gate of the bund ward and up the gentle hill toward the front of the prison, I figured that the superintendent had tired of waiting and now wanted to make a strong pitch for payment.

Inside the old gatehouse complex, a curved wooden staircase led to an oak-panelled office. It was like a Victorian headmaster's study except the bookshelves held no books, just mouldering files and time-polished leather registers.

Behind his uncluttered desk sat the portly superintendent, smiling and affable. In the front chairs sat two men in elaborate and expensive tribal dress. On a small, round table rested a colourful creamed sponge cake. There were decorated teacups ready. One of the visitors stood and turned to me with his arms open. This was Mir Noor Jehan, lord of the Magsi clan.

As we embraced, I could hear the voice of the superintendent in the background.

"Mister David," he was saying. "I had no idea you were here. I am angry with my deputies, they don't always have eyes where they must look. If I had known you were the friend of Lord Noor Jehan, well, we would be too-much friends by now." The chief warden prattled on.

I learned that a month earlier, Noor Jehan had been bailed on his mass-murder charges. Two wealthy Karachi businessmen had put up their houses as guarantees, backed by land owners from Baluchistan. Noor Jehan had come to know of my disappearance while inside, and then tipped as to my location. I turned and Noor Jehan embraced me, gleaming in white robes as usual.

"We have friends here," he said in confidence as we sipped sweet tea and I ate cake. "But perhaps give this pig a little money," he added making a light twist of thumb and forefinger. "I will do something for you."

I noticed that a guard standing by the closed office door with a rifle was not in uniform but in white robes. He was one of Noor Jehan's men. Noor Jehan had known of my disappearance, of course, and within a week of his release, had been told of my location – something unknown still to my other friends, lawyers and the courts.

Although afterwards returned to the bund ward, I was moved from my solitary cell to a large, almost empty dormitory, though without bed frames. That day, a bundle of bedding, clothes and food was delivered, arranged by my protector.

The new room held a range of misfits. Mostly those who might find enemies and a modest price on their heads if left to wander about the jail. A father and son pair of tribal hillbillies spent a night hoping to convince me that the murder of a village girl (a niece) had been an honour killing. I asked how the eighteen-year-old had disgraced the family. They became flustered, and I suspected they'd done something disgraceful between them that required her permanent silence. In another corner lived a man who was not allowed potatoes in his diet. The injunction against uncooked spuds had nothing to do with his digestion, rather his skills at carving and some literacy. He was notorious for crafting fake stamps on title deeds and court orders. Still, I could meet prison oddities anytime. I wanted more to find who had told Noor Jehan that I'd been disappeared to Hyderabad.

On the day of the Eid holiday, the internal prison sectors were opened allowing most inmates to roam. I suppose I was permitted from the bund ward to make arrangements for the 'little money' for the superintendent. I had no intention of paying a cent. I wanted to know what, if anything, my protector Noor Jehan, and separately, the superintendent might do next.

To help me with the search, I found a remnant of the British Raj who lived in a brick hut in a leafy open compound nearby. Tall and thin, Byron Stroud was in his thirties though maintained a bushy red moustache of an old colonel and lived alone, other than a servant, in his small rooms. He was the grandson of a couple who had stayed on after India's partition in 1947. He had no money to speak of, and his criminal career was eventful (he'd robbed a train with two Sindhi boys) but unrewarding. He'd gained his better accommodation the hard way, enduring hunger strikes and beatings. I think the moustache was to disguise the suture scars after stitching his lips when refusing food.

Byron took me to the main compound where we met with the remaining Russians from the '88 skyjacking case. They seemed lost but unbeaten. The Russians had learned more Sindhi than Urdu during their decade at Hyderabad, so Byron was translating as we chatted. Standing under the curved portico between bricked-up classical pillars, I was – as so often – distracted by the architecture of the jail. Surely, this was not always a prison, I thought. It looked as though some huge, ruined city from the Seleucid Empire had been walled and stone-filled into cellblocks by poor but industrious monks. In fact, merely the gardens and pavilions of an English park had been added to the prison and transformed using hungry refugees from the partition riots.

Some fuss at my side brought forward the sound of elaborate greetings. A small man, robed white, was bracketed by minions.

"Eid Mubarak," I greeted him, as Byron whispered background to me. The small man who moved with Napoleonic confidence was the leader of the Sindhi Nationalist Party. He knew me on sight.

"You're the friend of my friend, Mir Noor Jehan," he said. Eager hands (the Russian's servants) found a chair for the chief, as though particular to him as well as good manners. "What can I do for you, David?"

There was little the Sindh nationalist could do for me beyond that which he'd done already, although he then arranged cooked food for me each day. And he did wrinkle his brow when I mentioned the name of the judge in my case. Perhaps affordable, I wondered. As head of a party that sought independence for the province, government agencies had given him a difficult time, I later heard. He'd been held after his arrest (more like a kidnapping) for five months in a cellar, blindfolded and swaddled from head to foot in thick cloth with blanket mittens on hands and feet. On just one occasion, after three months, a night guard had taken pity on him. Led by his chains up to a quiet garden area, the guard knelt and unwrapped his feet for fifteen minutes.

"You can never know the feeling of that grass between my toes," he told me. "The kiss of each blade, the softness of the damp soil; even the grains of earth under my soles and the dew at my heels with the rich smell of evening was a gift of love from the land of my father's fathers." There were tears in Byron's eyes as he translated.

That prisoner of sensory deprivation seemed a different incarnation of this leader now in Hyderabad jail surrounded by his dedicated and respectful followers who waited for their moment. I could understand how these sons of the soil rained bullets upon those they saw as sham authority without fear of death.

10

In a walled garden, on yet another sunny day, I was drinking lime juice with a little gin, talking to Captain Arshad and a Christian tax collector when my servant announced that an Englishman lived nearby, held in the comfortable but parasitic grip of notorious Akbar Shah, the Amsterdam-based hashish smuggler and gambling addict. Akbar Shah was no longer in Europe, but with the only other Englishman held in Karachi's Landhi jail, as was I.

    Five weeks after the visit to Hyderabad by my tribal lord Noor Jehan, my fortunes changed. Without warning I was again bustled into a police van, driven to Karachi and produced before the customs court. There, I was beamed at by the diminutive and clear-eyed judge who welcomed me with what seemed like pride. He was entitled to feel that way. Frustrated by being ignored by those at Karachi Central Jail, he'd sent selected police to arrest the prison superintendent. His Honour made plain that either David would be found or the warden would remain in the court cells. The superintendent was released and I was found. It is a brave judge who takes on the cancerous growth of KCJ, and a rare one. I was given a court order for B-class status and sent to Landhi, the second-largest prison in Karachi. Before I left the court, I learned from my new lawyer that Billy Green had pleaded guilty and been sentenced to five years. (Noor Jehan had given him stern advice as he found him while looking for me.) My case was listed for judgement in two months' time. Robbie the Scot had arranged my lawyer, Rana Shamim, but the judge's stout heart had come from somewhere else. Perhaps from within.

The superintendent at Landhi was no less greedy than his colleague at KCJ, and – my court order notwithstanding – I was dumped in a pit for three days before moving to the neat and small B-class compound of eight rooms. A 'little money' (I now understood this more of a courtesy rather than a bribe) had given me a cool room, bed and new mattress along with the shared services of the bardashi of a new friend, a Pakistan Air Force captain under trial for a drugs conspiracy. However, I'd yet to survey the prison, although I was free to go as I pleased within the walls. On hearing the news of the new Englishman, I was asked by Ibrahim, the government tax inspector (corruption charges) if I wished to meet him at once.

"The sun is too low in the sky," I replied, not wanting to move from my chair. "Let's invite him to lunch. Sunday." I turned to Captain Arshad. "What can you tell me of this hashish man, our brother Akbar Shah?"

I dressed in western clothes for the Sunday lunch. Unaccustomed to the close fitting, I felt like a visitor myself. When the portly Englishman arrived – also named David – he paused on entry to our garden, looked to the colourful table array, then the faces smiling in greeting, unable to immediately identify who among us was his fellow countryman.

"Hello," I said, stepping forward. "You must be David. We were just about to send for you. I know B-class is hard to find."

David hugged me, not in the local style of feigned brotherhood but as though saved from perdition. There was a tremor in his voice as he mumbled greetings. He had been too long among strangers.

David Dufaur had come to Pakistan hoping to save £70,000 sent by a group of London villains with long-stalled plans to buy and ship a few tonnes of hash from Afghanistan to some Pacific island and then to Europe.

"When did the money go missing?" I asked our guest.

"The first lot or the second payment?" replied David, then changed subject. "You know I get good food living with, ah – my friend, but I haven't used a knife and fork in months."

Captain Arshad gave me a look of consternation. He was marvelling that anyone would twice send money unescorted into Pakistan. David was arrested at the Hyatt Hotel in Karachi not long after meeting Akbar Shah. No drugs were found anywhere. I asked if Shah had since asked for more money.

"No. He's been taking care of me here," David didn't sound convinced as he spoke. "We've got a good room with only six people. Still, I'll need twenty-thousand pounds for the judge. Looks like I'll have to sell the house." David was married with two children in London where he'd been a diamond trader. This was his first step into the drug world.

"Don't sell the house," I suggested. "In Pakistan, given time, everything turns to dust."

My last session in the customs court took place a few weeks later. The same judge, he who'd brought me from Hyderabad Jail, announced his ruling that there was no evidence of guilt for any crime; that Thailand had made no submissions with supporting evidence, and that I was free to go. Except that I wasn't.

Pakistan had a few years earlier formed its Anti-narcotics Agency. With little to do beyond add another layer of graft along the border, it was short on prosecutions to present to the courts. The agency's desk operatives began visiting local and provincial police for cases they could take. This usually meant a deal where regular police would find someone to set up for arrest. Fees and kickbacks were involved, of course, but the quality of the arrests was poor. On this, the national customs service would not play along. They were above all that; well, in a higher pay scale. So, the narcotics agency simply duplicated the customs court charges regardless of the outcomes there.

"But I've been found not guilty already, haven't I?" I asked my new lawyer Rana outside the court building.

"Absolutely. They must let you go," he assured me. "But there's a difficulty."

I'd become accustomed to the phrase, *'Absolutely – but there's a difficulty'* over the years. Rana explained that I'd have to face another trial on the same vague charges. Yet the new Anti-narcotics Agency court was packed with greedy low-level judges able to impose the death penalty. Worse, the even-newer Anti-terrorism Agency had taken the few available venues to use as courts, so the drug-related cases would be many years from commencement.

"You'll have to try for bail," Rana suggested. "Not easy for a foreigner."

I nodded, not easy.

Lunch with Akbar Shah and David at Landhi jail. A large but dismal pot of lentils and chickpeas with a suggestion of fatty meat. We were seated on the floor blanket of a small brick hut between rows of crowded dormitories. Akbar Shah with his sunken date-pit eyes kept watch on David while three nervy cellmates – with no possessions I could see – kept eyes on Akbar. He had just one servant (also resident) whom he scolded frequently, although privately spoke to with kindness. David took trouble to appear comfortable in the cell, as accepted and admired by all. He also joined in murmuring the Muslim grace before the meal. He laughed at now being called *motta* David (fat David) since *batala* David (slim David) had arrived. It was clear the English diamond merchant had fallen into a den of thieves. Akbar planned to eat *motta* David while the others looked like they'd been promised the crusts. A very small game for Akbar who'd once had a name as a high roller.

After lunch, I walked with David in the grounds.

"Have you seen the rest of the prison?" I asked. "The little temple, the big tree?"

David declined my offer of his own room in B-class. I then spoke of the twenty-thousand pounds asked for in legal fees, a figure claimed by Akbar.

"I suppose you're not planning to give that to a lawyer. Or someone in jail?" I suggested. "That's never worked for me."

"Akbar has to grease a few palms," David said without enthusiasm. "You know how it goes here."

"Yes, I do. Is it not too late to stop the sale of your house?"

It was.

Our gardener in the B-class compound was making a great show of planting wild flowers and saplings along the wall shrubbery. Captain Arshad had been granted bail and was due out within days. As that would leave only Ibrahim and me in the compound, the servants were all proving their worth. Keeping out of the way, we three sat in deckchairs on the veranda. Arshad leaned back, eyes closed in pretended exhaustion, yet talking softly. He'd made vague promises to some of the servants, all of whom had stalled cases. Most were hoping to make eye contact as a winsome reminder that they should not be abandoned.

Of course, I too, servant of another kind, had plans for the good captain. My second and duplicated case in the anti-narcotics court was now a mere single file, mouldering with fifty others, never to be examined. No judge, no dates set and no venue. I would need to have bail set, paid, and someone to ensure those orders applied on the ground. That ground being Landhi prison. I had no serious money, and no outsider and friend in Pakistan with a sharp knowledge of the land-pirates and ferocious officials who ate all those in need. Noor Jehan might have tipped my judge to my exile in Hyderabad but his commitments to his fiefdom (that is, himself) ruled out long-range gambles. However, Captain Arshad had agreed to do everything necessary for me. Fortunately, he'd had pleasant experiences with westerners – in business matters, at least. Arshad had control of a Dubai-based skipper who'd facilitated a six-tonne load of hashish to Canada. Soon after unloading at Quebec, the bricks were transferred to a dozen cars, two of which crossed into New Hampshire and New York State. Arshad was around for the payments and soon flew out. Yet not before being tagged by the American DEA, who'd requested his arrest in Karachi. His case was empty of evidence yet bloated with large numbers. Probably, it would drizzle for years of ten-minute hearings before being abandoned.

Perhaps my expectation was too ambitious that Arshad would, within weeks of his own release, use his own money to ensure others would offer property guarantees on my behalf, and then reward a dozen officials to do their jobs. Yet the captain had dreams of his own, most of which he hoped I'd fulfil. Of course, his costs would be repaid in cash, but I had grave doubts about more Afghan border crossings with a man already targeted by the DEA.

His final day in Landhi was no hour to remind my new friend of his duties – they would be done or not – but as we digested lunch, I kindled pale fire.

"I can tell you from sad experience," I said to Arshad. "The moment one steps from prison, it's as though waking from years-long anaesthetic – or a whack on the head. Only losses remain, with a real urgency to move on."

My attempts to add compulsion to Arshad's first days out fell on deaf ears. He couldn't shake off an earlier conversation about western bathroom habits.

"You're telling me most people don't wash their bums each time they use the toilet?" repeated Arshad. In the East, water jugs are kept to the side of squatting bowls. "So, they just smear the shit around their arse with a bit of paper?"

This was as though the captain's image of European civilization had been shattered. I tried at first to defend our own tribe.

"Okay, the rich have little bum-baths, bidets, but I have to admit water is mostly used for flushing the evidence."

Arshad and Christian Ibrahim looked at me wordlessly. I had only the dubious history card to play.

"And anyway, if you want to explore the world and conquer, you've gotta take being a bit smelly." Defeated, I added, "Naturally, I'm different."

I thought then that the chances of Arshad's help were no better than finding a pre-stamped passport waiting for me behind a bathroom mirror in Bangkok an hour after a jailbreak. Remote.

Part IV

1

The sky above the sea was overcast – no bad thing – and the wide beach almost deserted as I climbed the ridge at street level to return to the penthouse at Clifton. In the lobby, I passed the old major who advised me of a forthcoming residents' meeting about building services. The lift to the twentieth floor smelled faintly of sand and sun-cream. Inside the large apartment, I returned keys to my pocket and walked to a balcony. All quiet – Robbie had said he was going out to pick up a case of beer from a local wine shop. Looking over the city, I could have seen the walls of Karachi Central Jail if not for the haze of distant traffic. I was free of prison but had not moved far.

Captain Arshad had been good to his word. Properties valued at $50,000 had been given as surety for bail. Late afternoon, three weeks earlier, I stood at the inside-gate compound of Landhi jail with the two-dozen others who also were for release. I was the last to leave. The superintendent was having none of my release papers, though they were legitimate court orders. He'd demanded twenty-five thousand dollars, then left for the day. However, Arshad had wisely sent a mutual friend to collect me; had the captain himself arrived the super would have recognized him and been suffused with rapacity. The friend at the gate I recall as a religious scholar who'd once been jailed at KCJ. He was neatly bearded and white-capped, and told me he'd pretended to the guards at the gate that he was no more than a college driver.

"I said he could have the four-hundred from my pocket," my collector told me as he started the car. "I said there was no one else interested and anyway I didn't care if I got you or not."

After a year and a half, I'd been freed finally for five dollars.

Robbie the Scot had been bailed on his massive oil-pipeline corruption case and had rented the penthouse at Clifton Beach. Not simply for comfort but because he had unfinished business in Pakistan where appearances remain decisive. The apartment had six bedrooms on two floors, so Robbie's generosity allowed me the peace to finalize my case and assemble the devices to move on. A third occupant at Clifton was Tatiana, now Robbie's girlfriend. Robbie had kindly freed the Russian from the women's section of KCJ, a move in the Sindh High Court that coincidentally freed thirty-five other inmates sometime later.

For ten days, I explored Karachi on foot with a camera in hand finding spectacular tangles of wires nesting city streets. Unless with the background shadows produced by late afternoons, the resultant photographs were not as good as those taken indoors. Especially those with the layers of live mesh sagging from collapsed junction boards in sweating concrete carparks beneath the older high-rises. More than once, passers-by took me for some forlorn safety inspector and became nervous, as residents do when an outsider notices the obvious.

With little grace between the heat of smoky night and blistering noon in Karachi, I flew west and north for the slightest causes. A weekend with Noor Jehan and his retinue in Quetta, then northern hills with Captain Arshad in Muree, a summer retreat for generations. After listening to the captain's plans, and having reimbursed him the fix money for my bail, I returned south alone and slowly, river town to river town.

Karachi drew me back on several days when lawyer Rana had disposed of the second charge in the High Court. Seven slothful clerks and grasping court officials were as ever reluctant to clear the books, but with my training at KCJ and combined freedom, they didn't stand much of a chance. Even so, I was still without passports good enough for modern travel, so returned to wandering. On one side wanting to return fast to London and Eloise, though on another pausing in my walks to admire Raj-era suburbs such as Cantonment (in Lahore) along with parts of Abbottabad and Multan that – long favoured with homes for the military establishment – seemed curiously ideal for living beyond the net. The houses were yielded wistfully from 1947 to sentimental hands, trained in the old schools. Although careworn, their homes recalled my boyhood under 1960s Australian static summers where drifting acres of suburban houses made paralysis seem tranquil, and behind most doors the husbands and wives: baffled masters remaining bound to the gently enslaved.

Now free, I found myself almost entirely forgiving of behaviour in others regarded by most as avaricious and self-serving; a happy observer with no wish to be understood beyond my actions. For now, no action seemed best.

Shortly after my return to Karachi, I drove to the airport to welcome visitors new to Pakistan. They were Jeanette Dufaur and her two young daughters, Sophia and Ellie: the family of the imprisoned David I'd met months earlier in Landhi. By phone to London, I'd advised Jeanette against the trip as there would be nothing she could do to helpfully influence the case of her husband, which, I was sure would wither with time.

Leaving my rented *Vindaloo* (an old crock, though air-conditioned) in the carpark, I stood between the arrivals exit and the predatory taxi touts, ready to intercept. The little family appeared through the glass doors rattling a dozen suitcases on two defective trolleys, bunched and brightly dressed, laughing as though landing at Barcelona rather than the Islamic Republic of Pakistan.

Brushing aside a thicket of scammers, I introduced myself, dismissing Jeanette's apologies for lateness.

"An hour's not late in Karachi," I said, then looking at their suitcases. "You probably took the baggage handlers by surprise. Too sleepy at ten to steal much." The little girls, Ellie the seven-year-old blonde, and twelve-year-old Sophia, freckled yet darker, looked at me with amused disappointment. Perhaps their mother had given them different expectations. Jeanette was unreadable, and – to an outsider – they communicated telepathically.

After securing the visitors in the Avari Hotel, and planning for dinner, I saw that this venerable mid-city inn might not be suitable for a group with a holiday outlook. Beyond a meeting with father and husband David during his next court appearance (better than a jail visit as it would be outdoors), they would need entertaining. I had nothing more pressing.

"It was so bad to see David at the court," Jeanette said as we sat at the poolside bar of the Carlton Hotel, a complex planned as luxurious navy apartments before completion as a hotel to camouflage the military rich. "He was in chains."

"How was he?" I asked.

"Oh, David was just fine. Laughing like he was having a good time. He sent me to get chicken and pills from the shops for him and his friend. Like a picnic."

"It couldn't have been easy for him," I suggested. "Seeing you and the girls there while he's trapped. Maybe he was just embarrassed."

In fact, I'd witnessed the meeting. I'd driven across town and kept to the shadows. It would have been more humiliating for David if I arrived in charge of his family. Instead, unobserved, I watched Akbar and David, not chained but heavily handcuffed together. They sat on the rocky ground of the scrubby garden of the court, a young guard in his ill-fitting uniform with a carelessly slung rifle nearby, standing over a half-dozen prisoners. Akbar smiled at Jeanette as she stood with nowhere to sit and nowhere to go. The children were shy and comparing other trussed prisoners. I'd attended Landhi court twice myself from prison. Never shackled; with a prison guard who I'd send on errands while I dealt with the court. I mention this only because I knew well that Akbar could have easily – and cheaply – arranged much the same for himself and David. He clearly chose to demonstrate that for the cuffs to be undone, David's family must provide the keys.

Driving back to town I asked myself what should be my concern that another subject of mild terror was being fleeced. None, really – but I was here, on the spot, and that should mean something to the living.

Now, at the Marina pool, I kept silent as Jeanette told me of the failing marriage and her difficult past.

"I begged David not to come here," she said. "My witchy instincts told me it would all go bad."

Yet Jeanette came to this forbidding land to attend as a good wife.

Growling beyond the stony hills outside Quetta in a high Pajero four-wheel drive, I enjoyed the smoothest crossing I'd experienced into Afghanistan. Each checkpoint only a few seconds' courteous exchanges from half-opened windows. Our car held Arshad and a major of the army with his adjutant in civilian clothes. Less than ten miles over the border, we stopped at the small town of our purpose.

I tried to discard the chatter of my companions as we cruised through the village. Their talk, most-polite boasting and thin assurances, would count for nothing above ground level. Unlike most smugglers' towns, this stretched village had no strolling gunmen, few shuttered shops. More children with unaccompanied mothers than usual. The policing light, the few officers in barber's or tea shops rather than sotted and bunched protectively in cornered patrol vans as is usual in towns of any size. Under the Taliban, they'd changed uniforms, but recognizably policeman with every gesture. There was just one public call office, its operator alert. Public calls and privately monitored, I thought.

At the edge of town, we drove into a large, walled villa with heavy gates. I thought it completely deserted yet an impoverished servant family stirred from the outbuildings. Tea was brought to us after we settled in a gloomy living room. For large windows one must live in the cities.

"So, David," smiled captain Arshad. "Here, you can do what you want. We are law."

Before we left, I insisted on strolling the neighbourhood; to stretch my legs before the long drive back, I'd said. Nearby, another walled house but no sign of upper storeys. Passing, I heard the crack of what I took as a firework. My hosts looked concerned. At the slit of the gate, I saw a group of young men having a good time releasing drops of a liquid into a metal bucket which would then detonate with impressive force. The major gently moved me on.

"They have their *gora*, too," he said. Then reassuring, wagging a finger at the gate, "but they do nothing we don't know about."

They had their *gora*; their foreigner. And who were they? Men with black headscarves living in squared dormitories, never far from their guns. By contrast, at my side, the Imperial army abandoned by the British, and the confidence, two generations along, of princelings; casual rulers of a secret state that ran the length of Pakistan's western border. The military elite cared nothing for the tribal villains and torn fundamentalists who roamed and bullied both town and country. And they rewarded their superior selves the freedom to behave as urban sophisticates. If I built some brittle enclave of independence here I'd be a magic lantern: at first profitable wonder; then playroom Jack-in-the-box, and finally a light to attract pitiless hawkmoths.

In a crowded market beyond serene Clifton (if one overlooks the rare car bombing), I was shopping a week later for the makings of a roast dinner I'd cook at Robbie's apartment. The Dufaur family had moved to the Carlton Hotel but had joined me for the day. Under fabric-covered open-air stalls, we stopped at the chicken seller. The young girls looked doubtfully at the large cages of birds. Sophia with gathering repulsion; Ellie with growing fascination. Jeanette watched me interact with the girls, pleased. I wouldn't veil the process of food.

"So, whom shall we eat for dinner tonight?" I asked, inviting the girls to step closer as the chicken man pointed to the cage of his freshest. The four birds looked thin and irritable. "Should we take Frank or Melvin? Perhaps Joe or Tommy?"

Sophia wrinkled at the names I'd given. "They're not boys at all," she said. Ellie, the youngest, accepted the names immediately. I pointed at Joe. Somehow, Frank, Melvin and Tommy seemed to move in a flutter to the far side of the cage.

The chicken seller opened a small trap, and deftly wrenched a protesting Joe out by his feet. At arm's length, he swung the flapping Joe to a blood-blackened chopping block as their wing gusts cleared flies from a thin-bladed knife. The chicken man scooped the knife in a continuous movement, twisting around to a rusty 44-gallon drum, open-topped and encrusted with feathers where, in one stroke, he half severed the bird's neck, immediately dropping Joe into the drum to bleed out. This took a little time, with the drum pounded by death throes.

"I think Frank and Melvin are arguing," I moved back to the cage to provide distraction. "And now Tommy, not too bright, is asking what happened to Joe."

Sophia turned away while Ellie looked closely at Tommy. I pretended Frank-the-chicken's voice as he snapped at his cage mates.

"There is no Joe. There never was any Joe!" I mimicked. Ellie laughed. Yet she stopped in the thirty seconds it took the chicken seller to strip Joe's skin and feathers as one from his flesh, which he tore away as if removing a glove. Within a minute, he handed me two tied plastic bags, one holding the giblets. Both warm. I tipped the man for his correct slaughter. I thought I should next time find a more human slice of Karachi life for the girls. Even so, they ate Joe later happily enough, and like his cellmates, never referred to his name again.

On our way back to Clifton, I stopped briefly at the Hyatt hotel to run in and collect my dry cleaning. Closer to home, services often faked the cleaning with a brush-down and a bottle spraying of fumes. I took the scenic route through the lobby.

Loitering near a pillar like a house dick was Jeremy Cobley, a vice-consul from the British High Commission who'd once amiably palmed me my cash during visits while I was imprisoned at Karachi Central Jail.

"You'll get a better view if you take a seat and order coffee," I said as I moved to his side.

"David, I, er, didn't know you were staying here."

"I'm not. I'm just picking up my laundry."

"Me too," said Jeremy. "Dry cleaning."

I agreed. "Yeah, best in town. But I really am."

We took seats although I didn't want to leave the girls long in the idling (for the air-con) car. After chatting about those lately arrested at checkpoints and check-ports, I made a show of stealing a look at my watch, without explanation. Then, like I had all the time in the world:

"Jeremy, you know I met an American retired senator years ago, while waiting in a transit lounge. Twice, by chance. A southern gent. It was after the Gulf war. He, like all of us, was very impressed with the big field test. The green screens and smart bombs. That was then."

Jeremy just nodded. So, I went on, reluctantly.

"I hear a lot of the black-bandana kids are playing with their Chrissy presents. Chemistry sets, mostly."

"What? Here?" Jeremy, at least, didn't know of my travels.

"In the Hyatt ballroom?" I doubted as though considering the possibility of terrorists' convention. "No, the yokels around the border strip, not city boys. Hydrogen peroxide and hydrazine, at a guess."

"Really?" Jeremy gave me a dark look.

"Seems like it," I shrugged. "The old Messerschmitt rocket fuel, or close to it. Two liquids make contact and bang." I then had to make my motives clear. Self-interest seemed the most credible. I leaned forward.

"Jeremy, it's nothing to me what these people do to each other. And I'm not so sure if anyone gets upset when a few tourists get blasted. Makes the ragheads look evil."

Jeremy gave a good impression of bafflement which I hoped was just a lure and not real. I regretted opening this talk but went on.

"The liquids. Non-metal, low-density," I said. "Of course, I suppose a double pouch strapped around the gut of a fatty would likely detonate before any of them reached an airport, but planes blowing up makes my job a lot harder."

"You still at it?" Jeremy smiled.

"Not so's you'd notice." I gave up. Although, I added as I stood, "It's just as well that it's not easy to talk a fat man into becoming a suicide bomber. They'd miss their food."

Professional diplomats are right to be suspicious of anyone offering even general intelligence. Suspicion first lands upon the teller, and only the last and weakest action is taken against those creatures revealed. Fortunately, nothing, so far, has come of liquid bombs at altitude. A deserved triumph for the fat and idle, so often overlooked for praise.

Even then, I knew any warning from me would be ignored, but at least I'd said enough to seal a decision not to return to Afghanistan, a bridge now thoroughly torched as I left the Hyatt. Perhaps closing the door of that particular border was my unconscious motive in talking to Jeremy.

2

"What will you do when you get back to London?" Jeanette asked me as we stood looking at city lights from the portico of a large Palladian house on a hill.

I shrugged, "Find a house. Live." London seemed still far away.

The Karachi mansion belonged to a couple from old money; urban inheritors who for generations thought of themselves as displaced Indian aristocrats. Cultured and with a pedigree more noble, they felt, than any of the so-called twenty-two Families who owned Pakistan whom they thought farmers in city clothes. They also had their entitlement to a relaxed eccentricity. Yet Meera and Najib's chosen caprice was hidden. Sorcery, perhaps. The house did have gothic touches with towering drapes and dark, carved furniture. And when Jeanette drew my attention in the dining room to a clean patch on one wall where a painting had recently been replaced with a dull landscape, we thought of those '60s secret witches of New York City.

Over drinks in the living room, Meera spoke of the woman who frequently called upon Jeanette afternoons at the Carlton Hotel.

"I know her," she said. "She comes to my salon at the hotel." Meera owned and carelessly managed a hair salon at the Marina where she and Jeanette had struck a friendship. "Never has anything done. Not properly. Came from a good family, she does, but you wouldn't know it now. Married a crook," then Meera bobbed her head down. "Oh, I am sorry Jeanette."

Meera had been talking of Mrs Akbar Shah, the wife of the business partner of Jeanette's husband, David. She would often visit Jeanette's suite, to order food on the room service account, it seemed to me. Between mouthfuls she would pry into Jeanette's affairs.

Najib leaned back into his chair and added helpfully, "Akbar was a successful businessman years ago. His wife doesn't accept failure easily."

"I'm sure that woman is unlucky for everybody," concluded Meera. Then, "I should really cut her hair."

As Najib dropped his eyes at Meera, I made a little snipping gesture with my fingers to Jeanette, my hand half-hidden by a napkin. Jeanette stifled a smile as I made complimentary remarks about the house while swirling a flat palm over the imaginary lock of Mrs Akbar's hair.

"I suppose this place must have cast a spell over you two when you first saw it," I said admiringly. Jeanette gripped her napkin to her mouth to conceal a giggle, and choked.

"Are you alright my dear?" Meera stood suddenly at the table offering a glass of water, the remedy for all afflictions.

Despite the spooky atmosphere, the night on Karachi hill was suburban comfort compared to the days before in its flatlands. I'd planned to take a couple of days with Noor Jehan; say my goodbyes. I would soon be leaving Pakistan. I had a fresh passport in my own name. I'd not had one in that name in over twenty years since an old-style black British passport from the '70s. This new one was Australian, issued at Islamabad. When I opened it, and saw my own name in print, I didn't like the effect. Open, exposed, telling the world who you were. But it was time, I thought, to leave the smoking ruin of the past and try walking in plain view, which for me, is still a hall of mirrors.

Noor Jehan and I drove through the angry powder of Karachi's market streets to view a cousin's new venture (bankrolled by NJ): a concession of Subway, the sandwich shop. The installation of fittings in Karachi, no matter when visited, seemed always one of three snapshots: base, windowless concrete walls; dusty equipment bunched centre; or manic, improvised repairs as customers drift in, and never more than one worker in attendance. This Subway was of the last, and the customers, only the daring yet nervous relatives of his lordship, seated dutifully at booths despite the fact nothing was quite plugged in. That took an hour or so, and after a streaky wiping down of surfaces, we sat. After another hour, chicken buns were brought and Noor Jehan paused, his chilli-sauce bottle ready to drip.

"Is it safe?" his eyes flicking to the meat; the countryman's eternal distrust of city restaurants.

"Well, we are the first," I said taking a sniff before biting.

Kamran joined us, having just arrived from the street. I'd known Kamran as NJ's younger shadow since arriving from Thailand almost four years ago. Noor Jehan hadn't been disturbed by Kamran's possible involvement in cousin Iftikhar's kidnapping, so I buried the doubt. Today, he brought news that Noor Jehan sniffed at and dismissed in grunts, although I noticed he'd stopped eating.

The concern was this: some twice-removed friends of Noor Jehan had, over the past six months, transferred, willed or put up as collateral land and family houses. The properties had fallen into the hands of another tribal faction. Perhaps I'm putting a gloss on it. Fallen to a rival crook. Of course, there was no title-deed links to this leader, but there were links enough for Noor Jehan.

"Maybe they just got into debt?" I suggested to Kamran. "What do they say?"

"Not a lot," said Kamran. "None of them can be found." Kamran, still a young man, had developed a western sense of humour.

Having eaten, we drove to the house of NJ's opponent at the edge of the city. Just for tea, I was told, and it was so. The large, flat house was as so many: the living room overstuffed and grand while other rooms enduring cheap, battlefield furnishings with dusty floors. The chief was expecting us; these were not meetings one might attempt unannounced.

As we sat around the ill-aired living room, the talk was all polite, jokey and casual. The guts of the event took place in the seconds when Noor Jehan and his distrusted fellow leader eyed each other face-to-face. The steely glints above smiles slipped away as a gaudily decorated cake was brought before us. Noor Jehan narrowed his eyes further, this time at the cake as he was given a large wedge. I wolfed in anyway.

I didn't listen to the talk, as far as I could follow Sindhi, anyway. None of it would reveal more. Making uncomfortable shifts in my lounge chair, I excused myself to the toilet, as though leaving the grown-up talk to the men. Ostensibly to guide me in the right direction, one of our host's gunzels followed and pointed downstairs but edged back to the main room once I'd stopped to chat with one of the women pretending to clean. The aide was torn between ambition and security. Ambition won. He returned to the meeting. I cut my chatter short when my guide had gone and stepped to the ground floor below.

Dark rooms, mostly closed doors and even darker corridors even though it was high afternoon. At one corner an old refrigerator softly rumbling its works. Empty, apart from some unlabelled bottles of an almost clear liquid. I checked for ice. None, and the large compartment was packed with what looked like pale, plucked and plump pigeons, each wrapped in plastic. I closed the fridge door as I heard movement behind me. I pretended to look lost.

"Keep going," said a voice acting helpful. "Just a little outside." He meant the toilet was at the edge of the courtyard beside the kitchen. I turned to the voice.

A shaggy man in a dirty white shalwar kameez stood in front of an open door. Behind him a man crouched over crates of empty bottles. They must have been bottling from their home still, a similar enterprise I'd seen running at Noor Jehan's villa. The only difference was that NJ's Baluchis added labels. One stood in the room as though to block my line of sight. Ignoring the vague menace of their helpfulness, I bumbled out to the exterior bathroom.

In the car later driving along the coast I asked Noor Jehan if he'd had a good meeting.

"Maybe," he said, meaning, no. Then asked, "See anything interesting?"

"Not enough time," I replied. "What's Sindhi for rot-gut; cheap liquor?"

"*Pawah*," which meant, firewater.

"Kamran," I said looking to the back seat. "Is there much game-fowl to hunt nearby?"

That took some clarifying but the answer was not near Karachi, only north in the woods. What woods, I wondered.

The next morning at Noor Jehan's villa, I told him of my return soon to Europe. We agreed to meet the following year in Dubai.

"The thing is," I explained. "I'll be travelling in my own name. Mostly. I'm not sure if that is safe."

Noor Jehan looked up from a balcony recliner where he was lying on his back, digesting breakfast. "So, you'll never come back?"

"This *David* will never return – but we'll meet somewhere, for sure." I then asked if he'd settled his affairs with his rival.

"We have no business together," said Noor Jehan. "I can only think, never know. And I am tired from the thinking."

Not knowing was true. NJ would never ask directly of that mid-level bandit if he'd kidnapped or terrorized the missing friends into parting with their land and property. They were still signing documents after their disappearances, so they were alive. Noor Jehan had spoken of one of them at the meeting, musing that he hadn't seen him in months. This, to prompt any talk of ransom but it produced no admission, even heavily cloaked. I wasn't sure of the wisdom of the prompt. Kind of a glove slap with a furry mitten, a touch from a small creature to a larger predator. Yet Noor Jehan was undoubtedly the larger predator here.

Later that afternoon, we drove back to Karachi, stopping at the cousin's Subway. I doubted there'd be anything NJ could call profit in twenty-four hours.

"Maybe not," he said. "But if I don't come every week, I will never get anything but chickens."

The sky announced evening as we sat in a booth, keeping to the chicken that, at least, was not the same bird we'd munched on the day before. Kamran sat apart at the counter talking to the one girl who worked loading rolls into a warmer. There were half-a-dozen other customers, all take-away (or carry-home as they say locally) except for two young men at a table by the door.

I say now that I had a bad feeling that night but looking back, of course I'd say that. Maybe I get a bad feeling every time the sun sets, every twilight, but mechanically forget when nothing happens. Even so, arriving some place at dusk makes it difficult to scan the street, worse than streetlights under a black sky. Perhaps Noor Jehan felt the same way; we were both side-by-side facing the door, eating, not talking much.

A middle-aged man with a drooping moustache opened the door and walked smoothly to the counter as though to place an order. As he reached Kamran, he gestured to the counter-guy as though to emphasize some point, but sent sudden power into the right-arm swing, faking an accident that unbalanced Kamran from his stool. The trick worked. With nothing on the smooth benchtop to grip, Kamran twisted to the floor only in time to see a gun rise to fire at our booth. Noor Jehan and I had about a second on slow Kamran but it didn't do us a lot of good, wedged as we were at our immovable table and floor-bolted bench seat. I could tell that Noor Jehan, hands under the table, was fumbling for his own gun. He was buying a few milliseconds by looking reasonable and smiling at his assailant.

"You know where the money is?" NJ said.

Perhaps one of the gunman's shots had skimmed NJ's back after it passed through the table top.

The street was again busy with shoppers. Only three minutes had passed, and among the good citizens those few who heard shots and sensed danger had crept away. Yet for most amid the jangling traffic grinds and honks, the sound of shots had meant nothing and their numbers now swelled by newcomers. Noor Jehan walked casually across the street. Kamran walked out twenty seconds later. I gave him a look, meaning: there are many unknowns out there, I salute you. He figured as much.

He passed me his phone. "Call the last number if you need to," Kamran said with resignation, keeping his gun arm low, where the weapon was visible. I remained just inside the door, where the wounded had their own thoughts to occupy them.

By then, two cars opposite, sixty feet apart, stirred inside, probably containing enemies; cars that held men only; and were stationary – engines running – but had not moved on. Mid-road, NJ abruptly turned about, smiled at me and walked as though to return. Once touching the pavement, he changed course and moved quickly to a textiles shop, my left, to Subway. I could see part of the fabric shop through Subway's side window. Kamran was now on the far side of the street.

Noor Jehan touched some flat rolls of cloth, seemed to approve, then suddenly scooped up three one-meter offcut bolts, held them to his chest with one arm, swivelled fast and fired a clean shot into the forehead of an older man watching him who had pretended to be a customer. Noor Jehan must have pegged him earlier from Subway. Kamran, across the street, heard the shot but flicked his gaze back to his business side to look for reaction. One of the occupants of an idling car nearest Kamran began to climb out. That was enough of an introduction for Kamran who immediately plugged him in the chest. The man fell back to the car's rear seat.

My attention was torn back to Noor Jehan, by then striding across the street toward the second car, the cloth rolls now clutched firmly to his chest by his left arm, his gun held at eye level by the other. The cloth took a couple of slugs from the car window, Subway's window took two more. Noor Jehan downed a man (I'd not before noticed) who had produced an automatic rifle too slowly to result in anything but his own death. NJ was good at head shots.

I fought this distraction long enough to look back to Subway's floor, now sharded with glass. The groin-bleeder, though tied at the feet, was looking at his revolver, still a few feet away where Karman had left it. I scooted the gun toward the door with a toe, leaving it at my feet.

By my count, five of Noor Jehan's assailants were out of the game, as he'd just had a loud moment with the driver of the car nearest him. The car at Kamran's end had driven away at speed, or as much as could be gained along a busy Karachi road. Passers-by were no longer passing but sensibly keeping still and Kamran, sensible too, held his fire. Experience had taught him the futility of shooting at fleeing cars. However, two among the would-be assassins had fled – or now positioned themselves – deep in a narrow, high-walled walkway running off the far-side pavement between the shops. Noor Jehan picked up the fallen automatic rifle from the downed walker. One gun begets many. He then disappeared into the murk of that alley. I looked to Kamran who didn't like that anymore than I did, and he began furiously scanning the shops hoping for an unlikely way to get in ahead of Noor Jehan and so behind the gunmen. I told myself I must ask NJ later why he'd chosen to pursue those men, who surely would not come back. I looked to the gun at my feet. I wasn't concerned about fingerprints. Fingerprints, per the unofficial Karachi police manual, are what you apply to evidence with sticky tape, not things to be discovered through examination. I didn't pick it up. There'd be no time to gain an advantageous position, and I was beyond that point in life where simply looking like you're helping meant anything.

Kamran had disappeared. Into the maze of shops to seek a side entrance to that alley. Too late for that. I heard three bursts of automatic fire. A good sign, more or less. Then nothing. I quickly emptied the revolver at my feet of its remaining live cartridges, threw the gun under a table, pocketed the shells, and crossed the road. Halfway over, I was relieved to see NJ walk out of the alley without fresh blood stains (none of his own, anyway) and without the rifle but still his own automatic pistol, kept low and half-concealed in his left hand. He slow-winked at me. I'm sure his reputation as master of the decade-old massacre had weighed upon his enemies this night. Kamran caught up with me from the shops. Noor Jehan, I could see, was apologizing in his courtly manner to a family of shoppers for the disturbance. I returned Kamran his phone.

"I didn't need to call," I said. Kamran, though, was still occupied with sampling the street for any unaccounted enemy. He was good, and knew shootouts sometimes have a second act.

Yet not quite good enough for the imbecile factor. Kamran was looking for obvious desperadoes. To Noor Jehan's side came a chubby and young uniformed policeman, separated from senior colleagues who were beginning to arrive. He stopped a few feet from NJ, saw the gun resting in his hand, produced his own and promptly shot him through the ribcage. NJ didn't fall exactly, rather, doubled up, winced and doubled up again, then rapidly curled to the ground. The shopping family, just seconds ago relieved, now backed away in fear. The policeman put his gun away in his side holster as another might return a parking-ticket folder. His elders, senior cops, arrived thundering upon him a dozen kinds of abuse. Kamran paled. I could see he was breathless and, now, helpless. A minute later, as I saw Kamran come back to life enough to move cars and locate hospitals, I melted into the pockets of the street, closing the door on lives of which I'd no longer be part.

It was the next night that I'd brought Jeanette to the villa on the hill, home of the discreetly occult hair-salon owner and her aristocratic husband. Of course, I could say nothing of the day before and the long night as Noor Jehan died. Kamran had spent four hours with police almost until the minutes before his lord died in hospital – from internal bleeding and septicaemia. The senior police were most apologetic, not wanting to incur the possible vengeance of the Magsi clan. The young officer was an ignorant fool, they said, and simply reacted to the gun held in Noor Jehan's hand. In my last conversation with Kamran after midnight, he told me the attackers were indeed sent by the rival faction but their leader was not among the dead.

Jeanette and I were snacked out by 8:00 pm and with no dinner from Meera and Najib on the horizon and a rare cool evening from the Arabian Sea breeze, we took the otherworldly couple for a meal at the Marina club's best restaurant.

As the first course arrived, and we were just shaking out the starched white cones of our napkins to our laps, Jeanette joked that she half-expected Mrs Akbar Shah to appear and join our table for another free meal.

"She will know," Meera said, patting Jeanette's hand. "Two of her family work in this hotel. Her eyes are everywhere. David, I can't understand that woman. You know she has two cousins with the same police that arrested her husband." Najib dropped her a look of caution. He turned to me.

"David, who can say what are family matters and what are official matters only." Then to Jeanette, "I shouldn't worry my dear."

By eleven, Jeanette and I had escorted the couple to their car, and were again in the elevator to the third-floor bar where alcohol was served. As the door opened and we stepped out, I saw that Jeanette had left her scarf in the restaurant.

"Do you think Meera took it?" asked Jeanette. "To cast some kind of spell?"

I laughed. "No, I think she's a white witch. Only good things, mostly. It's Mrs Akkers you should worry about.

3

Each dawn triggers universal activity at a medium-sized walled town within Karachi, the work dedicated to one commodity: vegetables. The *subzi mandi* draws almost every cart and roadside seller of potatoes, carrots, tomatoes, cabbage, fruit and beans as well as city-wide grocers for pulses, herbs, spices and cereals. This might sound a lush abundance but the goods at *subzi mandi* come in mounds of just three forms: dried, withering and near-rotten.

Around a week after I'd attended Noor Jehan's funeral and edgy wake, I took Jeanette and her two girls to the vegetable market, arriving mid-morning before either girls or vegetable merchants started snarling at each other.

As soon as we entered the wide roads within the market – wide to accommodate caravans of mule-driven carts and awkward trucks – we were surrounded by young boys, each carrying empty rice-sack shoulder bags almost half their height.

"Pick one. No, make that two," I said to Sophia. "They'll carry our vegetables as we shop."

"Do we really need two?" asked Sophia.

"It's all they do for a living."

While Sophia settled quickly to one more assertive, Ellie, at seven, was taking her time. Jeanette smiled but said:

"You don't have to marry one, Ellie."

We began in the central five-acre tent, a poled canopy also stitched from nylon rice-sacks. Ellie disappeared at speed to explore. I directed her shoeless porter – about the same age – to stick with her. Jeanette tried, unsuccessfully, to supress a look of concern.

"Don't worry," I said. "A little blonde girl alone in a thieves' market in Karachi? We'll get her back. Or a fair price if we don't."

In fact, I knew that Ellie would be safer alone here than in the streets of London. A European child was so exceptional – and the traders so observant, that they'd be falling over each other to appear most noble. I explained another element of the market to Sophia.

"Our little bag carrier has a night-time job in the bag section where he lives. Tying and sorting the millions of small carry bags used here," I pointed to the only area without flies. "He was born in the *subzi mandi*, sleeps here, learns to read here. And his bed is no more than sleeping on the stacks of bags."

Sophia's expression showed doubt that such a life could be much fun.

"It's not so bad," I said. "He has the biggest family in town, and I'd say his bed is more comfortable than yours at the Carlton Hotel."

Even at the market, I was still trying to figure the image from the day before at the hotel where once again Mrs Akbar Shah had called by to see if Jeanette was alright. As usual, she ordered a table-load of food, remained almost silent until room service arrived, then sat at the edge of the bed gorging herself, smearing grease over her heavily cosmeticked face.

"So, you are doing the right thing, my dear," she'd said to Jeanette. "What is a few thousand pounds compared to the life of your husband?"

Why, I wondered then, was she pushing for the big payoff to the cops on Akbar's and David's case, rather than, say the courts? It didn't take so long to find out. I just wasn't sure when to tell Jeanette.

Ellie arrived back towing her bag-handler, as we'd completed our shopping – ten kilos of borderline veg rolling around in the oversized bag. Nothing in Ellie's, but in each arm, she held a baby goat, both all white and cute.

"Can we have these?"

In the car, Ellie was sullen. We'd denied her the baby kids.

"They weren't weaned yet," Jeanette explained to Ellie. "They need their mother, just like you did when you were a baby."

"Your mum's right," I said. "They'd starve, or grow up sick."

Ellie looked at me with surprise, for we were firm friends by then.

"Traitor."

A week later, I was again in my rented car as chauffeur to the girls. This time taking them to the airport for a return flight to London.

"I want to go with you," announced Ellie. She was teary with goodbyes, an inclination out of which she would grow with time.

"You can't, sweetheart," I said. Jeanette added colour to my claim.

"David has to travel on foot," she said. "Over the mountains and through the desert. For weeks and weeks."

Jeanette looked at me with sadness. Sophia looked at the car's roof, hoping some passing alien would beam her up to spare her both adult and childish nonsense.

After the bags were checked, and boarding passes issued, I took Jeanette aside.

"No more money to Pakistan, okay?"

"Yes."

"You say that but – look, David's case," I paused for clearer words. "There was no case until Akker's wife made one. She was the one who had David and her husband arrested."

After the London villains' money had been lost in Dubai, and it seemed silly enough to send more, word of this mother lode leaked through to Akbar Shah. (A link, at one point, no more than a sharp-eared waiter at an Emirates hotel.) Akkers told his wife in Karachi that she'd have the lioness's share to compensate for past neglect. However, when the second tranche reached Karachi, he re-directed it to Europe. That £70,000 went on the tables of Amsterdam's casinos, despite his later story to his wife that he owed Colombians there who would kill him if he hadn't paid. Of course, Mrs Akkers didn't swallow that. She knew well that if her husband didn't regularly survive unpaid debts to the mob, he would never have made it past his twenty-first birthday.

So, when Jeanette's David arrived in town Mrs A promoted a show-and-tell scheme where David might convince London to send a third lump. This time for transport and clearance. A month passed with no cash. She became convinced Akbar had, again, re-directed the money – even though none had been sent. She had one of her innumerable cousins fix the arrest of both husband and David. I'm sure she thought that would shake the money tree. I didn't know all of that as I spoke to Jeanette, but I knew enough.

"So, there were no drugs? No deal?" Jeanette seemed more exhausted and angry than if there had been a real deal. "How can you be sure it was his wife?"

"A friend of mine here. An ex-Air Force captain – apparently half of Karachi is laughing at this story. Except those in Landhi jail."

As I waved goodbyes to my little on-loan family, I thought better of saying more. I didn't know how Jeanette would take the news that Akbar himself knew everything of his wife's vengeance, just as he sat at the edges of a prison blanket feeding the man he thought just might have a few more drops of blood to give – *motta* David.

I didn't need more from Captain Arshad regarding David's case. Robbie the Scot was stuck in Pakistan for at least a year with hearings in the Banking Court and would channel the relatively insignificant costs to ensure David's freedom.

My last weeks in Pakistan that December of 1999 were tranquil and with an odd sadness that I'd not return. My Australian passport had been issued on the thirteenth of the previous month (I'm not triskaidekaphobic but its number began and ended with thirteen as well), and combined with other cautions I'd leave only with hand luggage for my return to Europe. Only the mountains of flight schedules and deserts of transit lounges to conquer.

"So, you'll be gone next week?" asked Robbie as he and Tatiana sat on the nineteenth-floor balcony watching the sun dissolve into the sea.

"Just about," I said, leaning over the railing. "Only one more thing to arrange before I leave."

"You'll miss Christmas in Clifton, yes?" Tatiana tilted her head in supplication. "We'll be the only Christians in Karachi!" In fact, there is a large population of Pakistani Christians who celebrate very quietly. Only the expat community and some nominally Muslim Karachiites go for the bells, decorations and Santa. The three groups don't much mix that week. Go figure.

"Looks like I won't be around for anyone this year," I said. "But keep your eyes out for Papa Noel."

Across the expanse of greater Karachi are cubes of flat rooftops, not gabled, so they catch more water than they repel. I suppose that's because, like those builders, we all do things the way we did them before - other than when by hazard, and almost never by calculated resolve. As many as those who stroll the streets evenings are those who pass time on the flat roofs where they enjoy cooler air or take in the night view.

In celebration of victories, birthdays or weddings, some revellers fire bursts from automatic weapons to the air. The bullets mostly fall harmlessly, perhaps annoyingly, depending on the angle of fire. Some, if sent vertically, on their return miles away reach terminal velocity, and a few have been known to kill. In addition to explosions of joy, a small number are aimed with determination, yet those too, mostly miss. Often the sound of directed fire will blend with the random.

Will it be fate's hand that delivers death to the chubby policeman whose own weapon killed Mir Noor Jehan Magsi? Not this night. For by chance or otherwise a 7.62 rifle bullet penetrated the skull of Deputy Chief Inspector of Customs, Ahmed Baboosh, known by those he interrogates as the torturer of Karachi Port. His was a quick death, a mercy born from professionalism rather than concern. Or, for all anyone knew, it could well have been the parting shot of a yearning groom about to take his bride after much ceremony. It is never easy to tell in the darkness.

4

Landing at Oslo airport, I hoped I looked the part: a businessman compelled to take an early flight from Athens, then stuck in transit until an onward connection to another part of Scandinavia. Of course, I was none of that, although I had flown from Athens. A peculiarity at the time of Pakistan International Airlines was multiple European stops after entry to the Continent, a schedule generated more by the needs of the airline executives and that country's ruling elite than based on passenger numbers. By the time the 747 landed at Oslo, it was almost empty. Since Norway is not part of the European Union, all passports are checked. Well, some are checked, EU passports are mostly just looked at.

I'd shed the moustache I'd grown for anonymity in Karachi, and had borrowed Robbie's mackintosh. I'd kept indoors of late but I suppose I still had a tan. I stood in line ready to present my new Australian passport in my own name. Yet moments before I would be seen I reached into the secret pocket of my jacket and slid out a British passport in the name of Northridge. I was not quite ready for McMillan. Just about the last thing I did before leaving Pakistan was to bribe an official in Karachi to give back the passport taken from me at Lahore two years earlier. (It would be poison only at entry through a British port.) The immigration officer at his desk looked at it briefly and welcome me in with a casual, "There you go," before returning the closed book. Looking through the thick glass of the terminal before the next flight at the bulldozed snow, I felt just fine.

Up to a point. After I arrived in Stockholm and settled in at a restaurant in Drottninggatan, I reviewed the damage. Two years in time, a steaming pile of money consigned to flames, another black concoction of imprisonment, fear, torture and accelerated cell death, lost identities, including that David with a fine but modest house in London, and I knew not what of Eloise Morse.

I didn't rate my skills high in dealing with Pakistan, however difficult. With the arrival at my table of a pale, trembling crème caramel at that Stockholm restaurant, I was taken back to those frozen and plucked pigeons I saw in the lonely refrigerator at the gangster's house in Karachi. Sure, I had but a glimpse yet I should not have needed Kamran to tell me later what they were: the severed and swollen hands of Noor Jehan's friends, the fingers kept ready to impress finger prints on bank documents, loan agreements and title-deed transfers. They would've been taken out, partially thawed and used time and time again for all important transactions that – still in Pakistan – demand thumb and fingerprints for validation. If I had been more perceptive, could I have changed anything? Could I have then persuaded Noor Jehan to deal with his enemy before all else? Worse, I probably precipitated the attack since those minions who saw me at the 'fridge would have assumed I knew what I was looking at. I paused at that thought – then spooned into my sweet dessert. True survival means never missing a meal.

Time to dive in. Or better, wade carefully in the shallows. I took ferries and trains to Zurich where I checked in overnight at a hotel where I taped my extra (non-McMillan) passport behind the red wheel of a fire hose on the top floor. As I closed the glass door covering the hose, I hoped no one in the next days would be careless with matches.

Passing through Swiss passport control the following day at the airport with a ticket to Istanbul I encountered the Frown. The

Frown is a countenance lasting about four seconds upon some officials after handing over one's documents. My Australian passport had that effect. I was politely taken aside. Swiss efficiency. Swiss chattiness over the next fifteen minutes resulted in the source: an Interpol blue notice. A note to authorities requesting they identify the traveller, his address, and forward details of his itinerary. I was permitted to leave after I gave my business card (an address in the Wan Chai district of Hong Kong) and ticket details. Not that I had planned to board the flight to Turkey in any circumstances, I still felt somehow miffed that Constantinople must wait. Making excuses to the airline, I left the airport, taxied to town, checked into the hotel next to my previous night's rest (the advantages of adjacent hotels are too many to list here), and returned via the garden to my original hotel and the fire-hose box. As I took out the Northridge passport, its maroon cover spoke to me.

'I knew you wouldn't leave me. Who do you think you are, anyway?'

5

Simon, my brother, tilted his head as though to speak, yet did not. We were sitting at one end of a large kitchen table in his house in north London. I'd arrived late. Cleared Heathrow at 10.00pm. Simon's wife, Annamaria, and the boys were asleep. Simon could have asked, 'How are you?'; 'What was it like?' After a long pause, he kept it simple.

"There are towels in the guestroom cupboard. I still eat Cheerios for breakfast, so there's plenty. I'm working from home tomorrow. We'll talk then."

The next day, by the time I'd dressed, Simon was in his home office, wedged among piled notes, two computer screens and an open phone line. He produced television documentaries at the time. Still does.

"There's an envelope on the kitchen table," he called over his shoulder, noticing I was already wearing a raincoat. "Let Annamaria know if you won't be back for dinner."

The Victoria-line tube took me to central London before a grey noon. I transferred to Gloucester Road and walked to the mews house. I caught a glimpse through a window and sounds told me there were people living inside, so I backed away. I walked to an internet café, logged on, and retrieved my address book from an unsent draft letter in an email account folder in a fake name where I kept my numbers. I then phoned the owner of my former home who lived in Oxfordshire.

"The police took everything," he said. "Furniture, clothes, everything." Not quite, I'd seen the furniture. "Except for a coat. You must come up to me some weekend when you're free."

"Just the coat?" I asked.

"Yes. But it's a good coat." He paused. "Penny and Brent are in the house now," as though I was one of the family. "You should come."

This wasn't an invitation to a set-up. My former landlord was simply being disarming. And I knew the man as a self-styled upper-class businessman. Now I saw he was all curiosity and wanted to know how my trade worked.

"Yep, I'll call you." I wouldn't.

At a restaurant near South Kensington station, I opened Simon's envelope. A visa card and a note. Beneath the PIN number, Simon had added, speaking for the card, 'Be gentle with me.'

At 8.05, the following morning, Eloise Morse stepped up to street level from her Fulham basement flat. She didn't pause at the pavement, just turned, head down, taking fast strides to her station. Most would have stopped briefly to look around. She didn't want to know. Eloise still moved through each moment as though she wanted to get it over before something bad happened. She was dressed for work. I waited until she'd cleared the first corner before stepping from the morning mist, crossing the street and taking a brief survey at her front window. No movement. The casual disarray of the bedroom revealed no other hand.

I didn't have time for more, and anyway, had learned enough for now. If she had a boyfriend – and she would have someone – he wasn't there. In the past, before me, they'd leave with her, if at her place, and if at his, she'd leave alone. Or so she'd said. I walked back to my waiting cab.

As I closed the door, the driver asked:

"So, what terminal then?"

"European flights. Germany."

I had five days until Christmas, had one more travel test to take, a friend to visit, and a need to be home – by which I mean at brother Simon's house – for Christmas Eve. The first passport test had tripped at Zurich, perhaps because I'd used an Australian document. I travelled this time again in my own name but with a British passport. I'd had one issued in 1998 when it was still possible to have them processed at foreign consulates. Today, even applications submitted in Commonwealth countries are sent to the UK for assessment.

This precaution made no difference on the ground. At Frankfurt, I was taken aside, held for forty minutes, and thoroughly lied to.

"We don't know why we were asked to stop you, I must say," said a bloated official as I waited for my passport to be returned.

I ventured a suggestion. "Maybe it's from that day I was chased down the street in Amsterdam by an angry prostitute?"

"Aha! Could be." Lots of jolly smiles, and I was eventually allowed to go. The Germans always double-check, especially when the notice says, do not arrest.

My friend Matthias lived in Bad Nauheim, a small town a half-hour from Frankfurt. He was a bachelor, edging towards his fifties, yet held his age by being small and never at any moment without a cocktail of drugs busily at work throughout every capillary and tissue of his body. One might not notice this, for his life was ordered; his house neat and comfortable. And most of all, Matthias could hold a civilized conversation in perfect English while technically unconscious.

From the local rail station, I walked the final three miles to Matthias's door, so not to bring any Frankfurt airport taint to his home. As I paused from time to time – Bad Nauheim has many plaques and notices to view commemorating Elvis Presley's army posting in the '50s – I was sure I was alone.

Once greeted by Matthias and both settled in the living room amid antique furniture (and decorated by that year's electronic toys) I gave an outline of the failed campaign in Pakistan.

"Well, you survived," he said quietly. Matthias (who in features and manner most resembled the actor Christoph Waltz) had spent eight months in an Afghan prison in the '70s after a suitcase attracted attention. He would write of that experience and more in, *Opiumessers Drachenjagd* [Inside Opium-Dragon-hunting] published under the name Viktor Mala in 2001.

"Yes," I said. "What doesn't kill you makes you just that little bit weaker."

In the kitchen, while eating the salads and cake I'd brought from the airport, I went on to speak of London plans.

Matthias gently interrupted my dry remarks. "There was a girl. What of her?"

"She's fine. A touch sad looking."

"So you'd like to think," said Matthias. "No big homecoming so far?"

I pushed at the olive bowl. "Well, I'm not quite sure how to present myself, or as what. On the face of it, everything I told her was a lie. Or, lies of silence, really."

"The smallest of sins, surely," Matthias pretended to dismiss my conduct. "Though, isn't there a special place in hell for sins of omission?"

"Matthias! Leave me alone. I'll patch it up. Somehow."

The last time I'd seen Matthias was in Dubai years earlier when we'd arranged our separate crossings to meet mid-journey in the transit lounge – even then, huge. At the business hub, we exchanged notes on a new contact, took on refreshments, and sat in peace.

"I always feel safe here," Matthias said. "It's like Switzerland, neutral territory. They don't want to arrest you. Whatever you're doing, they don't want to know."

"So, you don't want me to keep an eye out as you go through security?"

Matthias shook his head. "No, let's maintain that courtesy."

Once Matthias boarded safely, I checked into the 88-room hotel as my own flight was not until dawn. In the snug of a modest suite, a cocoon within a stateless cocoon, I peered through the thick-glass portholes at the soundless 24-hour shoppers below in the duty-free shopping mall. Was Matthias's life such a tragedy?

The only child of a war-ravaged couple thrown together in the wreckage of Berlin, Matthias had first grown into a member of a travelling theatrical troupe where he'd met his future wife. Unaccountably, by Matthias's observation, she took her own life in the fourth year of their marriage. Matthias didn't pine. He was simply perplexed. Yet he never married again, although there were later girlfriends, always held distant. On his terms, so no match would ever take.

Then there was the dope. Matthias had an unapproachable addiction to heroin. Top-shelf heroin his choice, so, beyond his inclination, his occupation as a low-level smuggler was, if not ideal, perfectly natural. A few kilos from Asia each year met his needs in every way. Matthias was regular in his habits: a line of coke to perk up after breakfast, a noseful of China-White heroin to reward the cravings; wine with lunch, then an evening toot of brown heroin (for the earthy aroma, the base punch): a whisky and a Xanax or a Dormicum for slumber come nightfall. The allure of close-call destruction was powerful for Matthias.

"There's no point in heroin without physical addiction," he'd once said. "Weekenders just suffer grogginess and constipation. Pointless. But for the addict, that assured sweet relief from threatening pain. There's joy for you." Sudden relief and rapid transitions (from stimulants) were the certainties in Matthias's life, and he'd come to view all other human desires as weakly disguised rituals seeking the same rewards. Friendship was his exception, one that of course was a business necessity.

This might seem morbid and loveless but Matthias's days were mostly serene and sure. Although he moved his lean cargo himself, he rarely faced arrest as no one knew of his plans (other than I) and his customers were just a driblet of old reliables.

I wondered then if such a life might be better for me. Although I don't have the constitution for such a high drug intake, maybe an untouched life would be less harmful to those around me. I could narrow the risk-taking with additional precautions, find a house somewhere calm near a good bakery, and confine love to comfort without deception. Not easy. There'd been no deception with Sharon yet I remained haunted by her almost casual aside in her letter after I abandoned her: *'I would have ended my life but you know I have my boys and so cannot...'* Clelia was ghost enough sovereign above the many who spoke to me among the dead. And now what would I do for Eloise? Walk away: or risk betraying her should I fall again? For even decades of stillness would never vanquish the demons of the past. I might have once smiled at smuggling as the wicked game but the deserted hearths of forsaken women seemed more wicked still.

Better perhaps to become the perpetual tourist, moving from hotel to hotel, city to city, leaving feint registers of false names. All human contact planned around the time it might take to consume a three-course meal. A happy wanderer, a timid explorer prepared for retreat within the baffles of misdirecting credentials and misleading papers.

Again, perhaps this doesn't sound very enticing. Perhaps men readily claim happiness with their sheds and Sunday leisure, the family a warm fuzz in the background, but women need more. Although, looking sideways, I imagined Clelia happiest at moments when I was simply in place, the house ordered, secure and quietly humming its certainty. Well, so it is looking from under the veil of memory.

Matthias had solved any yearning for loving demands by his choice of addictions. Knowing that if, thrice daily, he would descend into hell without morphine, he placed little cairns of supplies within the house, the nearby woods and beyond. Inns and post boxes around the world held envelopes that, never farther than four hours' journey, would save him from the abyss. Only once in a decade did I have to jump on a plane to come to his aid.

Morphine, a poor substitute for love, but a most predictable mistress.

On my last day in Bad Nauheim, Matthias and I walked out from his house to the forest beyond the war memorial, a massive statue with open arms. About a mile beyond, as the path forked, we stepped into the tangle of trees. Matthias took a stud finder from his pocket.

"Let me try," I said, taking the small metal-detector. "We'll see if your old instructions guide me over my natural stupidity."

I moved to what looked like a standout tree. Holding the detector around five feet from the ground, I guided the device over the bark. Nothing.

"Deeper in," prompted Matthias.

"Right. Never the first door."

At the trunk of the next large tree behind, the stud-finder chirped. Matthias joined me, and taking a pocket knife, levered out a one-inch square of bark at the signal point. It had been cut out and glued back over a large self-tapping screw sunk flush. This start point meant we should take directions by imagining a line from the screw to the footpath.

"So, one meter out," I began. "Ninety degrees left, and three meters on." That took us to cooler ground, still patchy from the snow of the week before.

"I hadn't accounted for snow," I said. "What am I looking for?"

"A straw man," said Matthias. "And anyway, you must go by the numbers." He gave me a small roll of tailor's measuring tape from another pocket.

After measuring again, I found the dry sprig surrounded by ice. "It doesn't look much like a man. A stick with arthritis, maybe."

Digging a foot deep into the hard ground with a garden spade, we exposed the two-inch top of a section of plastic plumber's pipe. The eighteen-inch long tube lifted clear easily enough, even though Matthias had buried it vertically. To remove the plastic cap, we had to grip an end each with our gloves and twist. From inside, three rolls of banknotes plopped out, and a fourth pod, one of Matthias's back up supplies.

"I'll just take two, if that's okay," I said, pocketing the rolls of 500-euro notes, valued at over $35,000 together. "Nice colour, I've never seen a five-hundred before." The euro had been introduced less than a year before. The money was a welcome-home gift. Good form would mean repaying it sometime.

"Anything to go back in?"

Matthias nodded and produced a cling film wrapped roll of US dollars, which he dropped in the tube along with a pod of white powder. Cocaine, judging from the colour. I was sure that wouldn't stay put for long.

I raised an eyebrow. "Part of your exercise program, I presume. A daily walk in the woods?"

Matthias replied with the smile of an optimist accustomed to failed resolve. You can bury that which you love, but you'll always dig it up. We reburied the tube.

After lunch, I left Matthias and Bad Nauheim. Three days, although pleasant, was not without personal jeopardy, given that Matthias was a generous host. In an open-doored glass cabinet in his dark living room, two flat squares of polished marble sat on a velvet shelf. Lines of heroin and cocaine lay separately prepared on each, chromium straws at the sides. Behind the slabs two blue-glass bowls held tablet remedies (naltrexone and lofexidine) against both soporific and stimulant when the soul demanded a return. Making my devotions at that shrine for two days was enough if I didn't want to risk taking up Matthias's addictions forever.

In London, I rented a furnished flat in Sloane Avenue, and spent Christmas at my brother's house where I was fondly mocked, which was what I wanted. Toys gifted all around with Simon giving his wife Annamaria a poster-sized enlargement of a Hubble astrograph. They'd met when Simon was filming a story in Hungary on Rubik's cube.

The day before New Year's Eve, I decided to phone Eloise. I couldn't recall her number, and it was not on my internet draft-page list. I must have mentally dumped her number like fuel from a crashing jetliner when I was consumed in Pakistan. Fortunately, I could still get to a private post box I'd had at a South Kensington phone shop. It was one of just eight in a musty corner near the booths and no one else had taken it recently. I found the envelope I'd left still sealed above a false panel I'd clipped flat inside the box. In the lobby of a small hotel nearby, I found a quiet place to call. There was a pause, an intake of breath from Eloise, as I announced myself. Then,

"I got your letter from the prison in Asia," Eloise said softly. "I didn't understand it. So, you're in London. Or so you say." This wasn't going to be a snap.

"Yes. I'm back. And I want to say I'm sorry."

"You betrayed me." Again, softly.

"Let's – let's meet. A couple of days' time, in the New Year."

I invited Eloise to come with me for lunch at my brother's house for the first Sunday of the New Year. I'd collect her from home. There was some calculation in all this: I wanted Eloise to know I was settled in town over the holiday break. No matter who she was with now, that thought would be with her on those transitional days.

The Thames was lit with decorated boats on the cold, rainless night as 1999 was rung out by Big Ben's iron clanging. People worried about – or gleefully anticipated – the predicted Millennium Bug that would wipe out the world's computer systems. I separated from my friends and squeezed to the crowded stone rampart overlooking the river.

I thought of the old warning that those who fail to learn the lessons of history are condemned to repeat it. That might apply easily to nations. But for each of us, we may learn the lessons of our histories yet still are condemned to blunder onward at every repetition with quite fresh and unique errors. Fate is too devious to allow prior knowledge to work as a shield.

6

Eloise was waiting at street level from her basement flat on Sunday when I called for her in a taxi. Although this was early – eleven – I was not invited into the home where once I'd be drawn by her extended arms. I ditched the taxi at South Kensington as we had an hour, and sought neutral but comfortable ground at a Café Nero. Our conversation was fluid but odd. We spoke as though we were casual friends separated by a war everyone knew too much about to discuss. I offered bland observations about resettling in London; how little had changed. Eloise was still at the Economics Frontier. That gave me an in.

"The new boyfriend. Is he a co-worker?"

"No," but she wouldn't say more. "I spoke to your landlord. It took me forever to find him. He said you would be executed."

I imagined the number of calls, and tried to guess the tone she might have adopted. "That story gets around."

"He said you'd been arrested in Thailand with two tonnes of cocaine. Was that right?"

"No, it would have taken longer to get back. That landlord is an ambitious man." I could tell Eloise didn't want details of Pakistan, and how could I explain that world to anyone?

As we were climbing into a cab for Finsbury Park, I asked if all was well at the Fulham flat. Eloise dropped to the car seat, staring ahead.

"I tore your picture to shreds. Threw the pieces in the bin."

Eloise went down well at Simon's house. Especially with the young boys – either side of ten – who were accustomed to me arriving with novelties, although this was my first human. They produced their terrapin and tried hard to amuse her.

After we ate, Eloise, still not entirely at ease in a lounge chair asked, "Why did you bring me here?"

"The food's good," I said. "And I live here, for now."

That was no longer true, but I wanted to present a picture of myself different from anything I'd given in the past. Living with family: yes, and at Finsbury Park, I knew no one (other than the kids) would say anything in direct praise. I wanted to appear small, unemployed, and with the manner a reprobate uncle. Nothing the least attractive. I even sent her home alone in a taxi.

"You think you'll get her back?" asked Annamaria as we stacked dishes in the washer. She had doubts.

"If she comes back to me after this, there must be something." Something wrong with her, or more likely something wrong about me.

I hadn't owned up to Eloise about my studio apartment in Sloane Avenue as – although near two of the best fish restaurants in town – it was no more than an upmarket bed-sit and a touch too pathetic, even for the image I was trying to give. I needed time as well to find ways to protect myself from the troubling Interpol notices. The Blue notice was puzzling. Why not a Red notice, requesting immediate arrest? Who would prefer me merely tracked as I moved about? That seemed too subtle for the Thais.

I contacted a London-Iranian property owner who rented me a large ground-floor apartment on the opposite side of the avenue to the studio. I'd keep both. Pre-revolutionary Iranians, long established in London, are naturally secretive. As well, I took some garage space nearby and bought a characterless Audi. This set up provided a place to maintain a separate identity as well as a clear line of sight of my principal accommodation if the need arose.

If a bolt-hole is what's needed, make it nearby; the longer it takes to get there, the greater the chances of detection. Besides, the studio-flat block had two entrances and five exits, and was accessible from the dim warren of an underground carpark. I rarely used the car.

Except for an occasional test drive. A test to see if I would be followed. There was nothing more certain than getting into a vehicle to make visible those behind you. (Well, that was so until modern cellular phones – the policeman's deputy.) I drove to Croydon where David Dufaur's Jeanette and girls lived. I was not followed, and anyway felt there would be no interest in my return to England no matter what my former landlord dreamed.

The Dufaur home was a large two-storey house from the '30s on a corner block with lead-paned windows. In winter, it appeared bleak under the rain but was alive with lights inside; and with the girls, of course. Jeanette in an apron enthusiastically fussed while preparing dinner. A small terrier and the girls jumped around showing me the rooms. With Jeanette in the kitchen, treating the dog at each stage of cooking, and Sophia and Ellie pointing out places to hide small toys and large (including people), I realized I'd forgotten that real people had houses they knew intimately. Places they'd happily grown into. For over twenty years in my world, every location had been a set constructed by others for torment, or by me for deception, and all scheduled for destruction. Yet I knew, too, the Dufaur home had been sold, and they must soon become accustomed to uncertain ways.

7

Copenhagen. Enough breeze from the Baltic Sea to hint at spring, keeping the air clear. I paused across the road looking at a side wall with a narrow gap that allowed discreet access to Christiania, the hippy town within the city. Most days, police in unmarked vans usually observed the main entrance gates on the far side but this gap was unwatched. If I was a cop, I'd ignore the public threshold and watch those who didn't like to be seen but Danes seem to observe the rules of chivalry unless you give them reasons not to.

Once inside, I wound my way to the centre court. Since last I visited before Pakistan, the shabby circle of stalls that sold exotic hashish brands had been replaced by well-built shops and converted, open-sided hot-dog vans that now sold packaged bars and plastic tubes of the same products. Harder drugs were around but never on show and always denied. I walked past and took the steps to the biggest pub of the court, looking behind the counter for the face I knew. He looked surprised to see me. I nodded a greeting.

"The boss is in?" I asked.

"At home. They're waiting for you."

I walked out, giving the place a quick scan.

Within the eight-acre site of Christiania are the pubs, cottage industries, a bicycle factory and many residences that amount to little better than hostels. I was not in one of those. On the fourth floor of an old warehouse an open plan duplex had been modernized and decorated in a style that would have sold for millions had it been on London's Southbank. With me, were the owners, Christiania nobility, once hippies, now underground urbanites who looked like tech venture capitalists. Floyd in a t-shirt and baggy pants took care of transport; Per Mögens, bearded, gruff and bear-like, was patriarch; and Florence did meetings, her slow, blonde rock of hair a perfect cover for misapprehensions by any watching investigators. We sat ourselves within large dark sofas in the room's centre, away from the walls.

"David, you haven't spoken to Emil yet?" began Per Mögens.

Emil was the reason I was in Copenhagen. He'd helped me when I was stuck in Karachi, and now he was in trouble. I dismissed the idea of visiting Emil.

"He's in prison. I can't see any point in taking that risk. And you know all that he knows. More, I hope. His wife told me that he still doesn't know why it all went wrong."

Neither did the Christiania group. Per tilted his head to one side, Florence dropped her sandals to the floor and hugged her knees. Floyd lit a cigarette. Did they think the disaster was Emil's fault?

The scheme had been big. Twelve tonnes of hashish from Afghanistan via Gwadar port. A place I knew well. A small coastal trader was bought in Lithuania and sailed from Europe. Loaded at Pakistan and refuelled at the Jebel Ali FTZ (free-trade zone) in Dubai, the ship sailed on, clearing port and canal, sailing past Gibraltar and onward to the North Sea. It was there, nearing the Danish coast that at least four police agencies squabbled and then drew straws as to which would make the seizure and arrests. Denmark won, I assumed, as this was the ultimate destination of the cargo. But how would they have known so early? Emil and eight others were soon to go on trial in a Copenhagen court.

"We can't find out where the trouble started," said Florence. "And it's too risky for us to go out looking."

And somehow less risky for me, they were sure. I wanted to know who was responsible for buying and loading the hash blocks at Gwadar.

"He's English," Per told me. "Pakistan-English, and he put in some money as well."

"Did he?" I already had doubts. "That's not good. I don't suppose he spent much time on the ground out there." If this deal followed the usual pattern, the Anglo-Pakistani would have made his arrangements long-distance. As usual, his timidity didn't save him or the deal.

"He's been arrested by the British police," added Floyd. "But he won't stand in a Danish court."

The Christiania group had good reason to stay within the enclave. If the Copenhagen police (who rarely stepped into Christiania, and only in force) lifted them outside, they'd be held in solitary until trial and certainly convicted. For all the kind treatment honest citizens receive from the state, those considered players by Danish police are held and kept, almost always convicted.

I took as much information as they were willing to give, and then readied to leave after settling on fees and terms. For one thing, I wouldn't be returning to Pakistan to poke about.

"That would tell us nothing, and I've done my time there," I said. "I won't be back here until this is played out. Nothing anyone could find out will change what happens in court. You have to accept that this is just so you – and Emil – will at least know why things went sour."

I took some side-turns checking mirrored shop fronts through the town centre before reaching Nyhavn and my modish hotel conversion by the port. I was alone. However, I was not by myself at the hotel, and I wanted to appear relaxed by the time my companion returned from her shopping lunch. Eloise had needed some convincing before joining me for this long weekend even though we were together again. That itself had been touch and go, rather than go and touch.

I'd done a fair job running myself down before her: the lunch at my brother's place with me as family oddball; the humble digs (well, comparatively) at Sloane Avenue. And I'd phoned only twice during the first month – and that, only while she was at work. I did my best not to impress. Was that less deceitful than I of my past? Maybe not.

Anyway, Eloise phoned one night around ten and she then called in. At the sofa, heads together in an embrace, I whispered, "this is just like we were back in those early, difficult months," I held her hair with open fingers. "Let's not go through that again. Just, when you're ready, give me a sign. Anything. I'm not as slow-witted as I was."

As we undressed for bed without words, I prepared myself for a night of chastity. Yet as I turned, I saw she was wearing the cream silk shorts I'd presented Eloise two years before in early hope. Now, as she half turned her face to a pillow, I pictured her selecting them from a drawer with care, and took that for a sign. I was not mistaken.

That was over a month ago, so travel, despite Eloise's fear of aviation, seemed manageable. To keep her relaxed, while I was at Christiania (of which she knew nothing), a school-teacher friend, Harry, took her in to town to eat and shop at Åhléns. I'd be sitting reading a paper in the hotel lobby when she returned.

Modern hotels are no longer places where one might learn all you need to know with a glance at the reception desk. For instance: key cards. Each guest has one and keeps it. So, when I let myself in, I was still in my overcoat as I rounded the short corridor to the bedroom to find Eloise sitting at the foot of the bed in her non-recovery position – knees together, head tilted down, and hands clasped.

"Sweetheart, you're back early," I said, knowing too late that's the worst thing to say, so quickly appending, "missed me too much, eh?"

"Where were you?"

"Aw, an old friend called, and I just popped out for a quick drink." The effect of my casual tone was spoiled as I frowned at the realization that in my left hand, I still held a small cellphone jammer that I was just about to turn off. An essential pocket accessory for meetings. Eloise wouldn't know what the unmarked black box was, but its two rubber-coated antennae seemed like the devil's horns in my hands. She trembled her eyes at the device. Had I been out vaporizing werewolves? I set the gizmo aside on a desk, and sat beside her, asking next with concern.

"Didn't you get on with Harry?" I'd told him not to let her leave on her own. "I thought he'd be fun."

"He was nice. I thought you had work to do here at the hotel?"

There was no credible way out of this, and truth was a pit without a ladder. I immediately abandoned words and applied intimacy. Caresses and soft murmurs; the reassurance of pulse against pulse, the loving consumption of another: at times, the cad's last resort.

With Eloise safe back in London – safe in a strictly physical sense – I was free to make enquiries as to why my friend Emil's tonnes of hash sailed into the hands of Danish police. Does it matter? When a deal goes bad, when you drive over that hill in the company of success only to descend to the blocked road of blue lights, can it help to know the details? And where does this fit into the long tournament that began twenty years earlier when I first saw DEA agent Bill Shenkmann cast his despairing curse upon me in the stone-shrouded wood panels of the Victoria State Supreme Court? To both questions: a little more, a little better.

8

I delayed further enquiries for a month. Poking at the survivors of any disaster immediately after the event yields too much talk or none; little that is accurate or helpful. Besides, as there were so many countries' police involved, some of them might have felt left out and looking for more bodies to throw on the fire.

Yet, even after the air had cooled, I didn't find much credible information. I knew the hashish had left the Makran coast for the Arabian Sea, and the ship – the *Kvedarna* – should not have attracted special attention in those smugglers' waters. The weakest links would've been, as usual, communications but the Scandinavians are close-mouthed by nature, while the Pakistani crooks often sound just as devious when talking about a lunch order or high treason.

I spent a couple of days in Vilnius talking to the Lithuanians whose arrested brothers had made up over half the crew of the ship. They didn't know much, and over drinks gleefully invented pointless detail to show that they, too, were willing to jump into anything new. They must have become accustomed to defeat over the years.

Another task was to clean out a self-storage room Emil kept at a site near Copenhagen airport. The company was one of only two in the country with just a few depots – and that was bad. Without much competition, the self-important operators would take a greater interest in their customers. By contrast, in the US and the UK, one might store a corpse without inspection.

In preparation, I'd visited the electronics shops in London's Tottenham Court Road. I left Eloise in *Paperchase*, sifting through the many grades of artists' paper. I didn't want to explain to her my need for auto-diallers, infrared alarms, silent cellphones and relay battery packs.

"Do you want to take all this now?" asked the clerk at *Electroworld*. "I've some boxes out back."

"No thanks," I said, scribbling an address on a card. "No time. Send it here. Gotta go."

When I returned to Eloise, I hoped I'd see her with half the store stacked for purchase on the counter. Instead, she was at the entrance with a thin *Paperchase* envelope, and a narrow expression.

"Now, I thought I was fussy," I said. "I was sure you'd go for a crate of Newton's and a ream of archive-grade."

"Didn't you find what you were looking for?" Eloise had been unsettled earlier in the day at the Imperial War Museum. Some letters by soldiers on show, I'd heard. In fact, a fine display of personal effects as well. Naturally, Eloise had been disturbed. Would I always have to be this careful with her?

I put that aside and said, "I found what I was looking for when I met you," a line that must be delivered with light-hearted sincerity but seems to work in any case.

A few days later I was in Emil's storage lock-up: Some furniture, a lot of boxes of crap; clothes and crockery, some tools. I figured most of that was merely cover for his notes and documents. He'd asked me to clear it all. I'd got inside as I'd rented another room along the same corridor yet had the combination number to Emil's lock.

Tempting though it was to sift through the material immediately, I knew better than to spend the afternoon in his unit. The ceiling of each storage room was open mesh, strong lights shining down from the metal A-frame of the building. There might have been cameras, although none visible. I'd planned to move the furniture (as cover) to my locker but it was distinctive and so might be noticed from above. Instead, I double loaded the boxes with

Emil's papers and stacked the now empty boxes in my own unit to give the place a used look. The caretakers wouldn't know they were empty. I took the full boxes to a holiday-let apartment I'd taken. Before leaving, I set a trap in Emil's room. If anyone entered, the infrared alarm would trigger an auto-dialler connected to a mobile phone that was now powered by a long-life battery. That would quietly dial a pager service in London that would alert me in minutes. A second cellphone in the unit had been set to silent ringing and auto answer, so if my pager went off I could dial in to listen to whoever had let themselves in. This equipment fitted into one of the cardboard boxes with just the infrared sensor peering from a small hole. Maybe all this was unnecessary. If anyone now let himself into Emil's unit at this late stage after his arrest, it could only be a traitor within the group or very slow police.

Among Emil's papers were receipts for antiques and photographs of paintings. He was a collector. Also, some sheets of figures – useful to any prosecutor in any trial. I thought, if you can't remember who you paid and how much you owed, you should find another line of work. And behind this, a photograph of the *Kvedarna* flying the registration flag of the United Arab Emirates. I burned the pages of figures and took the photos to a business centre, made high resolution copies, and then consigned the photographs to the flames. The SD card of the pix I mailed to myself in London. I then phoned a friend in Dubai to check on the registration of the ship looking for owners. I was sure the Danish police would have done the same. That night in my hotel room, I looked at the ceiling in the darkness from my bed. The picture of the ship looked like it was taken under northern lights. That might mean nothing. I slept well as I always do in hotels alone in foreign cities.

My last meeting that week in Denmark was with Emil's wife Lisa. We'd chosen the café at a small junction station south of Copenhagen.

"How's he doing?" I asked Lisa. Under Danish law, the only visitors prisoners awaiting trial are permitted are by close family, and even then, only by arrangement at a police station with cops sitting around, all ears.

"He's okay," Lisa said. "He's used to it. He was held twenty-two months on isolation one time years ago. He's tough."

"And how about you?" I asked. "Are you tough?"

"I've got a bone in my nose, as we say in Danish. I'm used to it, too."

I thought of Eloise. Soft bones. I then told Lisa about my visit to the storerooms. "Everything is safe now, as far as I can make it. Is there anything valuable there? The furniture?"

"No. That's all junk. He doesn't like to throw anything away. You can let it go."

Before we split our separate ways, I asked about the police station visits.

"How do you talk with the enemy in the room?"

"Very carefully."

Back in London I had an email from my Dubai friend. I called him from a phone shop. As I waited for my friend to come on line, I looked at the other customers in this cramped South Kensington phonery. Middle Europeans in the booths, expat moonlighters, mostly. Africans wearing out the fax machines, a couple of Poles at the till. Russians on the computers. It felt good knowing that everyone had something to hide but I wondered even then, as 2001 approached, how long it would be before these shops' lines would be tapped as a matter of course. Something big would need to happen to see funding for that.

Bashar came on the line. After some polite chatter, he told me: "The *Kvedarna* was never registered here, and there's no listing for anything except a payment for fuel."

"Well, that was careless of someone," I said. "What would it have cost to register the ship properly?"

"A vessel of that size? Maybe twenty thousand. Five by the back door."

By not registering the ship in the UAE anyone checking the background would come up blank. Not good. I wondered if the

Lithuanians or the Pakistanis had skimped on the registration. But Bashar had one more insight to add.

"Oh, and you're not the first person to ask about the *Kvedarna*."

"No, I guess not. The Danes must have checked soon after the arrests."

"They did. But even they were not the first. One month earlier, the Americans."

Great.

Moscow. I'd flown in ten days earlier on what I'd planned as a two-day mission. And now I was asking myself what the hell was I doing fooling around with this enterprise for such little reward. In London, I'd looked closely at the photograph of the *Kvedarna*, using software to crank up the colour saturation on the white-painted vessel. Where the name was clear on the bow, a feint shadow of a former name rose. The AN— something. The link I suspected was this: the Lithuanian group had been paid to buy a ship with a history of sailing in the Persian Gulf. They claimed they'd done this in the Emirates, and the *Kvedarna* was it. That now looked doubtful.

In Russia, I hoped to find out what was withheld from me in Lithuania, and I thought my old acquaintance Andreas might be able to find out. That is, the Andreas I'd met in Pakistan, leader of the prison-break skyjacking in the late '80s. He, and the remainder of his crew, had been repatriated to post-Soviet Russia, imprisoned at first, then released. The business of most Lithuanian crooks in Russia was smuggling and stolen goods. A business Andreas and friends had been drawn to for want of any other easy occupation. They'd found themselves out of their time, like wild-west gun slingers in prohibition Chicago.

I'd never been to Russia. I spent the first days like a dog with a new nose, sniffing around for atmosphere and admiring everything from light switches to preposterous cars. Such exploring is best done when without a purpose, and ready distractions got me tangled in Andreas's misadventures. All that has no bearing on this story, and I'd managed to keep clear. I was happy enough now that spring had begun to thaw April, and I sat at a café off Tverskaya with Alexei expecting news. Alexei was one of Andreas's survivors. The food, here as elsewhere, was bad and explains all the vodka.

I was interested to know what Alexei thought of Putin who had just been elected president.

"So, what do you think of Vladimirovich?" I asked.

"I like him," said Alexei. "He's old style, normal."

Traditionalists in Russia regarded former president Yeltsin a troublesome drunk who'd needed American power to stay in office. Alexei blamed Russia's new society for his gang's troubles. Andreas had been killed earlier in the week by new-style rivals. I wanted to leave Moscow as soon as possible to avoid the hungry orphans of Andreas's crew.

"What have you got for me?" I asked, returning to my shipping problem. Alexei paused, then answered.

"The Lithuanians, your friends. Big cigarette smugglers from Kaliningrad."

That wasn't a surprise. But the name of their ship had become well known a year earlier when it had been seized by Russian authorities when found loaded with stolen BMWs. The *Antonas*.

Eloise and I had been looking at houses. A cob, she wanted. To nestle, she'd said. A cob, usually a soggy pat of a country house with low, intimidating beams and often a thatched roof like a '60s mod haircut. As you can tell, I was against the idea. In such country mist, I would not nestle. Or maybe nights I'd nestle into a rocking chair with a shotgun on my lap and a plug of chewing tobacco to keep me awake.

The bad week in Moscow had ironed out any thoughts of mixing with careless crooks in need. I'd found out all I needed to know about Emil's forlorn shipload and had simply to deliver the news. I'd take the early flight to Copenhagen. No need to tell Eloise. I did anyway.

"I'll be busy out of town tomorrow," I said. "I'll be back by nine. Tired though, I'm sure. Unless you're awake late, I'll crash at my flat."

"Crash, will you?" said Eloise, with a smile. "How seventies."

I arrived in Copenhagen needlessly anxious about my meeting with the Christiania old-school hipsters behind the failed shipment. I'd taken my newest passport, each page blank. It held firm as I cleared the airport. Even so, most of us see through the gossamer tissue upon which fortune's contract is written, so I'd agreed to meet only Florence alone. Mid-afternoon at the refreshments bar of the *Palads Teatret* in the town centre. Its windows looked out to an open forum where it should be easy to spot unwanted lurkers. As the arrangement was by phone, we used 1-3 terms to disguise the times: that is, speaking of a day later than intended and a time three hours beyond. So, six on the phone is three on the day.

Florence was drinking coffee when I arrived. As far as I could tell she hadn't brought any unwanted company. I sat, and we made small talk for a few minutes until we could tear our eyes from the window where all was peaceful.

"The trial starts next week," Florence announced.

"Well, there's nothing I can tell you that will make any difference to that." I then got down to the ship. "You thought you were buying a clean boat from the Gulf, right?"

"You're telling me it wasn't clean?"

"It wasn't even bought outright. It was on loan."

I then gave Florence the details. The Lithuanians had pocketed most of the money for the ship. They'd just lost the *Antonas* with its stolen cars and untaxed cigarettes at Kaliningrad, Russian territory. For a fee, they then effectively rented the ship, had it repainted and named, the *Kvedarna* at Klaipėda. A small

Lithuanian crew sailed on to Dubai where some Pakistani sailors signed on, nursing a greater burden than their suspicions.

Florence nodded. "So, the Pakistanis let the story leak out?"

"No. For once the trouble was not exactly from the Pakistani side – although the *Antonas-Kvedarna* was noticed in the Arabian sea." A couple of US pickets had spotted the *Kvedarna* a day after it had left Pasni on the coast. Navy intelligence had been monitoring Gulf shipping closely since suicide bombers had rammed a small boat of explosives into the USS *Cole*, killing a dozen crew. The information was passed on and sideways as US Navy intelligence didn't view the *Kvedarna* as a threat. The details must have reached the DEA, as the agency was in place by the time the twelve tonnes of hash reached Danish waters.

"But knowing who to arrest on shore probably didn't come from the Americans," I said. "From the Lithuanians. Almost certainly from them keeping to the same phones. Never work with people who are too cheap to throw away their phones."

The Scandinavian phone-intercept network was then the envy of most western nations. They simply tapped without fuss (or special warrant) any number of interest. The calls would have revealed a web of treachery. My Russian friends had told me the Lithuanians had promised to cut out the Danes and waylay the ship back to Kaliningrad. Of course, they intended no such folly but wanted to keep the Russians quiet. An odd term, since all of this was discussed in feeble code words on contaminated phones.

"Florence, if you're up for it, go look at your ship in the sealed harbour berths. You can still see the real name through the paintwork."

"It doesn't matter, David. It's all over now." Florence looked down. "Thanks for looking."

"That's okay. You can give my fee to Emil. He'll need it now." I'd noticed Florence hadn't brought a bag with her, and no bulging envelopes in her pockets. I didn't mention that the Russians had told me of another link. Months before the *Kvedarna*-hash disaster, one of the Russians' key men had disappeared at sea in a pleasure yacht ten miles off Denmark's Køge Sønakke. There were over a million cigarettes floating around the waters of the wrecked yacht. No bodies. The yacht's details led to the *Kvedarna* – and that tip-off came from our friends at the DEA. Apart from that hidden link, here's the point: the Russian's man wasn't smuggling cigarettes. He had weapons on board. Some agency was arranging deaths. But that's the new way, along with renditions. I'd had enough; any arrangements for my death I would prefer to make for myself.

With three hours to kill before my return flight to London and spare luggage capacity, I decided to call by the storage rooms near Copenhagen airport. There was nothing other than empty cardboard boxes in my room but Emil's still held the dual telephone alarms, set to trigger if anyone chose to enter and poke around his old furniture. I'd dutifully carried the linked pager for a month, and not a peep. I'd checked it before I left Eloise and my flat that morning for Denmark. The pagers don't receive outside mainland UK. The equipment in the storeroom wasn't especially costly (£1800) but if abandoned some future cop would likely know what it meant. I stopped at the payphone before taking a cab and rang the second cellphone in Emil's lock-up. All quiet.

I would later come to know that at 9.05 that Saturday morning the pager, resting on a bookshelf in my flat, began to vibrate. The movement and sound caught Eloise's attention as it inched along the wooden surface. She stood and walked to it and – I'm guessing – frowned as the pager unbalanced on the edge and dropped to the carpet. She picked it up and placed it in the bowl by the door that normally held keys. She didn't read the display, not that this would have made a difference. If I'd turned Eloise into a girl other than herself, she might have known to alert me. But would that be the girl I'd loved?

In Denmark, as I crossed the threshold of the warehouse door to the cool concrete anteroom, I saw a carpenter working on the floor on some beams. This was the first time I'd seen anyone in the place other than the old caretaker in a far office. The carpenter was in his thirties and in good shape. He didn't look up, just began cutting with a small hand saw. Not much sawdust, I noticed as I passed. He was all wrong. As wrong as you could get if you held auditions for the part. I nodded at him in an ordinary way and chose the corridor to the office away from my own locker. There was a couple at an open room pretending to look inside. They were silent as I saw them but began chatting to each other like a couple without an obvious glance to me. The man, again in good shape, the woman, efficient somehow. Both wrong. It took maybe half a minute to walk to the caretaker's office. It surprises me still how much one can think in so brief a time. I had nothing to fear from my own locker. A few empty boxes. If I was asked about Emil's room, so what. No link there. And snide phone gear was hardly a crime. By the time I got to the caretaker, seeking confirmation, I was still puzzling over the timing – who would know I chose this day to arrive?

I said hello to the old concierge. His pudgy face instantly looked like I'd landed a family-sized cream pie clean into his mush. Surprised, abused and fearful. I spoke casually.

"Say, give me a couple of those fifty-krone boxes, will you?" I pointed at the packing materials behind his desk. "I've got some books in my car I want to bring in."

"Oh, okay,'" he said wiping sudden sweat from his face. "But you will go to your room now?"

I swallowed some obvious lines and said, "Sure, in a few minutes." Carrying the flat-pack boxes I took another corridor to the front door. More casual visitors appeared, most of them in greeting. Now, if only they'd be patient enough to see what I have in my car – not that I had a car – I simply wanted out.

As I approached the doorway, they pounced. All arm grips and headlocks.

"Danish police," said the woodworker. "You are under arrest!" A needless statement but I guess they enjoyed practicing it in English.

9

I left my office early on Friday. I pressed the keys for encryption on the computer and, as the machine shut down, gazed through the glassed walls at the electrical storeroom where a co-worker was assembling cable for an urgent job. Walking out to Pieter, a South African, I gave him the office keys.

"I won't be back today," I said. "Take care."

An hour later, I'd showered and dressed, and went to the large kitchen to check on a roasting chicken I'd began mid-morning, now sizzling in its tray with goose-fat potatoes and honeyed carrots. Then, I made a couple of calls, packed the roast under aluminium foil, and took everything downstairs to await my visitors. The gatekeeper, as the word translates from Danish, let me in to the visiting suite as my hands were full.

He smiled. "Your little girls have gone outside already. I don't know where."

"They'll be back for lunch," I said.

In the room, about the size of a cheap hotel suite, I put my tray on a table, and turned to lock the door. A voice behind me spoke. Jeanette Dufaur had just stepped from the bathroom.

"Well, David. This certainly isn't like any English jail."

True enough, Vridsløselille prison in Copenhagen was unlike most prisons but Denmark had still held me for eight months. At Vridsløselille, I had a well-furnished cell in a unit of thirty inmates who were serving between two and three years – terms considered substantial in Denmark. My job at the electrical repair station paid over one hundred dollars each week, enough to buy meat and groceries from a small supermarket within the prison. Jail policy insisted that prisoners cooked their own food and encouraged groups for sharing resources. The authorities did not want inmates to become accustomed to prison-style food or handouts. We paid for cable TV, and even contributed to a prisoners' union so wages might continue if we took strike action over prison conditions to which we objected.

However enlightened this might appear, such privileges were only for sentenced prisoners – which I'd been for five months – and a real contrast to the treatment of those awaiting trial. Suspects, such as I was from the moment of my arrest at the self-storage warehouse, are kept in solitary confinement until the conclusion of their trials. During that time, upwards of ninety days, a lawyer might visit the special remand prison, yet even one's advocate is not allowed to leave documents which may only be read to the accused. The lawyer is not permitted to contact family. As I'd learned from Emil's treatment, any contact with family or close friends must be made by appointment at a police station where the accused may sit for an hour with visitors as police listen. No talk of the case is permitted. Pleading guilty is frequent, and sensible, given the ninety-five percent conviction rate in Danish courts. The options make little difference to the sentence, capped at six years, unless a capital crime.

I hadn't killed anyone but my problems grew from the moment I was in custody. The phone-alarm set up was enough to allow detention for investigation. Although the police couldn't pin that on me, they still took their time. My first thought was that the caretaker of the storeroom had told the cops I was an odd customer, and they'd wanted to meet me. Yet this seemed thin, especially as they thought it was worthwhile to set up a stakeout, even though I rarely visited.

I'd told the police I was new to the country and was keeping a storeroom for the arrival of household goods as I hadn't found an apartment yet. And that I knew nothing of the earlier (Emil's) storeroom, and its telephone alarm. They didn't buy that – they'd already been given a story they liked better. Two months passed in an isolation cell before I heard it myself by which time my fingerprints had told them who I was. I'd spend my days in silence and an hour in the segregation yard. A circular pen with high walls divided as are orange segments, one prisoner to each. No talking allowed, although old hands inside had developed a whistling code that I never quite caught.

My lawyer had finally taken pity me on by telling me that the police already knew Emil had taken a storage locker somewhere in Denmark. Before they'd checked out the two possible locations, I'd been in and cleaned it out. When the police eventually visited, the caretaker had given them a photocopy of the passport I'd used to get my own locker. I'd never used the document for travel and the head shot gave a poor image (by adjusting colours to the same intensity levels, you can make a photo appear uniform grey in black and white photocopies), so who would recognise me? Still, in Danish hands, the picture had been added to the *Kvedarna* file and sent on to Washington. Would there be someone there who might recognise the muddy image? There was.

Anyway, that was the recent past. And now I was a convict, no longer a suspect and so could be treated kindly. I didn't have to use any creativeness to bring about the change. It came, as misfortune usually does, as a gift from the unknown. Those empty cardboard boxes I'd moved from Emil's room were not quite empty. They'd been soaked and dried with around 800 grams of cocaine. The Danes had taken a second look at them after a tip from Washington. I should have followed Emil's advice to get rid of everything, even empty containers. So now I was serving over a year for that.

And here was Jeanette and her girls visiting me from London. Why? Because we'd become friends. Her husband David was still locked up in Pakistan, the London house sold, with the little family settled in a semi-detached in Fulham. For me, Jeanette was merciful. She had weathered storms before and I didn't have to explain myself.

Within thirty minutes the girls, Ellie and Sophia, had returned to the visit room. We spread the food among the plates, although I had to tear the roast chicken apart with my hands as I'd forgotten to bring a carving knife.

"What do you do here?" Sophia wanted to know.

I shrugged. "Not much. Cook, play in my office, watch movies, take care of my laundry. I've two machines where I work. It's like being on a spaceship to Mars but stuck in orbit."

The girls nodded an unspoken 'weirdo' to each other, but Jeanette had more practical concerns.

"Did you manage to clear up before you left London?"

"No," I said. "There was plenty of mess. But I got word out."

I'd been sitting in solitary for three months knowing I had boxes to clear in London, a surely confounded Eloise, and a new apartment that wouldn't tolerate emptiness for long. Fortunately, an English friend who lived in Copenhagen was willing to brave an uncomfortable interview with Danish police to arrange one of the supervised visits at police headquarters. We sat across a small table as one of the detectives looked on and listened. Mark was fair-haired and thirty-five; he'd chosen Crookdom in calmer Scandinavia, and that cut an unhappy connection with some London villains. The quiet life. I'd chosen Mark mainly because he was a smoker, as well as reliable.

Although we were guarded in our conversation – keeping it light and peppered with false laughter – I had to pass him three post-it-note sized messages I'd written in tiny script. One note held information of my deposit boxes whose term was due to expire, another note concerning the stashes of papers and money in my flat; the third note a miniature scroll for Eloise. These I'd rolled into the emptied paper tube of a single cigarette, mixed then with others in my pack, those smokeable but less incendiary. The problem was that Mark had no forewarning of this play. I would have to reply on tiny gestures and taps to let him know.

"I can't get used to local brands," I said rasping out another unwelcome lungful of smoke. (Even then, I rarely smoked.) "Let me try one of yours." And that was as much as I risked saying of cigarettes. I took one from Mark's pack, toyed with it, went into a story about being lost in Copenhagen, made the switch, and put my message-laden cigarette into his packet – and then spent the rest of the hour forcing Mark to abstain, using nothing but hand signals. I can't be sure the policeman, only a few feet away, didn't twig to the idea we were up to something. Perhaps he thought Mark had brought me some drugs – in a small enough quantity to overlook.

Mark left with the notes, and my lawyer, a week later, passed on guarded confirmation that all was in hand. I wondered later what Eloise made of the tiny goodbye letter, sent by mail as I thought hand delivery would lead to hope. This time, I wanted none. I told her that I was no good for her. There's no honest way to write such letters. The important thing is to mean it, to be final.

In the visit room at Vridsløselille, we ate cakes, after which the kids grew bored – these were four-hour visits – and so disappeared to the icy streets outside. Jeanette packed up the tray of debris. She looked at me as I sat back on a padded chair, digesting.

"Now, don't think I'll be coming over here every month," she said. "I've had enough of visiting jails with David."

"How is he?"

"Okay I suppose. His lawyer says he'll get bail soon."

I nodded. "That'll mean the case is dead. He can leave Pakistan anytime he wants. They won't stop him. Or look for him later." I paused. "You want him back?"

Jeanette sighed but said nothing.

A few months later, I was taken to Copenhagen airport by city police, escorted on to a British Airways jet, and told never to darken Danish doors again. One of the detectives gave my passport to the flight captain, advising him to contact UK police before arrival in London. Once the plane reached cruising altitude, with the fasten seat belts sign switched off, the captain left the flight deck, sat next to me, and handed me my passport.

"You'll probably need this," he said. "I won't be saying anything on arrival."

I thanked the pilot, and we spoke for a few minutes about the wonders of modern travel. I then dozed for half an hour thinking about my next move.

On arrival at Heathrow, I went immediately to the airlines' ticket office, bought a ticket to Aarhus, and flew back to Denmark. After taking a fast train, I was in a bar with Mark before nightfall.

"There's something I didn't get a chance to ask you," I said after we'd made a cynical toast to freedom. "What did Bobby have to say about my arrest?" Bobby was my long-time American mobster friend.

"He said he'd tell you when he sees you," Mark said with a shrug. "But the interest came from an old sparring partner of yours."

I couldn't imagine DEA-man Bill Shenkmann still at his desk. Surely, he would have retired by now. "Well, that must wait. Travel is wearing me down."

Yet travel continued. I returned to England, staying with friends – a retired couple living on the south coast. The guest rooms were made from a large converted attic with sloped windows that made staring at the sea a pleasure. Evenings I could sit with a drink in my hand, looking over the channel and keep an eye on the French. I'd train to London a couple of days each week to secure money, documents, rare foods and music to bring back to the coast. Yet, I'd lost my old certainties about passports – the world was going on-line. Even so, I visited Matthias in Germany without being stopped. And in one passport, I was granted a US visa. For now, I would have no home. I thought often of Eloise, yet in reflections of my skeletal life, I knew this could be no match.

My touring discovered one or two homes that looked safe. A lakeside villa in Annecy, a sun-bleached house in Sicily. And I encouraged Michael to leave Australia but that was too late. He had been arrested following the seizure of a load of amphetamines in a storage locker of his own. Michael was conditionally free, though with health problems and had to report to the police. I suggested a way out.

"I can get you a passport if you're up for it."

"I should stay close to my doctors," Michael said with finality. "Don't know what it is. My blood is rebelling without the magic elixir." Michael had stopped using heroin a year earlier.

"That reporting must be a drag," I said. "You have a case officer?"

"Yes. He prides himself on probing questions every time he sees me, ready to have my bail lifted," Michael sniffed. "He has the foul breath of the non-smoker. Malodorous, with the fading yet pungent record of life's consumption." Michael didn't smoke, yet never took well to earnest questioning.

"Well, I'm always here if you want your last years in peace."

It was about time I stopped fiddling at the edges of the independent smuggling world. If Bill at the DEA could nearly have me put on some kill-list for nosing about a lost ship, then it was time to end the game. So many years were taken in a contest with no real purpose and few rewards, it must be time to escape the past. Could that be done?

10

Michael didn't take my offer. Instead, he died a few months later in summer 2001. Going against lifelong experience, Michael foreclosed upon all his vices. I like to imagine this abandoned the defences against cancerous blood, and leukaemia emerged triumphant.

Even in death, I still hear Michael's voice, often just a few steps to my left offering advice and the all-important ridicule that kept us level. *'Why do you care?'* This voice asked as I stood in line that autumn at Los Angeles International airport. *'Acting on a whim takes more planning than any military campaign.'* Maybe, but my trip to the USA was not business, just a loose end with Bobby Junior, who as ever remained in Mafia denial.

The city and another line of immigration made me think of the journey of the past twenty-five years. At its best when tied to no one, ultimately tragic when I cared. I was sure to face attack from time to time by authorities, somehow more likely when taking intense precautions. Eloise wasn't built to take that on. I hadn't made a big night telling her so. Just an honest lunch. None of the usual phrases and casual, parting promises. I fought hard not to say, 'Don't make a stranger of yourself,' or, 'I'll be around if you need me.' Such things turn a goodbye into a charade.

"So, this is it?" asked Eloise at some point. I nodded slowly. And meant it.

At the immigration desk, the officer finally stopped key-punching at his terminal, and smiled at me.

"Welcome to the United States."

The emphasis on welcome. I knew something was wrong.

Sure enough, just after I loaded my bags on a trolley, three US customs officers closed in. I was taken to one of those windowless rooms official buildings have in great numbers. My passport held up, as well as the tourist visa I had been given. The search was polite but very thorough, and I didn't prolong the act by making light conversation.

My hard-shelled suitcase was emptied and taken for an X-ray. Hand luggage sniffed and swabbed. A thorough pat-down for me and outer clothing checked. I'd made sure I carried less than $2000 in cash and had matching credit cards, and a hotel booking with a story for my journey. (Trade fair; electronics.) The woman customs inspector gave special attention to my soft leather suit carrier and began picking at the stitching before a sniffer dog gave the all-clear. Then, they gave up. They looked at my luggage and even at the empty trolley perhaps thinking they'd missed a bag somehow.

"Well, you can go," concluded the team leader. As I reloaded the trolley and rattled to the exits, it seemed odd that if I was known for who I am, why grant the visa? If the idea was to keep tabs on who I might meet, that should be clear within minutes at my hotel when followers take to their feet. For now, I sought out the car I'd rented from Avis – despite encouragement on the advertising plate of my trolley to use Hertz.

I drove north to San Francisco, checked in to a hotel, and took a walk. Nothing. That is, no-one following me. Not that I was up to special mischief, but it was sensible to block any link to Bobby Junior.

Without fuss, I flew east to Chicago, changed names, then on to New York. As it was late when I arrived Friday, another hotel night before morning with a new car rental and the drive to Bobby's Long Island house.

The place was full of people for a big lunch. Low-level mob fans, loads of family, a few hopeful film folk, and some young artists looking unimpressed while privately seeking a patron. It took some time to catch up with Bobby alone. In his study, he asked if I'd encountered any problems in my travels.

"None that I can talk about indoors," I said. "I was turned over arriving at Los Angeles. There's been no interest since."

We moved from the edges of a large desk to chairs before an unused fireplace. Bobby got to the point of my visits. He had information of the DEA's Bill Shenkmann. Bobby leaned forward.

"Not long after you were arrested in Denmark, the Agency was told. Shenkmann was about to retire – that'd be over a year ago, now. He remembered you, of course. My man in the Agency says Shenkmann told the Danes to go through everything. Gave them a list of the angles."

I wasn't sure what that meant. "I suppose they did. But they got me on one thing I never use. Cardboard." I explained the wax-coated cardboard boxes soaked and dried with cocaine found in the storage room. "Cardboard's been a thing in Asia for years. Dope-soaked bindings of books, mostly. Bill seems to go the extra mile for me. I suppose I owe him a night out sometime."

Bobby smiled. "Too late to thank him now. He died just a few weeks ago. If you'd been around you could've gone to his funeral."

"Natural causes?" I asked.

"His ticker. He's at Arlington cemetery if you want to spit on his grave."

"That wouldn't count for much. His people have been in my hair since I was eighteen. And the DEA is full of agents just as obsessive. Well, almost."

I stood and walked to the window. Bobby's friends were enjoying the late summer air. I nodded to the groups. "They staying?"

"Until tomorrow," Bobby said, joining me at the window. "I have to fill this house somehow." I was reminded of the gift I'd brought. I stepped back and took hold of the leather zip-folder I'd left on a chair. From inside, I removed a black package about half the size of a house brick. I offered it to Bobby.

"Here's something for your party. Straight from Peru. Best I've seen for years."

"Geez, Dave, thanks." Bobby sniffed at the package, almost excited in a childlike way. Then, a frown. "I thought you said you were stripped at LAX?"

"Near enough," I said, tapping the block. "This looked different then."

I didn't explain. Bobby was a little too talkative for a third-generation mob family son. Yet this was to my advantage that he was, for he gave me all he'd hear. And I knew that if he'd find out how I slipped through customs with half a kilo of coke, the method would spread, and once found, strangled in infancy.

I'd arrived at Los Angeles knowing the airport well. When I collected my bags at the luggage carousel, they included the expensive leather suit-carrier, the kind with a long zip at its centre and clips to carry it folded to a top coat-hanger. On the outside, it appeared a smooth surface of brown leather. In fact, the rear was a panel half-a-meter square that contained a compressed sheet of cocaine enveloped in plastic held by a millimetre thickness of ply veneer. Above that layer was another; not wood but a thin, magnetized rubber sheet. The kind you find on flexible fridge magnets. As I was being watched by CCTV at LAX, I walked to the rows of luggage trolleys, pulling one free. Back at the carousel, I hefted my suitcase onto the trolley platform. Beneath the trolley's bar handle, there's a hook. Just the kind of thing to hold a suit-carrier. I stood fetching my passports and tickets with one hand while adjusting the suit-carrier with the other. The trolley had, as I knew, a large flat rear panel between the upright bars that carried advertising. This is made of sheet steel, and allowed me to position the magnetized panel of the leather carrier against the advertising display of precisely the same size. Once in place, the suit-carrier peeled free, appearing essentially the same. The false panel needed just a few taps to sit edge-to-edge. Now in place, I moved on. Stopping once as though to adjust the suit-carrier over my suitcase. Pushing my trolley forward, I inspected my work. The outer layer of the panel carried the same green-print sign as the other trolleys, proclaiming Hertz to be #1.

During my forty-five minutes with US customs, they'd been through with my luggage and with me, but taken no interest in the trolley. The false panel held tight then and later as I wheeled it out to the carpark and my car. The green print colour didn't perfectly match the other trolleys – even by 2001, home printing was not quite to today's standard. For all the effort, half a kilo wasn't much. If sold today, I suppose it wouldn't pay much more than a holiday for two. Good as it was, around $20,000. But it was never for sale. I kept a little for me, and Bobby dined in on the rest. So, why take the risk? Well, despite twenty-seven years at odds with Bill Shenkmann and his DEA, I'd never taken a packet of any size into their heartland. I felt I owed it to those who had fallen.

A few days after leaving Bobby, I drove out of Washington to the four-hundred acres of Arlington cemetery. Only to enjoy the manicured gardens, I told myself – not to visit Shenkmann's grave. Besides, what were the odds, in all that expanse of finding one lonely plot? Slim. So, I checked at the visitor's office for the location. Only to give a mental map to my walk, you understand.

I walked for an hour, caught a lift on one of the golf carts that patrol Arlington, and by mid-afternoon brought myself to the simple white stone panel of William Henry Shenkmann. It's one of thousands in the columbarium, an open-air temple of the dead. I realized then that I'd never visited the grave of anyone I knew. Not even that of Clelia many years earlier when I'd been put off by the appearance of snooping police.

A wind flapped my raincoat around my legs. There were no chiselled words of praise or reflection upon Shenkmann's headstone. Just the name, Army details (CPL USA VN) and dates as a dry record. And the phrase, 'YOU WILL BE REMEMBERED'. And so, he is. Of course, despite Bill's strained and overzealous work over the years, I didn't credit my misfortunes on one man, no matter how timely his interventions. I should have been smarter or, more sensibly, not in the game at all.

A pair of suited men thirty feet away caught my vision. They were looking at another grave, though not with much interest. The feeling of mild satisfaction of being alive above the dead disappeared, and I ran the usual checklist of vulnerabilities. My documents were good, although I carried that day a small envelope of coke powder in my raincoat pocket. Minor, but a concern if the two police (if that's what they were) had intent as they slowly began to walk toward me. Discreetly, with one hand, I took the envelope from my pocket, flipped it open, and flicked the flakes into the white stone carving before me.

The two men passed by. As strangers in such places, we nodded at each other. One spoke.

"Family?" he asked.

"No," I said, edging away from the Shenkmann remains. "I think I've ended up in the wrong place. I should be in the Court number 9."

"Well, you're way off base here," he smiled. They glanced at each other and moved on. I casually walked back to the nearest high hill before looking back. The two visitors were no longer visible. I looked out across the serried ranks of white headstones, hill after valley. Even if Shenkmann was an exception, there were thousands before him, and assuredly, many to take his place.

I drove back to New York City to return my car, and checked into the *Pierre*, before buying a ticket to return to London. Fortunately, a flight was available the following day. Had it been a day later, the airline would not have flown. In a piece of brutal but effective showmanship, followers of Osama bin Laden had brought down the twin towers. The country was overwhelmed by thoughts of the dust of the levelling. People today may forget just how upset were those countries outside of the USA. Even those people I knew in cities where explosions and shattered bodies were a grim routine felt personally offended. New York is the city of universal aspiration; mass obliteration there hurt everyone's dreams. For me, I felt small, and not for the first time, feeling small felt safe.

11

Yet not safe enough.

Nine years later, a late-night event occurred at the Freedom Bar on Nai Harn Beach in Phuket. Lee Aldhouse, a British kickboxer resident in Thailand for four years, argued with former US marine Dashawn Longfellow. After more drinks and a run-around, both left the bar. Dashawn returned to his rented island apartment with his Thai girlfriend. Lee ran into a 7-Eleven store, picked up a couple of large kitchen knives and went after the former machine-gunner to make a final point. Dashawn was stabbed at his apartment door. He soon died from chest wounds.

Come morning, Lee got the urge travel. Leaving via Cambodia and Singapore, he flew to the UK, only to be arrested by police at London's Heathrow airport on an old weapons charge. Thailand soon made a request to Britain for the extradition of the Birmingham boxer. The request, if granted, would be the first successful extradition between Thailand and Britain in one-hundred years.

All of Lee's lawyers assured him his extradition was unlikely given the notoriously poor conditions of Thai jails. The Westminster court and two appellate courts disagreed. It cannot have helped Lee's cause that he'd killed a US marine, given

America's implacable desire that justice, of any kind, is served upon all those accused of killing its citizens.

Aldhouse was flown to Thailand in the custody of two Thai police officers, jailed and put in chains. Eleven months later he admitted murder, was convicted and sentenced to twenty-five years' imprisonment. Thai officials were happy - it was the first time in 101 years Britain had agreed to send any suspect to Thailand. At the suggestion of US and Australian police, the Thais turned to their next target.

For years, I'd been living peacefully in the suburbs outside London. Orpington is a middle-class town built-up after World War II. My life included Jeanette – we'd been together since after meeting in Karachi and her husband's early death. I was out of the business. Sometimes, that can be as dangerous as still being at it. All the rules for safety that you stick to don't apply when you haven't got an operation going. Over the ten years, I'd been arrested a couple of times. These days, it is not easy to manage a jury-acquittal when you have a past. Even when the evidence is thin, a past record swings the vote. I had a jury in my favour in one case until they went home for the night. They returned, having googled my name, and quickly convicted. Judges warn juries against doing that, but that seems only to remind them to do so. I was still arguing that case – a few grams of dope had been mailed to my house, supposedly from a big Karachi lawyer – when two grinning London cops appeared with an extradition warrant.

At first I was dismissive. Then I heard of the Lee Aldhouse case. I called in London's premier extradition lawyer, Henry Milner and a team from Matrix Chambers. Our problem was that Thailand had already had a success, and despite an appeal to the European Court of Human Rights, that success had stuck. In the London court, I presented two professors on politics and law who assured the judge I wouldn't get a fair trial in a Thai court. (I had never been convicted in any Thai proceedings.) Another witness told of the overcrowding and bad conditions of Thai jails. During the hearings, a Thai deputy attorney-general sat in court, sometimes accompanied by a pair of black suits who could have been Odd Job's younger brothers. My judge, a woman in her early 60s married to a conservative politician, was not persuaded. The found my entire life unlikely: that such things could have happened to anyone. When our experts visited the Thai jail to inspect and found the jailers had cleared the corridors and cells of all prisoners, the Westminster judge remarked, "They were probably embarrassed." This was a woman accustomed to her private girls' school and country gardening, not Asian prisons. She ruled against me. As did the UK Secretary of State. I moved the case to the High Court but kept in mind the probability that soon enough I'd be on a plane bound for Bangkok. There, I would be chained in the heavy, escape-proof thirty-kilogram links. I'd never be left alone. A cell with strong fluorescent strip-lighting throughout the night. Cellmates whose job was to watch my every move. At the Bangkok jail with jailers whose jobs and careers I'd harmed and threatened. If I survived whatever treatment officers planned for me, I'd be 76 before eligible for transfer to the UK on the prisoner-exchange scheme.

 This was an unusual situation for me. Usually, a disaster comes suddenly, yet always provides an alternative outcome. At first and best, escape. Yet this did not. I thought of the past. In the deserts and stone rubble of outlaw lands, one can do anything that comes to mind and hand. Standing at the moment of confrontation, those seconds of silence when all players, mostly armed and ruthless, eye the landscape and each other for the slightest advantage, your choices are simple. If your smart, you've made yourself too useful to kill. If you're smarter, then no one knows of what you are capable.

Yet the western world of 2016 is no easy badland where you can set the scene and improvise a battle plan. For someone trapped as I was, it is a world where law enforcement is complete with rich armour, maximum security prisons, steel transports, and speedy communication. More importantly, a determination to follow those who run to the ends of the earth until capture or death. If I escaped from London's Wandsworth prison, I would be hunted forever. That would mean abandoning family and friends. Since retiring from the game, I had opened my life and almost everything became known, and a potential target. Escape from Bangkwang or whichever prison I was kept, would be difficult and take perhaps years before I made a crack in the strongest security.

First, I needed privacy to think. Wandsworth is overcrowded and few had single cells. I befriended the most senior mental-health manager, a tall woman with short hair, discreet tattoos and a slightly swaggering manner that would keep her safe in a bikers' bar on Route 66. She knew I was kidding her, and liked me for it. I soon had my own cell. Bought my own bedding, stereo and the boxed sets of series I'd missed. Now comfortable, I thought through an immediate solution: TG911, the flight on which I would be taken, overflies airports along its route – including Faisalabad in Pakistan. It would be possible to have a passenger fake a heart seizure on board at a strategic point where the nearest airport for emergency landing would be in Pakistan. Once landed, the aircraft would encounter engine trouble. That would mean a crucial delay until an ongoing flight could be found. The Thai policeman would want only Thai airways, which would mean a road trip north to Lahore. On the ground, there would be some debate as to whose custody

I'd be in. Arrangements would need to be made so that I'd be arrested by the Pakistani police on some spurious charge that would keep me in Pakistan and send the Thai police on their way. Once in Pakistan, I would pay the same police to drop the charge. The Thais would then have to start the extradition process again. A Pakistan court is a place with which I am quite familiar. The extradition claim would fail.

The problems with this plan are clear. I'd be entirely dependent on others' trust. And finding someone capable of staging a convincing medical emergency would not be easy. And I would still be wanted by the Thais. A better plan would be to have the Thais abandon their wish to see me in a Bangkok court. Yet, how? The warrant issued by a Thai court in the weeks after I escaped in 1996 was due to expire in September 2016 but there would be nothing stopping the same court issuing another warrant. There would need to be a change of heart. A heart strong enough to withstand the goading of the foreign police agencies that prompted the Thais in the first place.

On Friday, the 16th of September around 6:30, my cell door opened. I was in my dressing gown about to settle in with the third season of *The Americans*. The officer at the door said: "You're going. You're released." Those are not statements any prisoner pauses to question. I had expected either this or two policemen ready to take me to Heathrow airport. Twenty-five minutes later, I walked into the night outside the prison to be then blinded by the lights of a car. Someone stepped through the light. It was Jeanette who had learned just that day from my lawyers that Thailand had withdrawn its request after almost two years. I was free.

I'm sure that the Thai officials were pleased with the result. They had won their case in the British courts. Yet they would know, too, that the many assurances given to the UK secretary of state concerning my proposed treatment once back in Thailand might mean little in the real world. The prisons run their own affairs like a mafia township. Orders from a distant office-bound hack would mean little. Eleven prison officers lost jobs and careers following my 1996 escape. In the isolated community of prisons, vengeance would be certain. If I was returned to Thailand, and then found dead, decapitated after slipping on a bar of soap, this would be an embarrassment for the diplomats who'd insisted on my extradition. As it is, the Thais have their victory without any consequences. I suppose I must thank someone with a cool head. In such a turn of events, a fellow would be a fool indeed to make claim that he influenced the Thai justice department from a prison cell. I try not to be a fool. Sometimes, I succeed.

Termination

The game had finished. Or, rather, that particular game.

Over the almost forty years of these events, the strongest engine that propelled them was my reluctance to accept a losing battle. Of course, I might have moved on to lose battles on fresh fields had it not been for Bill Shenkmann and his fellow enthusiasts. In the scheme of world drug smuggling, my contribution was small, and directed at the challenge of the crossings. The efforts of those working against me might be disproportionate but really amounted to no more than a few years' work over all that time. Yet their resources were and are great, so it's wrong to picture a fiery agency man up nights plotting my downfall. More, a lonely and driven man, one finger on the keyboard, poking remote vengeance for his own life's disappointments. Such are the people that cause the most distress in the modern world of agencies. And not just for riffraff such as I.

Even so, I am still alive, while many are not. Bill's dead but oddly that doesn't seem to matter. There's someone else at his desk.

Among the regrets, Clelia, of course, especially so as her death was due to my carelessness, to put it at its simplest. Michael Sullivan's death (leukaemia) was unpreventable and the saddest part of his life was that he survived on the thin ration of about five years of happiness until his wife Marie Escolar-Castillo's death with Clelia. For Michael, nothing ever made for happiness after 1981.

Of the Australians, some are still living, although George the Greek worried himself to an early death. Peter Dale is still in dreamland, others scattered or hiding. Brendan Healey, who stood trial with us in Melbourne and was acquitted, is a psychotherapist in Mullumbimby, and happy.

In Thailand, Tommy kept clear of the dope trade and runs a silk shop in Chiang Mai. Most of the people I knew at Klong Prem prison in Bangkok are dead; friend and first contact Lee died from a heart attack at 58. John Alford, the London minder turned courier, died from AIDs after seven years in the Thai prison. Sten, the Viking who helped me cut out of Klong Prem prison, stayed for his sentence and was repatriated to Sweden after four years. Served a total of twelve years; released, and has kept quiet since. Calvin, the Hawaiian fellow inmate in Bangkok, returned to the islands and his old life on the edge of the heroin scene. However, Charlie Lao, who had arranged my passport and exit after my escape, returned to Sydney where he opened a Lao restaurant. A little farther east, Lord Tony Moynihan (the fraudster and police informer) died in Manila in 1991, aged 55. The family remains cursed. In September, 2016, Moynihan's daughter Aurora was killed in the Philippines. Shot in a Manila street by someone she offended. Percy Hole, the fake SAS-commando who hoped to swindle us in a helicopter prison break, is still alive and tricking people at 66. As a butler in the UK, he sold his master's Bentley for £56,000 and then told the court he 'spent the proceeds on champagne, cocaine and prostitutes'. Despite what seems to me a reasonable excuse, Percy received a jail sentence. A couple of years ago, he was on company fraud charges and given a curfew. Tomas, my contact and friend in Stockholm, died from neglect while I was held in Pakistan. Although he lived comfortably in his flat, without friends, he didn't feed himself properly and ignored his health. While in Scandinavia, I should mention Mark, London crook relocated to Denmark: found dead with a naked girl (also taking the big sleep) in a hotel room in Copenhagen; a careless mix of chlorpromazine-laced brown heroin, tranquillizers and booze.

Iftikhar in Pakistan has kept clear of his late uncle Noor Jehan's tribal fights, became a teacher and lives in Karachi. My two close experiences of Lords: one the English fraudster Moynihan, and the other Mir Noor Jehan. I know which had the true nobility.

Of the many who had deep troubles there, some have survived, though not many. David Dufaur, then husband to

Jeanette, was freed, returned to London but died from an unexpected heart attack within a couple of years. Billy Green, who had invented an international-mafia history for me for Pakistani spooks that had me arrested, returned to Liverpool where he died a few years later from alcohol poisoning. Robbie the Scot left Karachi to find opportunity in the new eastern Europe. He took Russian Tatiana with him but the match didn't take. Andreas and the surviving members of the group that had escaped a Soviet prison (and had hijacked a jet to Hyderabad) were returned to Russian prisons. On release, they found themselves out-of-step with the new Russia. Andreas was killed in Moscow in a shootout, and all but two of the others fell in their own ways. I've made notes on their adventures for a book called, *White Russians*, but would anyone want to read it? Violent and depressing.

In the Americas, Diego, my helper in Colombia, has kept away from the coke world. He runs a taxi stand and fishes weekends. In the US, closet mobster Bobby Junior had a close call with a tax-fraud case, and had then moved to Florida. He was shot dead by his third wife in 2014.

Of my friends from that era, one to whom I was close was Matthias from Germany. In these pages, I had wondered if his solitary life of travel, comforted by his special blend of intoxicants, might be a fine balance for a man alien to his times. We had kept in touch – although while I was being held at Thailand's request in a London prison, communication was difficult. I hadn't heard from him, but I thought he was travelling as usual.

He was not. About a year ago, Matthias arranged his house and papers as if preparing for a long journey. He sent his home keys to a young cousin with a note asking that the cousin come to his house after he received the letter. The cousin drove to Frankfurt, let himself in, and found Matthias dead on a sheet of protective plastic laid across the living room Persian rug. A gun was at his side. The sheet had not prevented splatters of brain spoiling Matthias's neat housekeeping. From the notes, his death was certainly suicide. 'I am too old to travel in my business. I can't live in any other way,' said one.

Suicide is the most private of deeds. Who can say why anyone does not want to go on and then has the resolve to end his life? We can never truly know. Matthias was just 64, not too old to go on. His wife had taken her life unexpectedly decades earlier, only a few years into their marriage. They were then in their late twenties. Her death had simply perplexed him at the time. Perhaps that experience made for an option he'd not otherwise have taken. Yet, it's pointless to speculate – such a private, secret act will remain a mystery to those who live on.

Was Matthias a victim of the drug wars? Was my life wasted in this relentless pursuit? From one point of view, yes; we have a limited number of years and when sieved of all the routine demands amounts to a scrapbook of good days. Any careful planner would make careful use of that time. Yet we are born happy and ready to join any struggle that seems captivating and absorbing. The only good advice I can suggest after these years is not to take on a fight that cannot be won. Simply being alive while others have died on the trail is not winning – still, it is good to live long enough to tell the story.

Yet, that moment I left the grave of DEA agent Bill Shenkmann in Arlington, I realized the relentless pursuit had been my own as much as my detected enemies. And the search for a motive for those imagined enemies had led me through a maze as artificial as that in some cheap carnival hall of mirrors. As the image became clear in the single, undistorted mirror of time, my real adversary was in plain view: myself.

DMCM=MMCVII

INDEX

A GUIDE TO THE PEOPLE WE MEET

An essential list, especially in real life, where people often inconveniently share the same first names. Indexed by first names, when familiar.

A

Abdul - the Talib name adopted by Syed · *See* **Syed**

Adnan · 242 - Pakistani friend and advisor from Lahore.

Akbar Shah · 315, 318, 346 - drug-deal fixer and gambler in Karachi manipulating Jeanette's husband, David. *See also*, **Mrs Akbar Shah**.

Alan · 104 - Australian crook and police informer who helped police bug our house.

Alex · 148 - Alex Tsakmakis, who torched Barry in the Australian supermax; in 1988, he was clubbed to death in prison.

Alexei · 375 - One of Andres's gang of Moscow street bandits who had survived Pakistan jail & Russian return.

Alphonse · 61 - Colombian drug negotiator.

Andreas · 296, 374, 402 - leader of the Moscow street gang who hijacked a jet to Pakistan.

Anthony Moynihan · 93 - Lord Tony, British fraudster who lived and conned in Manila, Philippines under dictator Marcos. Died, Manila, 1991.

Arshad · 315, 322, 326, 346 - Pakistan Air Force captain who arranged my bail from Landhi jail, Karachi.

Azif Zardari · 301 - husband of Benazir Bhutto, imprisoned on allegations of murder, freed to become president.

B

Baboosh · 236, 269, 348 - Ahmed Baboosh, Pakistani anti-narcotics force officer who tortured me following my arrest in Lahore.

Barry · 148- Barry Quinn, inmate in Melbourne's supermax prison; torched by fellow prisoner Alex.

Bashar · 373 - friend from Dubai shipping, giving me information on the *Kvedarna* shipload of hashish.

Bill Shenkmann · 15, 71, 137, 167, 237, 267, 390 - DEA agent; my nemesis for 30+ years.

Billy Green · 275, 279, 315, 402 - Liverpool ex-boxer, arrested for drugs in Karachi; talked his head off.

Bobby C · 41 - US mobster and father of Bobby Junior.
Bobby Junior · 220, 388, 402 - son of Bobby C who kept me in the picture of New York business and US law.
Brendan Healey· 129, 136 - hippie co-defendant in the big 1982 conspiracy trial in Melbourne; acquitted.
Byron Stroud · 312 - lost Raj-era son in Hyderabad jail; helped me eat.

C

Calvin · 187, 401 - American minor drug runner in the Bangkok prison.
Captain Arshad · *See* **Arshad**
Carl · 296, 301 -Carl Parker - Canadian friend and bank-robber who came to help me while in Karachi prison.
Chalk · 170 - George Chalk; Australian Federal Police, visited me in Bangkok prison and reported to Bill Shenkmann.
Charlie · 185, 401 - Charlie Lao, Chinese-Lao friend who arranged my passport following the Bangkok prison escape.
Chopper Read · 145 - Cartoonish Australian 'prison identity'. Known for ability to survive repeated stabbings. Wrote fables of himself in successful books.
Christian · 229 - Danish friend with an independent smuggling operation.
Clelia Viganò · 18, 34, 124, 127 - my Australian-Italian wife during my twenties.
Colin · 142, 143 - fellow inmate at Jika supermax prison, Melbourne.

D

Danielle · 127 - agent provocateur and arsonist in Fairlea Women's Prison, Australia.
Daoud · 256 - translator and fixer in Kabul.
David Dufaur · 316, 325, 332, 345, 385 - Jeanette Dufaur's late husband, arrested then freed in Pakistan.
Dean Reed · 283 - fellow inmate at Bangkok's Klong Prem prison who fleeced my friend Lee pretending to help me.
Diego · 30 - Colombian driver and helper in Cali.
Duncan · 21, 81, 84 - Duncan Connor - Michael Sullivan's runner and helper who soon turned against him; state witness in the big trial.

E

Ellie Dufaur · 325, 328 - youngest daughter of Jeanette; travelled to Karachi after her father's arrest.

Eloise · 218, 353, 360, 362, 367, 378, 388 - Eloise Morse, girlfriend in London after escaping Thailand.
Emil · 366, 370, 371, 372, 382 - Danish friend and smuggler.

F

Ferdinand Viganò · 106 - Clelia's father.
Florence · 366, 376 - one of the Christiania (Copenhagen) players.
Floyd · 366 - another of the Christiania founders.
Francesco Turchurello · 40, 71 - Italian Mafioso with New York friends.

G

General Zia-ul-Haq · 277, 297 - Pakistani General; assumed power from 1978 until death in '88.
Geoff Macintyre · *See* Macintyre
George the Greek · 26 - early-period courier and ruinous gambler; became state witness.
Glen · 85 - Australian travel agent.

H

Harry · 368 - Danish friend; the teacher asked to distract Eloise in København.

I

Ian Hayden · 132 - Brendan Healey's lawyer.
Ibrahim · 316 - Christian tax collector held on corruption charges in Landhi jail, Karachi.
Iftikhar · 202, 261, 401 - Noor Jehan Magsi's cousin, kidnapped and later freed in Afghanistan.

J

Jeanette · 328, 331, 380, 398 - Jeanette Dufaur, former wife of David Dufaur; met in Pakistan when she arrived to help him.
Jeremy · 284 - Jeremy Cobley, consular diplomat at the British High Commission in Karachi.
Jet · 182, 190 - my head butler in Bangkok's Klong Prem prison.

John · 86, 88, 100, 138, 227, 401 - John Alford, London minder and one-time drug courier; arrested in Bangkok.

Josette · 200 - my French auntie who hid me in Autun following the Thai escape.

K

Kamran · 246, 333 - Noor Jehan Magsi's young bodyguard.

Khaled · 292 - head of the Murtaza-party splinter group in Karachi Central Jail.

L

Landhi jail · 315 - Karachi's second-biggest prison.

Lee · 2, 46, 169 - my first and best Thailand contact; loyal to the end.

Lee Aldhouse · 394 - British kickboxer, extradited and convicted of killing a former US marine in Thailand.

Lisa · 372 - the wife of my Danish friend Emil.

Lord Tony · *See* Anthony Moynihan

Lou Speechly · 20 - small-time thief in Melbourne; raided Michael Sullivan's house.

M

Macintyre · 275 - UK policeman who visited Karachi police torture cells and saved me from further damage.

Mahmood · 266 - fellow prisoner (briefly) in Lahore police station.

Mansour · 259 - Afghani air-force technician; helped during kidnap search for Iftikhar.

Maria · 154 - Scatty prison officer at a country open prison in Australia.

Marie · 20 - Marie Escolar-Castillo, Michael Sullivan's Colombian wife.

Mark · 384, 386, 401 - expat UK crook, living in Denmark.

Mason · 283, 294 - young American fixer in Karachi Central Jail.

Matthias · 354, 402 - German friend over many years; imprisoned in Kabul and later Karachi; often his house guest in Frankfurt.

Max · 130 - Max McCready, Melbourne friend, who with his wife, Jenny, helped over many years including risky journeys to Thailand & Pakistan. Jailed once following the fake helicopter escape plan from Victoria's biggest jail. He'd refused to fink.

Meera · 331 - wife of Najib; a couple Jeanette and I met in Karachi.

Michael Sullivan · 18 *(and throughout)* - my working partner in Australia during my 20s; life-long friend.

Mike Powers · 110 - American DEA agent whose wife Joyce was killed in Chiang Mai, Thailand.

Miraj · 187 - Indian people smuggler and unwilling cellmate during the 1996 escape from a Thai jail.
Montree · 186 - Thai lawyer for the 1993 drug charge; an eccentric fatalist.
Mrs Akbar Shah · 332, 344 - wife of Akbar Shah, notorious for manipulating the police.

N

Najib · 331 - husband of Meera, the wealthy couple met in Karachi.
Naveed · 248 - the Afridi informant helpful when seeking Iftikhar's kidnappers.
Noor Jehan · 6, 98, 200, 202, 239, 286, 332 - Mir (Lord) Noor Jehan Magsi. Tribal lord of Baluchistan; friend who helped free me from Hyderabad prison.
Norma · 92 - Norma Sullivan, sister of Michael. (Died in Manila, where her ashes were scattered over Manila Bay).

O

Operation Aries · 124 - Combined State-Federal police task force in '80s Australia, set to arrest McMillan-Sullivan.

P

Patrick · 234 - (Picklehead) Eloise's psychologist.
Paul Sigg · 87, 100 - Australian crook and informer in the 1980s.
Per Mögens · 366 - Danish underground banker in Christiania.
Percival Hole · 131, 401 - (Percy) British conman, duped into playing ex-SAS commando in phoney helicopter escape, Melbourne.
Peter Dale · 23, 36, 48, 86, 92, 94, 134 - the perfect courier; Australia 1980s; turned state witness.
Peter Howard · 65, 117, 123, 134 - Melbourne dope dealer and informer.
Pieter · 380 - South African friend in the Copenhagen prison.

R

Ralph Renard · 15 - my first family lawyer in Melbourne, 1970s.
Rana Shamim · 298, 316 - Pakistani lawyer, succeeded with my acquittal in Karachi; now a judge in Gilgit.
Robbie · 294, 298, 323, 346, 402 - Robbie the Scot, financier arrested in Karachi; friend who helped on court matters.
Rocky · 78, 206 - First Australian mentor and business partner.

S

Senator · 95, 203, 329 - unnamed US Democrat politician met by chance at airports whose words stayed with me over 20 years.
Shahid · 293 - prisoner-servant to Pakistan Steel boss in Karachi Jail.
Sharon · 162, 184, 207, 357 - girlfriend following release from Australian jail.
Shenkmann · *see* **Bill Shenkmann**
Simon Nasht · 352, 359 - my (slightly) younger brother, a TV-documentary producer.
Sohail · 304 - a medical student imprisoned in Karachi Central Jail.
Sophia Dufaur · 325, 383 - daughter of Jeanette and David Dufaur; with Jeanette & sister Ellie for two months in Karachi.
Sten · 182, 186, 192, 401 - Swedish friend in Bangkok's Klong Prem prison who helped on escape night.
Stratton Langslow · 132 - my Australian lawyer during the six-month 1982 trial.
Sue Noel · 37, 85 - (Secretary Sue) - Australian courier and later state witness.
Syed · 250 - cousin of Thai friend Lee who'd joined the Mujahedeen in Afghanistan.
Sylvia Troy · 225 - the good-looking American girl who tried to help me win Eloise in London.

T

Tatiana · 299, 323, 402 - Russian girl imprisoned in Karachi for drugs; freed and taken by Robert (*Robbie the Scot*) as a mistress.
Ted · 141 - Edward Eastwood, failed kidnapper of a busload of Australian kids; escaped and shot; recaptured and strangled rapist Glen Davies in prison. Released 1993.
Teresa · 79 - Teresa Viganò, Clelia's sister.
Tommy · 115, 122 - Thai smuggler; nephew of notorious **Uncle**, enemy of the DEA.
Tony · *See* (Lord) Anthony Moynihan
Trevor · 145 - Trevor Jolly, *the Artist* during the 1993 breakout from a supermax prison.

U

Uncle · 109, 117 - One of the *Big Three* heroin drug lords of Thailand's Golden Triangle; uncle to Tommy.

V

Vridsløselille · 380 - prison (now closed) in Copenhagen; held most of us foreigners as it was a walled prison.

Y

Younis Habib · 289 - Former director of Pakistan's Mehran Bank. Imprisoned in Karachi Central Jail for fraud. (Sentenced 10 years 'rigorous imprisonment'; released and later blabbed.)

Z

Zahoor Baloch · 290, 295 - a fellow prisoner at Karachi jail; later (& briefly), my lawyer.
Zia-ul-Haq · *see* General Zia-ul-Haq

Pakistan prison terms used:

- ***Bardashi*** — servant, cleaner
- ***Bund Ward*** — closed ward; solitary confinement
- ***Dhobi-walla*** — clothes washer
- ***Gora*** — a white man
- ***Muktadar*** — administrator; assistant

DEDICATION

for

Matthias Volker Lang — 1950 - 2015

(aka, Victor Mala)

ABOUT THE AUTHOR

Born in London in 1956, David McMillan spent his early years in Australia where, at 12, he presented a children's television news programme. After education at Caulfield Grammar School, he trained as a cine-camera operator, then briefly worked for Masius advertising as an in-house TV/Radio producer before joining the drug-law reform movement. In the late '70s, McMillan became a smuggler between Asia and Australia, then South America and Europe. Although, the contraband network was sophisticated, misfortune resulted in frequent arrests and imprisonment, twice resulting in potential death sentences in Asia.

McMillan has written of his escape from a Thai prison in ESCAPE (*Monsoon Books, 2007*) and his early misadventures in ESCAPE: THE PAST (Monsoon Books, 2012). He says of UNFORGIVING DESTINY, '— *probably the last book of autobiography for me. The remaining experiences from the criminal underworld are more safely told as fiction, and so that is next.*' The *Sefton Cooper* series will be published from 2018.

MORE IMAGES, MUSIC REFERENCES AND LINKS TO UNFORGIVING DESTINY
CAN BE FOUND AT HTTP://DAVIDMCMILLAN.NET

Readers who want more from David McMillan on the breakout from Bangkok prison turn to:

ESCAPE

Available at **Amazon** or direct from Monsoon Books

" Breathtaking stuff... the action rips along like a thriller."
Douglas Wight — News of the World

Printed in Great Britain
by Amazon